CHINA AND INDIA

CONTEMPORARY ASIA IN THE WORLD SERIES

CONTEMPORARY ASIA IN THE WORLD

David C. Kang and Victor D. Cha | *Editors*

This series aims to address a gap in the public-policy and scholarly discussion of Asia. It seeks to promote books and studies that are on the cutting edge of their respective disciplines or in the promotion of multidisciplinary or interdisciplinary research but that are also accessible to a wider readership. The editors seek to showcase the best scholarly and public-policy arguments on Asia from any field, including politics, history, economics, and cultural studies.

Beyond the Final Score: The Politics of Sport in Asia | Victor D. Cha, 2008

The Power of the Internet in China: Citizen Activism Online | Guobin Yang, 2009

Living with the Dragon: How the American Public Views the Rise of China | Benjamin I. Page and Tao Xie, 2010

CHINA AND INDIA

PROSPECTS FOR PEACE

Jonathan Holslag

COLUMBIA UNIVERSITY PRESS | NEW YORK

COLUMBIA UNIVERSITY PRESS
Publishers Since 1893
New York   Chichester, West Sussex

Copyright © 2010 Columbia University Press
All rights reserved

Library of Congress Cataloging-in-Publication Data

Holslag, Jonathan.
China and India: prospects for peace / Jonathan Holslag.
p. cm — (Contemporary Asia in the world)
Includes bibliographical references and index.
ISBN 978-0-231-15042-2 (cloth : alk. paper) — ISBN 978-0-231-52097-3 (ebook)
1. China—Relations—India.   2. India—Relations—China   I. Title.
JZ1734.A5714 2010
327.51054—DC22   2009030127

Columbia University Press books are printed on
permanent and durable acid-free paper.

This book is printed on paper with recycled content.

Printed in the United States of America

c 10 9 8 7 6 5 4 3

References to Internet Web sites (URLs) were accurate at
the time of writing. Neither the author nor Columbia University
Press is responsible for URLs that may have expired or
changed since the manuscript was prepared.

DESIGN BY VIN DANG

TO ANNEKE

CONTENTS

ACKNOWLEDGMENTS

IT TAKES A WHOLE COMMUNITY TO WRITE A BOOK. When preparing this work, I received generous support from the Flanders Research Foundation (FWO) and from the Vrije Universiteit Brussel, which facilitated my many field trips to East and South Asia. During these visits, I had the opportunity to interview numerous experts and officials. While most of them have been kept anonymous, I thank them all for their most valuable insights. Many academic institutions offered me the chance to exchange views with colleagues, to verify arguments, and to approach the relations between China and India from various angles. In China, they included the China Academy of Social Sciences (CASS), the China Institutes of Contemporary International Relations (CICIR), the China Institute of International Studies (CIIS), Fudan University, and the Shanghai Institutes for International Studies. In India, I benefited from seminars at the Institute for Defence Studies and Analyses (IDSA), the Centre for Policy Research (CPR), and the Institute of Peace and Conflict Studies (IPCS). Discussion sessions were also organized at the East Asian Institute and the Institute of Southeast Asian Studies (ISEAS), in Singapore, and at the Bangladesh Institute of International and Strategic Studies.

For constructive comments and suggestions at different stages of this book's development, and for encouraging me to uphold best practices of academic research, I am indebted to Bates Gill, François Godement, Gudrun Wacker, Gustaaf Geeraerts, Ma Jiali, Pan Zhongqi, Sujit Dutta, Zhang Yunling, Zhao Gancheng, and the anonymous reviewers of Columbia University

Press. I would like to thank particularly Andrew Nathan and Gustaaf Geeraerts for inspiring and encouraging me, and Anne Routon for helping me through the publishing process. I am also grateful to a large group of friends and family for being so patient and supportive during the solitary work of writing and the many stays abroad.

CHINA AND INDIA

SINO-INDIAN RIVALRY IN AN ERA OF GLOBALIZATION

IN THE LAST SIX DECADES the Sino-Indian relationship has been driven by an ambivalent mixture of common yearning for respect as prominent international actors and the mutual rivalry that their quests for power created in overlapping spheres of influence. It fell once into an open war, tottered at least five times on the verge of war, and on numerous occasions slid into a diplomatic war of nerves. This book demonstrates why the two Asian giants are still trapped in their protracted contest. Despite the impressive number of confidence-building measures, agreements, dialogues, and growing trade, the causes of conflict have not been tackled. Distrust of each other's intentions remains alarming, both sides keep all military options open, and no serious progress has been made on the final settlement of the border dispute. Moreover, while trade is often expected to weave states into a web of interdependence, economic ambitions seem to have added new impetus to the rivalry between China and India. The enormous pressure to make swift progress in domestic economic development makes competition inevitable and will lead to fiercer diplomatic wrestling for regional influence, at the expense of stability. This book explains why China and India will not grow without conflict with each another, and why there is such conflict in spite of their interdependence.

Piloting a third of the world's population into the global economy—that is the challenge that binds China and India. Despite euphoric reporting on their industrial growth and booming services sector, the reality is that half their labor forces, good for approximately 660 citizens, has to survive on the unpredictable yields of their farmland.[1] According to UN figures the average annual income of a "Chindian" in 2007 was only U.S.$5,105, not much more than the earnings of an inhabitant of, say, Botswana or Morocco.[2] Up to 54 percent of Chindians lived on less than U.S.$2 a day.[3] Despite the IT success in India and the higher education boom in China, less than 8 percent of their citizens have access to the Internet. Domestic consumption does not suffice to defuse challenges like jobless growth, rapid urbanization, and inefficient agricultural production. Consequently, there is a strong need to attract investment in labor-intensive sectors like manufacturing to boost exports and to obtain access to foreign reserves of raw materials.[4] The world is clearly in need of a second Chinese miracle to pull India out of its economic swamp, but China, too, still has a long way to go to become the well-off society Deng Xiaoping dreamed of.

Literature on Sino-Indian relations falls broadly in two main camps. On the one hand a large number of scholars focus on the security relationship. In his influential work John Garver elaborates meticulously on the evolving interaction of China and India regarding their border dispute, nuclear armament, and their overlapping zones of influence.[5] Garver's conclusion is that shifting power balances and geopolitical rivalry are not likely to abate.[6] This manifestation of realpolitik is extended and concretized to several specific cases. Gulshan Sachdeva, for instance, argues that India will work with Russia and Iran to balance China in central Asia.[7] Authors like J. N. Dixit and T. V. Paul emphasize China's bonds with Pakistan and the impact of this alliance on India's military power in South Asia.[8] Manish Dabhade and Harsh Pant argue that China and India are entangled in a contest for influence in Nepal.[9] Marie Lall sees a similar pattern emerging in Myanmar.[10] Chinese realists have been concentrating increasingly on the American attempts to pull India into its strategic orbit and are not confident about the motives behind India's improving relations with Japan and Russia.[11] In the past few years, scholars have also been viewing with suspicion India's military muscle flexing in the Indian Ocean.[12]

On the other hand, there is the extensive literature on economic relations. Whereas skepticism on cooperation prevails in the former, this category is more optimistic and emphasizes the intensifying economic cooperation on which the emergence of Chindia thrives. Rediscovering Prime Minister Nehru's initial esteem for China's swift growth in the 1950s, Indian politician and media commentator Jairam Ramesh was the first to revive Jawaharlal Nehru's Hindi Chini Bai Bai motto into Chindia, similarly hinting at the opportunities for cooperation and harmonious growth. In his 2005 book Ramesh advocates developing "the great trade route to China" and derides potential anti-Chinese hedging.[13] The Congress Party minister has also concluded that working together with China will be India's only chance to reach Chinese-like economic growth rates. "Emulation through cooperation" characterizes the Indian interpretation of Chindia. In Chinese publications, too, economic motives figure prominently. "China-India relations occupy a very important position in the diplomatic strategy of each country," claims ambassador-scholar Cheng Ruisheng, "the continuous strengthening of the trade and economic exchanges is conducive to the development of both countries."[14] Ren Jia and Wang Jiqiong highlight mutual economic expectations as the fundaments of the bilateral strategic partnership.[15] Both Chinese and Indian experts have come to the conclusion that the economic division of labor between the two states should be tapped to gain further profits. Authors like Mukul Asher, Rahul Sen, Biswa Bhattacharyay, Prabir De, T. N. Srinivasan, Yanrui Wu, and Zhanyue Zhou all emphasize the economic complementarities at the basis of a new, strong interdependence.[16] Several Chinese and Indian scholars elaborated on the various layers of this economic interdependence in a volume edited by Jayanta Ray and Prabir De, focusing on aspects such as bilateral investments, border trade, tourism, frontier development, and transport integration.[17]

Seldom are such economic studies of Sino-Indian relations merged with analyses that focus on the strategic and security dimension. There seems to be an analytical cleavage between realist skepticism and liberal optimism, resembling much what David Kang has called paradigm wars, pitting the different theoretical and disciplinary schools against one another and then attempting to prove one right while dismissing the others.[18] This book aims at bridging the two different theoretical approaches, analyzing the Sino-Indian relationship in a holistic way. It assesses to what extent deepening economic integration also fosters cooperation in other areas, such as security, and vice versa, and how far realist considerations allow commercial ties to develop. My aim is to examine whether growing bilateral trade and the increasing interest in a stable neighborhood will mitigate the "protracted contest," as scholars like Garver describe it. I also consider how much the security dilemma between both countries is preventing them from reaping the potential benefits that enhanced economic and diplomatic cooperation might generate. My analysis centers on a dialogue between theory and evidence. In the following chapters external relations are studied from the perspective of political economy and foreign policy analysis. This implies an assumption of states as the key actors in international society, but its particularity lies in the question of *how* this policy is formulated.[19] States are not considered as homogeneous billiard balls but as a complex amalgamation of actors, interests, and expectations. To a large extent, foreign policy is still a public policy. The state as a "metaphysical abstraction" is discarded, but the nation-state is still adhered to as the fundamental level of analysis.[20] Tracing strategies to various domestic interest groups and different public perceptions permits formulating more reliable conclusions with regard to future policy choices.

In addition, this book adds new empirical material to the debate on Sino-Indian relations. The largest part of this study starts at the point where the detailed analysis of Garver's *Protracted Contest* ends. Several of Garver's findings are tested against the changes in the Sino-Indian relationship between 2001 and 2007. For this purpose, intensive field research was carried out in Bangladesh, Cambodia, China, India, Indonesia, Thailand, and Singapore. Interviews with nearly a hundred officials, experts, journalists, and politicians provided new insights into the evolution of mutual perceptions and the formulation of policy objectives. Statistical reviews were carried out to study economic issues and public attitudes. Although for several reasons Indian policy making turned out to be easier to document, I tried to maintain a balance between Indian and Chinese sources.

The expectation to develop into a wealthy trading state can lead to opposite policy outcomes. On the one hand, there is the idea that rivalry can be tempered when states replace their fixation with relative gains with policies that focus on domestic welfare and stability, and that countries that engage in international trade will have more incentive for cooperation. "The natural effect of commerce is to bring about peace," Montesquieu wrote in 1748, "because two nations which trade together render themselves reciprocally dependent."[21] In a contemporary version, this argument has been mentioned several times by Indian and Chinese politicians. "In effectively addressing challenges," Manmohan Singh has stressed, "we [China and India] should avoid divisive policies and actions driven by the outmoded mindset of balance of power and instead strive for a more meaningful and inclusive cooperative framework in the region across a range of issues from security to trade and investment."[22] Chinese president Hu Jintao has added that "the development of China and India is not competition or rivalry" and that "working hand-in-hand, China and India will deliver enormous benefits to the 2.4 billion people in both countries."[23]

On the other hand, trade ambitions can also lead to aggressive and even hostile policies, in which states actively back national industries to make larger gains than their foreign competitors. This can imply defensive mercantilism, or, in other words, protectionist measures to fence off the domestic market from alien goods and services. Scholars like Robert Gilpin also distinguish a malevolent variant of trade policies that approaches in the international economy an arena for imperialist expansion and engages in aggressive economic behavior. Commerce here is perceived as a matter of conquest, either by persuasion or by force.[24] Such a zero-sum approach would also imply that the economic growth of one party is seen as threatening to the other, not just because of the direct balance of power but also because of former might be able to throw more weight into the scale to secure its economic interests at the expense of the latter.[25]

The main challenge is thus to discern the character of China and India's reform policies and their impact on diplomacy. How liberal or mercantilist are both states' strategies? How have trade interests affected the bilateral agenda? How complementary are both economies, and consequently what do these strategies mean for the intensity of actual and future economic competition? Do mutual interests affect threat perceptions? How are their ambitions interacting in their neighborhood?

The first chapter elucidates how China and India have gradually changed their inward-looking economic policies for the ambition "to unleash the productive forces," as Deng Xiaoping formulated it. The Indian and Chinese governments embrace economic openness as a new source of national coherence. Scholars like Chen Zhimin contend that such policy shifts entail a choice for "constructive nationalism" as a new unifying force for developing societies and as an alternative source of legitimacy for political elites.[26] This domestic change can be expected to have a fundamental impact on the foreign policy agenda. Hence the first assumption that will be tested is that constructive nationalism leads to a more constructive and cooperative posture in foreign affairs.

This leads us to the impact of trade on bilateral relations between China and India. Building on thinkers like Montesquieu, students of liberal international relations theory claim that setting commerce as a political priority makes states more reluctant to resort to violence in their interaction with other countries. Contrary to the Weberian state, Robert Cox has stated, governments become intermediaries between internal interests and external opportunities. Richard Rosecrance has argued that the expectation to gain from economic opening up makes states seek to improve their position in the context of interdependence and that, because of specialization, one state's attempt to improve its access to products and resources does not conflict with another's.[27] Thus, the second assumption implies that trade leads to specialization and complementarity, and that the resulting division of labor creates enough opportunities for multiple states to profit. This assumption is tested in the second and third chapters. Chapter 2 links the economic crises of the 1950s to the Indo-Chinese War of 1962. It explains how the realpolitik in the Cold War era between 1963 and the 1970s was rooted in the attempt of the central political elites to end internal disputes. This same struggle for survival instigated the national elites to embark on a gradual opening up to reap trade revenues and finally, in the 1990s, to create a well-off society that would become a new source of legitimacy. That consequently resulted in improving bilateral ties with economics playing an indirect role in the 1980s, becoming the centerpiece of cooperation in the 1990s, and finally led to the idea of an economically integrated partnership, Chindia. In chapter 3 an assessment is made of the depth of this emerging integration. How much are the two economies complementary? What are the prospects for deepening cooperation? What is the potential for economic disputes?

As a consequence of expanding trade relations it can be assumed that domestic influence will shift from economic conservatives and military cadres to new business elites and reformist politicians. Those persons will form the vanguard of new foreign policies and become the main stakeholders in stable and peaceful bonds with partner states. The more trade, proponents of neofunctionalist liberalism maintain, the more interest groups will lobby for broader and deeper relations with other trading states. Chapter 2 examines how the support for rapprochement has diversified from political actors at the national level to other players like local governments and large companies. Gradually, as domestic development improves and more people become directly or indirectly aware of the economic interdependence with other countries, the demand for cooperation instead of conflict becomes embedded in the broader society. Trade, tourism, information exchange, and people-to-people contacts may lead to what Karl Deutsch has called a "security community."[28] In such communities historical distrust and aversion make way for confidence and mutual understanding between nations. This process also fits with the constructivist idea that through positive interaction and mutually beneficial relations, societies will reconstruct their own identities through the lens of the other. Positive mutual perceptions can make public opinion recognize its own state as benevolent and cooperative instead of feeling humiliated or threatened. Chapter 4 gives an overview of the changing perceptions. It starts with a concise analysis of public attitudes. Subsequently, a critical assessment is made of the positions in the Indian parliament. Finally, light is shed on the attitudes of Chinese and Indian experts.

Expanding trade flows might also result in increasing mutual vulnerability and augment costs of offensive strategies. This thesis is as old as international relations has formed a subject of scholarly research. To name the most important current proponents of this idea, Robert Keohane and Joseph Nye have concluded that in a situation of complex interdependence, a state that threatens another will automatically injure itself, and consequently rational governments have a strong penchant for peace.[29] Military power remains relevant, but instead of deterring other states, the aim is now rather to dissuade nontraditional threats like piracy, terrorism, and armed rebellion. A consequence of embracing the market as the incubator of national growth is also that states feel less urged to develop military power and to deploy troops at the border in order to defend sovereignty. "The question of maps will become redundant," Indian national security adviser M. K. Narayanan has stated.[30] Yet, in a mercantilist scenario growing commercial stakes can also lead to a more robust deployment of power to unilaterally protect economic lifelines and assets abroad, so as to develop the capacity to ward off both traditional and nontraditional threats. Chapter 5 elaborates on the military dimension of Sino-Indian relations. It presents a critical evaluation of the border dispute. It also examines to what extent military deterrence still plays a role, in particular with regard to military deployment at the boundary, naval activity in the Indian Ocean, and nuclear armament.

At the regional level, trading nations can be expected to take more interest in a stable neighborhood to give leeway to traders and to promote a favorable investment climate. Regional economic integration is assumed to diminish the relevance of military deterrence and diplomatic balancing in third states. Growing economic interests abroad might lead to a resecuritization of regional policies, for instance with regard to nontraditional security challenges, but here the desecuritization of bilateral ties should allow China and India to join forces for a stable neighborhood.[31] Such a cooperative posture, though, cannot be taken for granted. On many occasions in the past, economic pressure has led regional powers to initiate hawkish strategies in which swift economic gains are pursued by playing a diplomatic tit-for-tat game with competitors. In this case, military predominance might not be crucial, but a favorable balance of economic and political power certainly is. In chapter 6 these options are tested against the case of Myanmar, Nepal, and Pakistan, three states in which Sino-Indian rivalry has been fiercest. It studies to what extent China and India cooperate to curb cross-border rebellion, smuggling, and drugs trade. As a key indicator of the quality of such collaboration, it also discusses whether they are able to deal with more comprehensive security issues like the need of good governance and inclusive economic development.[32]

In sum, the first two chapters present historical evidence for the convergence of interests that has taken place in the past two decades. After various episodes of war and serious military friction, both countries now aspire to becoming open trading nations and consequently have grasped the benefits of peace and cooperation. The subsequent chapters develop four main arguments for why improving relations and many common interests have not neutralized conflict, that even in an era of globalization the trading states of China and India are still stuck in a persistent security dilemma, and that in the end commerce tends to exacerbate rather than mitigate conflict.

Using these six issues as main variables, this book offers a critical assessment of the impact of trade on the relations between Asia's largest powers. Will globalization and the growing economic linkages mitigate great-power rivalry? Both liberalist and realist parameters guide us through a rich body of empirical information to down-to-earth conclusions relevant for both scholars and policy makers. In addition, the concluding chapter considers a few scenarios in case India or China does not succeed in persisting with the necessary economic reforms. What can we expect when economic complementarity declines as a consequence of similar economic policies? What will be the results if Chinese public perceptions of India change from the current ambivalence to a new suspiciousness?

It is not my aim to test the theoretical assumptions as such, or to evaluate whether either liberalist or realist paradigms hold true at large. Rather, international relations theory has to allow for the construction of a coherent study. Several elementary concepts, such as the security dilemma and interdependence, are applied as benchmarks for assessing the recent progress in the Sino-Indian relationship. As such, this study should be considered in the first place as a fact-based empirical assessment, but as a case study it certainly contributes to the wider scholarly debate on peace and stability and forms an experiment to enrich area studies via a facts-theory dialogue.

EMERGING TRADING STATES

STATES BECOMING A "TRANSMISSION BELT" from the world market to the domestic economy—it appears to be an unstoppable trend.[1] It is widely assumed that globalization fundamentally affects the raison d'être of states, and that they, if not replace, at least have to complement their traditional focus on rivalry for territory and military supremacy with the need to integrate into the world economy. Conquering states are thus expected to become trading states, focusing on the absolute gains of commerce rather than the relative losses. This chapter presents a concise historical account of how China and India have indeed set their ambitions on becoming such trading nations. The emergence of constructive nationalism, it is argued, has in many ways reduced the zero-sum thinking that was predominant during the Cold War and leads to new opportunities for cooperation.

During the past century, India and China have undoubtedly been the most dramatic examples of states that gave up their economic isolation for interaction with the global market. Not more than five decades ago the first fissures occurred in their fortresses of autarky and anticapitalism. Nowadays, both countries are among the world's most prominent proponents of a free global economy. No day passes by without affirmations of the commitment to liberalization and of the aspiration to become a prosperous trading state. The long-established pattern in which India and China identified their fate uniquely with the conservative and inward-looking interests of their vast peasant societies thus came to an end. For millennia this particular feature determined their interactions with the outer world. Economic self-sufficiency and social stability constituted the key sources of legitimacy for political elites and emperors. Both countries were reclusive civilizations, and external trade remained a marginal activity. Even though these states' contributions to the economic, cultural, and scientific cross-pollination between civilizations was substantial, it did not form a purpose by itself. Seldom was this pattern punctuated for a longer period. Traders, discoverers, and cosmopolitan minds were always counterbalanced by the vast interests of inward-looking peasants.

To trace the roots of this transition, one has to go back to the mid-1940s, the period that gave birth to modern China and India. For both states the independence they obtained did not mean more than a victory on an important political and symbolic battlefield. The struggle for the creation of coherent states had yet to start. In 1949 Mao Zedong stated: "Our victory is just a first step of a long march. Although we can be proud of this step, it is rather small. What we can be even more proud of lies ahead of us." After decades of violence, Chinese and Indian societies were traumatized. The secession of Pakistan and Taiwan aggravated political exasperation. Feudalism was a prominent characteristic and shattered both countries' huge territories into uncountable fiefdoms. Neither did the international context permit much optimism. Relations with the two victors of World War II were anything but amicable. With regard to the United States, Beijing came into direct confrontation during the Korean War (1951–1953). Washington's support for Taiwan was another thorn in China's flesh. Whereas India did not wage an armed conflict with the United States, it vociferously opposed the alliance with Pakistan in the framework of the Southeast Asia and Central Treaty Organizations (SEATO and CENTO). Even though the relationships with the Soviet Union were less hostile, Beijing and New Delhi remained on their guard. Mao perceived very well that the Kremlin considered China denigratingly as a little communist brother. The demanding conditions Moscow attached to its military and economic aid fostered an uncomfortable dependence. Following the death of Joseph Stalin in 1953, relations deteriorated even further as Mao and Nikita Khrushchev vied for the ideological leadership of communism. Neither let India take itself in tow. Unlike China, India did not experience a direct security threat from the Eurasian empire. Nehru characterized the Soviet Union as "harmless," but at the same time he continued promoting the Non-Aligned Movement as a middle road between the West and the Soviet Union.

From an economic perspective as well, there were obvious resemblances. To start with, the two economies were of a comparable size. According to Agnus Maddison, the 1947 gross domestic product (GDP) of the People's Republic of China amounted to U.S.$239 billion, compared to India's U.S.$222 billion. With 346 and 536 million inhabitants, respectively, India and China hosted the largest populations in the world. As 80 to 90 percent of their compatriots were small-scale subsistence farmers, this demographic scale posed an enormous challenge to the development agendas. In addition, violence and mismanagement ravaged agricultural productivity. Due to India's splitting up, vital crop areas such as those of jute, cotton, and wheat fell into the hands of Pakistan. The civil war in China resulted in vast stretches of fallow land and destroyed irrigation systems. The industrial sector in both countries was limited to what was left from the colonial presences. India inherited an extensive railway network and some textile factories in places like Mumbai and Calcutta. If not destroyed during the civil war, China could find a couple of plants erected by its Japanese occupiers. The two giants did not have much to expect from the international economy, either. Although they granted some limited economic aid, the superpowers targeted their external economic policies to other regions. Moscow focused on the Council for Mutual Economic Assistance (Comecon). Washington prioritized the reconstruction of western Europe and Japan as the two main pillars of its containment strategy vis-à-vis the USSR. The consequences for economic planning were clear. "The present international situation is likely to lessen to a marked degree our chances of getting capital goods," the Indian government summarized in 1948.[2] Mao similarly stated that China had to do more with less money. To a large extent India and China thus needed to rely on their own capacities.

This context considerably limited the options for state building. During the struggle for independence, frustration and hatred were an important source of coherence and mobilization. This dynamic was not tenable for the long haul. The objective was to turn negative nationalism into a more positive variant and to transform armed mobilization into political and economic commitment. In both countries the main catalyst of administrative and ideological unification was one-party governance. Although India was categorized as a democratic state, the dominance of Nehru's Congress Party was overwhelming.[3] The Congress Party knew to absorb most political opponents. Sardar Patel, Nehru's conservative alter ego, successfully developed a strategy to subjugate obstinate challengers such as the former princely states. Opposition parties sought influence via sympathetic groups within the Congress Party rather than through elections. Prior to 1967, the Congress Party never won less than 73 percent of the seats in parliament. Comparable to the Communist Party in China, the Congress Party became the main vertical structure that connected central decision making with the local level. At the grass roots, politicians were expected to widen the electoral base and to spread the Nehruvian ideology in return for promotion and economic incentives.

GROPING FOR STONES TO CROSS THE RIVER

Both Mao and Nehru assumed that internal differences, whether based on ideology, language, religion, or caste, would fade away with the onset of modernization.[4] Economic development was imperative for social coherence, and consequently for sustaining the young statehood. Necessarily this sustaining had to be *self*-sustaining. There was an outspoken skepticism toward an export-led growth track. From the outset it was clear that the state would be the guide to economic greatness. The government took control of several strategic branches and furnished itself with a planning commission in order to set out the priorities. A strong center was supposed to be a precondition for security and stability. Geographical and social redistribution of welfare had to temper centrifugal forces and to strengthen the government and the party in their positions as gatekeeper.

However, it is important to note that both regimes initially took a moderate stance vis-à-vis private initiative. India's first Industrial Policy Resolution recognized that "private enterprises, when properly directed and regulated, had a valuable role to play."[5] Mao shared this idea. Until the mid-1950s he promoted the principle of state capitalism: "We should introduce suitable readjustments in industry and commerce and in taxation to improve our relations with the national bourgeoisie rather than aggravate these relations. We must do our work well so that all the workers, peasants and small handicraftsmen will support us and the overwhelming majority of the national bourgeoisie and intellectuals will not oppose us."[6]

This prudence reflected the learning process that the new political elites went through. Although Mao and Nehru showed an outspoken penchant for socialism, they did not wish to copy any model blindly. The conception of a proper economic strategy rested on an experimental interaction between ideology on the one hand and several constraining contextual factors on the other. Second, there were still influential interest groups that showed themselves suspicious of sudden policy shifts. The national political establishments felt the necessity of strengthening their own positions first. Last, the cautiousness was also a matter of insufficient capacity. Mao and Nehru were well aware that the political elites did not possess the economic leverage to get the reform into stride. "At this stage," the Indian government concluded, "progress depends to a large extent on effort in the private sector."[7] Mao advised: "Make steady progress and avoid being too hasty!"

In 1951, India issued its first Five-Year Plan. China followed in 1953. The two plans clearly emphasized the industrial sector as the driving force behind economic growth.[8] In China it sounded as follows: "We must build up a number of large-scale modern enterprises step by step to form the mainstay of our industry, without which we shall not be able to develop into a powerful modern industrial country within the coming decades." "In order to realise this objective," the Indian government stressed, "it is essential to accelerate the rate of economic growth and to speed up industrialisation and, in particular, to develop heavy industries and machine making industries."[9] Industrialization was important from several perspectives. First, it was crucial to achieve self-sufficiency in order to prevent being subjugated by other, superior economies and, related to this aim, to build up a strong military industry. Second, factories were viewed as a means of generating the jobs needed to convert the two "backward" peasant societies into prosperous nations.[10] Third, industrial growth could also strengthen the network of new state-centric patronage as an alternative to the networks of powerful landlords and local baronages. Fourth, it was a matter of national security. In the context of an international arms race, an autonomous military industry was essential to enforce de facto sovereignty. Fifth, industry was considered as the foundation of technological progress. Finally, for the very long term, manufactures could constitute a source of foreign exchange.

Enormous amounts of resources were invested in key industries, with politics in control of both the input and the output. In India the Industrial Policy Resolution of 1956 dictated "to build up a large and growing co-operative sector . . . to reduce disparities in income and wealth which exist today, to prevent private monopolies and the concentration of economic power in different fields in the hands of small numbers of individuals."[11] It was ordered that the state should assume "direct responsibility for the further development of industries." India's industry was divided in three categories. The first consisted of activities of strategic importance: coal mining, iron and steel manufacturing, electricity generation, machine building, and so on. These had immediately to be brought under exclusive control. The second category was made up of industries that had to be progressively collectivized but in which private enterprise was also expected "to supplement the effort of the state." The third category included all the remaining industries. Their development was left to the initiative of the private sector. Both countries restricted entrance to the domestic market. In economic planning agricultural development was no longer the final end but a means to nourish industrialization and to embed it in a stable social environment.[12] The Indian Planning Commission even drew a parallel with the economic development of Europe, "which in the earlier stages of development was in a strong position because of the earlier revolution that had taken place in farming."[13] In addition, the political elites assumed that the further impoverishment of the countryside could lead to the weakening of their legitimacy base. In India, peasants formed the absolute majority of the electorate. In China, Mao's experience with guerrilla struggle made him concerned that an aggrieved countryside could still turn against its respective leaders.

Both India and China opted for *controlled communalism* as the chief strategy to activate the rural population. In 1955, the Indian government decided to divide the whole country into development blocs.[14] The point of departure of this Community Development Plan was that bottom-up initiatives should merge with top-down steering and support. Each bloc counted sixty thousand to seventy thousand people. Through bloc councils the government tried to convince the villagers of the benefits of new methods of cultivation, of infrastructure, and of effort pooling. In China this was mirrored by the more top-down cooperative system and the larger communes consequent to the second Five-Year Plan. Nehru and Mao captured this new economic reality with the term "state socialism." The first decade of China and India's development path was characterized by gradual reform that steadily came more and more under the control of political decision making.

A FORK IN THE ROAD

The converging courses suddenly separated following an episode of economic stagnation and political turmoil. In 1957, harvests in the two countries declined. In India floods, hailstorms, and drought caused severe food crises and pushed inflation rates to unprecedented levels. Moreover, the exchange crisis of 1957–1958 exposed the financial weaknesses of Nehru's economic planning. In addition to this economic mayhem, voices of political opposition against the central regime started sounding louder. Conservative Hinduist factions and liberal parties seized momentum. In Mumbai, Gujarat, and Rajastan the Swatantra Party called for economic deregulation.[15] The Congress Party also faced several complaints about corruption and nepotism. In China Mao came under fire from party members. In several cities, resistance was mounting and organizing itself. The Hundred Flowers Campaign (1956–1958) only incited more criticism. These similar political and economic stresses did not, however, result in the same answer. Whereas Mao decided to embark on a revolutionary episode of collectivization and isolationism, Nehru took the path of moderation and international cooperation.

China's second Five-Year Plan, also known as the Great Leap Forward, ushered in a period of intensive collectivization and resulted in a tenacious attempt to transform the "backward" agricultural society into a developed industrialized nation. Surpassing Britain and catching up with the United

States without having to do business with them became China's new maxim and at the same time a powerful tool for Mao to consolidate his power. In order to "activate" the abundant cheap labor, communes were established. Later, these communes were "industrialized" by erecting light industries all over the countryside. Mismanagement and extreme weather conditions caused the collapse of the entire project despite an impressive surge of productivity. Simultaneously, increasing friction with Moscow made Mao decide to further encase the industrial strongholds. In 1962, Beijing announced the so-called Third Line operation, a project that ordered strategic factories to move to China's hinterland in order to survive a Soviet invasion. The costs of this removal were staggering. The exasperation of the economic situation seriously undermined Mao's legitimacy, inside and outside the party. His reaction was to recoil from the international scene and to launch a harsh counteroffensive against so-called bourgeois elements with the Cultural Revolution as a climax.

The Indian government initially sent mixed signals on how it would deal with the domestic crisis. Among the first measures was the closure of the domestic market to imports. Although the balance swiftly tilted in favor of opening up the economy. In order to deal with the economic malaise Nehru agreed to an international assistance scheme. The Indo-Chinese War of 1962 (more about this follows in the next chapter) drove New Delhi further toward the United States. Thereafter, the Indian government pushed the door wide open to American economic and military support. The reluctant dilution of political guidance became more resolute after Nehru's death, in 1964.[16] Nehru's successor, Lal Bahadur Shastri, took various measures to liberalize the domestic economy. "As we function in a democracy, and democracy is the basis of our political structure, we cannot have a regimented type of economy," he explained.[17]

After Shastri's unexpected death in 1966, Indira Gandhi took the post.[18] Crop failures and the war with Pakistan in 1965 resulted in another balance of payments crisis.[19] Stimulated by the Bretton Woods institutions, Gandhi decided to devalue the rupee by 36.5 percent, liberalizing India's tight system of import licensing and relaxing industrial licensing.[20] This turn appeared to usher in a definitive split between a dark red China on one side and an opening India on the other.

THE FUNDAMENTALS OF REFORM

However, instead of a straight track, the reorientation process took a zigzag path. At the end of the 1960s, Gandhi decided to reverse the liberalizing trend in India's economic policy.[21] By leaning more to the left and choosing the camp of the weak segments of society, the premier hoped to save her position against the background of antireform opposition and a dwindling Congress Party. Immediately after the devaluation of 1966, the political left, industries, and bureaucracy cried foul and accused the prime minister of undermining social stability. In the 1967 elections, the party's share declined to 41 percent. This result demonstrated the erosion of the stable, vertical linkages that the Congress Party elites had used to gather their dependents. Instead, citizens started organizing themselves horizontally by their perceived class, caste, communal, and regional interests.[22] The 1969 split between Prime Minister Gandhi and the Syndicate, a group of powerful leaders from the states, also contributed to the dismantling of the Congress bastion. The party ended up divided into two rival sections.

To reinforce the patronage networks necessary to uphold Gandhi's broad but unstable voting coalition, the government expanded trade protection and state regulation of the economy. Charles Hankla has described in detail how Gandhi was able to harness the financial means to sustain her precarious voting base.[23] Through tight industrial licensing she obliged companies to fund the Congress Party's campaigns. For the same purpose large state companies were formed and all banking activities were brought under the Reserve Bank of India. Import licenses became more expensive and tariffs surged.[24] Instead of relying solely on elite intermediaries, decentralized patronage networks, or a strong local organization, the prime minister also spoke directly to voters of the need to "abolish poverty" (*garibi hatao*).[25] At the height of the legitimacy crisis, Gandhi resorted to political repression and declared, in 1975, a state of emergency. Militarism became another instrument. Undoubtedly, the military reaction against Pakistan's operation in Bangladesh and the experimental detonation of an atomic bomb in 1974 were intended to prop up Gandhi's leadership. Consequently, Gandhi further sacrificed the original mobilization structure of the Congress Party for personal cult and populism.[26]

While India's political and economic climate continued to deteriorate, Mao curbed the vagaries of the Cultural Revolution and paved the way for more moderate successors. At the beginning of the 1970s, the leader felt his physical condition weakening. He even showed himself prepared to admit some mistakes from the Cultural Revolution.[27] In 1973 Mao decided to rehabilitate Deng Xiaoping, who had been persecuted during the Cultural Revolution. Following Mao's death, in 1976, the Gang of Four tried to preserve the revolutionary spirit, but the pragmatists and reformists prevailed and took advantage of the frustration among the bureaucracy, industry, and the military. In 1978, Deng was fully rehabilitated and invested with a broad mandate to pilot China into international society. Openness became the core of his reform policy.

This shift was enabled by a silent pact between, on the one hand, the elite, which was in an existential crisis and struggling to survive, and, on the other, the millions of Chinese citizens desperate to escape poverty and arbitrariness. To start with, there was the collective trauma following an era of mayhem and economic exasperation. Mao had brought his country to the verge of ruin. After his death, even the National Bureau of Statistics admitted: "Economic progress got stuck between the 1950s and the 1960s as a consequence of political turmoil, notably the Great Leap Forward and afterwards the Cultural Revolution. When the Cultural Revolution ended, the national economy was in a state of collapse."[28] The Great Leap Forward resulted in total failure and a famine that took between 10 and 30 million lives. Industrial development and technological progress were also hampered due to the emphasis on self-reliance: the Chinese economy had to be able to rely on its own capacity, and as a result of several periods of political isolation China had not many more options but to resort to *self-sustainment*.[29] This seclusion became even more apparent after the Third Line operation.[30] The Cultural Revolution was the fatal stroke.[31] During this period industrial output was nearly zero. Consequently, between 1960 and 1970, China's GDP showed an average annual increase of only 1.8 percent, whereas Japan and South Korea enjoyed growth figures of 14.5 and 7.7 percent, respectively. However, it was not only on the socioeconomic level that Mao's policy turned out to be disastrous. The military, too, was bitterly aggrieved because of the injury it had had to endure. During the turmoil of the Cultural Revolution, compatriots of the Red Guard, Mao's revolutionary militia, even attacked several units of the People's Liberation Army.[32] In addition to the economic chaos, it also became clear that, with his death, Mao had left the Communist Party with a huge legitimacy gap. Since the proclamation of the People's Republic in 1949, the entire political elite had relied on the cultivation of Mao's revolutionary leadership; personal cult and ideological indoctrination constituted the glue that kept China together.

Hence, the pressing question arose as to how to fill the gap. On the one hand it appeared that nobody among the senior party members *could* follow in Mao's track; on the other hand an obvious consensus was formed that nobody *should* try to emulate Mao's dictatorship. His political legacy nearly brought the entire party to collapse. Deng stated that China should "avoid mistakes of the Great Leader in his later years."[33] Deng's personal experiences during the last days of the Cultural Revolution made him resolute to end personal capriciousness and the gravest excesses of political intrigue.[34]

A new person-based regime turned out to be neither achievable nor desirable. Hence, economic liberalization and the promise of "getting rich" can be considered as an alternative legitimacy base that had to foster new esteem for the party as the sole guardian of the nation's interests. Besides the internal factors, the exterior environment also lent itself to openness. Better relations with Washington meant Beijing had one fewer potential challenger to fret about. Deng was well aware of the increasing interest of foreign investors in China. Japan, for example, needed cheap labor to compensate for the rising wages in the domestic market. Deng confided to his Japanese counterpart that he "should appreciate it if all enterprises in your country—large, medium-sized and small—strengthened their cooperation . . . China is short of funds, so that it has been unable to develop many of its resources. If they are developed, we shall be able to supply more of Japan's needs."[35]

In the meantime in India the headstrong policies of Indira Gandhi were also brought to a halt. The outcome of the general elections of 1977 gave a clear signal that the prime minister had gone too far. The Bharatiya Lok Dal, an alliance of seven opposition parties, amassed 43 percent of the votes. Gandhi's National Congress Party ended at a historical low of 35.5 percent. During the campaign, Gandhi even altered her policy from leftist populism to a World Bank–approved liberalization program in an ultimate attempt to win the ballot and to deal with another financial crisis. All in vain, however: she lost her credibility among the poor and did not succeed in satisfying the business elite.[36] The new government, led by Prime Minister Morarji Desai, was a loose construction of ideological and regionalist interest groups. Endless quarrels and internal divisions paralyzed the policy-making process. Economic growth stagnated. The oil crisis of 1979 brought the economy into even more dire straits. India again faced serious inflationary pressures, a foreign exchange crisis, and a food crisis. The combination of public grumbling and intragovernmental bickering caused a split in Desai's Janata Party. In June 1979 Charan Singh briefly took over as premier, but a few months later parliament called for new elections.

Gandhi succeeded in capitalizing on the weakening of her opponents and claimed victory with 42.7 percent of the votes. Despite this electoral triumph, the sociopolitical fragmentation continued and divisive forces gained strength.[37] The ballot brought the emergence of five new political parties. Among the twenty-five parties that ran in the national election there were eleven regionalist participants with strongholds in one particular state. Communist groups collected nearly 10 percent of the votes in total, religion-based parties as much as 25 percent. The Congress Party's traditional coalition base of upper castes, backward castes, untouchables, and Muslims eroded in the Hindi-speaking northern belt, where Hinduist parties were gaining ground. Premier Gandhi picked up the thread of deregulation, the policy she had ultimately resorted to in 1977. Because Gandhi's main objective was to counter the Janata Party, which had overwhelmed the Congress Party in the Hindu belt, her mission became less secular and populist and more communal and business-oriented.[38] This communalism took the form of favoring Hindi movements in their struggle against the Sikhs in Punjab.[39] The probusiness strategy aimed at harnessing the economic elite for propping up the Congress Party.[40] It operated directly, through campaign funding and bribes, and indirectly by stepping up economic growth and providing government revenues. In this regard, Dani Rodrik and Arvind Subramanian have underscored that the probusiness strategy did not imply opening up India's market to external corporate actors. Real liberalization "favours new entrants and consumers," whereas probusiness measures focus on "raising the profitability of established industrial and commercial establishments."[41] Amid escalating communal violence, Gandhi was assassinated by two of her Sikh body guards on October 31, 1984.

Immediately after, her son, Rajiv, was promoted to the office of prime minister and leader of the Congress Party. The elections of 1985 resulted in a marked victory. The fresh premier was determined to consolidate the frail attempts of his mother, giving domestic companies more breathing space.[42] He reinterpreted the country's obsession with self-reliance: "Self-reliance does not mean autarchy. It means the development of a strong, independent national economy, dealing extensively with the world, but dealing with it on equal terms."[43] The seventh Five-Year Plan called for a more effective "resource mobilization" by curbing subsidies, stimulating internal competition in order to raise quality standards, and by stimulating exports. Income and corporate taxes were cut and the Licence Raj, used to thwart competition, was partially dismantled in order to promote investments. The cabinet spent substantial efforts modernizing the electronics industry. Despite these changes, the economic straitjacket was not removed. Rajiv Gandhi chose to stay with the probusiness tack and to only slightly open the market to new players and external competition. Nevertheless, the modernization program came under a harsh assault from labor unions and untouchables movements. The Bofors corruption scandal encouraged them in their claims. Ensuing ethnic violence in Punjab, Karnataka, and Andhra Pradesh was grist for the mill of Hindu extremists. During the extremely violent election of 1989, Gandhi's Congress Party lost more than half its seats in the Lok Sabha. These events took place in the context of a deteriorating economic climate. The trade deficit widened, inflation accelerated from an annual rate of 5 percent, in 1985, to 8 percent, in 1988.[44] Public savings went down and external debt increased to more than 60 percent.

Meanwhile in China, Deng had been making headway with his reforms. Deng's preference for a more open Chinese market had already become obvious during the Mao era. From the beginning it was also clear that he favored a pragmatic approach in which the opening up had to be embedded in an interior economic configuration. In 1963, for instance, he asserted: "So long as we know the existing industrial foundation, proceed from the reality and review the experience gained in our country while drawing on foreign experience, we can achieve greater, faster, better and more economical results in industrial development as is required by the general line."[45] When he came to definitive power in 1978, this cautious analysis resulted in the prioritizing of a stable domestic framework as a basis for subsequent liberalization.

On the political level this implied that the primacy of the state should be upheld: the party was to remain at the helm of society and actively guide the economic transformation. "What is essential," Deng stated, "is that the party, government, army and people throughout the land work wholeheartedly for national development, taking it into account in everything they do." Nonetheless, several adaptations were made in order to grant sub- and nonstate actors more scope for implementing the national aims. For example, the five-year plans were drafted in more flexible terms: fixed production targets were abolished and fixed prices became subject to international market prices. In 1980, provincial authorities received substantial autonomy to concretize national guidelines to their own specific geographic, social, ethnic, and economic circumstances.[46] The objective was thus not to foster a full-fledged market economy but to replace the tight centralist dirigisme with a more relaxed regime of "planning through guidance."[47]

At the socioeconomic level Deng had to recognize that the People's Republic was still a predominantly agricultural society. A first batch of measures guaranteed that the interests of the farmer corps would not collide with the effects of the expected massive industrialization.[48] Consequently, in 1979 peasant communities were re-formed and farmers were allowed to retain surpluses. As a result, China's agricultural output rose 49 percent in five years and peasants' household incomes increased significantly. In addition, several initiatives were taken to establish public infrastructure for attracting investors: the transportation, communication, and energy grids were upgraded and extended, and the mining sector was revitalized to furnish the necessary raw materials. Special emphasis was also laid on capacity in the field of research and development and on the rejuvenation of the educational system. Last but not least, Deng ordered the military to do its bit. The defense industry was ordered to integrate itself into the civil economy and to contribute its share to research and technological innovation. Moreover, the entire military doctrine was explicitly fitted into the economic venture. After the invasion of Vietnam, the People's Liberation Army took a more cautious stance in the execution of its active-defense strategy: a stable and secure neighborhood was a prerequisite to attracting foreign investors.[49] Even though full-fledged conflicts did not occur, the navy undertook several operations to enforce Beijing's claim to the Spratly and Paracel islands in the South China Sea with the aim of securing energy sources in China's disputed littoral periphery. Altogether these industrial, agricultural, military, and scientific aims were assembled into the so-called Four Modernizations.

In this context the Open Door Policy was launched to entice foreign entrepreneurs to invest their cash and skills in China's huge market. This "invite-in" strategy contained several far-reaching measures and legal modifications. In 1979, the investment law was relaxed: companies were discharged of corporate earning taxes the first two years after arrival or in the case of their putting this return back into the Chinese economy. The same year, the so-called foreign exchange retention system was established, permitting local governments and companies to retain a part of the foreign currency earned on exports, for the purpose of enlarging industrial output and stimulating the importation of technology. Whereas foreign investors were initially compelled to set up joint ventures with their Chinese counterparts, a new directive, in 1986, also allowed the establishment of 100 percent foreign-owned daughter branches. In 1984, the first Special Economic Zones, Open Coastal Cities, Inland Cities with Expanded Authority, and Open Coastal Economic Areas were created. A century before, during the time of imperial China, trade ports barred alien merchants from entering the interior market. This time, these zones had to draw in foreign entrepreneurs—the more, the better. From the outset, it was clear that most investors were not interested in the local consumption market, in which purchasing capacity was very modest, but rather in China's abundant cheap labor.[50] The People's Republic developed into the world's assembly factory: by the end of the 1980s more than half its GDP consisted of export earnings. Alien processing companies employed 70 percent of China's urban labor force.

To stimulate exports, Chinese companies were allowed to engage directly in international trade. In 1988 export planning was reduced. A system of import and export licensing was established to permit the government to go along with the exigencies of the interior and international markets. On the one hand, caps on exports of most manufactured goods were removed. On the other, the drain of scarce natural resources such as copper, aluminum, and oil was plugged. In addition, Beijing decided to keep the yuan at low rates to outcompete other exporting nations.[51] In brief, the takeoff phase was expected to convert China's obsolete industries into a modern, export-oriented production capacity.

In both India and China an episode of social unrest and political delegitimation laid the foundation for a cautious attempt to open up their economies. The political catharsis subsequent to the Cultural Revolution and the coup by the Gang of Four obliged the Communist Party to reinvent itself and to look for a completely new development model to secure its position vis-à-vis a population that longed for stability.

The 1977 general elections in India and the increasing segregation of the power structures of the Congress Party also led to a search for new options to harness public support. However, there was a fundamental difference between the two reform tracks. In China reform served mainly the party's legitimacy indirectly. Although politics retained its planning mandate, many direct ties with business were cut. To a large extent, the role of state companies as a source of social promotion and patronage was lost. Instead, liberalization was aimed at a fast private export- and FDI (foreign direct investment)-led industrialization generating jobs, tax revenues, and technological progress and indirectly strengthening the party's reputation. This was the recipe for Deng's new economic nationalism. Social promotion was to be guaranteed on an individual basis, "only according to a person's work, not according to his politics or his seniority."[52] Through legislation and state-owned banks, the party maintained valuable levers for its use. In India, economic reform's chief task was utilizing domestic companies as a direct source of revenue and patronage. At the same time, reform's aim of deflecting outside competition was intended to reassure India's uncountable small and medium entrepreneurs.

PRUDENT DEREGULATION

After Rajiv Gandhi's defeat in the 1989 elections, the Janata Dal Party formed a new government coalition with the National Front. The result was a double agenda. Janata, represented by Prime Minister V. P. Singh, tried to secure its support among the poor rural population in northern India. To this end, he decided to implement the so-called Mandal report that advised positive discrimination for backward castes and non-Hindu entities. The Hindu members of the coalition counteracted this move by rallying extremist movements and pitting Hindus against Muslims in the Ayodhya debate. This bifurcation swiftly led to a political collapse, and, in May 1991, Gandhi reentered the scene after national elections. Following Gandhi's assassination during the electoral campaign, Narasimha Rao was appointed as the new leader of the Congress Party.

After another fierce balloting, Rao's government announced a drastic shift toward liberalism representing a thorough change in India's economy. During the balance of payment crisis of 1991, the determination to reform strengthened dramatically. The contrast between India's humiliating financial bailout by the International Monetary Fund and the showy success of the Southeast Asian countries emboldened the proponents of liberalization. With his new economic policy Finance Minister Manmohan Singh attempted to open the market by removing import controls, easing approval for foreign investments, allowing the rupee to fluctuate, deregulating the industrial licensing policy, and so forth.[53] The aim was to accomplish the reform agenda by stealth.[54] Prime Minister Rao put it this way: "What it really entails is a complete U-turn without seeming to be a U-turn."[55] The government therefore tried to avert attention and refrained from touching tricky issues such as agricultural subsidies and industrial reform.

The Rao government succeeded in curbing inflation and getting real GDP growth back above 6 percent, and, by 1995, trade had risen 23 percent. The most striking product of reform, however, was the impressive boom in services and IT development. Bangalore, in Karnataka, emerged as the Indian Silicon Valley thanks to massive investments by Indian migrants in the United States and elsewhere. However, beyond these economic achievements inequalities sharpened. According to Mustapha Kamal Pasha, the government paved the way for the transformation of the Indian economy and society in such a way that it empowered both the upper-caste urban elites, who dominate national politics, and the agricultural elites, who dominate local politics, at the expense of the urban and rural poor.[56] The poor were mostly affected by cuts in public expenditures such as subsidies on food, transportation, utilities, and fertilizers. Differences in development among states were widening as well. Regions like Uttar Pradesh and Bihar fell far behind the average growth rate. Economic assistance schemes were not sufficient to stop the government's popularity from plummeting. Opposition parties decried the Rao-Singh policies as the end of economic self-sufficiency, arguing that the reforms were the route to unemployment and inflation and meant nothing more than an opportunity for a small elite to be corrupted by foreign luxury goods.[57] In 1995, the Bharatiya Janata Party (BJP) accused the government of sacrificing Indian consumers' interests after the government granted an energy project to the American Enron Corporation. A Kentucky Fried Chicken restaurant was shut after two flies were discovered in the outlet's kitchen.[58] These incidents were just two of the several protests against "Western-style

decadence" and "American-style consumerism."[59] The grievance was carried
forward by several groups: peasants who feared losing their subsidies on fer-
tilizer, workers employed in inefficient public-sector enterprises, bureaucrats
who profited from the endless red tape, and the poor in general, who wanted
more aid allocations.[60] With substantial political hostility against economic
changes, a falling GDP growth rate, and the straitjacket of deficits, the pace
of reform decelerated. On the whole, opposition was most outspoken in the
impoverished Hindu belt. Here, the foundation was laid for the victory of the
BJP in the general elections of May 1996.

The BJP sought to replace the inclusive, secular Nehruvian idea of India
with the principle of Hindutva. This referred to a unified, homogeneous
Hindu political identity that, in its turn, would create a "strong and prosperous nation." From this perspective globalization was considered an un-
dertaking (Hindu) India had to take up to assume its rightful place in the
international community. Just as this was accomplished in the global security
field with the nuclear tests in 1998, so would India's technological progress
and business acumen allow it to thrive in the global economic field as well.[61]
The loose coalition government did not stand for long but collapsed when the
parties from Tamil Nadu left. After another interlude of the United Front, a
loose leftist BJP coalition including thirteen smaller parties won a sweeping
victory in the 1998 national election. The credo of Hindutva was resuscitat-
ed and translated into the slogan India Shining.[62] The government tried to
maintain a subtle balance between nationalism oriented to the Hindu majority and careful reform. Therefore it made backdoor policy changes rather
than implementing them through overt decision making.[63]

Prime Minister Atal Behari Vajpayee was typified as a "master of ambiguity" who "sends different sometimes wholly incompatible messages to different communities."[64] Several strategies entered into force to anchor India
in the international market.[65] Special economic and export processing zones
would help India live up to its alleged status of a "trading superpower."[66] The
Industrial Infrastructure Upgradation Scheme established transport, communication, and energy infrastructure in industrial clusters with high growth
potential.[67] Customs tariff rates were reduced from peak rates of 150 percent,
in 1991, to 25 percent, in 2003. In January 2004 they were brought down
again, to 20 percent for nonagricultural goods. The import licensing system
was further dismantled and quantitative restrictions on imports and foreign
investments were phased out two years ahead of the World Trade Organization (WTO) schedule. At the same time, however, Hindus were stimulated to
close ranks through their participation in the Rashtriya Swayamsevak Sangh
(RSS), an old Hindu nationalist mass movement aimed at "ensuring entry

and access to every Hindu, irrespective of his caste, to their homes, temples, religious places, public wells, ponds, and other public places."

Shining Hindu nationalism did not, however, succeed in turning eyes away from the poor conditions in the countryside. Whereas technological growth accelerated, the rural population experienced several setbacks. Even though the poverty rate dropped, many of the poor became worse off than before. Food subsidies were curtailed and price guarantees to farmers were restricted. Sectors like the mining industry and manufacturing saw a net decline of hundreds of thousands of jobs.

In the 2004 elections, it was these issues the United Progressive Alliance (UPA), an alliance of fifteen parties led by the Indian National Congress, took advantage of. With the mantra *bijli, sadak, pani* (power, roads, water) the Congress Party castigated the BJP for neglecting the poor.[68] To convince rural electorates, the party stressed the need for social investment and support for the agricultural sector in economic policy. The program of the new government was based on a clever division of labor. The fate of the poor was addressed by Congress Party president Sonia Gandhi. She was a driving force behind the Common Minimum Programme. This program had as its most important component the Rural Employment Scheme, which guaranteed one hundred days of work a year for every rural household at the minimum wage. In addition, the agenda focused on credits for enterprises in the informal sector, the stimulation of village industries, and education and health projects for the poor.[69] These projects were balanced by a national cabinet that assembled a "dream team of reformers."[70] The tandem formed by Premier Manmohan Singh and Finance Minister Palaniappan Chidambaram took the lead and focused on further liberalization: "Our strategy for achieving rapid growth," Singh explained, "involves making our economy more open, with a rising share of trade to gross domestic product . . . We must move to a new stage of development. We must integrate into the world economy."[71] The Special Economic Zone Act of 2005 created further tax breaks and other measures to promote the creation of these special zones. The revised Foreign Direct Investment Policy of 2006 abolished the requirement for government approval for projects pertaining to infrastructure, activities with export potential, and large-scale employment, agribusiness, technological innovation, and so on.[72]

China's liberalization has always been accompanied by state interference. However, with the ascent of the fourth generation of party leaders, the political establishment became more inclined to make use of its power than it used to do under Jiang Zemin's reign. This had much to do with a shifting legitimacy base. Whereas Jiang curried favor with liberalist politicians and interest groups, Hu Jintao and Wen Jiabao shifted more to the left. The third generation had its geographical power base in the affluent coastal regions, whereas the fourth generation was, from the beginning, more associated with the impoverished regions in the hinterland. Under Jiang economic growth was an absolute priority. Hu set his sights on harmonious growth, spread over the entire territory and equally benefiting all economic sectors: "We must uphold the scientific approach in achieving economic and social development of the country." He explained: "We must put the people first, making the fundamental interests of the broadest masses of people our point of departure and endeavoring to satisfy their growing material and cultural needs to pursue the comprehensive development of man."[73] In 2006 he launched a new version of the Chinese work ethic: profits are allowed, but not at the expense of national unity:

> Love, do not harm the motherland.
> Serve, don't disserve the people.
> Uphold science; don't be ignorant and unenlightened.
> Work hard; don't be lazy and hate work.
> Be united and help each other; don't gain at the expense of others.
> Be honest, not profit-mongering at the expense of your values.
> Be disciplined and law-abiding instead of chaotic and lawless.
> Know plain living and hard struggle, do not wallow in luxuries and pleasures.[74]

This policy shift was also driven by increasing resistance to the inequality growing along with economic opening up. Between 1995 and 2005 China's GINI inequality rate increased from 30 percent to 47 percent. The 2007 *Human Development Report* clearly showed that in China the divide between urban and rural and between coast and hinterland was gaping as never before. Even the Chinese government admitted that the rate of job creation was not sufficient to absorb the flood of migrants flocking each year into the coastal cities. Moreover, most estimates have confirmed that, despite the 10 percent annual economic growth, unemployment has been rising during the first years of the twenty-first century.[75] Consequently, intraparty opposition mounted as new leftists joined traditional conservative interest groups in their lambasting of the so-called undermining of Chinese coherence in general and the party in particular. On the streets resistance began to grow as well. According to official figures the number of large "public order disruptions" increased from forty thousand to eighty thousand incidents. Thus, the concept of "harmonious society" became a crucial attempt to make the current growth process sustainable and allows the party to strengthen its legitimacy among the masses experiencing the increasing uncertainty accompanying

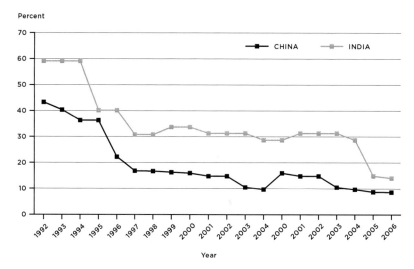

FIGURE 1.1 Average Import Tariff Rates on Nonagricultural and Nonfuel Products (in Percentages). *Source*: UNCTAD, *Handbook of Statistics*, 2007.

globalization. Additionally, the liberalization of several strategic branches was put on the back burner. Whereas China's accession to the WTO brought several conditions concerning the banking sector, the party did not intend to give up its control over state banks, through which it is still able exert far-reaching influence on companies.[76] The same applied to services such as energy, communication, and transport—all instruments for sustaining the capacity for "prudent deregulation."

In China as in India, the 1990s saw increasing efforts to carry forward economic liberalization. In India, the humiliating financial crisis of 1991 created a tipping point in the country's economic policy. Even though economic reform had been drawing harsh criticism during every election campaign, and although it was the main cause of electoral defeat for both the Congress Party and the BJP, liberalization continued gaining momentum in all national cabinets after 1991. At the same time in China, Jiang sped up the program to convert state enterprises, which accounted for a third of industrial output, into corporations owned by private shareholders. Trade barriers were lowered and investment regulations relaxed. The determination of Beijing to join the WTO despite formidable admission criteria emphasized the commitment to open the People's Republic further to the international market. This evolution in both countries is clearly seen in their import tariff rates. Between 1992 and 2006, China's tariffs were slashed by 80 percent, India's by 75 percent.[77]

In the same period foreign direct investments in the two countries increased by 9.1 percent and 12 percent, respectively.[78] At the beginning of the new century, however, rising inequalities and social tensions resulted in more attention to growth favoring the poor. The Hu-Wen and the Singh-Gandhi duos recognized that growing uncertainties were undermining public support for greater interaction with the global economy. The result has been a more balanced strategy in which a continued opening goes hand in hand with more programs for the poor such as redistribution of revenues in the form of extensive assistance programs and rural development schemes.

CONSTRUCTIVE NATIONALISM

The economic logic behind the emergence of trading states is clear: integrating into the world economy is the most optimal way for countries to validate their comparative advantages. In the cases of China and India these assets had always been related to their huge reserves of cheap labor. However, in the first decade after their establishment, the two countries were reluctant to engage with the international market. This was due mainly to an interaction between historical economic identity and the international economic structure of that time. The interests characteristic of their agricultural societies were deeply rooted. Most citizens were used to the idea that with plenty of natural resources and an affluent domestic market, trade was a "dangerous" activity. The destructive consequences of the struggle for independence and the pressure of demographic growth heralded a brief period of reflection and engendered some interest in attracting foreign capital. Both Nehru and Mao considered a pragmatist coalition with the outward-oriented "bourgeois" to gradually reconstruct their shattered countries. But distrust of the two key players in the Cold War and their neglect of India and China in favor of Japan and Europe rapidly made New Delhi and Beijing close the door. *Self-sustaining* became the buzzword in economic planning. At the end of the 1950s, this policy came under severe pressure, and consequently also the legitimacy of Mao and Nehru.

Yet, their responses differed significantly. The former opted for a counteroffensive against criticism, whereas the latter chose to step back and reduce the political grip on India's economy. Two decades later both countries seemed to be in a similar position again. The personality cults of Indira Gandhi and Mao ended in chaos and disarray. The crises brought political catharsis, which in turn resulted in a drastic economic reorientation. The subsequent period of reform was not propelled by the masses, not even by the economic elite. The opening up was promoted by the political establishments in order to secure their positions. They had to shift their source of legitimacy from progress based on isolationist dirigisme to a more outward-looking economic nationalism. From that point, opening up in China coalesced unabated. In India, however, it took until the 1990s until steps to genuine liberalization were taken.[79]

This detour was due to several factors. First, Indian industry was in a much stronger position than China's. Even during Gandhi's state of emergency, factories remained "holy cows" that had to be protected.[80] On the contrary, after Mao's revolutionary excesses there were scarcely any factories left, so the necessity of fencing them off against outward competitors disappeared automatically. Investments from Japan and the Chinese diaspora were considered the only chance to achieve industrial revitalization. Second, as in any democracy, there was the electoral exploitation of uncertainty that, in this case, coincided with economic restructuring. Third, the links between markets and mass welfare were not made clear in Indian public opinion.[81] Few politicians emphasized the relationship between markets and mass welfare, whereas in the case of China reformers such as Deng and Jiang continuously underlined that the economic success of the country and individual progress depended on market-oriented growth. Fourth, the gradualist approach to reform led to a delayed flow of profits that weakened the perception of benefits and consequently support for liberalizing measures.[82] Fifth, attempts to reform were mostly reactions to crises. Given the need for quick results and international donors' insistence on shock therapy, the responses were too impetuous and too unbalanced to be acceptable by most interest groups, whether they concerned farmers, middle class entrepreneurs, or factory managers.

It is important to stress the role of "New Delhi" and "Beijing" because the move to liberalism and the option for constructive nationalism in both countries is pushed forward mainly by the central political establishments, the Congress Party and the BJP in India, the Communist Party in China. What explains their alteration? To start with, negative nationalism in terms of class struggle and isolationism, their initial source of legitimacy and mobilization, came under pressure. In China this culminated in the power vacuum after the failed Great Leap and the Cultural Revolution. In India the atrophy of support occurred in different dimensions and at a different pace for the two main parties. In both cases the failure to fulfill economic ambitions played a significant role; or, as Gramsci signaled: "Immediate economic crises of themselves produce fundamental historical events; they can simply create a terrain more favourable to the dissemination of certain modes of thought, and certain ways of posing and resolving questions involving the entire subsequent development of national life."[83] From this perspective, constructive nationalism permitted national elites to reinvent themselves. Second, and related to the former, was the drying up of the financial resources that were needed to coax citizens indirectly through economic support or directly by bribing them. This lack of means also reduced the capacity to influence sub-state actors and local governments. Opening up to foreign capital provided new sources through customs taxes, levies on increasing productivity, and so forth. In India, the national government has strengthened its position as economic gatekeeper as it continues to tightly administer nonagricultural production, corporation, and customs taxes, and it consequently remains the first to pick the fiscal fruits of foreign investments and increasing exports.[84] Even though China's provinces, in size comparable to India's states, have more fiscal scope than their Indian counterparts, the constitution reserves an important redistributive role for the national government.

The economic transition gave birth to a new brand of constructive nationalism. This positive, pragmatic nationalism regards the economic isolation of the prereform years as the source of economic deficiency and advocates participation in the positive-sum game of international economic interdependence.[85] It seeks to redirect the people's energy to strive for their *own* economic welfare through *national* greatness. Constructive nationalism does not rely on the mobilization of the masses through collectivist ideology but via private interest and the creation of structural incentives to meet those interests. Unity and support for the national government are less and less created by means of *direct* patronage, indoctrination, or compulsion; they are promoted *indirectly* by connecting the national reform agenda to tangible economic improvements in citizens' personal life spheres.

In India constructive nationalism emerged during the Rao administration, but as important was the fact that the subsequent Hindu nationalist members of the Vajpayee government continued this line and partially adapted their Hindu chauvinism. The emphasis of the BJP's official discourse shifted from Swadeshi, which implied a resistance to globalization, to Hindutva, which in fact supports globalization. In 2004, the BJP explained that Hindutva could "trigger a higher level of patriotism that can transform the country to greater levels of efficiency and performance" and thus make "India a global economic power."[86] Moreover, Prime Minister Vajpayee stressed that Hindutva was all inclusive and even synonymous with Bharateeyata, a notion of "Indianness" that bridges ethnic and religious differences. At a party meeting in 2003, he stated that India belongs to all and all belong to India, and that all Indians have equal rights and equal responsibilities.[87] A few months later the BJP launched the India Shining motto: "India Shining is all about pride. It gives us brown-skinned Indians a huge sense of achievement," the chief campaign strategist summarized.[88]

After 2004, the UPA coalition tried to follow a more secular interpretation of nationalism. The central message nevertheless remained the same. Deng's metaphor of the red cat and the white cat clearly reveals China's shifting nationalism. Pragmatism, patience, and pride became the key instructions for party propagandists. Accordingly, three key nationalist agendas were adopted: economic progress, sovereignty, and a more prominent place in the international arena. Economic development is the precondition for fulfilling all other tasks.[89] Thus, reform is no longer a vehicle for promoting cultural or ideological particularism. Particularism evolves into a utensil, a superficial wrapping for selling economic reform. In general, New Delhi and Beijing transformed from bulwarks for protecting the domestic economy from harmful influences into transmitters between the global and domestic economies.[90] By transforming gradually into trading states, China and India shifted policy doctrine from a reactive agenda to a progressive one. From a defensive posture international engagement evolved into a pragmatist and integrative stance.[91] The next chapter studies how this shift has affected bilateral relations between China and India and how much the expectation to benefit from globalization has reduced mutual fear.

TWO

THE EVOLUTION OF SINO-INDIAN RELATIONS

CHINA AND INDIA EMERGE as two ambitious trading states that priori-
tize growth through interaction with the outside world instead of isolation.
The question arises whether this engagement with globalization will be benevolent or malign. After all, gunboat diplomacy and imperialism, too, are
possible expressions of outward-oriented economic aspirations. In the past,
constructive nationalism in the domestic realm turned out to be perfectly
complementary with harsh mercantilist strategies abroad. Both New Delhi
and Beijing indicate that this is not the case. "In effectively addressing challenges," India's prime minister Manmohan Singh assured, "we should avoid
divisive policies and actions driven by the outmoded mindset of balance of
power and instead strive for a more meaningful and inclusive cooperative
framework in the region across a range of issues from security to trade and
investment."[1] Likewise President Hu Jintao has urged turning the China-India relationship "into a bond of good-neighborliness and mutually beneficial
cooperation."[2] This chapter reconstructs the recent history of Sino-Indian
relations and demonstrates how their fixation with economic growth has indeed reduced geopolitical tensions.

For countries that profile themselves as trading states, the propensity for
a benevolent relationship can be traced back to several dynamics. First, there
is the prediction that through the *low politics* of trade, relationships between
states can be transformed or even reversed. By participating in global trade,
states will specialize in the domain where they hold a comparative advantage
and that will consequently reduce the possibility of economic and political

competition.[3] This Ricardian interpretation is complemented with the idea of structural economic openness. Advanced capitalism mitigates anarchy between states because it creates such high prospects for absolute profits that they are less obsessed with relative gains or losses.[4] Third, there is the neofunctionalist assumption that emphasizes the need for national political elites to cooperate and maintain peace in order to safeguard the domestic reform agenda.[5] Finally, trading states are assumed to engender more diversified societies in which interest groups look across borders for alliances to defend their interests. As a result, not only the political elites nurture cooperation; bilateral ties become manifold and thus stronger.[6] These entrenching economic interests prevail at the expense of *high politics* and promote the desecuritization of sensitive territorial or military questions. As Benjamin Cohen has summarized, the difference between the two types of economic nationalism, benevolent and malign, lies in the willingness of a country to identify its own national interest with an interest in the stability of the overall international system. "Benign nationalism acknowledges the connection between self-interest and systemic interest; malign nationalism ignores or denies it."[7]

The recent history of Sino-Indian relations appears to confirm the extension of constructive nationalism in national politics to a more benevolent posture in their bilateral relations. During the past six decades, there has been a clear linkage between economic priorities and shifts in foreign affairs. The general trend is that of accommodation due to intensifying economic interdependence. During the 1950s, bilateral relations did not go beyond a loose relationship based on the ideological conviction that both countries had to secure their sovereignty vis-à-vis the two superpowers. Ties were nurtured as far as they suited the personal power bases of Mao Zedong and Jawaharlal Nehru. This personalization of foreign policy contributed significantly to the outbreak of violence along the border in the early 1960s.

In the two decades after, India and China dug themselves in. The combination of distrust and internal instability made any rapprochement impossible. During the 1960s and 1970s, realpolitik enabled the central political players to concentrate on their domestic opponents. Shifts in economic priorities instigated a more constructive stance toward other countries. As economic opening up, although at different velocities, prevailed in both countries as the ultima ratio for internal stability, peace at the borders became more important, and that in turn resulted in improved bilateral relations. In the 1990s, economic interests developed into the centerpiece of mutual engagement. Expanding economic interests paved the way for numerous agreements in other branches. This evolution culminated, at the beginning of the new century, in the idea of borderless integration. The following sections look closer into these different phases.

THE 1950S: ACCOMMODATION AND STRUGGLE

"Are we going to invade others? No, we will invade no one anywhere. But if others invade us, we will fight back and fight to the end. The Chinese people adhere to this stand. We are for peace, but are not afraid of war. We are ready for both."[8] This statement by Mao clearly illustrates his young state's obsession with territorial sovereignty. The first decade after the declarations of the Republic of India and the People's Republic of China, the chief ambition of both countries' diplomacy was indeed to defend their immature independence. At the basic level this implied territorial restoration. Demarcation was not only a matter of enabling administrative control; for Mao and Nehru it constituted part of their roles as defenders of national interest and unity. Mao repeatedly declared that a strong China needed to control the territory that the Qing dynasty (1644–1912) had governed at the height of its power. Therefore apostate regions such as Inner Mongolia, Manchuria, Xinjiang, and Tibet had to be recovered. Nehru, too, identified Indian territory with the former imperial realm, in this case the empire of the Raj. Remote areas such as the northeast and Kashmir had to be called to order. Even the Portuguese settlement, Goa, which had not been a part of the former British imperium but was, according to Nehru, a last remnant of colonialism, had to be liberated. Also in this regard, the partition and creation of Pakistan in 1947 was perceived to be but a temporary breach in the historic unity of the subcontinent.[9]

Besides their administrative and nationalist importance, pushing the borders forward fulfilled a military function. Peripheral areas formed an important buffer zone against security threats from abroad, at least if they were brought under control. If not, they risked becoming strongholds from which alien powers could project their power. In India's northwest, the passes of the Hindu Kush and Karakoram mountains had been repeatedly the gates through which conquerors raided the plains around the Ganges. In China the remote Tian Shan in the west and the wide-open steppes in the north formed crucial corridors that had to be controlled in order to secure the Chinese heartland between the Yellow and Pearl rivers.

Sovereignty also meant avoiding dependence on external superpowers. Although China leaned to the side of the Soviet Union and India received help from Washington, the two countries saw the diversification of their diplomatic contacts as a clear demonstration of their independence. For China this goal was not only a matter of political autonomy but it also related to the quest for legal sovereignty as it sought to quell the Kuomintang in Taipei as the official government of China. Thus, Beijing and New Delhi prioritized amicable contacts with western European, Latin American, and African countries. Additionally, the ties with Asian countries were intended to prevent isolation and containment. Most Asian states were suspicious of the intentions of China and India; China and India, for their part, perceived these countries as a potential springboard for great-power intrusion. Amicable diplomatic ties were therefore imperative to avoid this mistrust's resulting in alliances directed against them and to constrain the superpowers' offensiveness. The Bandung Conference, in 1955, certainly has to be studied from this perspective. Generally, the conference was directed against the divide-and-rule strategy of the Soviet Union and the United States. One specific goal, however, and Nehru most prominently advocated this, was to integrate China into the "Asian community" and prevent its becoming an aggressive actor and a threat to regional security.[10]

The aversion toward the Soviet Union and the United States also fulfilled a role in the construction of national identities. In the initial stage of state building, nationalism was a negative notion essentially directed at external threats, among which imperialism and great-power offensiveness were the most apparent targets. Anti-imperialism constituted an instrument of political mobilization. Maoism articulated China's profound sense of humiliation and dissatisfaction. It aimed at channeling this grievance into national unity via the promise of internal stability and the capacity to fend off new attempts of external intrusion.[11] Mao perceived the internal impoverishment as "the result of the collusion of foreign imperialism and domestic feudalism." These two evils had to be eradicated if China was to be restored to a prosperous and self-respecting nation.[12] Nehru's claims were similar. Nonalignment and Swadeshi, economic independence and self-sufficiency, would restore national pride and to a certain extent a chauvinism on the part of Indian citizens after having gone through an era of subjugation.

Foreign politics well suited the buildup of Mao's and Nehru's personal influence and status. Both leaders saw external affairs as a source of internal legitimacy and as a powerful lever for strengthening their ideological leadership. Whereas domestic politics remained the realm of various opposing interest groups, external relations could be easily monopolized. Nehru claimed foreign politics as his personal realm. After the death of Sardar Patel, the charismatic deputy prime minister who had earned the title "iron man" for his tough line, Nehru became uncontested in his international aspirations and ideology. Besides his premiership he retained the portfolio of External

Affairs, and intermittently the mandate of defense minister, president of the Congress Party, and chairman of the Planning Commission.[13] His personal style led to simply neglecting the authority and the opinions of the cabinet and Cabinet Committee on Foreign Affairs. Except for a few senior diplomats, the External Affairs was involved in only everyday and marginal issues. The personalization of diplomacy also prevailed in China, where Mao had the exclusive command over principle and policy. Unlike Sardar Patel in India, Zhou Enlai, who was at the same time prime minister and minister of foreign affairs, did not enjoy high moral credentials of his own. Each personal dictate of Mao's diminished his charisma and authority. Zhou was forced to maneuver within the narrow scope Mao granted him.[14] This supreme centralization of foreign policy making became tangible in the Korean War. Mao's determination to go to war ran counter to the advice of both the military command and the Ministry of Foreign Affairs. During the conflict he maintained direct strategic and tactical command, even to the extent of orders to privates on the battlefield, which at times arrived too late to allow for appropriate action. Mao himself is reported to have compared this position to the Mandate of Heaven of his imperial predecessors: he lent his authority to his personal ability to protect the country from interior and exterior threats. His failure to live up to this conviction weakened his power.[15]

Sovereignty, ideological prestige, and power were the main forces behind foreign policy making in the 1950s. The economic dimension of Indian and Chinese diplomacy was negligible. Except for natural resources the two countries had little to offer, and most parts of the world were putting their capital into the reconstruction of their own economies. The United States and the Soviet Union were the only shops in town with their doors open. But, as mentioned in the previous chapter, they prioritized their investments to Japan and western Europe. As a result, the emphasis was on aid, not trade. In 1950, for instance, China received a Soviet-funded loan of U.S.\$300 million, compared to U.S.\$550 million in export revenues.[16] The U.S.\$600 million credit granted by the United States to New Delhi in 1957 amounted in value to 43 percent of India's total export revenues that year. Even though both Mao and Nehru encouraged the import of technological know-how, the results were disappointing.[17]

The foreign policy of China and India in the 1950s was characterized by a mixture of struggle and accommodation. The notion of *joint* struggle dominated their bilateral relations. Although Nehru was anticommunist by principle, he identified the needs of his country with those of the People's Republic of China. According to his assessment the founding of the PRC was a victory of nationalism and a demonstration of Asia's emerging emancipation rather than a triumph of communism. The ferocity with which the country expressed its nationalism he deemed a result of China's isolation. India therefore had to foster direct ties with Beijing and attempt to temper diplomatic collisions with third parties.[18] During the 1940s, Nehru sympathized with China's struggle against Japanese imperialism and decided to dispatch a medical team to China.[19] Although New Delhi supported the Kuomintang (KMT) throughout China's civil war, Nehru fiercely lambasted the American backing of the KMT regime after it retreated to Taiwan. His two visits to China left a sincere esteem and respect. After a visit of twelve days in 1939, Nehru concluded that "a new China" was "shedding the lethargy and weakness of ages, strong and united."[20] In 1954, he returned from a trip to China deeply impressed by the "energy of Chinese workers" and by the "terrifying strength" the central government gave China.[21] Nehru repeatedly asserted that both countries had a shared destiny and that they might form the two pillars of a pan-Asian order.[22] "The future of which I dream," Nehru stated, "is inextricably interwoven with close friendship and something almost approaching union with China."[23]

Beijing, however, was not keen to accede to these expectations. Mao's personal posture toward India was characterized by a feeling of superiority and distrust. This distrust was raised mainly after New Delhi became a recipient of American aid and because he saw Nehru's moral crusade under the banner of a nonaligned pan-Asianism conflicting with his own ambitions to become Asia's ideological and political shepherd. Nevertheless, Zhou Enlai was allowed to travel to India, with the primary task of achieving a breakthrough in the debate about the status of Tibet. On the one hand Mao saw no reason to discuss this issue, since the Himalayan district was considered as an inseparable part of the country. On the other, Beijing wanted to avoid bringing the question to a head and letting tensions with India undermine its attempt to gain regional influence. The result of this bargain was a pragmatic eight-year agreement recognizing Chinese claims over "the Tibet region of China" without reaching a final settlement of the delineation of the entire Sino-Indian border. Both sides remained at odds over the final status of Arunachal Pradesh and Aksai Chin, the two most disputed areas. This text was in turn wrapped in the five principles of peaceful coexistence:

1. Mutual respect for each other's territorial integrity and sovereignty
2. Mutual nonaggression
3. Mutual noninterference in each other's internal affairs
4. Equality and mutual benefit
5. Peaceful coexistence[24]

The morality of these standards obviously reflected the arduous task of nation building and referred to the optimal international context enabling the two young states to meet their objectives. Nevertheless, the Sino-Indian boundary soon reemerged as the front line of overlapping interests. New Delhi had agreed that Tibet as such was a part of China, but its borders remained a subject for discussion.[25] In the west, China and India disputed over control of the Aksai Chin plain, a strategic corridor between China's autonomous regions of Tibet and Xinjiang. In the east, Nehru asserted that the border had to be based on the McMahon Line that was mapped out in the 1914 Simla Convention and defined the eastern section of the border between British India and Tibet. China challenged this idea and plotted the border southward of the McMahon Line. Although Zhou tried to break the stalemate with a conciliatory proposal in 1959, the scope for negotiation had been reduced significantly.

Beginning at the end of the 1950s, social and political tensions climbed in both countries. In China the failure of the Great Leap Forward drove the Communist Party into a corner and challenged Mao's legitimacy. This quandary was intensified by the souring relations between Mao and Moscow. The impact of the financial crisis (1957–1958) in India was aggravated by the three subsequent drought years of 1959, 1960, and 1961. Nehru's self-sufficiency policy fell dramatically short in dealing with the economic disarray. With these crises economic progress as the most important column of nation building began to crumble. Consequently, the maintenance of national unity came increasingly to rest on the management of foreign issues. Moreover, since multiple persons and institutions were involved in internal politics, the centralization of external affairs meant that Nehru and Mao were even more confronted by their own self-confident promises and high expectations. More than ever the two leaders were the focal point of politics and accordingly also of criticism.

In this context, the pressure to stand firm on the border question only intensified. In India Nehru came under fire from the Lok Sabha, where several members accused him of lacking toughness in dealing with China. The China policy in fact became the lens for a whole spectrum of criticism; all manner of policies, attitudes, and personality were called into question.[26] The border dispute gave political adversaries a stick for lashing out. Hawkish figures within the security community seized on this distrust to push their own agendas through.[27] When the 1959 Tibetan uprising was suppressed by the People's Liberation Army, the exodus of the Dalai Lama to India with thousands of refugees in his wake provoked a storm of protests in several Indian cities. In Beijing, the National People's Congress began scrutinizing the party leadership on the Indian "interference" in the administration of Tibet.[28] When Indian border troops discovered a Chinese road on top of the disputed Aksai Chin plateau, the parliament cried foul and demanded that the road be "bombed out of existence."[29] Nehru was obliged to veer and respond to these calls with nationalist rhetoric. Whereas hitherto the border had not been a matter of national interest, the Himalayas now became the "crown of India" and part of her "culture, blood, and veins." Subsequently, in 1961, a "forward policy" was launched, which ordered Indian troops to patrol as far as possible.[30] A combination of interior pressure and wrong assessments finally led, in 1962, to an open war.

Built on the shaky foundations of two young states, foreign politics had a highly symbolic value. Lacking substantial economic and commercial interests abroad and missing social stability inside, diplomacy was about emancipation, and this emancipation was personalized by the two leaders, who drew on foreign policy as a source of prestige and nationalism. With the economic setbacks of the 1950s, the prospects for development and national unification started to fade, which made the appeal of gaining status and prestige abroad stronger than ever. In these circumstances, each affront was amplified by a diplomatic snowball effect that finally resulted in an armed collision.

THE 1960S AND THE 1970S:
TWENTY YEARS IN THE TRENCHES

The outcome of the Indo-Chinese war impeded Nehru in his continued efforts to extract legitimacy from his idealist diplomacy, whereas Mao felt strengthened in his foreign policy leadership. The Indian defeat shattered the idea of a nonaligned Asia as guarantee of peace and security. Even though Nehru and his successors Lal Bahadur Shastri and Indira Gandhi continued paying lip service to the principle, their foreign policies were shorn of the benevolent sentiment and idealist attitude of Nehru's original thinking. Blunt chauvinism started to dominate their diplomacy, while at the same time they resorted more than ever to foreign aid.[31] New Delhi knocked at the door of every possible supporter, whether it concerned London, Moscow, and Washington for military aid, or Canada and Australia for grain deliveries. In August 1963, when Nehru was still prime minister, the socialist leader Ram Manohar Lohia stated: "One minister of this government clings to the United States, another to Russia, and the magician tries to hold the balance by his charm. They call this non-alignment?"[32] The actual support from Washington and Moscow, though, was disappointing, so that India had to step up its own capacity to secure its interests. In 1963, Nehru doubled the Indian defense budget. After Nehru's death Shastri continued refurbishing the army. In his public rhetoric he combined appeals for economic opening up and modernization with a strong focus on India's increasing military strength. In April 1965, Shastri gave a green light for the preparation of experimental nuclear explosions, an attempt to demonstrate India's military might not only to Pakistan and China but also to his Indian compatriots.[33] The Second Indo-Pakistani War (April–October 1965) gave a boost to the prime minister's patriotic policy.[34] Addressing the nation on August 13, 1965, Shastri, referring to Pakistan's threats, stated: "Force will be met with force." Two days later, during the celebration of Independence Day, he added: "It does not matter if we are destroyed. We will fight to the last to maintain the high honour of the Indian nation and its flag." The Indian victory boosted Shastri's status to unprecedented heights and reoriented the public focus from domestic economic hardships and the new plague of hunger afflicting the country to the battlefield on the border with Pakistan. Jai Jawan, Jai Kisan (Hail the Soldier, Hail the Farmer) became the new motto merging Shastri's militarism with a call for modernization of the countryside. When Shastri died, in 1966, Indira Gandhi sought to continue this line.[35]

For the Chinese leadership, victory in the 1962 war was absolute. Troops of the People's Liberation Army had penetrated deep into Indian territory but then suddenly retreated. While the Indian regiments were overwhelmed by this stroke, Mao unilaterally announced a cease-fire and declared that India had "learned its lesson." This taste of success encouraged him even more to appeal to foreign issues for raising his domestic esteem, which was still under siege as a consequence of economic decline and rivalry within the political elite. Moreover, Mao decided that the total collapse of the flawed China-India axis in the nonaligned movement brought the need for a more revolutionary mode of neutrality.

Beijing resolutely opted for an independent foreign policy and blew up its bridges with both the Soviet Union and the United States. This militant neutralism was expressed in words and in deeds. Mao launched an aggressive propaganda campaign against imperialism. He urged the Third World, that is China and the developing countries, to shake off the subjugation of the First World, that is the two superpowers. The principle of struggle and active resistance thus emerged as the alpha and omega of China's diplomacy. Rebel movements all over the world were applauded and supported by means of financial and military aid. China's posture vis-à-vis imperialist "intrusion" into its periphery became irascible. In 1965, Beijing reacted ferociously to the coup of the rightist General Suharto in Indonesia. In 1968, political and armed communist resistance was supported in Malaysia, Indonesia, and Thailand. A year later, troops clashed with Russian border patrols at the Ussuri River.

In the end, instrumentalization of external relations for nationalistic ends became prominent in both countries. This was also the case in their bilateral relations. Between 1962 and 1965, India's political debate was entirely oriented toward the People's Republic. China's nuclear explosion in 1964 only strengthened the Indian obsession with the "Chinese peril." Especially in northern India, sentiments of distrust were deeply rooted in the collective memory of Chinese troops on Indian soil. This time, however, direct confrontation was avoided. Instead, rivalry was channeled mainly through Pakistan.

Such was the case during the Indo-Pakistan War of 1965. China actively supported the Pakistani side in its claim to Kashmir. When Zhou called on Pakistan in February 1964, the two countries signed a joint communiqué supporting Kashmir's partial secession from India.[36] In 1965, Zhou went further and asserted to Pakistan's president Ayub Khan that "if India commits aggression into Pakistan territory, China would definitely support Pakistan."[37] In September, at the height of the war, Beijing ordered troops to take frontline positions along the Tibetan border with India. On September 17, Chinese diplomats warned that the Indian presence in the disputed border state of Sikkim could trigger a Chinese military intervention. China clearly sought to relieve Pakistani troops by threatening India with a two-front war. China also assured Pakistan that it would block harmful resolutions from the UN Security Council. In China the state-controlled media portrayed India as a new colonialist power that needed to be curbed, and the case of the Kashmiri resistance was portrayed as an act of revolutionary struggle against imperialism.

In the 1960s, for both India and China the element of *struggle* gained importance at the expense of *accommodation*. A new open war between India and China was averted only because of the military successes of the Indian army and because Pakistan's president Khan and Prime Minister Shastri realized that an armed intervention by the three major powers would be detrimental for both parties.

Six years later, Beijing again chose the side of Islamabad in Pakistan's third war with India (1971).[38] When New Delhi decided to back East Pakistan in its struggle for secession, Beijing immediately increased its military presence along the Indian border, obliging the Indian command to diffuse its attention.[39] Apart from Pakistan, China also sought to trouble India by encouraging the Naxalite uprising in India's northeast. The Naxalites, described by Mao as "spring thunder," took the Great Leader's revolutionary style as a model and urged peasants and the lower classes to abolish landlordism and upper-caste supremacy. The cleavage between India and China further widened after each entered into an alliance with one of the two superpowers. In 1971, India and Moscow signed a Treaty of Friendship and Cooperation, a move that Beijing denounced as a "tool of Soviet expansionism." China simultaneously had replaced its militant neutralism for a realist alignment with the United States. In 1972 Indira Gandhi summarized her distrust vis-à-vis China in a *Foreign Affairs* article: "Simultaneous or subsequent developments, such as China's systematic support of Pakistan against India—her provocative criticism of India for alleged subservience to the United States and later the Soviet Union, and her persistent though futile efforts to promote internal subversion—leave us no option but to infer that the border dispute was the outcome of a more complex policy which aimed at undermining India's stability and at obstructing her rapid and orderly process."[40]

At the time of her writing the article, the victory in the Indo-Pakistan War of 1971 had boosted India's confidence and Gandhi's leadership. This euphoria was short-lived, however, as the opposition did not temper its criticism. The economic crisis between 1972 and 1973 aggravated social tensions. In this context Gandhi was forced to focus entirely on the domestic situation, nonetheless "external factors" were mentioned ceaselessly to explain the deteriorating internal situation.[41] Gandhi's Congress Party portrayed itself as the only party capable of maintaining India's integrity against powerful outside forces. India's first nuclear test, in 1974, symbolized this message and at the same time sent a warning to both China and Pakistan. Until the late 1970s, Beijing and New Delhi maintained a policy of counterbalancing. China continued its support of Pakistan's military build-up and contributed significantly to the development of the country's nuclear program. Between 1970 and 1980, China spent approximately U.S.$450 million on loans and grants to Islamabad. In 1971, Mao invited Sri Lanka's prime minister Sirimavo Bandaranaike to Beijing and provided her government with a U.S.$30 million long-term loan. That same year, Ne Win, head of Burma, visited China. Between 1972 and 1973 China launched a charm offensive toward Nepal, resulting in an official call by King Birendra, in December 1973, and a visit by Deng Xiaoping to Kathmandu five years later. In 1977 Bangladesh's strongman Zia Rahman was received in China and signed an agreement on economic cooperation. India, for its part, sympathized with the Cambodian rebel leader, Heng Samrin, who, in 1978, assaulted the Beijing-backed regime of Pol Pot. India also entered into an informal alliance with China's archenemy Vietnam, a country that New Delhi perceived as a vital buffer against Beijing's influence in Southeast Asia.[42] In 1975, it induced the Himalayan state of Sik-kim to join the Indian Union.

During the 1970s, China and India pursued a cold war in its purest form. Except for a border clash in 1975, in which China reasserted its military power on India's frontier, the emphasis was on deterrence, containment, and countercontainment.[43] The two countries acted as zealous errand boys of Washington and Moscow's divide-and-rule strategy in Asia. Realpolitik had become the basis of diplomacy. This modus of foreign policy brought a sense of predictability that permitted the political elites to shift their attention to the domestic front. As stated in the previous chapter, China's Communist Party was taken up by the reinvention of its own position and the restoration of the country after the turbulence of the 1960s. In this way foreign and do-mestic policies mutually reinforced the paving of the way to gradualism and pragmatism.

The failure of Mao's personality cult brought moderate leaders such as Zhou Enlai and Deng Xiaoping to the political fore. Without a doubt, Zhou used his regained authority to convince Mao to ameliorate contacts with the United States, Japan, and western Europe. The visit of American president Richard Nixon and Japanese prime minister Kakuei Tanaka highlighted the diplomatic momentum. The fact that this political rapprochement was ac-companied by intensified economic contacts consequently strengthened the reformers' domestic agendas. The 1971 Canton Trade Fair attracted two thou-sand foreign investors, among which were fifteen hundred Japanese. By 1973 commercial relations with noncommunist countries had reached 80 percent of China's total trade volume. Thus, the combination of domestic and interna-tional changes brought about a dramatic alteration in China's external policy. It gave rise to a reassessment of foreign policy priorities, from the exportation of class struggle to the import of capital and know-how. At this stage, deter-rence remained instrumental in the sense that it prevented the Soviet Union from interfering with China's interior transition and from drawing China against its will into violent conflicts. In this way, cautious diplomacy became a vehicle for economic development and vice versa.

In India, great-power trench war permitted the concentration of all at-tention on the social and political mayhem. Despite her harsh anti-U.S. and anti-China rhetoric, Gandhi expended efforts on restraining her domestic rivals. In the running up to and during the state of emergency (1975–1977), Indian armed forces were deployed for subjugating strikes and protests in-stead of for patrolling the border with China. Thus, the interaction between domestic and foreign policies was such that it catalyzed moderation. It allowed Prime Minister Gandhi to concentrate all means and attention on her personal power struggle. After the state of emergency, diplomatic prudence facilitated domestic rehabilitation, as was the case in China. The elections of 1977, entirely against her own assessment, brought a temporary end to Gandhi's rule. Her successor, Morarji Desai, stressed that domestic reconstruction needed stability along the borders. Prudence dominated foreign politics, and good-neighborliness became the centerpiece of Desai's foreign policy. In addition, the new government sought to curb its "unbalanced alignment" with the Soviet Union.[44] In 1978, Desai paid a visit to Washington, during which he underscored the "crucial importance" of a closer relationship. Simultaneously, New Delhi revived negotiations with Pakistan. This evolution broadened the scope for interaction significantly.

China and India seemed confident in their attempts to ease bilateral tensions. In 1976, China reopened its embassy in New Delhi, and India consequently sent an ambassador to the People's Republic. A year later, Beijing offered to start talks for resuming border trade. In 1978, it invited Foreign Minister Vajpayee to discuss bilateral political and economic relations. At the same time, China modified its pro-Pakistan stand on Kashmir and appeared willing to remain silent on India's absorption of Sikkim and its special advisory relationship with Bhutan. Beijing also offered to open Mount Kailas and Lake Manasarowar, in Tibet, the mythological home of the Hindu pantheon, to annual pilgrimages from India. Although Desai sincerely welcomed these initiatives, his scope for positive response was severely constrained. The opposition, including Gandhi, blamed him for soft-soaping China and being weak.[45] Nevertheless, he resisted calls for more assertiveness. Desai refused to exploit the development of nuclear arms, explaining that "a nuclear race with China would retard India's economic and social programs, weaken the country internally, and eliminate its political influence." In the 1970s, realpolitik gained the upper hand, making Sino-Indian relations more predictable. Gradually, the need for domestic rehabilitation and foreign stability became mutually reinforcing and paved the way for cautious deviations from power politics.

THE 1980s: COOPERATION WITH ECONOMICS AS A FACILITATING FACTOR

At the end of the 1970s, China took the lead in easing the strained relations. Desai welcomed this gesture, but he was still hampered by harsh criticism. Nevertheless, as soon as Gandhi regained power in 1980, she continued the line of appeasement herself, despite anti-China criticism and ardent lobbying by pro-Soviet interest groups.[46] This shift was decisive, since it allowed new, frail links to be sustained. In 1981, China's minister of foreign affairs, Huang Hua, was invited to India, where he made complimentary remarks about India's role in South Asia. When receiving a delegation from the Indian Council of Social Science Research in 1982, Deng Xiaoping stated: "We cannot afford not to understand each other and promote the friendship between us. The problem between China and India is not a serious one. Neither country poses a threat to the other. The problem we have is simply about the border. If we want to change the international economic order, we must, above all, settle the question of relations between the South and the North, but at the same time we have to find new ways to increase South-South cooperation."[47] Despite the symbolic and strategic sensitivity of the dossier, India and China held eight rounds of border negotiations between December 1981 and November 1987. In 1984, a trade agreement was reached.

After Indira Gandhi's death, Rajiv Gandhi instantly faced a crucial test case of his stance toward rapprochement.[48] In December 1986, the Indian parliament announced the creation of Arunachal Pradesh as a member of the union. This démarche enraged the Chinese government. Deng warned India not to take possession of disputed terrain. In the months following the act, troops mobilized on both sides of the border, and media reports even mentioned new armed skirmishes.[49] However, this time violence did not escalate, and both countries backed away after the Indian and Chinese ministers of foreign affairs met in New York. In May 1987, the Indian External Affairs minister was sent to Beijing to bring to an end this brief episode of unrest. This event clearly confirmed both countries' adherence to appeasement and dialogue. In 1988 Rajiv Gandhi paid a historical visit to China, despite opposition from the media and several Congress Party members. During the call he had lengthy conversations with Deng. Deng clearly identified China's internal quandaries with those of India:

> The world is changing, so people's minds have to change with it. Because of mistakes made in the past, especially during the Cultural Revolution, we have wasted about twenty years when we could have been building our country. After the downfall of the Gang of Four, everything has been changing here in China too. For example, we have changed from taking class struggle as the central task to concentrating on modernization, we have changed from stagnation and a closed-door policy to reform and a policy of opening to the outside world, and we are carrying out all sorts of reforms. I think your country will also encounter this problem of change. Development means change; without change, there can be no development.[50]

The visit of Deng's "young friend" deepened mutual trust at both states' highest levels of policy making. Annual diplomatic consultations between foreign ministers were set up to intensify this atmosphere of confidence. In addition, a working group was created to deal with the boundary question. Six rounds of talks of the Joint Working Group on the India-China Boundary Question were held between December 1988 and June 1993, resulting in several concrete confidence-building measures, including mutual troop reductions, regular meetings of local military commanders, and advance notification of military exercises. China and India also made progress with regard to economic relations. They signed three agreements on economic cooperation and established a joint ministerial committee on economic and scientific cooperation and approved direct air links.

What allowed this progress was the fact that the many sectoral negotiations were uncoupled. For instance, the time-consuming bargaining on territorial issues did not preclude the improvement of economic and political talks. The easing of the Cold War allowed India and China to partially distance themselves from geopolitical zero-sum thinking. Another contributing factor was the gradual depersonalization of foreign politics. Both Deng and Gandhi stayed at the center of diplomacy, but, unlike their predecessors, they did not make use of their positions to nourish personality cults. Gandhi duly followed the course mapped out by his foreign secretaries, the charismatic Romesh Bhandari and later A. P. Venkateswaran. Deng perceived diplomacy as just one tool among others for promoting domestic economic growth, which he saw as his main source of legitimacy.

During the 1970s, deterrence and realpolitik had enabled the political elites in Beijing and New Delhi to concentrate on their domestic power base. In the 1980s, the shift to appeasement was to a large extent the consequence of the *economization* of foreign politics. This did not mean that China and India anticipated becoming main trading partners. After all, save some border trade, the potential for direct commercial interaction was negligible. Nevertheless, even when commercial expectations were modest, joint economic initiatives became a means to foster mutual trust. Border trade, for example, was an important confidence-building measure. Bilateral trust and cooperation in turn contributed to the stability and predictability necessary for attracting foreign investors. Without peace at the borders, Deng would be thwarted in his plans to transform China into an appealing investment market, and Gandhi would be hindered in his attempt to involve overseas companies in his project for high-tech growth. Hence, economic security rather than military or territorial security became a core principle of the two countries' strategic planning.[51]

THE 1990S: CONTEST AND CONTINUATION

"I am confident that we have still to tap the full potential of the possibilities that exist for our two large economies to interact in the economic sphere," India's prime minister Narasimha Rao uttered when he visited China in 1993. "We could consider several modalities to realise this immense potential."[52] With Rao's becoming the new prime minister, India's diplomacy more than ever developed into economic diplomacy. Raja Mohan has described this as the crossing of the Rubicon: a transition from domestically focused socialism to a globalized free market economy, a de-emphasis on politics in favor of economics, an abandonment of New Delhi's earlier infatuation with Third Worldism and nonalignment, a rejection of anti-Westernism, and a loss of idealism.[53] Focusing on economic modernization and keeping a low international political profile became the central themes of India's foreign policy. In the late 1980s, Rajiv Gandhi took the first steps toward releasing diplomacy from the double straitjacket of nonalignment and the defunct alliance with Moscow. The shock of a new financial crisis in 1991 and the end of the Cold War strengthened the tendency toward openness.

These events increased the need and the international maneuverability for a more pragmatist approach in which economic interests gained the upper hand. In 1997, Prime Minister Inder Kumar Gujral stressed: "Our country is undergoing a veritable revolution in economic policy and in giving economy growth dynamism by integrating with the world economy. Our external relations have to fully reflect this new emphasis."[54] During the 1990s, the further economization of diplomacy was most obvious in several institutional reforms in the civil service.[55] The Ministry of External Affairs revamped its Economic Relations Division and created both a new Economic Coordination Unit and an Investment Promotion Unit. The ministry also became permanently involved in the National Steering Committee on Economic Reforms. Gradually, the diplomatic focus shifted from a preoccupation with Moscow and Islamabad to an orientation toward the world's main economic centers, the United States, the tigers in Southeast Asia, Japan, Europe, and China. Embassies were beefed up in these places to attract more investment and know-how.

In China, the crackdown in Tiananmen Square and the subsequent reaction of the international community led to a short period of hesitation and political introspection. A year later, however, the Chinese government enthusiastically started an invigoration of its external relations. The new generation of Chinese leaders, led by Jiang Zemin, accelerated the pace of liberalization and stepped up efforts to comply with international norms and standards. This was clearly illustrated by China's voluntary adherence to the stringent requirements put forward by the WTO and its individual member states. Based on participation rates in international institutions, Alastair Johnston has concluded that, during the 1990s, China became "overinvolved" for its level of development.[56]

The increasing importance of commercial interests in China's external affairs also resulted in a profound organizational reconfiguration. From the highly centralized decision making within the State Council and the Politburo, authority more and more dispersed over several other institutions. On the national level, the Ministry of Foreign Affairs and the newly created Ministry of Foreign Trade and Economic Cooperation in particular gained influence as they became the main sources of expertise in an increasingly complex international setting. Another trend was the decentralization beyond the national level. Provinces and major cities were allowed to expand the capacity to promote their own economic interests abroad. Professionalization and decentralization became the main characteristics of China's foreign policy making. Simultaneously, Beijing clarified its foreign security policy. The New Security Concept, issued in 1996, stressed the necessity of "seeking common security through consultations, coordination, and cooperation." Sovereignty remained the baseline, but to maintain it, economic security prevailed over military strength. "We should promote trust through dialogue, seek security through cooperation, respect each other's sovereignty, solve disputes through peaceful means and strive for common development."[57]

These institutional and conceptual changes fixed the diplomatic process. However, commercial interests now also started to dominate bilateral relations directly. China's spectacular ascent and India's more hospitable posture toward foreign entrepreneurs awakened an interest in exploring each other's markets. Between 1990 and 1999, the bilateral trade volume multiplied tenfold. In 1992, consulates reopened in Mumbai and Shanghai. In June 1993, the two sides agreed to open an additional border trading post. Under Rao's government the two sides prepared memorandums of understanding pertaining to the avoidance of double taxation, banking relations, and coal. In 1995, trade between China and India exceeded U.S.$1 billion for the first time.

High-level political exchanges continued. In 1993, Rao made a visit to Beijing. The two governments signed an Agreement on the Maintenance of Peace and Tranquillity that provided for troop reductions along the border and confidence-building measures. This political interaction continued under Rao's successors. In 1996, Prime Minister Deve Gowda hosted Jiang Zemin for a four-day state visit. This was the first visit of its kind by a Chinese head of state to India since the establishment of diplomatic relations. The respective militaries followed a similar course. In July 1992, the Indian defense minister paid a visit to Beijing, the first ever. The two countries' armed forces agreed to develop academic, military, scientific, and technological exchanges and to schedule an Indian port call by a Chinese naval vessel. In 1993, a senior-level Chinese military delegation called on India to concretize the confidence-building measures that had been agreed to earlier. That same year, border units organized the first joint meetings, and command-level exchanges began. In 1994, troops were reduced along both sides of the Himalayan frontier.

The second half of the 1990s saw the heightening of friction between economy-driven constructive engagement and negative nationalism based on military strength. In China these tensions were vented with two waves of missile tests above the Taiwan Strait. Whereas in the months prior to May 1995 Beijing had sought to revive informal interchanges and softened its stance on Taipei, the visit of President Lee Teng-hui to the United States precipitated a new crisis. The "official character" of this visit was perceived by China as a blunt provocation. The necessity for Jiang to prove his leadership, an assailing media campaign, and belligerent proposals from the military persuaded him to order a series of military exercises and short-range ballistic missile salvos near the Taiwanese coast.[58] This took place despite opposition from senior Foreign Affairs officials.[59]

In India, similar strains instigated the testing of five nuclear devices, on May 11 and 13, 1998. Whereas the cross-strait crisis stirred Indian public opinion only indirectly, Indian politicians provoked China directly by referring openly to it as a key threat. The Indian agitation toward China started to resurge in 1997. Members of parliament cast doubt on China's fulfillment of the earlier agreed confidence-building measures. Opposition spokesperson Vijay Kumar Malhotra, for instance, claimed "heavily armed" Chinese troops had crossed over into India and photographed territory in Himachal Pradesh. External Affairs minister Inder Kumar Gujral reacted stating the reported intrusion into India's frontier state was a "serious matter." Gujral was the first Indian foreign minister since the 1970s to publicly air national concerns over China's nuclear activities and its links with Pakistan. He declared that during President Jiang's visit "India proposes to engage in a comprehensive security dialogue with China and not just discuss development cooperation," and that "India can no longer ignore the activities of a full-fledged nuclear power in its neighborhood."[60] After Gujral became prime minister in 1997, his posture became more ambiguous. On the one hand, he struck a moderate tone. In his diplomatic manifest, he argued, "It stands for reason, therefore, the two largest developing countries in Asia should seek mutual beneficial cooperation. I am committed to working for a significant expansion and diversification of economic cooperation with China . . . We need to create a vested interest, through greater economic linkages, in each other's development and prosperity. There can be no surer guarantee of peace and stability."[61]

At the same time, however, he disclosed to U.S. representative Robert Cox his suspicion of China's exercising a pincer movement on India. He pointed specifically to the deployment of nuclear missiles in Tibet, the alleged submarines in the Indian Ocean, the impression that Burma had been turned into a stronghold of the Chinese army, and China's military assistance to Pakistan. The so-called Gujral Doctrine thus acquired a Janus-faced aspect. This policy prioritizing a stronger presence in India's immediate periphery can be interpreted not only as an attempt to deepen economic integration but also as a strategy to ward off China's influence in the area. Hence, in the second half of the 1990s the positive expectations of Rao and Gowda were sifted into an ambiguous mixture of optimism and distrust.

After the general elections of 1998, Sino-Indian relations trembled in the shock waves of India's nuclear experiments. Ever since the failed test of 1974, politicians had been toying with the idea of a new experiment, but either they were impeded by financial constraints or they did not want to face the diplomatic consequences.[62] What convinced Prime Minister Vajpayee to give the green light? After the dispute with Pakistan, the development of a nuclear force has always been a key issue in the BJP's security policy. The endeavor was first and foremost a highly symbolic mission. It was about national strength and pride and opposed what has been called the nuclear discrimination by other powers. From the mid-1990s, this opinion was reinforced.[63] The electoral fragmentation obliged the major parties, the BJP and the Congress Party, to distinguish themselves. Both endorsed the need for further economic reform and opening up, and, similarly, they needed to make substantial concessions to smaller parties if they hoped to form a government coalition. Under the slogan For a Strong and Prosperous India, the BJP's 1996 election manifesto clearly accentuated the "strong" part and stressed that India should be armed with nuclear weapons in order to become a true world power.[64] The issue was brought to a head after China and the United States joined forces to approve the Comprehensive Test Ban Treaty (CTBT), a move that Vajpayee denounced as "nuclear apartheid."[65] It has been reported that after only fifteen days into his premiership, Vajpayee ordered, in May 1996, preparations for a new nuclear explosion, but, because of a lack of time, the plans were stalled. The issue was brought up again during the general elections of March 1998. In its manifesto, the BJP assured that it would "actively oppose attempts to impose a hegemonistic nuclear regime."[66]

After the party succeeded in forming a new cabinet, the popular media affiliated with the BJP threw attention on the nuclear policies of countries such as China and the United States. The argument was that they, respectively, supported Pakistan and Israel while prohibiting India from developing nuclear weapons.[67] Such opinions became even more pronounced in April, after Pakistan test-fired an intermediate-range ballistic missile, allegedly assisted by China.[68] On May 11 and 13, several nuclear devices were detonated in Pokhran. Unlike the Taiwan crisis, the detonation directly threatened the bilateral relationship. The successful tests were not only celebrated as emancipated muscle flexing but also, in the subsequent weeks, explicitly targeted *against* Pakistan and the People's Republic. China ended up in the path of a rhetorical storm. On May 18, Defense Minister George Fernandes referred to the northern neighbor as the "potential threat number one" and contended that "the potential threat from China is greater than that from Pakistan." On May 29, Prime Minister Vajpayee continued along the same line: "There is a threat, a primary security challenge from China . . . We are for a better relationship with China even today. But at the same time, you should not forget that unless we prove our might, unless we prove our strength, peace is not possible."[69] Later, in a letter addressed to U.S. president Bill Clinton, he wrote:

> I have been deeply concerned at the deteriorating security environment, especially the nuclear environment, faced by India for some years past. We have an overt nuclear weapon state on our borders, a state which committed armed aggression against India in 1962. Although our relations with that country have improved in the last decade or so, an atmosphere of distrust persists mainly due to the unresolved border problem. To add to the distrust that country has materially helped another neighbour of ours to become a covert nuclear weapons state. At the hands of this bitter neighbour we have suffered three aggressions in the last 50 years.

These two events displayed several similarities. First, Jiang and Vajpayee were under strong internal pressure to strengthen their political positions. Vajpayee sought to rally voters to accrue more weight in the negotiations for a new government coalition. Jiang, the first Chinese president who had not served in the armed forces, needed to gain credibility with the military, especially after he announced plans to push through another round of troop reductions. There was a need to confirm the People's Liberation Army as the ultimate guardian of the state's sovereignty. Second, both leaders faced a point of no return. As a consequence of earlier policies and statements, the subjugation of Taiwan and a nuclear power status were considered sine qua non conditions of rule. Third, they both felt pressure from external actors: China and the United States in the case of the pending CTBT, and the United States in that of Taiwan. Finally, both in China and in India, decision makers were deeply divided over the handling of the questions. Jiang faced firm opposition from senior Foreign Service officers, industry leaders, and top party members, who feared that the maneuvers would affect China's investment climate. India's new prime minister faced skepticism not only from competing parties but also from high-ranking military commanders. One general stated: "We simply cannot afford to antagonize the Chinese at this point . . . We are fully stretched in combating insurgency in the country and if we have to deal with renewed tensions on the LAC, the army could well break down."[70] Thus, deterrence was to a large extent for electoral and even personal use.

In the matter of the Pokhran tests, however, the additional question arises as to why China was brought up in the public arena as the main scapegoat. After all, bilateral relations were improving, and, among the BJP's leadership, a consensus existed that ties with the People's Republic should be further strengthened. The first argument, and of course the baseline of nuclear deterrence, was that a nuclear capacity would prevent the repetition of the 1962 scenario. Second, a minimal nuclear deterrence would strengthen India's bargaining position in dealing with issues such as the boundary settlement. Third, it was assumed that India needed a nuclear umbrella from under which it could project its influence without having to fear a violent clash with China's regional aspirations; nuclear power would enable a regional sway on an equal footing.[71]

However, these three arguments did not go unchallenged. It was contended, in the first place, that its northern neighbor might risk a new invasion. Former prime ministers Gujral and Gowda had openly refuted such a scenario, and they were supported in this stance by several leading strategists.[72] Unlike the 1960s, India's conventional capabilities were now reckoned to be strong enough to block a military offensive.[73] China would not, therefore, risk the costs of a full-scale war. In addition it was emphasized that India could change Beijing's mind by playing the Tibet card, that is, by supporting armed Tibetan resistance, or by launching short-range conventional missiles at border cities such as Chengdu and Kunming. It was also questioned whether India's strategy of minimal deterrence would really work, since India lacked adequate middle-range missiles and China had the capacity to carry out a decisive first strike.[74] Finally, doubts were voiced that the nuclear umbrella could strengthen India's regional position, as nuclear muscle flexing would, rather, foster distrust more than respect. Thus, whereas the nuclear tests as such were not surprising, the reference to China in legitimating them certainly was.

Therefore, the causes of the rhetoric against the People's Republic must be located beyond strategic considerations. Although it is not possible to precisely trace them, several additional explanations can be offered. First, there were the personal convictions of leading figures like Vajpayee and Fernandes. Vajpayee undoubtedly had not forgotten that China declared war against Vietnam in 1979 just at the moment he was paying a visit to Beijing as minister of foreign affairs. Fernandes, for his part, had never made a secret of his aversion toward the Chinese subjugation of Tibet. From early in his political career he was known for his blunt statements and stubbornness.[75] Second, China placed itself at the center of India's nuclear debate after the major nuclear tests in June 1996 by playing a prominent role as a defender of the CTBT and by continuing its support of Pakistan's missile development project. Third, at the time, the Ministry of Defence was duly prepared to endorse the China-threat contention, since it was struggling under budgetary constraints. Finally, China's military transition and its relations with Pakistan were an intriguing and rewarding issue for the Indian news media. Consequently, even though there was not a consensus about the actual merits of nuclear deterrence vis-à-vis China among experts and policy makers, several less-explicit promptings, desires, and aims determined the rhetorical setting. China was more the provider of ad-hoc justification for the process than its cause.

The aftermath of the nuclear upheaval confirmed India and China's inclination toward peace and cooperation.[76] Beijing's self-restrained reaction in particular demonstrated its propensity for dialogue and stability instead of confrontation. The initial response to the first round of tests was silence. The official press agency Xinhua only reported the news, without comment, and the spokesman for the Ministry of Foreign Affairs refused to respond to questions pertaining to the incident. Only days afterward did the Chinese media start to decry the incident. After the second round of tests, the ministry stated that the Chinese government was deeply shocked and expressed "its strong condemnation."

Yet, China refrained from criticizing the nuclear explosion as such, given the sacrosanct premise of sovereignty and the fact that the supreme party leadership did not consider it an important challenge to its security.[77] Instead, the Chinese government endeavored to avoid further damage to the partnership. By means of its mouthpiece, the *People's Daily*, it advised New Delhi to "treasure the fruits of the bilateral relations." Moreover, the official media displayed understanding for the "internal dimension" of India's nuclear nationalism and pointed to the personal opinions and interests of hawkish figures such as George Fernandes more than to India as a whole. In addition to this rhetorical restraint, China did not unilaterally resort to punitive measures. Nor did it choose to counterbalance the event with more support for Pakistan's nuclear testing. It used the incident instead to beef up its status as a responsible international actor and preferred multilateral action within the framework of a UN Security Council resolution.[78]

One month after the blasts, India started to mend fences. On June 11, the Indian Defence spokesman Jaswant Singh explained: "About these areas of concern we have engaged with the People's Republic of China meaningfully and seriously over the past some years, and that process of engagement and discussion shall continue. Our approach to China is not of trepidation. These are two great civilizations. They do not approach each other with anxiety or trepidation."[79] It took four months for the agitation to calm. During the winter of 1998, Indian diplomats traveled to Beijing to resume the Sino-Indian dialogue. President K. R. Narayanan declared, in his February 22 speech, that India sought to "strengthen and deepen its historic and friendly relations with China."[80] These friendly remarks were immediately reported by the Chinese news media. Later in February, consultations at the director general level between the two foreign ministries were held in Beijing, which served as a starting point for improvement of bilateral relations and paved the way for the resumption of the Joint Working Group at the vice ministerial level.[81] Thus, rather than being a turning point, the aftermath of India's nuclear tests confirmed the mutual willingness to restore the progress that had been made in the first half of the 1990s; the nuclear blast did not result in a diplomatic fallout.

A new eruption of Indo-Pakistani violence in Kashmir presented a new test case for the revitalizing relationship. In May 1999, Kashmiri militants, with the support of the Pakistani military, crossed the Line of Control into the Kargil area in the India-controlled state of Jammu and Kashmir. The Indian army launched military operations seeking to repel the intrusion. In June, the conflict escalated into a full-scale war. At this boiling point, India's foreign minister was invited to Beijing and assured that China would not back Pakistan's offensive.[82] Foreign Minister Tang Jiaxuan acquainted visiting Pakistani foreign minister Sartaj Aziz of China's "great concern" regarding the present situation in Kashmir.[83] Later the same month Pakistani prime minister Nawaz Sharif called on Beijing seeking greater Chinese support for Kashmir. Jiang refused to give in to these demands and explained to Sharif that he expected that India and Pakistan would jointly seek a solution.

For the Sino-Indian relationship, the 1990s was a period of both contest and confirmation. Between 1991 and 1996, bilateral ties flourished like never before. Economic expectations in particular created a new drive for interaction that was carefully nurtured by Beijing and New Delhi. Nonetheless, a new crisis in the Taiwan Strait and India's nuclear ventures in 1998 proved that this motivation was not without contest. The fusion of internal tensions and remaining external threat perceptions resulted in dramatic challenges for the maintenance of the bilateral dialogue. However, the striking difference with, for example, the early 1950s and 1960s was that these challenges were not allowed to blow up the bridges. China's calm reaction to the 1998 crisis especially demonstrated an ability to separate a short-sighted act of aggression from the fundamental need for stability. In this sense, the 1990s represented an important stage of confirmation rather than reversal.

THE ERA OF CHINDIA

In the closing years of the twentieth century, economic expectations had been a key stimulus for the rapprochement between the two countries. The central governments in particular carefully cultivated the idea of mutual gain. At the beginning of the new century, this impetus became self-sustaining as other state and nonstate actors actively promoted stronger commercial ties as well. Whereas economic cooperation had been pushed forward mainly by the political elites, bilateral ties now started to branch into other levels. The large companies that had been maturing in the protective economic environment of the 1980s and 1990s especially aimed at expanding their activities beyond the border. The Indo-Chinese forums that had been established in the preceding decade lobbied strongly for more openness and integration. Another drive came from local authorities, notably in border provinces that hoped to unlock their remote economies. Even the military appeared to engage in mending ties. More and more, security issues and border problems moved to the background of public and diplomatic discourses. In both the official discourse and in that of influential companies, borders and barriers made place for deepening interaction. The cooperation of the prior decade paved the way for the idea of deepening synergies.

After the 1999 elections strengthened the BJP's leading position, the Indian government launched a charm offensive to amend for its offensive posture of the late 1990s. The period between 2000 and 2005 saw a boost of high-level visits. Only four months after the installation of the new BJP-led government, commerce and industry minister Murasoli Maran traveled to China to study the Special Economic Zones. He himself referred to the visit as an eye-opener: "After studying the success of these special economic zones, I have decided to have similar SEZ in our country. The idea of SEZ is new to India, hence I modelled it on China."[84] In May 2000, President Narayanan followed. In 2001 and 2002, several exchanges of ministers and senior members of both countries' parliaments took place. In the meantime, Hu Jintao had been taking over the party leadership from Jiang Zemin. In the run-up to his presidency, Hu repeatedly emphasized the need for continuing the "normal development track."[85] This intention materialized when Beijing extended an invitation to former China basher Defense Minister George Fernandes. The Indian and Chinese media gave to this highly symbolic visit to Beijing more coverage than that for all visits in the previous years together.

A few months later, the charm offensive reached a new highpoint when Prime Minister Vajpayee journeyed to the People's Republic for a five-day state visit, during which agreement was reached on "qualitatively enhancing the bilateral relationship at all levels and in all areas."[86] Compared with Jiang's mission to India in 1996, the results of this meeting covered a wider array of issues and matters that were more concrete and technical. The parties signed nine memorandums of understanding encompassing issues from phytosanitary measures for trade in mangoes to energy cooperation. The joint declaration stressed the need to intensify interaction at all levels: President Hu was invited to visit India, it was decided that the foreign affairs ministers would hold annual consultations, and that personnel exchanges between ministries, parliaments, political parties, and the militaries of the two countries should be further enhanced.[87] The issue of a boundary settlement was moved entirely to the background as the two countries chose to appoint a special representative to explore the framework for a boundary settlement. The two officials, Indian national security adviser Brajesh Mishra and Chinese vice minister Dai Bingguo, met several times without media coverage.[88] "We both wanted to take the discussion away from the microphones and look for solutions in practical and technical details," a senior Indian diplomat summarized.

This mind-set endured the Indian general elections of 2004 smoothly. Unlike in former campaigns, neither China nor the symbolic border question in particular made it to the rostrums. The BJP and the Congress Party election manifestos struck the same tone and appealed for maintaining the path of cooperation. The former underlined the "amazing speed" at which economic cooperation had been growing.[89] While the Congress Party has not shown the munificence to give credit to the BJP-led coalition for improving relations with China during its tenure in office, it has refrained from criticizing the BJP's handling of relations. Its manifesto called China "the most important factor affecting Asian security and stability," and its foreign policy program confirmed that "the Congress will continue and increase the momentum of the initiative that the Congress Government took between 1988 and 1996 to ensure a stable and mutually cooperative and beneficial relationship with China."[90]

In 2005, new prime minister Manmohan Singh invited his Chinese counterpart, Wen Jiabao, for a visit, which led to the conclusion of a strategic partnership and a new series of rather technical arrangements on economic and border issues. With the announcement of a strategic partnership, Beijing symbolically confirmed India's status as a friendly power. This recognition was encapsulated more concretely in Wen's overt support for India's claim to a permanent seat on the UN Security Council, in the formal recognition of Sikkim as a part of the Indian republic, and in a first "strategic dialogue" at the vice ministerial level.[91] A year later, the presidential aircraft touched down in New Delhi. Hu and his hosts placed this visit in the light of "making cooperation irreversible." Therefore, apart from trade, discussions focused mainly on stimulating interaction between policy makers, diplomats, students, and military officers.[92] Also significant was the announcement to intensify cooperation at the regional level, notably in a trilateral framework with Russia, within the Shanghai Cooperation Organization (SCO), a central Asian forum dominated by China, and the South Asian Association for Regional Cooperation (SAARC), in which India does most of the talking. With an annual average of nine state-to-state visits at the ministerial or presidential levels and a multiplicity of other official stopovers, the beginning of the new century heralded an unprecedented diplomatic momentum.

Simultaneous with the diplomatic charm offensive, corporate initiatives developed as a new, autonomous motion for intensifying cooperation. In particular, both countries' new generation of national champions started to explore additional options for going beyond the borders. Since 2002, Indian software and information companies such as TCS, Infosys, Wipro, and Satyam have set up branches in China.[93] Zensar Technologies, as another example, established a Global Development Center in Hangzhou and trained a thousand Chinese software project managers in India.[94] In 2005, the influential Indian firm Tata reported increasing its turnover in China to U.S.$200 million.[95] China's leading consumer electronics group TCL laid down U.S.$150 million in an Indian plant to produce televisions, DVD players, and air conditioners. Haier Group is also planning to set up a factory to make home appliances. In 2006, Haier assembled about twenty thousand TVs a month in India under contracts with Indian companies. More than 130 entrepreneurs from China and India took part in a China-India CEO forum in 2006, most from leading enterprises like Huawei, ZTE, Sinosteel, China Minmetals, CMEC, Tata, Mahindra and Mahindra, Jubilant, and SRS.[96] Just previous, the BusinessWeek

CEO Forum in Beijing concluded that the two countries "should establish more co-operation mechanisms in order to complement their strengths."[97] Various chambers of commerce had been outpacing the government's euphoria. Prior to 2000, most Indian economic confederations and chambers of commerce had been apprehensive about the increasing imports of cheap Chinese goods and the growing competition from China in exports to neighboring markets such as Sri Lanka, Bangladesh, Nepal, and Myanmar, and the South-East Asian countries.[98] "In all our global industry interactions, it is no more China or India," Confederation of Indian Industry (CII) director general Srinivasan asserted, "it is now China and India. In the coming years we see it as China with India."[99] The CII took several initiatives "to educate Indian entrepreneurs and opinion makers about China."[100] The Federation of Indian Chambers of Commerce and Industry (FICCI) organized numerous meetings with its Chinese counterparts, such as the China Council for the Promotion of International Trade.[101] The Indian government issued modified guidelines for the quick granting of visas to Chinese nationals and extensions of their stay in India. These changes were due to considerable pressure from Reliance Industries, the largest business entity in the country, which wanted to hire Chinese contractors for a construction project.[102]

Another impetus came from substate governments. In both China and India, provinces and major cities had a leading role in promoting opening up. In 2000, the foreign affairs office of China's southeastern province of Yunnan launched the Kunming Initiative, which sought to assemble experts from India, Bangladesh, and Myanmar to "revive the ancient Southern Silk Route between Assam and Yunnan."[103] What started as an informal academic project developed into an influential lobby for more cross-border ties.[104] In 2006, Beijing and New Delhi approved the rejuvenation of the Stilwell, or Ledo, Road, after strong appeals from Yunnan and the landlocked Indian states of Assam, Arunachal Pradesh, Meghalaya, Manipur, Nagaland, Mizoram, and Sikkim.[105] During a conference in 2005, these remote states also urged the central government to invest in two other infrastructure projects, the Gangtok–Nathu La and Sevoke-Gangtok roads, and to put in place adequate credit infrastructure for trade in agricultural goods.[106] That same year, the vice secretary general of the Yunnan government proposed an air link to Calcutta and announced plans to make his province an attractive destination for Indian travelers.[107] Sichuan, another southern border province, made eyes at India as well. With West Bengal, it agreed to promote commercial exchanges.[108] Its capital Chengdu especially is ambitious to attract Indian IT companies to replicate the success of Bangalore, the so-called Indian Silicon Valley.[109] On the Indian side, Sikkim hopes to reap profits by profiling itself as a trade corridor.[110] West Bengal presents itself as the maritime front for China's land-locked provinces in the south and a chief supplier of steel products.[111] In 2006, it signed a trade pact with Hunan province and revealed plans to establish a special investment zone for Chinese companies.[112] Earlier, West Bengal had explored possibilities of getting Chinese support to transform itself into "the toy manufacturing capital of the country." Apart from these conterminous regions, several other states and provinces joined the scramble. Between 2002 and 2006, five Indian states sent a delegation to China, among which Gujarat organized a mission headed by the ultra-nationalist chief minister.[113] In China, provinces as far as Jilin explored commercial opportunities in India.

This proliferation of mutual interest, political and corporate, resulted in new and larger steps to deepen economic cooperation and hesitant moves toward commercial integration. [114]To start with, several measures were taken to dismantle tariff and nontariff trade barriers. In 2000, China offered to cut tariff rate quotas for agricultural products and phytosanitary measures on pharmaceuticals, two product categories in which India had a comparative advantage. During Vajpayee's visit in 2003, Beijing and New Delhi agreed to exchange trade preferences under the Bangkok Agreement. Under the agreement, China offered tariff preferences on 217 items, including foods, chemical products, drugs, textile products, and machinery items. India offered tariff concessions on 188 items, including primarily chemical, paper, steel, rubber, electric machinery, railway products, and toys. In addition, China vowed to facilitate the import of Indian fresh fruits and vegetables. Since 2004, China in particular has been urging to go further. In 2005, China's ambassador in New Delhi announced his country was ready for a free trade agreement.[115] A month later this sentiment was echoed by Prime Minister Wen Jiabao.[116] In 2005, the Joint Group on Economic, Trade, Science and Technology Cooperation suggested a China-India Regional Trade Arrangement instead, including trade in goods and services, investments, identified understandings of trade and investment promotion and facilitation, and measures for the promotion of economic cooperation in clearly defined sectors, with safeguards in the form of tariff rate quotas.[117] Subsequently, the two sides agreed to appoint a joint task force to study in detail the feasibility and benefits.

Second, transportation links are a part of the attempt to foster economic integration as well. In 2003, India and China agreed to reopen Nathu La Pass, a mountainous trail at an altitude of more than four thousand meters. Unlike the Shipki La and Lipulekh passes, which were opened under the border trade agreement of 1991, Nathu La is expected to channel a larger volume of trade and to reduce transport time.[118] From the outset, expectations were high. A study by Jawaharlal Nehru University, in New Delhi, predicted trade through the pass would increase from U.S.$48 million, in 2007, to U.S.$527 million, in 2010.[119] Although only regional goods were allowed for transit, given the limited payload and the fear for competition, both New Delhi and Beijing decided to develop communication links via the passes.[120] In China, a new border market was established and the Qinghai–Tibet Railway was extended to Shigatse and Yadong, a town near Nathu-La Pass.[121] The India Border Roads Organisation took the responsibility for widening the Gangtok–Nathu La road, for completion by 2010. Moreover, in 2006 the Indian government revealed plans to construct a 608-kilometer road through five states in order to develop infrastructure and trade links along the Indo-China border.[122] The same plans contained the administration's intention to upgrade the Indian section of the so-called Stilwell Road, a historical thirteen-hundred-kilometer-long connection between the northeastern city of Ledo and the Chinese province of Yunnan.[123] These plans announced a significant shift. Until then, the Indian government had been unwilling to develop transportation links along the frontage with China because it feared it would give the Chinese military an advantage in the event of hostilities. In addition to these road connections, China and India also decided, in 2003, to enhance air links. In 2006, Manmohan Singh and Hu Jintao approved an increase in direct flights from seven to forty-two per week.

In 2006, a new milestone was reached when India and China signed five memorandums of understanding in the area of oil and natural gas. As India's petroleum minister Mani Shankar Aiyar explained, "Both China and India recognize that unbridled rivalry between them only results in the seller of the assets being benefited irrespective of which of the two countries wins the bid."[124] The agreement came after Indian and Chinese oil companies wrestled for oil concessions in Angola, Nigeria, Kazakhstan, Ecuador, and Myanmar. One memorandum provided for the establishment of a joint committee in which representatives from both countries' oil industry are to exchange information on bids for overseas oil and gas contracts. The other documents stipulated the intention of Indian and Chinese state-owned energy enterprises to team up in the areas of research, exploration and refining, and pipeline construction.[125] In 2005, another new step was taken. India's Ministry of Oil proposed that China participate in the construction of a transnational gas pipeline connecting the extensive deposits in Iran with India and China.[126] A year later, a prominent expert from the influential National Energy Leading Group, the committee in charge of China's energy strategy, disclosed plans to build a pipeline linking both India and China to Russia's oil fields.[127]

Although these initial plans are not yet concrete and remain without obligations, they show that both sides are prepared to distance themselves from the zero-sum approach that dominates the international energy market. They also reflect a substantial degree of interdependence. Beginning in the 1990s, the two industrializing countries became net importers of oil, and they both face suppliers that try to capitalize on the competition for their assets. Moreover, in the race for resources, India and China are equally confronted by the dominance of strong Western oil giants. Concerning the two pipeline proposals, such projects not only imply a de facto consumer alliance, but they would also deepen energy interdependence, since India would partly rely on China as a corridor for Russian oil, and China on India for Iranian natural gas. In November 2006, energy collaboration went beyond mineral fuels. At that time a joint statement on civilian nuclear cooperation was made public.[128] Although the substance of this declaration remained opaque, it marked China's acceptance of India as a responsible nuclear power. It significantly desecuritized India's nuclear program and shifted attention from the military perspective to the commercial dimension. After all, Beijing showed itself interested in providing know-how and infrastructure.

Fourth, economic ties were tightened in the financial sector. In 2003, Beijing and New Delhi agreed to enter into a financial dialogue with the purpose of exchanging information and best practices on monetary policies.[129] This was seen as a matter of necessity. As the two economic powers' influence on the international monetary market increased, an unfortunate coincidence of policy decisions by their central banks could trigger severe financial shocks that would do harm to both.[130] If, for instance, New Delhi and Beijing decided simultaneously to stockpile a strategic reserve of commodities, this could lead to booming oil prices and surging inflation. Competitive devaluations of national currencies are another scenario that is to be prevented. If India, for example, decided to strengthen its position as an exporter by lowering the rupee, China might decide to follow suit and provoke a race to the bottom that would overheat both their domestic economies.

Finally, India and China teamed up to defend their interests toward international trade regimes.[131] During the negotiations for a new world trade agreement, the so-called Doha Round, the two states took the vanguard in an assault against agriculture subsidies in the United States and the European Union. Jointly with Pakistan and Hong Kong, they also stalled talks on assistance for smaller textile-producing developing countries.[132] With regard to intellectual property rights, Chinese and Indian representatives blocked Western proposals for tight enforcement procedures. They also successfully opposed the European Union's call for new negotiations covering foreign investment, competition, customs rules, and government procurement. In 2006 India's commerce minister Kamal Nath and his Chinese counterpart

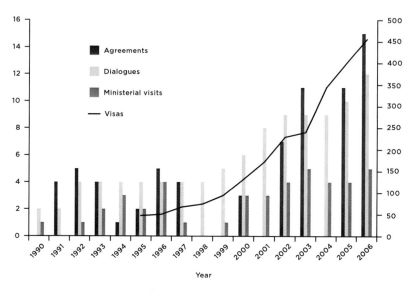

FIGURE 2.1　Measuring Interdependence. The graph shows (*left axis*) the accumulated number of bilateral agreements and memorandums of understanding, the accumulated number of bilateral track I and II dialogues, the annual number of ministerial visits, and (*right axis*) the annual number of visas granted. *Sources*: Indian Ministry of External Affairs; Chinese Ministry of Foreign Affairs; Chinese embassy in New Delhi; *China Statistical Yearbook, 2008*; and Indian Ministry of Tourism.

Bo Xilai announced they intended to continue this synergy.[133] On a lower level, this posture was reflected in a cooperation memorandum between the influential Shanghai WTO Affairs Consultation Center and the FICCI.[134] In this case of the international trade regime, China and India clearly take a position at the center of the bargaining process.

From the beginning of the twenty-first century, the idea of two separate but linked economies gradually made room for a notion of integration, integration that would enable the two countries to exploit their division of labor. Politicians, heads of industry, and several news media organizations replaced China and India with the idea of Chindia. Instead of *competition, complementarity* became the new buzzword. Chinese officials in particular capitalized on the Ricardian expectations. Visiting India's IT miracle in Bangalore, Prime Minister Zhu Rongji proposed joining forces: "You are number one in software. We are number one in hardware. If we put hardware and software together, we are the world's number one."[135] When several Indian industrialists stated that the People's Republic barely imported manufactured goods, Wen Jiabao riposted that bilateral trade "expanded from pure import and export of commodities to multifaceted and multidimensional cooperation including engineering contracting, technology trade and two-way investment."[136] In a similar way, Hu Jintao promised to "diversify the trade basket" and particularly stirred the expectations of Indian steel, IT, and biotechnology concerns. In order to tap the comparative advantages more efficiently and to increase the trade volume to U.S.$30 billion and later to U.S.$40 billion by 2010, New Delhi and Beijing ordered the drafting of a Five-Year Plan for China-India All-Round Trade and Economic Cooperation. Thus, the numerous new interest groups have proved to be a fertile breeding ground for expectations to continue to grow as they team up with the central political elites to deepen cooperation.

ON THE HIMALAYAN TRACK

Sino-Indian relations have followed a Himalayan trail. It is a bumpy road marked by sudden changes in the landscape. In the past twenty years, however, there has been more continuity in the complex bilateral relationship. Despite the dramatic nuclear tests of 1998, economic interests have been the key conductor of appeasement, accommodation, cooperation, and the first steps toward integration. Both discourse and deeds confirm that the attempt to transform India and China into open trading states has abated tensions and stimulated expectations about the economic gains of peace and deepening exchanges. Figure 2.1 illustrates the deepening political ties and confirms that, especially after 1998, the political willingness to consolidate the relationship gained momentum and resulted in an increasing number of agreements and high-level dialogues. The figure also reveals that, after 1998, political exchanges grew to an unprecedented level. This is also the case with the number of bilateral visits by Indian and Chinese citizens, as is also shown in the figure. The idea of a lucrative division of labor gained importance. Accordingly, China and India's obsession with growth has little or nothing to do with an economic balance of power. Economic ambitions are inward-oriented. The fact that the Indian government hopes to emulate China's success originates from its encounter with Indian voters rather than with this neighbor's increasing power. In both China and India, the national political elites have been taking the lead in the quest for a common ground. Since the beginning of the new century, this drive has been strengthened by several new substate and nonstate actors: provinces, major cities, think tanks, companies, chambers of commerce, and so on. Is economic interdependence the winning formula for peace? In the case of China and India, the assumptions related to the impact of interdependence appear to be valid.

Yet, it remains to be seen how deep the economic interdependence really is. The bilateral commercial flows have been expanding significantly, but as a share of India and China's overall trade, they are modest. Moreover, the current trade pattern seems to benefit China more than India, since the latter exports mostly low-value-added raw materials. Is this division of labor indeed mutually beneficial? How will it evolve in the future? What will be the consequences if India fulfills it plans to beef up its export-oriented industries? What if China achieves growth in economic branches in which India has hitherto had a comparative advantage? The following chapters look closer into these issues.

THREE

RICARDO'S REALITY

IN THEIR QUESTS FOR NATIONAL UNITY India and China have em-
braced economic development via openness as a new sort of superglue. By
piloting their enormous labor reserves into the global economy, both countries' political establishments aspire to continue the arduous task of nation
building and to enhance their legitimacy through job creation and a swift
improvement of living standards. In turn, these high expectations result in a
diplomacy that prioritizes the attraction of investments and access to foreign
markets, with stability at the borders as a precondition. These dynamics have
also propelled the amelioration of bilateral relations between the two Asian
giants. This chapter examines how much the two countries can gain from
cooperation at the economic level. It will posit that such profits indeed prove
to be substantial in the short term, but that integration is fostering competition, and that for the longer haul this new competition might become of such
a proportion that it halts further integration.

The current concept of Chindia, a complex of two integrating markets,
is to a large degree founded on the idea of economic complementarity. Each
country possesses particular comparative advantages and has thus the potential for specialization. If states concentrate on specific niches, a division of
labor will materialize that is mutually beneficial, that optimizes the effective-
ness of production, and stimulates commercial exchanges. India's minister of
commerce and industry Kamal Nath, for instance, described India and China
as "twin engines of growth" and underlined that the complementarities were
reflected in the fact "that India had a comparative advantage in IT software
and China in IT hardware. Similarly, India's strength in auto components,

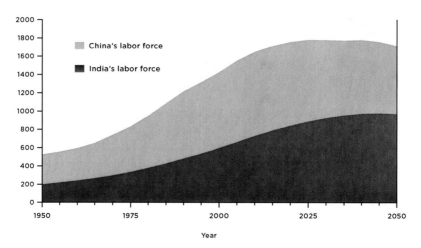

FIGURE 3.1   Projected Development of the Labor Forces (between sixteen and sixty years of age [in Millions]) of China and India According to UN Population Division's Medium Fertility Scenario. *Source*: United Nations Population Division, 2008.

pharmaceuticals and chemicals and machine tools were complemented by China's strengths in electronics, toys and machinery." "Therefore," Nath continued, "I do not see this as an India *versus* China debate, but rather in an India *with* China context."[1]

The pressure for swift economic development will not lessen in the coming decades. The first challenge relates to the expanding labor force. Figure 3.1 shows that China and India's combined population in an age range between sixteen and sixty-five will grow at least until 2030. The natural growth of this labor force obliges China to create an additional 55 million jobs between 2010 and 2020. For India the figure is 316 jobs by 2045. At the apex of their demographic curves, to be reached in 2025, the two countries together need to provide 225 million additional jobs.[2] This comes on top of the present un- and underemployment rates. Comparing national figures on these indicators is problematic given the different definitions and methods of calculation used by the monitoring agencies. For China the unemployment rate is assumed to be somewhere around 8 percent, in India it is 9 percent.[3]

Applied to their current labor force, this would result in 100 million unemployed citizens.[4] Underemployment, too, is a daunting burden, especially among rural dwellers. The area of fertile ground available to an average farmer amounts to only 0.27 hectares in China and 0.56 hectares in India.[5] In most cases this is just enough to sustain a family and to bring a limited part of the yield to market. The Chinese government estimated that, in 2007, at least 120 million peasants needed to find work in the secondary or tertiary sectors in order to raise their living standards and to make agriculture more productive. Figures of 2005 for India show that 8.5 percent, or 25 million, of its farmers are underemployed.[6] All in all, if one takes the natural growth of the labor force into account, the 2006 level of unemployment, and the dramatic underemployment in the countryside, India and China will have to create 450 million more jobs by 2050. If this were not enough, the generation of new employment will be hampered by the fact that production is becoming less labor intensive.[7] Thus, more growth will be needed to create the same number of jobs. The question is whether the Ricardian formula is the winning one. Will India and China be able to overcome their domestic economic challenges without outwitting each other?

COMPETITION AND COMPLEMENTARITY: EXPORTS, FDI, AND NATURAL RESOURCES

To find an answer it is essential to compare the two countries' economic strategies once again, now with the aim of determining actual and future complementarities or similarities. Basically, the policy answer is simple: reallocating redundant labor from the countryside to industry and services. From a socioeconomic perspective this conversion must diminish the gap in incomes between the primary sector and other niches. Indian and Chinese farmers' annual incomes are still 5.6 and 6.1 times lower, respectively, than the average incomes in the secondary and tertiary sectors. The economic rationale for this shift is that a reduced demographic burden on the agricultural branch might allow the necessary increase in agricultural productivity. In the past decade, total factor productivity in the primary sector hardly increased.[8]

The released labor consequently forms an advantage to attract foreign investors in industry and services. Both countries count on the global market to keep this reallocation process going by providing investments and through the purchase of final goods and services. Their economic policies are export- and FDI-led. Even for China, which already has made much more progress than India, this remains true. The following paragraphs elaborate on the relevance of exports and FDI. Subsequently, an assessment is made of the increasing need for natural resources stemming from industrial aspirations.

For both India and China exports are a key target in economic planning. First and foremost, sustaining exports is vital for keeping the factories running. In 2007, 54 percent of China's industrial output was exported. In India this figure amounted to 28 percent. Domestic consumption is still far too

low to absorb the domestic production of goods, and this is likely to stay so
for many more years as their average annual growth rates of industrial production outpace the growth rate of domestic consumer spending. In 2006
China's consumer spending grew at a pace of 12 percent, compared to an industrial output increase of 20 percent. In India this was 6 percent compared
to 10 percent.

Moreover, export-oriented companies are considered as a crucial source of
jobs. In China export-oriented factories are estimated to provide 75 percent
of the employment in the industrial branch. Barry Eichengreen has argued
that the country has to stick to its export-led growth for a decade or more.[9]
The National Development and Reform Commission has confirmed this:
"We will continue to give scope to the competitive edge of labor-intensive
industries."[10] India's tenth Five-Year Plan also stressed that "Indian industry
has to discard its inward-looking approach and become outward-oriented."[11]
It goes on: "Demographic projections suggest that about 60 per cent of the
population would soon be in the 15–59 year age group, leading to a substantial increase in the workforce. Unless jobs are created in the more productive manufacturing sector, the unemployment situation could become quite
alarming."[12] Therefore the government vows to dismantle "existing barriers
to industrial growth" and to create an "enabling environment" that limits the
"rigidities" in labor policies, estate laws, bankruptcy and foreclosure regulation, and restrictions on the interstate movement of goods.[13] The minister
of commerce and industry summarized: "Export-oriented production has a
huge potential for generating jobs."[14] In fact, the Indian government aims at
a strategy similar to Deng Xiaoping's approach in the 1980s. By opening up
it hopes to apply India's huge labor force on the international market and to
replace the principle of self-sufficiency to a large extent with the goals of an
export-led economy.

Last, export-oriented production is a vital source of revenue. At first sight
this seems to be most applicable to India. In 2007, it reached a record trade
deficit of U.S.$92 billion. Between 2003 and 2007, GDP growth was due
mainly to debt-funded consumption.[15] The country's negative trade balance
therefore strengthens the necessity for trade revenues. With its surplus of
U.S.$160 billion and a total foreign reserve of U.S.$990 billion, China is in
a more comfortable position.[16] Nonetheless, even for the People's Republic,
these financial resources are no luxury, since they will continue to suit the
government's policy of building up strategic energy reserves, compensating
for rising commodity prices, limiting inflation, amassing funds for an aging
population, buffering international financial shocks, revitalizing the banking
sector, and so on.[17] Indeed, export revenues are necessary for keeping impor-

tant trade partners importing. With U.S.$727 billion of Treasury bonds by the end of 2008, China is the second largest creditor of the United States and thus contributing to the conspicuous living standard of American consumers.[18] As China at least needs to maintain its current export levels for many more years, it will also need to have the cash to pay the entrance ticket to the American consumer market.

FDI inflows were the fuel for China's takeoff in the 1980s. Even two decades after the launch of Deng's opening-up strategy, the People's Republic still attracts between 19 percent and 38 percent of Asia's total FDI inflow.[19] India, too, makes eyes at FDI as a catalyst for its interior development. Minister of Finance Palaniappan Chidambaram stated that even if the domestic savings rate were up to 30 percent to 31 per cent, his country would still require an FDI component equivalent to 4 percent of its GDP, which implies a sextupling compared to its current inflows.[20] The Planning Commission calculated that in 2020 the amount of FDI as a share of GDP has to climb from 0.1 percent to 3.5 percent.[21] For India these investments are indispensable, and they will continue to be encouraged and actively sought, "particularly in areas of infrastructure, high technology and exports and where local assets and employment are created on a significant scale." The central government estimates that U.S.$150 billion needs to be invested in improving the country's infrastructure over the next ten years. Also in China, a country with an abundance of liquidity, alien investors will still be needed. The Eleventh Five-Year Plan calls for more foreign investment in China's remote west and the northeast rust belt, which are currently lagging far behind the coastal regions in attracting foreign investment. Therefore, despite the emphasis on quality, the document says the government expects foreign investment to keep rising in the next few years. The government will also stimulate investments in relatively new growth areas such as agribusiness and services.[22] For both states foreign direct investments are vital contributors to technological innovation. Since the two countries do not yet have the full capacity to make their way into foreign consumer markets themselves, they will have to rely on the export channels, the distribution networks, brands, and the marketing strategies of their corporate guests. Moreover, once investors are anchored, they will make up a part of the pro-China lobby groups in the West and counterbalance the influence of protectionist voices. Consequently, if a substantial disinvestment occurs in the near future, it will cause not only a financial drain but also, and more important, a cutoff from incentives to trade and to innovate.[23]

What, then, is the impact of these similar needs? How are China and India's ambitions to ramp up their exports and to soak in FDI interacting? Currently the export profiles of China and India are complementary. The export

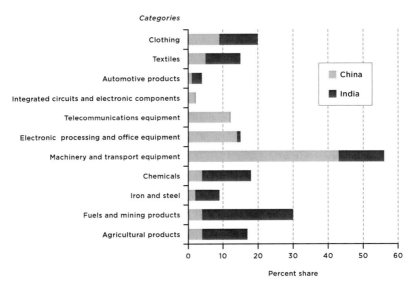

FIGURE 3.2   Export Categories as a Share (in Percentages) of Total Export Volume (2007).
Source: WTO, *International Trade Statistics*, 2007.

complementarity index concerning goods surged from 0.38, in 1996, to 0.61, in 2007.[24] The chief explanation is China's specialization in fabricated products, representing up to 81 percent of total exports of merchandise, and India's strength in raw or semiprocessed commodities, constituting 70 percent. With commercial services included, the specialization is even more obvious. Whereas China gathers only 8 percent of its export revenues in the tertiary sector, in India this figure reaches 42 percent.

This complementarity, however, is likely to dilute if the two countries succeed in their aspirations to modify the composition of their export flows. India, for its part, wants to enlarge its exports of labor-intensive goods.[25] The Tenth Five-Year Plan states: "Raw materials and low technology products dominate India's export basket today." "The ratio of high technology products to total manufactured exports in the case of India is only one-fifth of that of China and one-tenth of South Korea and Taiwan. Modernisation and technological upgrading would, therefore, lead to value addition and diversity, lending resilience to our exports."[26] Recently, the government set its heart on several industrial sectors that are currently dominated by China. With regard to textile products it envisages increasing exports to U.S.$50 billion by 2010.[27] The minister of finance hinted at making India a manufacturing hub for the auto industry, nearly at the same time Beijing stated its plans to boost the export of automotive goods to U.S.$70 billion in 2010.[28]

Likewise the Ministry of Commerce launched a plan to make the Indian electronics/IT hardware sector globally competitive through a beneficial tax policy, export support, the development of hardware manufacturing cluster parks, and special incentives to international companies that relocate their production activities to India.[29] With the National Programme for the Development of the Machine Tool Industry, New Delhi is also eyeing the sector that represents 39 percent of China's export volume.[30] The Confederation of Indian Industry estimates that manufactured product outsourcing, mainly in auto components, consumer electronics, pharmaceuticals, and others, could reach U.S.$50 billion by 2015.[31]

The Chinese government, on its side, wants to steer its growth process more in the direction of economic branches in which India takes the lead.[32]The Eleventh Five-Year Plan announced significant investments in the development of integrated circuits and software.[33] All 251 tax items related to IT products adopted zero duty. According to a January 2005 report from Yu Guangzhou, vice minister in China's Ministry of Commerce, the Chinese software industry has developed rapidly, with an average annual growth rate of 30 percent for the past five years. Software exports grew a whopping eight-fold between 2001 and 2007. In addition, sales revenues from China's software grew from U.S.$6.2 billion, in 2001, to U.S.$80.8 billion in 2007.[34] Beijing also strives to become a major base for international service outsourcing. It has consequently introduced a favorable fiscal policy and invests billions in foreign language teaching and technological education.

Besides the reorientation in the secondary and tertiary sectors, several changes in the primary branch will contribute to the flattening of complementarity. If India's industrial leap consolidates, its specialization in exports of raw materials and metal semifabricates will erode in favor of domestic production of fabricates. Competition is also likely to rise in agricultural exports. Hitherto China has been mainly a net food importer, but the Ministry of Commerce hopes to see the country's farm produce exports grow by at least 7 percent a year, for a worth of U.S.$38 billion by 2010, and raise the sector's competitiveness in the world market. For its part, India is trying to sustain its competitiveness and hopes to double India's share in world agricultural trade between 2006 and 2011, inter alia by establishing agri-export zones.[35]

Apart from the blurring complementarity, export competition might intensify due to other factors. First, there is the problem of overcapacity. As governments continue backing industrialization, production can be increased even if profits are sinking because of the relative saturation of consumer markets. Nowadays China is already struggling with large surpluses in textiles, causing wafer-thin profit margins, ranging between 2.5 percent and 3.1 percent. Vehicle production capacity outpaced China's domestic demand by 1.8 million units in 2007. According to the plans made by the major auto manufacturers, China is expected to produce, by 2010, 18 million autos, 8 million units more than the expected sales.[36] Thus, in several sectors rising domestic consumption will neutralize excesses only to a certain extent. Second, the labor intensity of manufacturing is decreasing continuously owing to a larger production scale and more efficient technologies. More output for the same employment will put even more pressure on the importance of escalating export volumes. Finally, there is a rising mood of protectionism in Western consumer markets. If this trend persists, China and India will have to vie ardently for the remaining open partner regions.

With regard to FDI, the two giants are likely to enter into more competition as well. Between 2000 and 2007, the accumulated FDI inflows in Asia surged by 6.2 percent compared to the prior five-year period. In China the increase was 34 percent and in India as much as 73.8 percent. However, if we look at the nature of these FDI flows, only a third pertains to labor-intensive activities such as industry and agriculture. Services draw 62 percent of all FDI inflows, among which business and banking represent 50 percent.[37] As much as half the worldwide FDI increases between 1990 and 2007 have been the result of projects in banking, trade, and business activities.[38] Only 8.3 percent was due to investments in the secondary sector. Consequently, competition for labor-intensive investment projects is not going to ease.

What about China as an emerging international entrepreneur? Expectations are mounting with regard to China's role as an outward investor, also in India. In 2006, Ashwani Kumar, India's industry minister, even set a target of attracting U.S.$50 billion in Chinese investments by 2010. Undoubtedly China's outward direct investments are rising significantly. In 2007 the outward FDI stock reached U.S.$87 billion, an increase of 210 percent compared with 2000. Nevertheless, New Delhi need not expect its neighbor to become Asia's next flying goose. In the near future it is likely that China will invest more in its neighborhood, but contrary to Japan in the 1960s and 1970s, these FDI flows will not automatically contribute to industrial growth and much job creation. Chinese companies have enough cheap labor at their disposal to keep manufacturing activities within national borders. Several studies confirm that Chinese investors are interested mainly in seeking new export channels, avoiding domestic competition, securing resources, and obtaining technology.[39] Specifically in India opportunities are situated in the metallurgy, contracting for transport and telecommunication infrastructure projects, trading branches, and banking. There will be an FDI spillover from China to India, but it will not have the same catalyzing effect as the investments from Taiwan, Hong Kong, and Japan triggered on China's east coast.

The supply of natural resources is another precondition for economic growth. China and India have developed into the world's most voracious consumers of all kinds of raw materials. Fossil fuels are at the top of their menus. Between 1996 and 2005, China's use of fossil fuels increased from 960 million to 1.55 billion tons of oil equivalent. India's consumption climbed from 285 million to 385 million tons. In both countries, 60 percent of this increase was made up of coal. Although mineral oil and natural gas are swiftly gaining in importance. Between 1996 and 2005, the consumption of oil grew from 174 million to 324 million tons in the case of China and from 81 million to 116 million tons in India.[40] China surpassed Japan as the second largest oil consumer. India ends up in sixth place. During the same period, the use of natural gas grew from 18 billion to 47 billion cubic meters and from 20 billion to 36 billion cubic meters, respectively.[41] The U.S. Energy Information Administration predicts oil consumption to double by 2030.[42] By then, the consumption of gas will have quintupled in China and quadrupled in India. The two countries will see their rural populations switching from traditional sources of energy to fossil fuels. In 2007, more than 44 percent of Indian households still relied on wood, dung, and crop residues as their main heating sources. The expanding number of private cars is another explanation for these remarkable increases. In 2007, only 15 per 1,000 Indians and 44 per 1,000 Chinese citizens owned a motorized vehicle. By 2020 this is expected to rise to 30 and 65, respectively, still only a fraction of the car ownership in the West. The continuing industrialization will also contribute to the voracious appetite for liquid fuels. Although the energy intensity of China's industrial production is diminishing, booming outputs will keep demands high. If the Indian government succeeds in starting a new stage of industrialization, India's demand for fossil fuels will grow at unprecedented rates.

Apart from mineral fuels, several other primary commodities feed the soaring productivity. China consumes nearly a quarter of the world's metal production and, in 2003, became the largest consumer of total main metals. In comparison, India's position is minor, since it consumes less than 3 percent of the world's metals, ten times less than China. Moreover, whereas China has used these commodities directly to feed its production of manufactured goods and the modernization of its infrastructure, India has sought rather to cash in these goods by exporting them to countries like China. For the middle long term, it is expected that Chinese demand for metals and ores will continue to grow. Its southern neighbor's mining outputs will be gradually reoriented from external customers to domestic consumers when its industrialization accelerates.

Timber and agricultural commodities form another category. The booming furniture industries in China and India have resulted in an insatiable craving for timber products—from tropical hardwood to Russian lumber for chipboard. Between 1998 and 2007, their consumption of these goods quadrupled, making China the leading and India the third largest consumers in the world.[43] China's rubber consumption has also accelerated, rising at a rate of 16 percent, owing to strong economic growth, rapid industrial development, and the increase of new vehicles. Both in India and China, economic growth has expanded the need for raw materials. Although India's growth figures for most commodity categories are spectacular, China's are unequalled. For all important minerals and several agricultural products, the People's Republic has developed into the world's main consumer. India may follow this trend as soon as its ambitious economic plans start to materialize.

It is clear, however, that domestic production of raw materials cannot meet the soaring demands. India consumes more than three times more oil than it produces. China's oil production is only half its consumption.[44] In the case of gas, the deficit is not that dramatic, but as the two countries seek to curb emissions, the consumption of natural gas as a carburant for vehicles and power generation will increase swiftly. China and India's reserves of oil and gas are not negligible. Their proven oil deposits are the largest in South and East Asia and their gas reserves rank third and fourth, respectively.[45] In China the wells of the Tarim basin in the western region of Xinjiang have just started to yield. In the early years of the twenty-first century offshore prospecting projects tracked several new reserves in the East China Sea. Indian energy companies discovered oil and gas in the littoral waters of the Arabian Sea. Nonetheless, the amount of energy represented there does not at all suffice; at the current level of consumption China and India's proven oil reserves would be depleted within less than seven years.

Likewise, the deficits in mineral ores and metal is widening. China in particular consumes more than it produces of all important types of this commodity group. India has no such dramatic shortages, but again this is due to its relatively low degree of industrialization. If the country starts to increase industrial production, its deficits may even surpass those of China. India's domestic reserves are smaller than those of China. According to the authoritative U.S. Geological Survey, China owns significantly larger deposits of iron ore, copper, cobalt, titanium, zinc, and so forth.[46] In addition, rapid deforestation has endangered the two countries' timber supplies. In 1998, the Chinese government imposed a total ban on logging. New Delhi is also toying with the idea of restrictions.

These shortages have resulted in rocketing imports. Between 1998 and 2007, China and India's foreign supply of oil increased five and four times, respectively. The International Energy Agency assesses that, by 2030, dependence on foreign wells will rise to 80 percent and 94 percent, respectively, of their total oil imports. A similar evolution is predicted for six categories of metal ores, but for these commodities China is by far the largest importer.

How will the two countries face these challenges?[47] China and India's resource policies are based on three pillars. To begin, they both aim at curbing demand as much as possible. This implies more efficiency in industrial production. In 2007, President Hu, for instance, stressed: "China should take substantive measures to shift its focus from pursuing speed to improving the quality and efficiency of economic growth." A second pillar is the diversification of the resources basket on which economic development depends. In the energy branch this means investing more in alternatives for oil and gas. In the late 1990s China and India embarked on an ambitious program to expand nuclear power generation. China brought ten new reactors on line between 2002 and 2008, and plans at least another thirty by 2020. India, likewise, is aiming for thirty, with seven due to come on line by 2008. Renewable energy as well is considered as a vital element in their diversification strategies. Addressing the Indian Science Congress in 2007, Minister of Finance Chidambaram underscored the need for a "second Green Revolution" and for extending the application of science and technology to forest conservation and management and new models of water conservation: "India must find alternative sources of energy supply. We will need bio-fuel, solar energy, photo voltaic, nuclear and almost all sources, which do not burden the conventional sources of energy supply."[48] In 2006 China passed a renewable energy law to encourage the growth of "clean energy companies." That same year, Premier Wen Jiabao pointed out that renewable energy was strategically important. China plans to raise its electricity installed capacity for renewable energy to 10 percent of its total power capacity by 2010 and to 20 percent by 2020.[49] Outside the energy sector, China is also experimenting with fast-growing bamboo as an alternative to precious timber. It has rediscovered adobe as a means for easing the shortages of cement. Despite these measures for more efficiency and diversification, the security of supply will remain in its traditional place, namely access to foreign commodity reserves. On Chinese and Indian shores, new oil and gas terminals have been erected to take delivery of overseas supplies. Both countries are harnessing their mining companies to go abroad. The question arises as to how China and India will try to get control over foreign wells and how their ambitions will interact. These issues are dealt with in subsequent sections.

Hitherto there has been an obvious division of labor between China and India. The former specialized in export-oriented industrial production, whereas in India commercial services have been the main driver of economic growth. Cheap Chinese manufactured goods more and more find their way to Indian middle-class households, whereas Indian raw materials feed mainly China's factories. However, such an assignment of work is not static. India has become aware that the division of labor is in fact a *hierarchy* of labor in which China is much more successful in generating jobs and reaping export revenues. This awareness is starting to affect the political economy of the relationship profoundly. At the bilateral level, pledges for trade protectionism against China are impeding the liberalist government's pushing through its plans for more openness. India and China also vie for access to the same countries and regions for exports and attracting investments. The two countries are entangled in a race for foreign oil and gas concessions. In the following paragraphs I take a close look at these issues.

IMPLICATIONS FOR ECONOMIC RELATIONS

Bilateral Trade Relations

The examination of bilateral trade flows in this section builds on statistics from the UN Comtrade database, which in turn relies on reporting by the Chinese and Indian governments. Incongruence between both countries' calculations of imports and exports amounts in some years to as much as 25 percent; therefore, I use the average of the figures as registered by India and China. Between 1998 and 2007, bilateral trade grew from U.S.$1.7 billion to U.S.$37 billion. Especially for India, China's importance as a trade partner increased significantly. Figure 3.3 shows that China's share in India's total trade volume jumped from 1.2 percent to 6.5 percent. On the other side, India's part of China's trade flows mounted from 0.6 percent to 2.9 percent. These tendencies raised high expectations. According to a research report from the FICCI, China may replace the United States as India's largest trading partner.[50] According to the India-China Joint Study Group (JSG) evaluation of Sino-Indian economic relations, "there is a huge potential for enhancement of bilateral trade between the two countries."[51] During his visit to New Delhi in 2006, President Hu confirmed the aspiration to double bilateral trade, to U.S.$40 billion by 2010, and, in 2008, this was elevated to U.S.$60 billion.

Even plans for a free trade agreement (FTA) were put on the table. In answer to anxiety about Chinese goods harming domestic producers, Prime Minister Singh stated: "There is a misconception that India and China are competitors, this is not true."[52]

With such soaring trade figures, absolute economic gains for both sides have been substantial. Yet, moving beyond this picture, the outlook is less rosy. India's trade deficit grew to U.S.$12 billion in 2007. What is more, the composition of China's exports to India is more advantageous to China than to India: the People's Republic gets what it wants. It is supplied with vital natural resources such as metal ores, iron, and steel, necessary for realizing infrastructure works and supplying numerous factories, from the automobile industry to shipbuilding. Raw materials and iron make up 80 percent of India's exports to China, whereas India's imports cover mainly finished goods such as machinery, office machines, and telecommunications. Figure 3.4 depicts, taking the average of both countries' reporting to UN Comtrade, the export composition of both states. Consider the U.S.$23.3 billion growth in bilateral trade between 1998 and 2006. Of this increase, 7.1 billion dollars relates to iron ore and its derivatives (SITC 27, 28, 67, 68, 69) coming from India and U.S.$13 billion concerns finished goods (SITC 6, 7, 8) imported from China. In 2006, India sold merely U.S.$53 million in machinery products (SITC 7) compared to China's U.S.$7.2 billion. China only partially permits India to achieve its ambitions. The current bilateral trade composition impedes India in stimulating its labor-intensive productivity. Exports of agricultural products (SITC 1 and 2) are limited to 2 percent. The value of paper and textile products (SITC 64 and 65) even shrank. Two comprehensive econometric research projects predict that also in the near future new incentives to augment bilateral trade will be limited.[53] Mahvash Qureshi and Guanghua Wan foresee that India will be able to increase its exports to China only within product categories such as agricultural goods and minerals. However, Beijing, too, is eyeing the agricultural industry as a new growth niche.[54] Cropping conditions in China's southeast are similar to those in India; if China succeeds in transforming its fragmented agriculture, opportunities for Indian products will diminish.

Simultaneous to the increasing efforts to intensify economic relations, several actors in India slammed on the brakes. That the passionate desire for an open trade relationship is not shared by everybody became most visible in India's reaction to China's proposal for an FTA.[55] As mentioned in chapter 2, Beijing tabled the idea for an FTA for the first time in early 2004. New Delhi's immediate reaction was restraint and an emphasis on the importance of more selective liberalization measures as steps toward a gradual

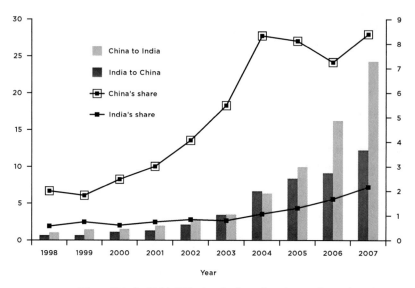

FIGURE 3.3   Bilateral Trade (U.S.$ Billion) and Bilateral Trade as a Share of Total Trade (in Percentages). *Source*: United Nations, Comtrade, 2008.

opening up. Consequently, the Ministry of External Affairs proposed a Bilateral Investment Promotion and Protection Agreement (BIPA), one aimed at protecting and promoting foreign investment through legally binding rights and obligations. In the meantime, the JSG continued searching for common ground. The step proposed by the JSG, in 2005, was a regional trade agreement (RTA), a step beyond a BIPA, but it would still include several limits on free trade. The Indian members of the JSG, however, demanded this option be discussed further by a joint task force. In July that year, India's minister of industry and commerce expressed his skepticism about a swift liberalization. "For a FT with China," Kamal Nath stated, "both countries should have market economies."[56] The inking of the BIPA during Hu's visit to India clearly did not satisfy the Chinese side; officials continued repeating their preference for an FTA.

This tempering of the official eagerness for opening up was rooted in the prudence of influential corporate lobbies and think tanks. Although these groups were in the vanguard of the evolving economic partnership, an FTA appeared to be a step too far. Arguments arose in several quarters. The Federation of Indian Export Organisations highlighted that "unfriendly" Chinese labor policies and the reservation schemes for the small-scale sector hampered India's industry and lambasted the state for its support via the low-interest

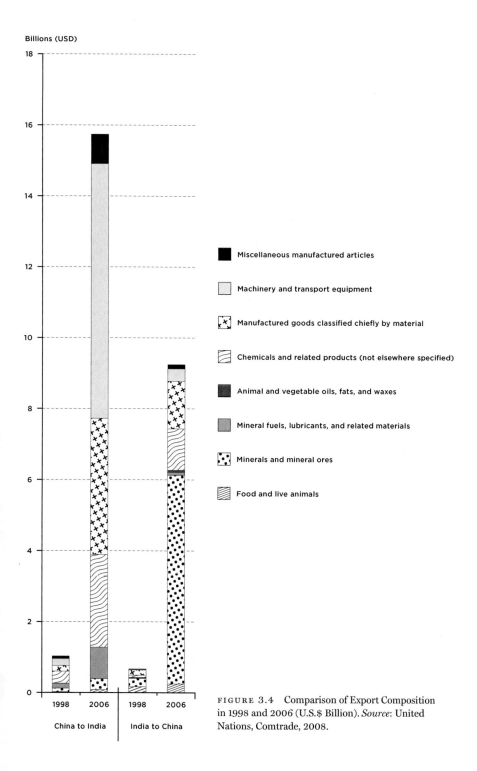

Billions (USD)

Miscellaneous manufactured articles

Machinery and transport equipment

Manufactured goods classified chiefly by material

Chemicals and related products (not elsewhere specified)

Animal and vegetable oils, fats, and waxes

Mineral fuels, lubricants, and related materials

Minerals and mineral ores

Food and live animals

1998   2006   1998   2006

China to India   India to China

FIGURE 3.4   Comparison of Export Composition in 1998 and 2006 (U.S.$ Billion). *Source*: United Nations, Comtrade, 2008.

lending by government-controlled banks.[57] Biswajit Dhar, of the Indian Centre for WTO Studies, said: "The Chinese have done wonders using economies of scale . . . The Chinese are stamping their presence even in the high-end segments of market such as those for white goods. Where does the Indian industry see an advantage in getting a deal such as an FTA with China? Indian industry is completely unprepared for an FTA."[58] Other leading groups went less far but nevertheless confirmed that the Indian economy was not ready. Saroj K. Poddar, president of the FICCI, stated: "India is talking to China on an RTA, for which we are quite keen. However, we should be gradual towards a full fledged FTA."[59] Amit Mitra, secretary-general of the FICCI, suggested that India and China could only gradually work toward an FTA.[60]

Alleged Chinese dumping practices were the main consideration that nourished the aversion to an FTA. Between 2002 and 2008, the Directorate General of Anti-Dumping, of the Indian Ministry of Commerce and Industry, filed most of its antidumping cases against China. Of all the developing countries, it was the leading complainer to the People's Republic. For example, in May 2006 India charged one hundred Chinese exporters for dumping silk and satin. This démarche was due to pressure from several weaver associations via local members in the national cabinet.[61] Consequently, New Delhi imposed import tariffs ranging between 57 percent and 116 percent. The Automotive Components Manufacturers' Association and the Society of Indian Automobile Manufacturers also exerted pressure on the ministry to ward off a far-going trade pact with China.[62] Another reason for the Indian dislike of an FTA was the fact that Indian companies already enjoyed a lax import regime in China. Swapan Bhattacharya and Biswa Bhattacharyay have argued that at the time of the FTA-proposal, tariffs in China were fairly low and that Indian producers could not expect serious additional market benefits from an FTA.[63]

Apart from the tensions surrounding the FTA, several other issues were brought to the fore. The Indian government was taken to task for selling off the country's natural wealth to China.[64] "Allowing exports of iron ore is absolutely against national interests," B. Muthuraman, managing director of Tata Steel, asserted. Companies like Tata Steel lobbied intensively to discourage exports of unprocessed iron ore or crude iron plates in order to strengthen the international position of domestic steel producers. In March 2007, the decision to increase iron export duties triggered furious reactions in China.[65] Large Chinese importers such as Sinosteel started a boycott and urged the Indian government to rescind the measure. The Indian government was also pressured to limit the number of items covered under duty-free treatment provided by the Agreement on Border Trade. India allowed duty-free treatment of only fifteen product items, among which were yak hair, yak tail, goat skin, and cashmere.

Is this hardening stance about the growing pains of a maturing relationship? Can it be considered as the rear guard of India's notion of Swadeshi? Or is it ushering in a new stage of heightening competition as India develops its manufacturing sector? It is clear that the idea of a corporate vanguard in Sino-Indian relations has to be nuanced. Interviews with several representatives of leading companies and industrial associations have confirmed two things. First, the corporate interest in free economic exchanges is pushed forward mainly by large banks, IT, services, and trading companies. Second, the leading chambers of commerce, such as the FICCI and the Associated Chambers of Commerce and Industry of India, acted somewhat autonomously when they launched several programs with their Chinese counterparts. Indian manufacturing companies were involved only to a limited degree in the rush for China that started in the late 1990s. They were simply too small or did not have any competitive advantage in the Chinese market. A government eager to trade and a couple of companies able to deliver the merchandise formed the perfect duo. It appears, however, that reality is more complex. India's economic policy is a balancing exercise amid different interests. The more the Indian government counts on the development of a strong domestic industry, the more protectionist measures are likely to prevail, especially as it will take time to develop a manufacturing sector that is competitive abroad. Yet, the state also has to take into account the wishes of its current premier economic league: the Jubilants, the Infosys, and others. Then it also remains to be seen how China will deal with India's hesitation. Several bilateral agreements concluded after 2000 are centered on Indian expectations. The memorandums on trade in mangoes (2003), grapes (2005), bitter gourds (2005), and rice (2006) clearly favor Indian exports to China.

The future evolution of the bilateral Sino-Indian economic bonds will depend on several factors. How will New Delhi maintain the balance between the demands of manufacturing on the one hand and sectors like services and trade on the other? Will China bring economic interdependence to a higher level by investing in India's industrial growth? If Chinese investors are allowed to participate in infrastructure projects, will they employ local workers and avoid the frustration of Chinese contract laborers? Will Chinese demand for agricultural goods permit India to develop new niche markets? In any case, keeping the economic partnership on a positive track will increasingly necessitate political maneuverability and mutual understanding about the domestic economic challenges.

Keeping Up the Ends: A Case Study of the Race for FTAs in Asia

When it comes to the promotion of exports, the different modi operandi vary between liberalization and gunboat diplomacy. If these two approaches are considered as the ends of a continuum, the role of the state forms the main variable. On the one end, authors like John Hobson point to imperialist practices. The interplay between overproduction and protectionism among industrialized countries can spur them to open and monopolize other economies by political coercion and military force. On the other end, the state's role is viewed as minimal by scholars who claim that states cannot and should not interfere in export promotion. They contend that globalization and the transnationalization of economic interests weaken the position of the national polity, or they assume an international consensus on the merits of free trade. In between these two theoretical poles, an extensive body of literature has developed that focuses on commercial diplomacy.[66] Commercial diplomacy is a government service to the business community that aims at the development of *socially* beneficial business ventures.[67] It is about the aptitude to persuade partner countries to open their markets by inducement. The different outcomes of this exercise can vary in terms of the degree of reciprocity and achieved trade openness. Unequal reciprocity can, for instance, imply that the country that has most interest in free trade agrees to certain exceptions for another country that is hesitating. This imbalance can also develop from a situation where a particular state has a degree of dominance so that it can sway the other party into an indulgent position. The openness of bilateral trade can be categorized on several levels; complete openness is achieved in an FTA. In this case, two or more nations approve the elimination of all tariffs between them but maintain their external tariffs on imports from the rest of the world. More selective are economic partnership agreements (EPAs), which comprehensively liberalize and facilitate trade in goods, services, and investments and strengthen bilateral economic cooperation. A preferential trade agreement directs preferential tariff reduction to only a few goods. Other possibilities, such as trade and investment facilitation agreements and bilateral investment promotion agreements, are rather more precursors to an EPA or an FTA.

The economic rationale for these commercial démarches starts with the idea of trade creation.[68] There are three direct effects at work when a pair of countries signs an agreement that lowers import barriers. First, domestic firms are faced with greater competition from foreign firms. This is expected to stimulate efficiency. Second, domestic firms gain more access to foreign markets. Third, domestic consumers benefit from lower prices resulting from competition. The political approach, however, focuses mainly on the second outcome, strengthening domestic companies' position abroad.[69] This can be a positive motivation when states are confident that they will build up their economic influence, but the aspiration for opening up can also be defensive; one state can be afraid of losing a part of the consumer market in a second country, because a third country is trying as well to get more access to it by means of a trade agreement.[70] For states, national export revenues are the barometer of success, in both absolute terms, that is, increasing export revenues, and in relative terms, maintaining a positive trade balance. Moreover, the idea of intensifying competition and stepping up efficiency is, however, perceived as a perverse effect that threatens domestic employment and social stability. This is the reason full-fledged FTAs tend to exist only in name. Liberalization almost always concerns a selective opening up. Instead of trade creation, it results rather in trade diversion, which means that prices of goods remain above international price levels because of restrained competition.

Numerous scholars have addressed China and India's commercial diplomacy and studied their engagement in bilateral and regional trade negotiations with third countries.[71] Although the interplay between the two countries in engaging other Asian markets has been underexplored. What kind of commercial diplomacy are India and China pursuing to promote their exports? To what extent are their ambitions competing? The following paragraphs discuss Beijing and New Delhi's rush for trade agreements in Southeast Asia, South Asia, and central Asia.

The Association of Southeast Asian Nations (ASEAN) is Asia's largest trading bloc and also the economic constituent on which India and China have set their sights.[72] In 2005, the ten ASEAN member states represented a GDP of more than U.S.$884 billion and a total trade volume surpassing U.S$1.2 trillion.[73] Between 2001 and 2006, the region saw its GDP climb at an average annual growth rate of 8.1 percent.[74] China and India started to recognize ASEAN's economic importance in the early 1990s. In 1991, India's prime minister Narasimha Rao formulated his "Look East" policy with the triple aim of increasing India's exports of pharmaceuticals, metal products and services; attracting investments from Singapore; and strengthening ties with the diaspora of Indian entrepreneurs in the region.[75] In 1992, India was accepted as a sectoral dialogue partner of ASEAN in the fields of trade, investment, tourism, science, and technology. At the ASEAN ministerial meeting in July 1991, China's foreign minister Qian Quichen expressed Beijing's interest in deepening economic cooperation. In the prior decade, Beijing had already signed bilateral investment treaties with three ASEAN member states.[76] During the 1990s, not many concrete measures were taken because of consecutive domestic political shifts in India and several Southeast Asian countries, ensuing tensions between Indonesia, the Philippines, and China over the South China Sea, and the turbulence caused by the financial crisis of 1997 to 1998. In the meantime, however, Beijing ordered its many think tanks to study formulas for economic cooperation, among which was the idea of a China-ASEAN free trade agreement (CAFTA).

CAFTA was tabled for the first time as an official proposal in 1999. In November 2000, Prime Minister Zhu Rongji publicly declared: "In the long term, China and the ASEAN countries can also further explore the establishment of a free trade relationship."[77] He also proposed the creation of an expert group within the framework of the China-ASEAN Joint Committee on Economic and Trade Cooperation to study the feasibility of such a trade agreement. Eight months later, at a meeting of senior ASEAN and Chinese economic officials in Brunei, China made a strong push, proposing tariff reductions and the facilitation of cross-border investment. In November that year, Premier Zhu formally made the proposal for the foundation of a China-ASEAN free trade association by 2010. In order to induce his hosts, Zhu offered to open China's market in some key sectors to the ASEAN countries five years before they reciprocate. The People's Republic would also grant preferential tariff treatment for some goods from the less-developed members, notably Cambodia, Laos, and Myanmar.[78] By November 2002, a framework agreement had been signed, launching the process of establishing a free trade regime. The document foresaw a progressive elimination of all barriers for trade in goods and a gradual liberalization of trade in services. Beijing consented to special intermediary measures for ASEAN's weakest members. In 2005, the tariff reduction process started, with the final goal of bringing tariffs on all goods below 5 percent with Brunei, Indonesia, Malaysia, the Philippines, Singapore, and Thailand by 2010, and with Vietnam, Laos, Cambodia, and Myanmar by 2015.

China has good reason for its coaxing approach to the economic conglomerate.[79] To start with, its 500 million consumers are a target for its soaring exports. Between 1991 and 2000, ASEAN's share in China's foreign merchandise trade increased from 5.8 percent to 8.3 percent, putting ASEAN at the fifth largest trading partner of China. China's share in ASEAN's trade grew from 2.1 percent, in 1994, to 3.9 percent, in 2000, making China the sixth most important trading partner of ASEAN. Chinese products with low prices and reasonable quality especially were assumed to sell better than expensive ones from the developed countries.[80] China's landlocked province of Yunnan in particular lobbied for lowering trade barriers.[81] The importance of ASEAN as a consumer market is heightened furthermore in the context of looming protectionism. If the United States and the European Union imposed even minimal measures to curb imports from the People's Republic, the impact on employment and social stability in the Chinese industrial growth poles would be detrimental. Therefore, markets like ASEAN are an important focal point in Beijing's attempt to diversify its export flows. Another factor that has awakened China's interest is the stranded Doha Negotiation Round for a new world trade agreement. In this regard the subregional grouping is targeted as a direct customer of Chinese goods and services and as an intermediary market through which protectionist measures elsewhere can be circumvented. Chinese textile traders have said: "Due to frequent limitations from the United States and the European Union, Chinese textile export still faces huge frustrations when entering the two largest markets after the elimination of global textile quotas in 2005, insiders said. The significant textile tariff reduction will not only expand Chinese exports to Southeast Asia, but also help them to enter Western countries through bypass means."[82] China's economic advances were also a reaction to Japan's economic primacy in the region.[83] Apart from Southeast Asia's potential as an export market, the region had proven to be an important source of investments. ASEAN became the sixth largest investment source for China by 2000. By 2001, ASEAN's direct invested projects in China reached 17,972, with a cumulative value, in 2007, surpassing U.S.$26.3 billion. At the same time, China had invested in 740 projects in ASEAN countries, with a total investment amount of U.S.$650 million. China also looked with interest on the technological expertise present there. Finally, ASEAN was expected to feed China's voracious appetite for raw materials. Already by the 1980s China had developed into one of the top consumers of Malaysian palm oil, Thai rubber, Burmese teak, Philippines copper, and so forth.

In November 2002, two years after China's proposal, India tabled its plans for an FTA with ASEAN. However, compared to the People's Republic, it was much less enthusiastic to enter immediately into a full-fledged open-door partnership.[84] Whereas China is well aware of its rising economic agility, India's economy would face much more competition. In the industrial sector, the comparative advantages of Indian export-oriented companies are modest. New Delhi's aspiration to develop a competitive industry in consumer goods such as electronics and cars might collide with increasing imports from the east. ASEAN's edge is clear from the fact that its exports to India increased much faster than vice versa. Between 1991 and 2001 India's exports to ASEAN increased more than five times, to U.S.$5.7 billion from U.S.$1 billion, while its imports from ASEAN increased nearly seven times, to U.S.$7 billion from U.S.$1.3 billion during the same period. Moreover, foreign investors might consider ASEAN as a springboard for upping their exports to India, rather than in the other direction. UPA president Sonia Gandhi cautioned that the interests of domestic farmers should not be at stake. Nor can New Delhi expect that the Indian diaspora in Southeast Asia will be able to emulate what Chinese emigrants did in the 1980s and 1990s. While there are fairly well-established ethnic Indian business communities in Singapore, Malaysia, and Thailand, they are not as large, rich, and influential as the ethnic Chinese equivalents in those countries. Rather than of direct gains, India's moves are prospective and can be explained by the assumption that India would develop into a leading export-oriented industrial nation later. New Delhi wants to buy the entry ticket now to avoid closed doors in the future. This defensive approach also related to the fear that India's trade with ASEAN would be harmed if China succeeded in making a preemptive entry via its Early Harvest Program. This program offers mutual tariff concessions on several commodities, so that India's exports of agricultural and maritime products in particular would suffer from export diversion.[85] The Ministry of External Affairs also explained that the free trade proposal was an effort to "upgrade" India's political partnership with ASEAN and "to bring it at par with" the partnerships of China and Japan.[86]

India's modest economic strength made it reluctant to meet the demands of its counterpart. Under pressure from the Lok Sabha and prominent members of the National Congress Party like Sonia Gandhi, the Indian government presented a long list of goods that were expected to be exempted from zero duties.[87] In 2005 this negative list included 1,140 products, both industrial and agricultural. In 2006 the catalogue was brought back to 900, and in 2007 to 490 items. But that was not enough to please. The sensitive list still contained goods such as palm oil, pepper, rubber, coffee, tea, and rice, weakening the incentives for countries like Malaysia, which exports mainly palm oil to India, or Thailand, a major exporter of rice. Palm oil alone forms 20 percent of India's imports from ASEAN. ASEAN not only demanded trimming the negative list, but it also required bringing the end date forward by which tariffs on highly sensitive items needed to be reduced.[88] The rules of origin were another thorny issue. India wanted to prevent third countries from taking advantage of the FTA.[89] This anxiety was grounded in the impact of an earlier FTA with Thailand. While Thailand's export of electronic products to India jumped 130.2 percent in 2006, India's exports to Thailand increased by just 27.3 percent. The fear is that the sparkling growth of Thai exports of these items was due to Japanese firms and that India may not be capable of shielding its domestic industries from a proxy Japanese foray. Products such as TV sets, air conditioners, cathode-ray tubes, polycarbonates, and auto parts turned out to be manufactured by Japanese subsidiaries in Thailand and not by Thai companies. For instance, in the automobile sector, Japanese firms account for about 80 percent of the Thai market and in consumer electronics, even more.[90] In November 2008, India and ASEAN finally agreed on a draft text of a limited FTA.

This reluctance contrasts with India's posture toward other trade agreements. Whereas Indian negotiators have been taken in tow by their ASEAN counterparts, New Delhi pushes for open borders within the South Asian Association for Regional Cooperation (SAARC). India has been the main supporter of the Agreement on South Asian Free Trade Area, signed in 2006 by the seven SAARC member states. While India vowed to cut its import tariffs by 2013, it granted Sri Lanka a delay of one year. The least-developed countries are required to cut these tariffs by 2016 in a phased manner. Then, it comes as no surprise that India dominates the commercial transactions within this South Asian grouping. India's exports to SAARC member states make up 77 percent of total intraregional trade volume. The same goes for the Bay of Bengal Initiative for Multi-Sectoral Technical and Economic Cooperation (BIM-STEC), where India's exports represent 62.5 percent of the trade flows.[91] The seven-country forum aims to develop its own free trade area by 2017. In 2004, the leaders of the group agreed on a first line of action: transport infrastructure, energy, communication, tourism, trade, and fisheries. Several working groups were set up to move the agenda, with India lobbying hard to advance its strongholds in services and "affordable pharmaceutics." The director of the Ministry of Commerce and Industry explained: "We are planning to open our market for the pharma and services industries, as we have a strong comparative advantage in these sectors over the other BIMSTEC countries. Initially we will open up a few sectors in which we have a comparative advantage."[92]

India has also sought to reach deals on a bilateral basis. A country-to-country approach holds several advantages. More maneuverability and flexibility are possible during the negotiation process. Instead of having to take into account long lists of desiderata from many partners, bilateral trade agreements allow for more picking and choosing. India's bilateral trade liberalization can be categorized into two clusters. On the one hand, there are the FTAs with neighboring countries over which India has a clear economic edge. In the case of Nepal and Bhutan, India clearly confirms its position as the only shop in town. For landlocked Bhutan, India is the destination for 57 percent of its exports, and its territory forms the only all-weather connection to the Indian Ocean. India in turn represents 40.4 percent of the Himalayan kingdom's imports and has a trade surplus of 11 percent.[93] The economic relationship with Nepal is similar. Commercial transactions with India make up 47 percent of Nepal's trade volume. The natural barriers with China, the geographical proximity of the densely populated Ganges Plain, and the presence of an extensive network of Indian merchants result in an overwhelming Indian domination. This position is strengthened by Nepal's reliance on its southern neighbor for the supply of energy. The FTAs that New Delhi concluded with these two countries confirm India's position as the geographic gatekeeper and as sole trade agent.[94] India assures both countries a free passage of goods; Nepal and Bhutan in turn open their markets to Indian products. The FTAs with Sri Lanka and the Maldives also reveal India's economic confidence in South Asia.[95] In 1997, at the time New Delhi and Colombo were preparing the agreement, Indian exports to Sri Lanka were valued at U.S.$650 million, while the value of Sri Lankan exports was a meager U.S.$43 million. The Indian business community was in particular attracted by the island's copper mining and hoped to further increase exports.[96] Indian investors could also take advantage of the European Union's trade package with Sri Lanka, which gives it access to European markets at low duty rates. Immediately after the India–Sri Lanka Free Trade Agreement was implemented, in 2000, India started to push for a new treaty that would also encompass services.[97] Farther southward in the Indian Ocean, India concluded a preferential trade agreement with Mauritius. India's direct stake in penetrating the islet state related to the export of pharmaceuticals, agricultural machinery, automobiles, and spare parts. But what makes Mauritius especially interesting is that it can act as a bridge between India and Africa. While Mauritius, with its 1.2 million inhabitants, is a small market for India, it belongs to two regional African economic blocs, Common Market for Eastern and Southern Africa and Southern African Development Community, which provides preferential access to a large number of African countries. Moreover, its membership in the EU-ACP (European Union–African, Caribbean, and Pacific) community opens possibilities for reexporting goods to the European market.

On the other hand, New Delhi also strengthened its commercial ties with Asian countries that are more competitive. Since the beginning of the new century, free trade talks have been initiated with Malaysia, Singapore, and Thailand. What propelled India to engage these leading Asian trading nations? First, the country considered these markets as an ideal center for Indian companies to raise capital and know-how from local industrial titans.[98] For instance, the CII expected that a Comprehensive Economic Cooperation Agreement would propel tenfold investments from Singapore.[99] India also saw opportunities in the Southeast Asian "wonder trio" as a fishpond for American and Japanese investors. This intermediary function also applied to exports.[100] Since Malaysia and Singapore had concluded FTAs with the

United States, India could make use of these states as an export hub without having to engage in direct trade liberalization.[101] Nor were the three partners' domestic consumer markets neglected as an economic opportunity. For example, India sought to step up its exports of services, agricultural goods, and jewelry. Unlike countries like Sri Lanka, New Delhi worked to limit the scope of the partnerships as much as possible and pushed its partners to offer concessions to India to reciprocate at a slower pace. Hence, for India economic bilateralism has a double function. With regard to small markets, it is a means for projecting economic power and for fully exploiting its limited competitive advantages. In the case of the South Asian countries, deepening state-to-state commerce also turned out to be a stepping-stone to the negotiation for a regional free trade area in which India could take the lead. Toward stronger economies, trade pacts reflect rather India's reluctance to enter into a full-fledged regional free trade partnership. Here, New Delhi resorted to bilateralism as an assurance of selective liberalization and as an entry into third markets.

Compared with China and India's commercial diplomacy in Southeast and South Asia, the efforts in central Asia are just starting to develop.[102] Measured against the U.S.$2.755 trillion and U.S.$4.074 trillion GDP, respectively, of the former two regions, the U.S.$973 billion of the seven central Asian states is rather modest. In the 1990s, China had been focusing mainly on energy and security challenges in the region rather than the consumer market. Indian vendors have a long presence in the area, but geographical barriers and insecure land corridors have been seriously hampering trade. Since 2000, however, Beijing has been throwing all its weight into the scale to step up its exports. From that time, embassies have been beefed up to pave the way for Chinese trading wares. In 2003, Prime Minister Wen Jiabao surprised his colleagues when he launched such a proposal during a summit of the Shanghai Cooperation Organization (SCO).[103] Even though Russia is member of this group as well, it has been clear to all parties that China is the economic center of the association. In 2007, it represented 59 percent of the intraregional trade; oil omitted, this amounts to 35 percent. Kazakhstan, Kyrgyzstan, Uzbekistan, and Turkmenistan, the four central Asian nations that are members of the SCO, are of vital importance as a source of raw materials such as mineral oil, natural gas, cotton, and mineral ores. Apart from that, the group is a key export market, in particular for China's landlocked western provinces.[104] Compared to the eastern growth poles, industry in regions like Xinjiang remains underdeveloped, but its unadvanced manufactured goods and food products fit well into the demands of the neighboring countries, where competition with other exporters is limited.[105] As mining production boosts these states' incomes, Chinese expectations are high for expanding trade further. The Indian government, too, is recognizing the need to invest more in export promotion in this region. "India is about to lose its share in the Central Asian market of pharmaceuticals, machinery and tea," a senior Indian official stated, "we have to work to break through the many logistical obstacles to reach the place, but at the same time we need to foster the will with local governments to lower the political barriers." Although New Delhi established a joint commission on trade, economic, and technical cooperation in several countries, the outcome in terms of concrete agreements was negligible.

Asia is on a keen quest for trade partnerships. China is eager to show its economic leadership and throws all its weight into the scale to entice surrounding groups into an open trade regime. In this race for trade agreements Beijing and Tokyo have set the pace and New Delhi tries to keep up. China clearly aspires to full-fledged FTAs, whereas India sticks to extensive negative lists and tries to compensate for its lack of lenience toward regional groupings with bilateral pacts. Initially this pursuit was propelled by the fear of being locked out. Now that regional free, or *freer*, trade has begun to develop, the apprehension is no longer being excluded but that the other might reap relatively more profits and set the economic agenda. In terms of exports, actual competition between India and China has been limited. The main reason is that the export flows from both countries consist of different goods, and India has not yet developed the industrial capacity to fully exploit the potential of the surrounding consumer markets. More than China, it hopes to attract investors from economic powerhouses such as Singapore and Malaysia. India's engagement is prospective; it aims at keeping the channels open for the moment and looks forward to having the industrial agility to become a chief exporter of manufactured goods.

Paving the Way for Influence

Whereas commercial diplomacy has to pave the political way for increasing exports, numerous logistical challenges remain. India and China have therefore embarked on an impressive road diplomacy that approaches neighboring countries' governments to participate in cross-border transport infrastructure projects. China and India's interest in more logistical ties with the rest of Asia started to grow in the mid-1990s. The initial aim was to unlock remote regions to potential consumer markets abroad. Growing trade was expected to stimulate manufacturing, raise prices of local agricultural goods, and consequently to elevate the level of development of these sectors. In China these

plans coincided with a so-called Go-West strategy, a policy that aims at reducing the wealth gap between the east and the hinterland.[106] In India, this
interest is rooted in the first Border Area Development Programme, of 1986.
Since then, the national government has been authorizing an increasing
number of so-called land custom stations, reaching a total of 138 in 1994 and
141 in 2003.[107] In 1998, a new Border Area Development Programme was
launched focusing on the trade potential of Myanmar, Nepal, and Bhutan.[108]
In 2003, Prime Minister Vajpayee came up with the buzzword *connectivity*,
and in 2006 Foreign Secretary Shyam Saran restated his country's willingness to transform its borders into "arteries of commerce, exchange and movement of people." In November 2006, the Cabinet Committee on Security for
the first time gave the green light to building roads in the rugged terrain of
the Himalayan borderland. According to officials of the Home Ministry, the
allocation for infrastructure development increased from U.S.$80 million, in
2005, to U.S.$130 million, in 2006. In 2006, the central Planning Commis-
sion held out the prospect of a further increase, to U.S.$2.5 billion, on the
condition that all border states prepared an action plan for the development
of infrastructure.

Southeast Asia is again the main target of this road diplomacy. Myanmar
in particular is eyed as an important transit zone to more affluent countries
like Thailand, Malaysia, and Singapore.[109] The country borders four landlocked Indian states and China's province of Yunnan. In 2006, India and
Myanmar inked a final agreement on a multimodal transport corridor between the state of Mizoram and the Myanmar port of Sittwe, on the Bay of
Bengal. New Delhi budgeted U.S.$103 million to refurbish the port infra-
structure at Sittwe, dredging the Kaladan River and building a road from
Kaletwa to Nalkawn, the terminus of Highway 54. Initially, Myanmar vowed
to contribute U.S.$10 million, but since Myanmar was unwilling to invest,
India agreed to provide a soft loan.[110] Earlier, in 2001, India's Border Roads
Organisation completed a 160-kilometer-long road from Tamu, on the border
of the Indian state of Manipur, via Kalewa to Kalemyo, heading toward Mandalay, an important trade center. In July 2004, Myanmar and India signed a
memorandum of understanding on India's provision of a line of credit worth
over U.S.$56 million for upgrading Myanmar's more than 600 kilometers of
rail between Mandalay and Yangon, on the Andaman Sea. The entire U.S.$23
million project was a "gift" from the Indian government. India also took on
the costs of maintaining the track until 2009.[111] In 2007, India revealed new
plans for several more links. The Rail India Technical and Economic Services
presented a study for the construction of a rail link between Jiribam-Moreh,
in India, and Tamu-Kalay-Segyi, in Myanmar, a project worth U.S.$11 mil-

lion. That year, the Border Roads Organisation finished its feasibility survey on a 150-kilometer-long road link from Rhi to Tiddim, across the Mizoram border. The Indian government foresaw U.S.$133 million to U.S.$177 million for the new infrastructure.[112]

China has also made its way into Myanmar territory. A 651-kilometer-long road between Kunming and the Chinese border city of Ruili was completed in 2007. China is assisting Myanmar with upgrading another, 170-kilometer section. Both countries also agreed to complete a missing railway section between Dali and Lashio. China supports a road improvement project connecting by road Lashio and Chiang Rai, Thailand. In addition to road and railway construction and improvement programs, Southeast Asia's rivers are also vital in unlocking China. In Myanmar, China focuses on the Irrawaddy River, which is navigable for cargo vessels from Bhamo, near the border with Yunnan. Linked with the above-mentioned land routes, the Irrawaddy could take cargo destined for China from maritime shipping through the narrow and dangerous Strait of Malacca. Further downstream, the river is also reported to be linked with two seaports on the Bay of Bengal, Sittwe and Kyaukpyu. In 2002, Beijing spent U.S.$5 million on dredging a 300-kilometer section of the Mekong River along the Myanmar-Laos border. This improvement project will triple the freight capacity by ship, even during the dry season.[113] Myanmar is not the only passage. China upgraded the railway link and built a parallel highway between Kunming, the capital of Yunnan, and Hanoi. The railway project reduced travel time by nine hours and increased annual freight capacity from 4.6 million tons to 200 million tons. China also invested in a new connection between Kunming and Laos, a project for which forty-two tunnels and 260 bridges were built to cross the mountainous landscape, and financed a third of the highway that will connect the China-Laos border with Thailand.

In the Himalayas, China and India funneled millions of dollars into transport projects with Nepal. In 1996, New Delhi and Katmandu concluded a bilateral agreement for the construction of twenty-two bridges on the Kohalpur-Mahakali sector of the East West Highway in Nepal. In 1992, the two states agreed to improve the road between Tanakpur and Mahendranagar, though it took eight years before the work was begun.[114]

In 2005, India's Container Corporation opened a new inland container depot in the Nepalese city of Birgunj.[115] In 2007, the Indian government ordered a study for five railway links to Nepal. According to the *Himalayan Times*, the proposed lines will run from Nepalgunj to Uttar Pradesh, Nautuna to Bhairahawa, Jayanagar to Bardibas, Jogban to Biratnagar, and New Jalpaigudi to Kakarvitta. On the Chinese side of the Nepalese border, Beijing financed the extension of the Lhasa railway, completed in 2006, to Xigaze.[116] In 2007, China started the construction of a new highway between Syabrubeshi and Rasuwagadhi and immediately offered to build two more roads, connecting the eastern part of Nepal with China, Koshi to Kimathanka and Jomsom to Lumanthang. The Chinese ambassador in Kathmandu explained: "Goods and services from Lhasa and even the inner part of China will be coming to Nepal much more easily and at cheaper prices." [117]

In China's western region of Xinjiang, the two ancient Silk Road cities of Kashgar (Kashi) and Ürümqi are experiencing a spectacular renaissance as trade hubs between the Far East and central Asia. In the late 1990s, Beijing proposed construction of a rail line from Kashgar to Kyrgyzstan and lobbied the Asian Development Bank for financial support to connect this branch with the iron roads in Uzbekistan.[118] Simultaneously, the People's Republic completed a new railway stretching from Ürümqi to Kazakhstan via the Ataw Pass. In 2004, China and Kazakhstan agreed to build a second rail link to Almaty. In addition, both countries teamed up to develop a fast railway from China's eastern littoral zone to Kazakhstan's most western border, with the aim of reducing the usual freight time to Europe: instead of fifty days by sea or fifteen days on the Trans-Siberian Railway, this route is reported to take eleven days.[119] China's vice minster of communications also stated that a cross-country road will be built from Shanghai to Khorgos, including the world's longest tunnel, with a length of eighteen kilometers.

China's tarmac diplomacy has also extended into Pakistan.[120] In 2001, both sides signed a cooperation agreement for the development of the deep-sea port at Gwadar. Beijing provided U.S.$50 million as a grant and another U.S.$150 million in the form of three low-interest loans. In the first phase of the project, China assisted with the construction of three multipurpose berths and the dredging of a four-and-a-half-kilometer-long approach channel. China has also agreed to participate in the second phase, including four container berths, one bulk cargo terminal, one grain terminal, one ro-ro terminal, and two oil terminals.[121] In June 2006, the Pakistan Highway Administration and the China Roads and Bridge Corporation signed a memorandum of understanding to rebuild the Karakoram Highway, a project worth more than U.S.$500 million, and to expand its width from ten meters to thirty meters.[122] In 2007, Islamabad and Beijing began exploring options to link the Karakoram Highway to the southern Gwadar Port, in Balochistan, via the Chinese-aided Gwadar-Dalbandin railway, which extends up to Rawalpindi.[123]

Since 2003, India has been focusing on the Iranian port of Chabahar as a logistical hub for central Asia. That year, Teheran and New Delhi signed a protocol on transport cooperation. The joint project aims at the rejuvenation of the port infrastructure in Chabahar. In addition, India and Iran vowed to connect Chabahar with Bam, a main transit city in the Iranian central railway system, and to Zaranj, in Afghanistan. In 2004, India's Border Roads Organisation started with the construction of a 218-kilometer road connecting Zaranj with Delaram, a central node in the Afghan highway network. The project, worth U.S.$70 million, is entirely funded by the Indian government. In 2003, India's External Affairs minister Jaswant Singh concluded an agreement with Uzbekistan to build a highway linking the Afghan border town of Khairaton with Herat.[124] Under the different agreements Indian goods enjoy duty-free access to Chabahar and tax reductions in Afghanistan. The trilateral project reduces the distance from India to central Asia by fifteen hundred kilometers and transit time by days. The new connections are also integrated into the plans for the so-called North-South Corridor running from Mumbai via Pakistan and Iran to the region around the Caspian Sea.[125] Indian expectations for this land bridge are high. The CII, for example, has stated that "the corridor will not only boost India's trade with Russia and Iran but also that with the Baltic states and the Central Asian countries." In November 2005, the railway nexus of the North-South Corridor was in turn incorporated into the Trans-Asian Railway, making India a central transit country between Southeast and central Asia.[126] For security reasons, all India's initial plans circumvented Pakistan. In 2004, however, New Delhi and Islamabad reopened several cross-border transportation links. While these measures aimed in the first place at confidence building, the two states also initiated talks on the shipment of goods.

How far are India and China playing a role in each other's road diplomacy? Are the emerging trade corridors built with the purpose of economic balancing? These questions have been taken up by several scholars and journalists.[127] There are indications that maintaining a balance may be the purpose. Especially after China made efforts to unlock Yunnan via Myanmar, Indian officials voiced their apprehension of too much Chinese economic influence. In 2007, Minister of State for Defence Pallam Raju was quoted referring to China's presence as a main argument for Indian investments in Myanmar transport infrastructure: "We need to be much more active in our region. China is expanding its presence all over the globe."[128] Interviews with members of India's Foreign Service revealed a consensus on the fact that India cannot afford to leave the Myanmar market and the Southeast Asian consumer markets in general to Chinese exporters.[129] The transportation links were perceived as a necessary investment to keep up with China's economic presence, or at least to keep the options open for India's rising ambition as a trading nation. The same goes for China's involvement in Nepal. Apart from security considerations, Nepal has always been considered as a buffer against military aggression from China; officials feared that India would lose its commercial edge if China were to overcome the current physical barriers. The "top priority" plans for the five new railways announced in 2007 are clearly a reaction to China's new trade corridors.

Yet, other interpretations are possible. Instead of acting as tools for counterbalancing, the emerging transnational transportation corridors can also contribute to economic integration. The new links in Myanmar not only penetrate the Myanmar market or reach potential consumers in other conterminous states. but they also constitute a new land bridge between Yunnan and India's northeast. In April 2007, New Delhi took an important step toward the completion of this Sino-Indian corridor. After years of hesitation it commenced converting a 680-kilometer stretch of the dilapidated Stilwell Road into a six-lane highway. At the time, the People's Republic had finished another 1,000-kilometer section of the route. The completed road forms a direct connection between Kunming and Ledo. The Myanmar railway grid also contributes to this connectedness. Jay Prakash Batra, chairman of the Indian Railway Board, explained: "Since Myanmar is getting a rail link with China, to be completed in around three years, a link with Myanmar could help India reach China and then right up to Russia."[130] Similarly, Nepal, too, might form a transit zone when the different infrastructure programs link up.[131] The idea of a Trans-Asian Railway promised that, as a new logistical center, India might improve its attractiveness to foreign investors.[132] India's increasing interest in transportation links in Myanmar, the Kaladan project in particular, should also be related to escalating security problems with Bangladesh. Although China undoubtedly had a role in New Delhi's plans, the new Myanmar transport arteries became even more imperative after Bangladesh turned out to be unreliable as an outlet for such landlocked states as Assam and Manipur.[133]

Since border roads are but a means to step up exports to neighboring countries, the final impact of road diplomacy cannot be separated from the changing trade flows. What is the impact of the new connections on export competition? One might expect that the picture at the different microregions reflects the level of competition at the national level. If economic competition is already strong, new outlets would be expected to intensify this as trade volumes increase. Building on earlier conclusions in this chapter, it is likely that China will profit most from the new transportation links, because it has more capacity to nourish these arteries with various goods. Moreover, whereas Kunming is profiting from the new link and developing into a new industrial powerhouse, the manufacturing base in India's northeast is hardly expanding, so that China strengthens its lead. The same goes for Yunnan's horticulture.[134] In this sector the Chinese provinces have the same geographical and climate conditions as India's northeast. Nevertheless, the growth of Yunnan's production and export of various crops outpaces that of India's secluded region significantly.[135]

"All ways lead to China," remarked a Thai official. This idea indeed is becoming ever more real. China is developing itself into Asia's logistical center. India is trying to penetrate the markets of neighboring economies, but its efforts are clearly outpaced by China's transportation projects. Undoubtedly, the new regional arteries play a vital role in increasing the two countries' relative economic influence; yet, it is premature to speak of a road war. Several new infrastructure projects will also connect the Asian giants, and India simply does not have the capacity to fill the wagons and trucks with goods that can compete with Chinese products.

Natural Resources: Fueling Competition?

China and India's policies related to foreign commodities is hotly debated and the subject of numerous publications.[136] There is discussion about the extent to which the governments succeed in conceiving and implementing coherent strategies. Beijing University professor Zha Daojiong, for instance, has argued that China has had great difficulty finding an appropriate mechanism for governing its energy industry and refers to the frequent re-formation of its energy ministries.[137] The Brookings Institution holds a comparable view on India: "India has developed a cluster of energy policies rather than an overarching energy strategy . . . Attempts at integrating energy policies have been hindered by separate entities overseeing each type of energy source."[138] Even when these shortcomings are taken into account, however, the two states are clearly capable of setting benchmarks.

Both India and China opted for a control-over-the-well-strategy because they do not have confidence in the liberal approach of the commodity market. First, upstream activity, the excavation of recourses, is seldom liable to free-market principles but rather is in the grip of monopolies and state control. It is still the hosting governments that have to grant concessions to foreign companies eying *their* resources. Ninety-three percent of the worldwide oil deposits are owned or controlled by state and national oil companies. Often exploitation contracts require much more than a strong market position: political and geostrategic reasons also play a predominant role. Second, they do not want to be dependent on the dominant *multinational* concerns as their suppliers. Third, control over the upstream processes also permits keeping downstream prices in check. Whereas Beijing and New Delhi are aware of the fact that market-tied prices of petrol, gas, iron, and other commodities are crucial for curbing overconsumption, the limiting of inflation is even more imperative: rising prices and low wages are a dangerous cocktail threatening social unrest. Fourth, Chinese and Indian companies involved in upstream activities are often junior players in the international market. Hitherto, they were chiefly occupied with interior resources; since these domestic sources are depleting fast, they have to make up lost ground swiftly and carve out their own part of foreign assets. Finally, a foot on the ground in resource-producing countries also permits sketching out a long-term policy and anticipating trends in interior demand.

Thus, the desire to have a certain control over supply will spur New Delhi and Beijing to stimulate their companies to hunt for a share of the commodity market. Nevertheless, it will simultaneously open up its markets to *foreign suppliers*. International concerns are stimulated to invest in downstream activities such as processing and distribution, as well as to participate in upstream activities. These investments are beneficial in terms of the infusion of capital into expensive infrastructure projects such as the construction of pipelines and refineries. They are also necessary for bringing know-how; China and India have little experience and expertise in offshore excavation, for example. The two Asian titans have to strike a balance between the long-term strategic objective of fostering a certain degree of *trade ownership* on the one hand and, on the other, the necessity of involving foreign or international concerns with the purpose of making swift headway to meet the immediate needs of their burgeoning economies. Cooperation cannot be shunned. Yet, for the long haul, the need is for competitive devices with the purpose of pursuing an autonomous and energetic foreign trade policy.

State companies are still in the vanguard. For many years, the central government of China has been trying to regroup its fragmented mining branch into a limited number of leading companies able to play a significant role on the international scene.[139] As one senior official stated, state-owned mining companies have to "expand in volume, optimize in structure and grow into leading world businesses" and gain influence over international mineral prices.[140] Under the banner of "grasping the large, releasing the small," Chinese entrepreneurs are barred from starting new companies. Instead, thousands of small firms and mines have already been closed or absorbed by "national champions." In 1998, Beijing amalgamated the shattered domestic energy industry into three large companies, each with a particular responsibility.[141] It is these three companies, China National Offshore Oil Corporation

(CNOOC), China National Petroleum Corporation (CNPC), and Sinopec, that are also reaching out to foreign wells. In 2002, a similar development took place in the metals sector when sixteen companies joined forces under the umbrella of China Nonferrous Metals International Mining (CNMIM).[142] Nowadays CNMIM presents itself as the "forerunner in carrying out the go-out policy" and controls a vast share of China's copper and nickel imports.[143] A year later, the China Aluminium Group was founded as a new aluminum-sourcing consortium consisting of aluminum producers.[144] Among the mining companies, Minmetals is the central government's favorite. This "flagship enterprise" leads the country's mineral mining. It took over eighteen smaller Chinese companies and has representation in seventeen countries.[145] In 2005 Minmetals received a U.S.$2 billion credit line to prop up its overseas activities.[146] Even though several state-owned companies have carried out initial public offerings, the government keeps a tight rein. Not only has it maintained at least a majority stake and guaranteed its position as chief financer, but also the government's State-Owned Assets Supervision and Administration Commission appoints all company managers.[147] In 2005, a so-called energy leading group was established in order to foster more coherence in policy making. The group functions directly under the State Council and is chaired by the prime minister.

That same year India set up a similar body, the Energy Coordination Committee (ECC). The ECC was established to formulate a synchronized policy response cutting across ministries so as to improve the overall energy strategy. The committee is chaired by the prime minister and consists of the ministers of finance; power; petroleum and natural gas; coal and nonconventional energy sources; the deputy chairman of the Planning Commission; the national security advisers; and others. Like the approach in China, the Indian government exerts control by means of personnel appointments, price setting, and production targets. In 1997, New Delhi identified four energy companies and the Steel Authority of India, a dominant actor in India's metal market, as part of the *navratnas* (nine precious stones), a group of companies that will receive special advantages and political steering. While the government has already restructured some of the state-owned companies (the Indian Oil Corporation, for example, bought out retailer Indo-Burma Petroleum Company and refiner Bongaigaon Refinery and Petrochemicals Ltd.), there have been other proposals to merge more state-owned companies with more competitive actors. Compared to the Chinese mining sector, India hardly attempts to foster a new generation of state-owned conglomerates with an international scope. Whereas India's private metal companies, such as Tata Steel, are world players, they contribute nearly nothing to the supply of ore to the

Indian market. An Indian mining expert summarized this situation ass follows: "All in all, our country [India] still perceives the national mining sector as a milking cow for foreign revenues. It does not appear to be aware that, for the future, our own deposits will be insufficient, but then we will not have the players to secure overseas deposits."[148]

The quest for oil has repeatedly pitted Indian against Chinese companies. Usually, the Indian bidder suffers defeat. In October 2004, India's Oil and Natural Gas Corporation (ONGC) was outbid by CNOOC in Angola; in January 2006, the same happened in Nigeria, where the latter succeeded in securing an offshore concession. Also in Ecuador, Kazakhstan, and Myanmar Chinese oil giants have edged out their Indian counterparts. Prime Minister Singh concluded: "China is ahead of us in planning for its energy security. India can no longer be complacent." Compared to their Chinese competitors, Indian companies are hampered significantly by a lack of financial means. In the case of Nigeria and Angola, CNOOC simply added a couple of billion dollars to its initial bid, which obliged ONGC to throw in the towel. In addition, the Chinese government seems to be more agile in combining several levers to curry favor with decision makers in resource-rich countries.

New Delhi's reaction is to try to steer away from direct confrontation and to cultivate a sense of energy interdependence between China and India. After the Congress Party–led government took office in 2004, it proposed to Beijing making joint bids to avoid being played off each other by oil-producing countries.[149] During a visit to China petroleum minister Mani Shankar Aiyar stated: "Unbridled rivalry between Indian and Chinese companies for the acquisition of overseas hydrocarbon assets is to the advantage only of the seller of the assets." In January 2006, the proposal was accepted by Beijing and consolidated in five memorandums on energy cooperation. Most of them deal with information sharing and cooperation between companies. Additionally, a joint bilateral working group is to be set up to monitor the progress of cooperation, with the focus on four main regions: the Caspian Sea, central Asia, Africa, and Latin America.[150] Furthermore, India has also tried to engage China in joint pipeline infrastructure. Aiyar again took the lead and presented a plan for a gas pipeline from Iran through India to China: "We need to shed the confrontationist approach . . . and leverage the power of offshore and onshore gas for the benefit of our continent, for which India can dip into its vast reserves of foreign exchange for investment in pipelines."[151]

Is a Sino-Indian energy partnership emerging also in action? The initial reaction of the leading figures in Chinese oil companies was positive. CNPC vice president Zhou Jiping agreed to India's proposal for going together in Africa, central Asia, and Latin America. He went a step ahead and announced two nodal officers for identifying areas of cooperation even as the Indian team was floundering for names. Sinopec vice president Zhang Yao-cang suggested two-tier cooperation. At the government level, he proposed an energy cooperation committee for establishing a dialogue mechanism and a network for information, while at the company level he suggested a strategic cooperation agreement for joint bidding and equity participation in third countries. With such cooperation, Yaocang believed any large project could be handled jointly anywhere and thus India and China could have "more say" in the international pricing mechanism. In January 2006, ONGC and CNPC signed an initial deal covering exploration and production, while the state-run gas company, Gas Authority of India (GAIL), concluded a pact with Sinopec, CNOOC, and Beijing Gas.

Since 2006, these plans on paper have also been translated into action. In February of that year, CNPC and ONGC jointly acquired a U.S.$580 million project in Syria. In August 2006, ONGC and Sinopec formed a joint-venture company to invest U.S.$850 million to buy a 50 percent stake in Omimex de Colombia, which has assets in the South American country.[152] In 2006, the Chinese media announced a U.S.$2 billion bid jointly made by ONGC and a Chinese company for more than 400 million barrels of Kazakh deposits owned by Nations Energy, although the outcome of negotiations with Nations Energy failed. Apart from joint bids, other initiatives indicate an emerging partnership. In 2006, India, Russia, and China held official discussions on a trinational pipeline. A senior research fellow with China's National Development and Reform Commission stated that the "project is very likely to succeed." In January 2007, CNPC started the construction of a sixteen-hundred-kilometer-long east-west pipeline in India.

Skeptics maintain, however, that rivalry will finally gain the upper hand.[153] The Sino-Indian competition for Myanmar gas appears to be a clear counter-example of cooperation. Though ONGC invested in the exploitation of the Shwe gas field in the Bay of Bengal, it was CNPC that finally succeeded in hammering out a contract for buying a large part of the output of this project. In 2006, Yangon signed an agreement with CNPC under which Myanmar's Ministry of Energy agreed to sell 6.5 trillion cubic feet of gas through an over-land pipeline to Kunming for a period of thirty years. With this agreement Myanmar effectively relegated India's offer for a westward pipeline to the storeroom.[154] That same year, ONGC teamed up with a Russian oil company to exceed Sinopec's bid for Udmurtneft, in eastern Siberia. Regarding the Iran-India-China pipeline, Beijing also tends to establish its own channels. In 2006 Beijing and Turkmenistan's government agreed to build a connection linking up with China's east-west pipeline. It would be a small effort to extend the project beyond the border with Iran.

Only in the late 1990s did the Chinese and Indian governments slowly, and often inconsistently, start to make efforts to guide their companies in setting up new projects abroad, as well as to stimulate the development of large national mining companies. China eyes all kinds of raw materials; hitherto, India has been focusing on oil and gas only. Their initial strategies reveal marked skepticism about cooperation. They approached the international commodity market as a zero-sum game dominated by mercantilist ambitions. This explains why Beijing and New Delhi have made great efforts to foster a squad of powerful state-owned enterprises capable of getting foreign deposits. Gradually, however, both states have slightly modified this policy and begun to experiment with forms of cooperation. Paradoxically, competition fostered a new sense of interdependence; the two countries discovered repeatedly that they were being played off each other by oil producers. The costs of this divide-and-rule game mounted to billions of dollars and came at the expense of the companies' profitability and respective state treasuries. India and China also realized that their mining giants' expertise and experience were still inferior to those of other companies. While Chinese firms surpassed their Indian counterparts, they frequently fell short in competing against Western oil companies, or even mining concerns from Brazil, South Africa, and Australia. This new awareness lay at the foundation of a partial policy reorientation. On the one hand, the two countries opened their markets for more cooperation with multinational enterprises; on the other, they undertook several joint initiatives that can be considered as building blocks to a bilateral buyer's alliance toward influential energy suppliers and cartels.

As Robert Axelrod has incisively concluded, countries can team up as "rational egoists."[155] Although not many concrete projects have materialized thus far, there are encouraging signals that the formula is working. First, these ventures are widely supported by the governments of both countries, company leaders, and other actors such as think tanks. Second, the joint bids in Syria and Colombia reflect India's acceptance of China's leadership. In both projects, the Chinese company was the main bidder and has the largest role in their implementation. Finally, India and China have also begun investing more political efforts into the creation of a trans-Asian energy grid. As for the contest for Myanmar natural gas, it has to be seen in its context. The fact that China finally received the contract was due mainly to India's incapacity to table an acceptable counterproposal.[156] Moreover, China's plans to build oil and gas pipelines to the Andaman Sea are not a move against India's aspirations. Prospecting for this energy corridor has been going on for many years. Yet, the development of a solid partnership for natural resources cannot be taken for granted. Whereas the notion of interdependence is becoming stronger, cooperation has yet to be institutionalized in bilateral working groups with a clear mandate or permanent joint ventures. Beckoning short-term gains will stimulate cheating. The appeal of bid-and-take démarches will further increase as import dependence mounts further and supplier countries try to capitalize on this.

WHITHER CHINDIA?

This chapter presented an assessment of the extent to which the idea of Chindia is based on reality. In order to measure the degree of integration, economic observations were consistently placed in their political context. After all, competition and integration might be beneficial from the perspective of economic theory; it is not necessarily so that governments perceive them to be suitable to their agendas. Several indicators support the thesis that economic integration is progressing. The composition of bilateral trade is complementary, and export competition in third markets is limited. India and China's regional trade policies did not result in economic conflict, nor did their ambitious cross-border infrastructure projects. Even in their quests for natural resources, New Delhi and Beijing took measures to join forces. However, two key points arise from this positive picture. First, the fact that economic tensions were limited is due mainly to the fact that India takes an inferior position to China's industrial development. Second, as India tries to catch up in the industrial sector and China at the same time strengthens its commercial services, the current complementarity is likely to lessen, which will result in fiercer competition. In chapter 4 it becomes clear that despite the initial optimism, many Chinese and Indian politicians and experts have begun to recognize these potential tensions.

SHIFTING PERCEPTIONS

THE RELATIONS BETWEEN CHINA AND INDIA are lauded with optimism by officials and key political leaders from both sides. Apart from the nuclear crisis in 1998, the partnership has intensified steadily throughout the last three decades. This friendship has pushed its way through narrow elitist paths. The nurturing of bilateral relations occurred mainly within ministry departments and business offices. From these leather-seat establishments mobilization campaigns were launched to adjust the perception of actors who felt less involved in the narrative of Chindia. The following pages make clear that the confidence of public opinion, experts, and political leaders is still low and that distrust persists at all levels of society.

In both countries governments remain the central node, where varying aspirations and perceptions are amalgamated into a national foreign policy. Although states need to play a two-level game, mediating between internal and external players.[1] If one wants to assess how steadfast a certain diplomatic course is, it is also necessary to map out the whole domestic constellation of interests and opinions. There are several examples of situations in which the willingness of the Indian and Chinese governments was held back by domestic forces that did not follow the way of pacification. In the 1950s, Prime Minister Nehru overestimated his ability to keep the national parliament and the security community in line with his euphoric project of Chindia. During the 1980s and 1990s, political games in parliament further hampered the different cabinets in their desire to strengthen ties with China. During the reign of Mao Zedong, public opinion and internal power struggles constrained options to deal with India's Forward Policy, which was launched to step up control over the boundary. These examples indicate that a sanguine vanguard can be forced to revise and alter its policies if public opinion and influential constituents in society are not supportive. We thus move down from the neofunctionalist approach of international relations, in which self-interested elites are the main object of analysis, to the domain of *sociological liberalism*, where the making of foreign policy is broadened to the society as a whole.

Sociological liberalism implies that diplomatic stability, predictability, and peace can be assured only when a certain foreign policy is legitimized by a broad domestic consensus. To begin with, support for peaceful relations can be strengthened by increasing the extent of communication and transactions between societies. The more transnational relations, Karl Deutsch has contended, the stronger will be the notion of a *security community* and consequently trust, mutual concern, and even identification.[2] Second, connectedness will also lead to a stronger experience of a common interest in peace.[3] At the basic level this implies that citizens become aware that, from the perspective of their private lives, maintaining peace is better than conflict, even if it means a relative weakening of national power. At a more advanced level, it indicates strengthening bonds with another country affects their own lives in a tangible and positive way. Finally, sociological liberalism is about mutual perception. Especially in a context where two countries share a history of overt violence and diplomatic nerve wars, public opinion's ability to overcome this legacy is of utmost importance.

PUBLIC OPINION

To what extent then have these positive expectations become engrained the Chinese and Indian public opinion? Did the growing interdependence result in reduced threat perceptions? Reconstructing public attitudes is a delicate task given the lack of coherent quantitative surveys over a long period. Nevertheless, the scarce material that is available does allow verifying the main assumption. A survey carried out by the Chicago Council on Global Affairs of more than six thousand Chinese and Indian respondents in May 2006 reveals a positive to ambivalent posture in China and an ambivalent to negative attitude in India. Responding to the question whether it was a "good thing" that their neighbor gained economic power, 56 percent of the Chinese answered positively, 26 percent negatively. In India the response was less positive: 39 percent yes, 46 percent no. With regard to military power, Chinese citizens had identically the same opinion as on India's economic influence. Indians were more apprehensive; as much as 46 percent considered China's increasing military prowess a negative evolution, compared to 39 percent

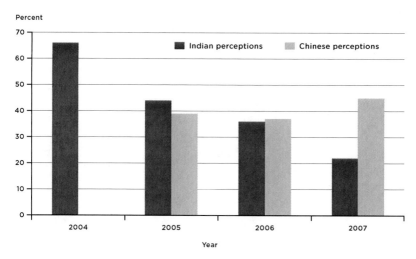

FIGURE 4.1   Share (in Percentages) of Chinese and Indian Respondents Labeling Their Neighbor's Increasing Influence as "Mainly Positive". *Source*: BBC World Service polls, 2005–2008.

on the positive side.[4] The BBC World Service poll, surveying thirty-six hundred respondents in December 2007, revealed similar perceptions, with 47 percent of the Chinese views on India's influence being mainly positive and 39 percent mainly negative. India's hesitation became visible in the fact that more than 60 percent of the Indian respondents could not choose between a positive and negative appreciation: 22 percent gave a negative rating, 18 percent evaluated China's growing influence as positive.[5] Another study by the Chicago Council on Global Affairs confirmed India's uncertainty. Asked to indicate their feelings about China on a hundred-point scale, Indian citizens gave an average rating of 54 percent.[6] Thus, both surveys demonstrate that the optimism of the political and economic elites has not completely trickled down.

If we study these observations from the perspective of earlier surveys, this ambivalence appears to be the result of two different trends. In 2004, a BBC World Service poll calculated that 66 percent of Indians saw China's increasing influence in the world as "mainly positive"; this positive response declined to 44 percent in 2005, the year that Wen Jiabao paid his widely covered visit to the country. In a new BBC poll in December 2006, carried out only a few weeks after the cordial visit by Hu Jintao, this share shrunk further, to 36 percent, and in 2007 to 22 percent. This appraisal was considerably less positive than that of other Asian countries that were studied. For China, I found comparable figures only for 2007, 2006, and 2005. Chinese perceptions improved slightly. In 2005, 39 percent of the respondents believed that India's growing clout was positive; two years later this opinion was shared by 45 percent of the Chinese.

While the short time frame and the undetermined trend do not permit us to conclude that China's public opinion has been positively affected by improving elite perceptions and growing interdependence, it is obvious that Indian citizens did not buy their government's win-win story; while New Delhi stepped up its efforts to improve relations with China, public attitudes did not follow. On the contrary, between 2004 and 2007, trust in China's growing power eroded quickly. Rajiv Sikri, former secretary of the Indian Ministry of External Affairs, concluded: "The latent mistrust of China, which was well entrenched in the security agencies but of late was missing in the public perceptions and within the strategic community, has now resurfaced at a popular level."

THE INDIAN PARLIAMENT

The lack of public confidence weakens the legitimacy of the constructive China policy that New Delhi has pursued in the last years. It makes Indian leaders an easy target for criticism from political opponents or even from parties within the government coalition. Because of limited public support the government's maneuverability depends to a large extent on the leeway that it obtains from other political parties. This section focuses on the scope for further rapprochement that other parties are prepared to give and assesses the position of the Indian parliament with regard to Sino-Indian relations. The decision here to concentrate on the Indian parliament and not, for instance, on China's National People's Congress is justified for the reason that the latter enjoys only a very limited mandate to interfere with the government's foreign policy at its annual sessions, not to mention no information on the debates is available.

In general, China is not a key issue in party programs. From the public policy papers issued by the ten largest parties in parliament between 1999 and 2007, only three gave attention to China. Predictably, the National Congress Party and the BJP were two of them. Whether they headed the cabinet or were in opposition, their official line on China has been pragmatic. They both favored closer relations and called for intense commercial bonds. On the border issue, the two vowed to continue relations but remained vague on the terms and conditions. During the 1999 and 2004 elections, only three parties mentioned the relations with China in their official manifestos. In its 1999 campaign agenda, the BJP and its partner, the National Democratic Alliance (NDA), stressed the need for "good neighbourly relations with *all* neighbouring countries," subtly referring to the People's Republic.[7] In 2004, the NDA explicitly stated that it vowed to "expand economic cooperation with China and to continue the dialogue process with China to achieve a mutually satisfactory resolution of the boundary issue, which is an objective of strategic interest."[8] The National Congress Party presented the enhancement of relations with China as a historic task: "Historic confidence building measures in relation to China were taken by previous Congress governments. These will be consolidated and expanded, while recognising that we have border disputes with China that need long term negotiations in mutual good faith."[9] This message was also present in the Common Minimum Programme, a program drafted by the Congress Party and others of the UPA: "Trade and investment with China will be expanded further and talks on the border issue pursued seriously."

Apart from the BJP and the National Congress Party, only the Communist Party of India (CPI) mentioned China in its program, and similar to the other two, it contended that it would give "special attention to improve all-round relations with China."[10] It alleged that "the danger to foreign policy is real as the United States has long term plans to draw India into a strategic alliance to subserve its global designs against China and Russia."[11] Other parties took a similar stand. Statements in the press and interviews with party members revealed that China was not a divisive issue. The seven largest parties, apart from the BJP, the National Congress Party, and the CPI, affirmed their support of continuing the closer relationship that had been developed between 1999 and 2007. They also approved the government's steps toward bilateral trade facilitation. Although six of them believed the UPA government needed to take a stronger position toward China's claim on Arunachal Pradesh. The Bahujan Samaj Party, for one, stood strong on the border issue, but in 2005 it showed itself prepared to pursue constructive talks on the demarcation and to deepen economic relations.[12] Two parties insisted on paying more attention to the economic impact of Chinese imports on local entrepreneurs. The DMK, for example, asserted that China was being allowed to dump TV sets in the Indian market at the expense of local firms.[13] In general, however, these criticisms appear to be automatic responses to specific incidents instead of initiatives that originate in a thoroughly conceived China policy. Between 1999 and 2007, only two of the seven medium-league parties paid attention to the People's Republic in their party programs.

This positioning also appears to be reflected in parliamentary questions. These questions form a clear indicator of the attention given to a particular issue.[14] Between May 2004 and May 2007, thirty-one parliamentary questions pertaining to China were submitted to the Ministry of Commerce and Industry; the same number as well to the ministries of Defence and External Affairs. With ten questions, the military evolution of China received nearly as much attention as archrival Pakistan. Although the interest in defense and security issues has to be nuanced. In terms of the content of the questions, the border issue and China's involvement in Pakistan were mentioned only three times. Most questions related to subjects like bilateral maneuvers and military exchanges. In addition, the attention given to diplomatic relations with China was modest compared to that for other countries. Whereas only nineteen questions to the Ministry of External Affairs referred directly to China, seventy focused on Pakistan, twenty-five on the United States, and twenty-three on Bangladesh. Regarding trade relations, more anxiety was evident. Fifteen queries expressed apprehension about the evolution of Sino-Indian trade relations, especially regarding the unbalanced composition of the trade basket.[15] Only three questions articulated willingness to deepen commercial interactions and to increase exports of rice, fruits, and tea. Hence, the total number of thirty-one questions in three years' time is limited, and it also becomes obvious that security issues declined in importance compared with trade matters.

Another way to look at the parliamentary agenda regarding China is to study the reports of the Standing Committee on External Affairs. Poring over twenty-nine reports issued in the thirteenth and fourteenth Lok Sabha between March 2000 and April 2007, it appears that throughout this period, the committee tended to endorse the agenda of the Ministry of External Affairs. It approved grants for all three China-related projects tabled by the Foreign Service: the establishment of a cultural center in China, special financing for the Institute of Chinese Studies, and the building of a new consulate in Shanghai.[16] The committee agreed to special funding for the Joint Working Group on the India-China Boundary Question and the India-China Eminent Persons' Group.[17] Several "observations" and "recommendations" affirmed this supportive stance on the government's efforts to strengthen ties with China. Seven months after the NDA government was installed, the committee concluded that "it is heartening to note that our relations have reached a degree of friendship and cordiality" and that India and China were "going ahead in areas of cooperation in various fields like trade, economic cooperation, cultural operation and people-to-people contact."[18] In 2001, the committee emphasized that it "would like the Ministry to strive to increase the interaction between India and China by facilitating people to people contacts and mutual exchanges of Parliamentarians, scholars and experts in various fields."[19] It also suggested the Ministry of External Affairs to "sponsor bilateral visits" to "convince them [China] of the need and desirability of having India in the Security Council as a Permanent Member." In the following legislation, the Committee stated that it "appreciate[d] the steps taken by the Government to improve our relations with China."[20]

Apart from the questions and the activities of the Standing Committee, the submission of discussion proposals is another barometer. Between May 2004 and May 2007, only two debates in the Lok Sabha and three in the Rajya Sabha focused on China. Nevertheless, these sessions were widely covered by local media, given the harsh criticism from opposition parties like the BJP of the government's China policy. During a Rajya Sabha discussion on November 23, 2006, leader of the opposition Jaswant Singh accused the government of keeping the country's foreign policy and territorial integrity "mortgaged" to the Communist Party, which had yet to condemn even the Chinese aggression of 1962."[21] This incident occurred at the moment Chinese president Hu Jintao was winding up his four-day stay in New Delhi. Earlier, the Chinese ambassador in New Delhi had hinted that Arunachal Pradesh was not exclusive Indian territory. A half year later, in 2007, opposition leader L. K. Advani went further and derided the "tentative" and "apologetic" answer of the government to China's alleged attempt to contain India. "If we don't voice it and if we don't recognize it, we are not recognizing a reality," Advani stressed, adding, "the extension of the railway line to Lhasa, the extension of road communication from Myanmar, the lease on Caucus Island, negotiations on the port of Chittagong with Bangladesh, also the initial moves with the Sri Lankan Government, the Construction of the Port of Gwadar, the strategic alliance with Pakistan is a string of pearls around India."[22]

Indian political parties and parliament display an ambivalence that is similar to overall public opinion. On the one hand, party programs are positive toward the People's Republic, and in parliament China does not attract more attention than other countries such as Pakistan and the United States. On the other, political parties are increasingly concerned about China's growing economic prowess and the positive language in party programs is overshadowed by sharp sinophobic criticism of government policy during parliamentary debates. In effect, the government obtained parliament's blessing for continued expanding ties with China, but its scope for enhanced interaction with China on trade and the border dispute is constrained by persistent fear and suspicion.

THINK TANKS

While polls plot general public perceptions, a more qualitative review of experts' assessments allows tracing the issues that form these attitudes. Moreover, in circumstances of ambivalent views, experts might table new arguments that could further alter public and political positions in a more favorable or hostile way. As John Kingdon has demonstrated, experts can have a strong impact by linking a problem to its proper discourse and subsequently by making a direct appeal to policy makers, or indirectly by mobilizing public opinion. In this section, I look at the discourse of twenty leading Chinese and Indian scholars. The selection of these privileged spectators is based on their position in the policy-making process. Some are involved in bilateral working groups; others have a voice in advisory bodies of the national government.[23]

Figure 4.2 gives an overview of expert perceptions on seven issues. A review of recent writings of the target group of twenty specialists confirms that overall attitudes are anything but positive. Comparable to the findings pointed to in the preceding, Indian respondents tend to be more suspicious than Chinese. Fifteen experts view their neighbor as a competitor in international affairs and believe this will remain so in the future. Most believe their neighbor poses a threat in the areas of regional influence and border security. Twelve think there is a security threat. On economic issues like energy security and trade interests, a growing commercial interaction has not resulted in a strongly positive view. Chinese and Indian watchers are divided over the risks and benefits of economic cooperation.

"Both India and China are exploring each other very gingerly." This idea of sniffing at each other was articulated by Sujit Dutta, senior fellow at the IDSA and member of the India-China Eminent Person Group.[24] This observation sets the tone for most of the other Indian China experts. There is a consensus that economic aspirations and the yearning for a stable regional setting make peaceful relations with China more precious than ever, but several doubts remain. "Chinese foreign policy has transited into a post-conflictual modus" says Alka Acharya, head of East Asian studies at New Delhi's Jawaharlal Nehru University, "but nevertheless there is an abysmal lack of confidence in each other. There is just no trust."[25] This perception branches into several specific concerns. To start with, the perception exists that Beijing does not take India seriously. "China would do well to develop greater sensitivity and understanding of India's genuine concerns," Ajit Kumar Doval, senior fellow at the IPCS and former head of the Intelligence Bureau, bemoans.[26] Brahma Chellaney, member of the prime minister's Policy Advisory Group, continues: "China's lecturing on the values of openness is like an Al Capone instruction

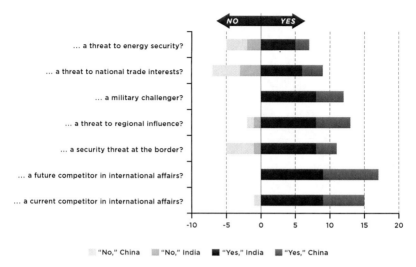

FIGURE 4.2 Expert Perceptions (in Number of Experts) in Answers to the Question "Do You Perceive China/India as . . ." *Source*: Review of writings (2005–2007) of ten Indian and ten Chinese experts.

on law and order."[27] There is also the impression that the People's Republic is not sincere and uses trade incentives as a carrot to divert attention from its attempts to strengthen its power. "The Chinese initiative so far has stressed on economic cooperation and friendly political ties, but has been woefully short of substance in areas that shape the dynamics of the relationship," Sujit Dutta claims, concluding, "the Chinese were more interested in keeping India isolated and moves towards improving the relationship through trade and commerce were cosmetic in nature. It was pointed out here that the path of politics and economy were not necessarily intertwined."[28] This decoupling of several layers of the relationship, economic and political, is also present in the discourse of Nimmi Kurian, research professor at the CPR. Kurian stresses that the Sino-Indian partnership is still precarious and that New Delhi needs to pursue a balanced policy, combining both competitive and cooperative approaches.[29]

Chinese opinion leaders accept India's status as a regional power and as a strategic partner. In this regard, Ma Jiali, one of China's most prominent India experts, has argued that Sino-Indian relations were moving out of the shadow of a "cold peace" to a process of "hot cooperation."[30] According to Ma Jiali the South Asian neighbor had obtained the status of *zhong he guoli*, a comprehensive national power.[31] Sun Shihai, deputy director of the Insti-

tute of Asia-Pacific Studies, CASS, endorsed this line of thought and contended that "the two Asian giants are adopting more mature and pragmatic
approaches."[32] Economic interests are generally recognized as the driving
forces, but it is also stressed that the rapprochement is propelled by "similar
views on world order," multipolarity to be specific, and a common interest in
regional stability.[33] Nevertheless, despite this progress, most of the surveyed
authorities stressed that there is still a significant lack of confidence. "India
and China lack mutual trust," maintains Sun Shihai, adding, "this has been
hindering the development of bilateral relations."[34] The reasons for this hesitation are many. Scholars like Zha Daojiong, an adviser to the government
and the party, allege that the economic interdependence is still too premature. He asserts: "China and India are really seeking each other out," saying,
however, "so far the economic link between China and India is very weak, so
let us see how market forces play out."[35] Another argument on the enduring
hesitation is India's swift military modernization, which is not proportionate
to the country's low socioeconomic development. The expansion of its naval
presence in the Indian Ocean is especially a point of concern. Chinese experts
also leave two options open for India's further economic growth. On the one
hand, analysts like Sun Shihai underline that despite the "overriding strategic task to provide a stable environment" the two countries' pressing needs
will "almost certainly involve them in a contest for influence," especially in
resource-rich states.[36] On the other, specialists take into account that the
economic basis of India's resurgence is not solid and that failure to deliver the
promised affluence could result in a new negative patriotic backlash. Consequently, the commercial propulsion of the current rapprochement might
sputter and, at the worst, result in a confrontation similar to the nuclear incident of 1998. Finally, China's captains of thought tend to share the skepticism
of their Indian peers on the border dispute.

Taking a closer look at mutual perceptions of this issue, on both sides of
the Himalayas experts approach the negotiations on the border conflict with
mixed feelings. Only a few voices subordinate the importance of territorial
demarcation to the overall commercial interests and believe for this reason
that a final settlement is within reach.[37] For example, B. G. Verghese, senior
fellow at the CPR and member of several official Indian dialogue groups, asserts that "the term *border* is often conversationally employed as a synonym
for *boundary*, whereas in fact it describes a zone of transition from one regime to another, whether in terms of people, language, culture, the economy,
or environment. Ultimately what matters is the nature rather than the fact
of a boundary."[38] Arguments like this one are rare. Although most watchers agree that both Beijing and New Delhi need to take a more constructive

stance, the general opinion is that both parties beat about the bush and that the talks are still more about appeasement than about finding pragmatic and realistic solutions.

Whereas the status quo, in which India would keep Arunachal Pradesh and China Aksai Chin, is accepted as the most plausible outcome, several concerns remain. On the Chinese side, five of the ten surveyed specialists indicate that India should yield the region of Tawang to China.[39] Tawang is a small part of the current Indian state of Arunachal Pradesh and forms an important corridor between the Chinese provinces of Tibet and Yunnan.[40] "Tawang is central to the resolution of the Sino-Indian border issue," Ma Jiali states, adding, "India should return Tawang to China."[41] Zheng Ruixiang, senior researcher at the CIIS, stated that New Delhi's stubborn position on the small mountainous area impedes "building a real and sustainable relationship" and that it now has to "correct its past mistakes."[42]

Indian observers, for their part, emphasize that it is equally important to secure the borderlands as to demarcate them. Ajit Kumar Doval, for instance, points to the military risks of making the borders redundant. China's new railway infrastructure in Tibet near Indian territory is enhancing China's combat capability and the capacity to transport hardware for military offensives, he warns: "India has to factor it in its higher defence planning and match the capabilities."[43] This assessment is affirmed by Phunchok Stobdan, senior fellow at the IDSA and former director of the National Security Council: "China has become emboldened over Tibet. They have a strike hard policy because nobody dares to raise the issue with them. Of course that won't stop Tibetans leaving."[44] Brahma Chellaney adds that China's sway over the Himalayas will allow it to "divert the waters of rivers flowing southward from the Tibetan Plateau" and that "a future conflict over the sharing of interstate water resources can no longer be ruled out."[45] The two countries share the impression that their respective diplomatic approaches fail to understand the limited domestic maneuverability on this sensitive question. Surjit Dutta, for example, urges the Chinese side to have more understanding for the "coalition of hard-line forces that have deeply influenced boundary policy."[46] Zheng Ruixiang, in turn, has explained that "my Indian friends tell me: 'We can't hand back one single inch of territory or the coalition government will fall.' But they fail to understand that even in a one-party state like China similar popular constraints exist. We live in the internet age. Now Chinese people have a say, unlike in the fifties and sixties. That is progress in our politics."[47] Likewise, Ma Jiali indicates that New Delhi should take into account that "the Chinese central government could face problems from local Tibetan people" if Tawang became officially part of

India. Thus, for most experts, mental barriers run parallel with the disputed Sino-Indian border.

This discussion is extended to the significance of the Sino-Indian partnership in an international setting. Optimists argue that the two giants will form a tandem to pursue their common interests. Nagesh Kumar, a member of the India-China Joint Economic Group and director of the RIS, signals that "the China-India strategic partnership can help Asia regain its place as the centre of gravity of the world economy that it once was."[48] Arvind Virmani, adviser to the Planning Commission and director of ICRIER, goes further and declares that "Europe will fade away" due to the formation of an "Asian Economic Community," of which China, India, and Japan will form the engines of growth.[49] This notion of an enhanced China-India partnership in a context of intensified regional integration is echoed by several colleagues. B. G. Verghese, for example, predicts that economic ties between ASEAN, South Asia, and East Asia will prevail in geopolitical and geoeconomic predicaments.[50] Other observers renounce the idea that China plays a divide-and-rule game in South Asia. On this, Sujit Dutta pledges "to take a more balanced view of Chinese military support to Pakistan."[51] G. V. C. Naidu, a senior fellow at IDSA, says that the "age of military alliances is over, and hence there is no question of India joining any military alliance" and that India's other partnerships "would not be aimed simply at confronting China."[52]

A similar number of thinkers show more skepticism over the departure from realpolitik. Brahma Chellaney claims that "China has set up proxy military threats against India" and insists that the government should "ensure that China does not continue to exercise a cost-free containment option."[53] Lalit Mansingh, senior fellow at the IPCS and former foreign secretary, uttered lyrically that even though positive sounds dominate the discussions about China, the country's increasing diplomatic and military influence in Asia is "like the ghost at the banquet—an unspoken presence that no one wants to talk about," and concludes that India should balance China's sway in the region.[54] Nimmi Kurian joins in this plea and warns that China is "pulling the region into its orbit," an appraisal that Phunchok Stobdan focuses on central Asia, where China is allegedly trying "to counterbalance India's rising profile."[55]

Chinese opinion leaders, for their part, point to India's military muscle flexing in the neighborhood. "Beijing cannot be expected to welcome India's measures to upgrade its naval facilities at the Andaman and Nicobar Islands or post-Sept. 11 joint patrols of the Malacca Strait," writes Lan Jianxue, research fellow at CASS, indicating in particular the risks when this presence becomes incorporated into American attempts to restrain the People's Republic.[56] Ma Jiali echoes this reasoning: "India's military might is rising and it is accelerating the process of military modernization. Its international influence is also expanding rapidly. While strengthening its relations with the big powers, India is also trying to improve its ties with its neighbouring countries."[57] Sun Shihai adds, "The US always said it wants to use India to balance China," referring to India's entry into an alliance of democratic countries, that is, the United States, Japan, and Australia. Zha Daojiong agrees that some aspects of the "Cold War structure" were continuing in the form of a subtle "proxy war" and that "India . . . would like to take advantage of ideas which are coming from America," but he doubted that India would comply with Washington's strategic designs.

Only a few well-known figures take an optimistic position. Zhang Yunling endorses the analyses of Virmani and Kumar and foresees that bilateral trade and investment initiatives involving China and other key players in Asia would "gradually bring all countries together" around common objectives.[58] Zheng Ruixiang contends that China and India's stance in the region reflects "a new type of strategic cooperative relationship" that does not target a third country. Hence, he asserts, "China's policy towards South Asia has been gradually accepted by South Asian nations," adding that China will "develop balanced relations with Pakistan and India."[59]

In conclusion, what are the ideas about further economic cooperation? There exists in both China and India a consensus among opinion leaders that the absolute gains of growing commercial relations are substantial enough to continue with the promotion of bilateral trade. Most of the Indian experts caution, however, that India could be overwhelmed because of China's economic leadership. S. D. Tendulkar warns that the People's Republic will continue to be "the major competitor" of India in labor-intensive exports. Shankar Acharya, professor at ICRIER and economic adviser to the government, asserts that Indian services companies may be outpaced by their Chinese peers. These concerns have their impact on the enthusiasm over the desirability of an FTA. All Chinese opinion leaders agree that an FTA with India would be lucrative.[60] Their Indian colleagues are less keen. Rajiv Kumar maintains that India may rather need an FTA with itself before concentrating on liberalizing commerce with other countries. Most Indian experts make a case for a cautious and gradual opening up. Arvind Virmani claims: "Given the current costs of production in the two countries, it would be foolhardy to enter into a zero tariff arrangement with a country like China." He therefore advises his country should adopt "a graded approach to opening up trade with China. First remove the barriers (visa and language constraints) that limit Sino-Indian commerce and reap an additional 6 billion USD in potential trade, then think of the next step."[61] Nagesh Kumar suggests first stimulating joint ventures to extend production networks to each other.[62] Nimmi Kurian believes that India should continue developing logistical links and business-to-business networks but warns that the diversification of trade flows is a precondition for new steps forward.

China and India's intellectual elites are not promoting the tale of Chindia unequivocally. Experts from both countries recognize that progress has been made in the restoration and improvement of bilateral relations, but a persistent wind of fretful intelligence gusts through the amicable atmosphere. Distrust and uncertainty make most analysts hesitant to abandon their cautious discourses. Whereas economic gains are accepted by a number of observers as an important motivation for nurturing the partnership, fears of military designs and conflicting diplomatic ambitions result in a pledge for prudence and restraint.

Realists nowadays find only a limited interest among government officials, except for the defense community; these thinkers appear to be better able to peddle their message indirectly. The Indian media in particular is eager to pick up salient accounts about Chinese intrusion into the Himalayas, stories that are much easier to sell than abstract promises about economic integration. In fact, further research might well be carried out to assess the impact of the news media in the public perceptions between India and China. This goes also for Indian and Chinese Internet forums. Realists can also capitalize on a strong collective memory about past conflicts, whereas liberalists have no precedent of success to build on. These intellectual checks and balances may allow the political elites to continue writing the Chindia story, but they do not mean that symbolic issues will sink into public ignorance. Moreover, the unabated skepticism among many thinkers may catalyze a sudden reversal in the political or public debate.

IF ANYTHING CHARACTERIZES China and India's perceptions of each other, it is ambivalence. Compared with the 1980s, public attitudes, political positions, and expert assessments evolved from apprehension and hostility to a mood of uncertainty and hesitation. It is clear that only a limited part of Indian and Chinese societies give credence to the optimistic advocacy coalition formed by the government and several corporate actors. At the time of this writing, perceptions of each other's growing influence were more or less equally divided among a camp of optimists, a group of undecided citizens, and a party of pessimists. In India attitudes have become even less positive.

The same picture became visible among experts and analysts. The number of proponents of deepening cooperation increased, but only as a complement rather than replacement of the prominent group of skeptics. Neither intellectual camp appeared to dominate the debate on the future course of the Sino-Indian relationship. Concepts like balancing and military deterrence remain appealing and are not making way for the enthusiast pledges to make boundaries history via regional integration and intensifying trade.

This indecisiveness undoubtedly reflects the state of transition in Indo-Chinese relations. The bonds are clearly recovering from a period of conflict and aggression, but it is not yet clear in which direction they will evolve during the coming decade. The circumstances are simply not conducive to a *determinateness of mind*. Economic relations are at a crossroads, and either competition or cooperation is a plausible scenario. Incidents like the nuclear flare-up in 1998 unveil the volatility of India's political transition. Many Indian observers, on their side, worry about Chinese nationalism. For China and India it is not clear where the redefining of the other's identity as a regional power will lead. As self-images, ambitions, and diplomatic identities are in a state of flux, so is the perception by one of the other.

Yet, shifts in attitudes and perceptions are not based solely on the evolution of their subject. The channels that deliver information and ideas, the most important building blocks of perceptions, are also of importance. The fact that many Indians and Chinese citizens do not have an outspoken opinion might indicate that they are not or do not feel connected to the changes in bilateral relations. After all, local news medias, which are still much more popular than national outlets, offer only a narrow window onto international issues. In addition, the impact of expanding trade flows is barely noticeable in daily life. Although the number of bilateral visits increases every year, traveling remains for only a happy few.[63] The number of Chinese employed in Indian companies, and vice versa, is negligible. The new jobs generated due to rising exports make little difference. Thus, the lack of information and the minor tangible gains mean that bilateral affairs only rarely penetrate into households.

The perception of minimal gains also has to be brought up in relation to the marked suspiciousness in relevant news stories. Whereas bilateral trade generated more jobs than the few thousands of Chinese temporary workers would have taken away in India, the spat over the permission to dispatch four thousand Chinese technical executives in 2006 drew more political and media attention than the fact that the Chinese contractor for the project, CNPC, made by far the cheapest bid. This also relates to the public attention cycle. Whereas the media tends to be less eager to take up gradual increases in economic benefits for news stories, exciting news facts like trade rows, military maneuvers, Chinese ventures in Pakistan, and so forth, do make the front pages. Often these reports appeal to memories of the time when bilateral relations were less rosy and consequently contribute to a form of intellectual atavism.

This brings us to a final point. As Robert Jervis has stressed, individuals tend to see what they expect to see and to assimilate incoming information to *preexisting images*. Thus, India's memory of the Chinese strike of 1962 and repeated provocations in the two decades after still influences perceptions. Similarly, Chinese experts still refer to Nehru's unreliable posture on the border issue to argue that India is not a trustworthy bargaining partner nowadays. On the other hand, self-perception, how identity is translated into national interests and objectives, forms one of the lenses through which another country is viewed.[64] In this connection, both countries see themselves as a regional power and find that they have the right and plight to extend their influence to larger parts of Asia. The interplay of overlapping spheres of influence therefore tends to be perceived as a zero-sum game: intrusion by one player is automatically seen as a disregard for the other's entitlement and aspirations.[65]

The construction of attitudes, whether those of society as a whole or of individual experts, occurs through an intricate process in which political psychology and rational choices both have a role and often enforce each other. Facts, communication, and personal dispositions are at the basis of the limited trickle down of optimism in Indian and Chinese societies. Negative images that were constructed in the past may gradually erode when relations have been sustained for a long period and society as a whole has felt their benefits.

All these factors make it unlikely that public attitudes will soon shift from hesitation to trust. It will be a lengthy process in which room for diplomatic maneuvers will remain limited. Further convergence will be a matter of a delicate balancing exercise. Openness will create many new economic opportunities, but overeagerness to liberalize trade may result in complaints about dumping and unfair competition. The need for a border settlement is accepted, but too much permissiveness could stir nationalist sentiments. Regional cooperation is inescapable for both India and China if they want to maintain stability in their peripheries, but ignoring the balance of influence in Asia will undermine the governments' credibility as guardians of national security. The political will and economic interests are strong enough to absorb setbacks, but the process is not irreversible. Public opinion on both sides of the

Himalayas is volatile. As elucidated in the following chapter, many remaining territorial disputes and the military buildup are like fuses in a powder keg, and there are many opinion leaders able to light them. Political elites can perhaps neutralize ignition to some extent, but the final impact will depend mainly on the sensitiveness of the surrounding powder.

FIVE

THE MILITARY
SECURITY DILEMMA

"WE SHALL NEVER FORGET 1962." Gazing at the impressive collection of writings on India's foreign policy, it was striking to find these letters penciled on one of the reading tables of the library at Jawaharlal Nehru University. Lively discussions with students at the university indeed revealed that the Sino-Indian War figured prominently in their thinking about China. Most thought that a war with the People's Republic was still possible. This chapter looks a bit closer at this issue and studies to what extent growing economic and political synergies between the two countries allow them to neutralize the military security dilemma. They have already made progress with various confidence-building measures, but do we also see a decreasing tendency toward military balancing? Are the proliferating military exchanges making an arms race or an armed conflict less likely? Looking more closely into the demilitarization of the border, naval developments in the Indian Ocean, and the modernization of India's nuclear arsenal, it appears that growing interdependence has by no means neutralized the military security dilemma. The distrust highlighted in the previous chapters seems to be the cause of a military tit-for-tat game that, though possibly not as aggressive as in past decades, remains worrisome.

FROM PACIFICATION TO CONFIDENCE BUILDING

The Sumdorong Chu incident, in 1986, was the last massive troop mobilization along the border that brought China and India to the verge of war. Nearly two hundred thousand Indian soldiers were sent to the strategic valley in the north of Tawang after the discovery of a newly built helicopter platform and an increased presence of Chinese infantry. During the subsequent two years of gradual diplomatic rapprochement, the first initiatives to prevent any new saber rattling started to take shape. During Prime Minister Rajiv Gandhi's visit to the People's Republic, military exchanges were discussed but not formalized in an agreement. In 1990, the Chinese and Indian militaries hesitatingly started mending fences by exchanging middle-rank officers from the National Defence College, in New Delhi, and the National Defense University, in Beijing.[1] The 1991 Communiqué on the Maintenance of Peace and Tranquillity along the Line of Actual Control (LAC) expressed the hope to enhance confidence building. Five months later, Sharad Pawar called on China, the first visit ever by an Indian defense minister, and reached an agreement on the further development of academic, scientific, and technological exchanges.[2]

In 1993, during Narasimha Rao's stay in Beijing, this initial engagement was cemented into a more operational agreement. The two delegations exchanged general information about the positions of their troops in the border region and decided to include senior military officers in the Joint Working Group that had been established earlier to prepare a final demarcation. Article 1 of the agreement stated that both sides would refrain from using violence. Other clauses provided for a gradual reduction of troops, improved communication between commanders, a mutual pullback of troops in forward areas, limits on military exercises, and measures to prevent air violations. This breakthrough was followed by a significant increase in high-level visits. In December that year, the vice chief of the People's Liberation Army (PLA), General Xu Huizi, traveled to India, followed by a visit by the defense minister, Chi Haotian, in September 1994. From the Indian side, chief of army staff General B. C. Joshi and naval chief of staff Admiral B. S. Shekhawat paid visits to several defense facilities in China in 1995 and 1996. In August 1995, the Joint Working Group decided to pull back four border posts in the Sumdorong Chu Valley, where troops had been deployed at a disturbing proximity. Also during this period, the Joint Working Group institutionalized frequent meetings of military area commanders from both sides, at Bumla and Dichu, in the eastern sector, Lipulekh, near Pithoragarh in the middle sector, and Spanggur, near Chushul in the western sector. Commanders on both sides were also provided with telephone hotlines to ensure consultations in case of intrusions or other emergencies.

In 1996, another landmark document was signed to improve stability. During Jiang Zemin's visit to India in November that year, the two countries inked the Agreement on Confidence-Building Measures in the Military Field along the Line of Actual Control. The agreement included specific provisions for reducing the military presence, such as the withdrawal of offensive weapons like mortars, tanks, howitzers, surface-to-surface and surface-to-air missiles. Exercises involving more than a division were prohibited, and all maneuvers with more than five thousand soldiers needed to be announced in advance. Combat aircraft were banned at a distance of ten kilometers from the LAC except after prior permission. Article 6 prohibited "any use of hazardous chemicals . . . blast operations or . . . guns or explosives within two km" of the LAC unless it is "part of developmental activities," in which case the other side shall be informed "through diplomatic channels or by convening a border personnel meeting, preferably five days in advance." Article 7 stated that the two sides would increase "meetings between their border representatives at designated places," expand "telecommunication links," and establish "step-by-step medium and high-level contacts between the border authorities." China and India also agreed to pull back their forces from the disputed area by two hundred meters on either side, pending a final clarification of the LAC.

Only two years later, the Indian government detonated new experimental nuclear devices in an atmosphere of xenophobic China bashing by key politicians. Yet, the calm Chinese reaction to the Indian nuclear tests in 1998 was a strong reassurance to the political and military elites in New Delhi that China had diverted its confrontational hostility. Military exchanges were restored a year after the crisis. With the Indian defense minister George Fernandes's seven-day visit to Beijing in 2003, new initiatives related to joint military exercises and the combat against terrorism came to the fore. In October of that year, six Indian ships from the Eastern Naval Command set a course for Shanghai for a joint maritime search-and-rescue exercise and a port call. In August 2004, Chinese and Indian border troops held a joint mountaineering exercise in the border area of southwest Tibet, the first of its kind between the two armed forces. Another first was China's invitation for an Indian military delegation to attend a PLA military exercise in Henan province. These exchanges developed steadily in the following years, reaching a new height when the Chinese and Indian armies joined forces for the first time in a military exercise on land, in China's province of Kunming, in December 2007. Earlier, in 2006, Indian defense minister Pranab Mukherjee and his Chinese counterpart, General Cao Gangchuan, signed a memorandum of understanding in Beijing that formed "the basis for the defense and military exchanges that have been taking place between the two countries in the last few years." The memorandum formalized the "regular and institutional contacts between the armed forces and defense officials and experts." Both sides also vowed to establish an annual program of exchanges, a plan for study tours for each other's senior and middle-level officials, to organize an annual defense dialogue, and to hold "joint military exercises and training programs in the field of search and rescue, anti-piracy, counter-terrorism and other areas of mutual interest."

Today rusty barbed wire and checkpoints still taint the snowy, rocky landscape along the many passes through the Himalayas. Nevertheless, both sides have made progress in giving the border zone a less militarized look. Troops were trimmed and main offensive systems redrawn. Especially in the eastern sector, border meetings became routine and less tense. Cultural events, mountaineering expeditions, and sports helped to break the ice. These changes all seem to herald the development of true "mountains of peace," as Indian prime minister Manmohan Singh likes to articulate.

EVALUATING THE DEMILITARIZATION OF THE BORDER AREA

Despite the absence of large-scale troop movements since the 1991 communiqué, minor incursions continue to agitate bilateral relations. Every month, the Indo-Tibetan Border Police reports around a dozen unannounced Chinese military patrols in the disputed border area, and this number has not decreased over the last decade. Most of these incidents are inoffensive. Often, border guards do not even make direct contact but leave subtle traces of their presence like piles of stones, cigarette packages, or cans. From time to time Chinese military officers reportedly enter the Indian side of the LAC in civilian clothes and vehicles. Nearly on a weekly basis, small Chinese boats tour around on Pangong Tso Lake, in Ladakh. Most of these movements have been concentrated in the western sector of the boundary. Between 2000 and 2007, the annual number of violations observed by Indian border troops increased from ninety to one hundred forty.

From time to time these routine infiltrations do cause diplomatic agitation, although the public reaction of the Indian government is to downplay the incidents. In 2003, an army report registered that Chinese expeditions on foot in the area of Trig Heights, in Ladakh, were replaced with vehicle-mounted patrols.[3] In July 2004, the Ministry of External Affairs confirmed reports that a Chinese patrol had temporarily arrested an Indian intelligence team kilometers inside the LAC in Arunachal Pradesh's Subansiri district.[4] In August 2007, the Indian army was alarmed over a number of intrusions in Bhutan and a flight by a Chinese helicopter over the LAC in the western sector. In November that year, the news media broadcast an alleged demolition

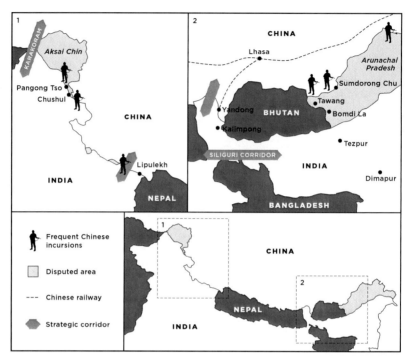

FIGURE 5.1   The Sino-Indian Border Area.

of unmanned Indian forward posts in the Dolam Valley, in Bhutan. These Chinese maneuvers in the Chumbi Valley into Bhutan stirred public outrage and reawakened the phantom of the 1962 invasion, which had pushed its way through the same passes. Bhutan has always been considered a strategic buffer for the Siliguri Corridor, which connects India's northeastern states with the rest of the country. The Chinese, for their part, claimed that India had built "facilities" on its side of the boundary. According to the Ministry of Foreign Affairs this was "a violation of the agreement between China and India on maintaining peace and tranquillity in the border region." This claim came a day after Indian government sources said Chinese army personnel demanded the removal of two bunkers on the border in Sikkim.

China's maneuvers aim more at reinforcing claims over certain parts of the frontier than at deterring India. Most incursions occurred in regions that Beijing in any case does not want to yield to India, such as Tawang or parts of Ladakh. China responds to criticism of its incursions by emphasizing that these military deployments are not made in Indian but in Chinese territory.

Yet, the incidents in Bhutan and Sikkim cannot be justified by such arguments, since Beijing recognized Sikkim as a part of India and Bhutan as a sovereign state. Interviews at the Chinese and Indian foreign affairs ministries disclosed that local military officers might have acted on their own initiative and that the Chinese minister of foreign affairs has complained that the military ventures there went too far. Whatever the exact motivations were, the actions were perceived by the Indian security community as acts of aggression. Not only did they reveal the vulnerability of the Siliguri Corridor, but the incidents also accentuated China's mobility in this rough terrain, approximately forty-four hundred meters above sea level.

In fact, the whole demilitarization process has to be put into perspective. While the presence of troops in the direct border area has decreased, the buildup of conventional forces has gone on a bit farther. On the Chinese side, the military regions of Chengdu and Lanzhou saw a significant modernization of their capacities, after being overlooked for many years. Compared with the other five military regions, the two bordering India are still modestly equipped. Together they constitute only four of China's eighteen group armies, but their approximately four hundred thousand troops still represent 20 percent of the country's total military manpower. After boosting the firepower of the units along the east coast, Chengdu and Lanzhou have now moved up as a priority for new rejuvenation schemes. The 13 Group Army, for example, has developed into a modern rapid reaction force with enhanced logistical capacity, mobile artillery, air defense, communication and intelligence, special forces, and intensive training in warfare under exceptional conditions, such as high-altitude combat.[5] Airfields in the Chengdu Military Region underwent an upgrade in the late 1990s. In 2001, the 33rd Air Division was reinforced with Su-27UBK aircraft, which are currently based in Chongqing. These long-range air defense fighters are equipped with a state-of-the-art radar system, display increased maneuverability, and are, given their payload of eight thousand kilograms, better suited to high-altitude tasks.

Closer to the border, China has reportedly built signal intelligence installations in Aksai Chin and on the southern edge of the Tibetan Plateau. Since 2002, it has conducted several counterterrorism operations and exercises near the LAC, among which one with the participation of Pakistan. As far as open sources reveal, China has been carrying out a program to make its military units in Tibet better equipped for rapid-reaction operations by investing in new wheeled armored vehicles and artillery, specialized training, and helicopters equipped for missions in the heights of the Himalayas. Since the mid-1990s, the Chinese air force has renovated its fourteen airfields in Tibet with new communication and command infrastructure, longer landing strips, and depots.[6] Several sources indicate the experimental deployment of Su-27 multirole fighter aircraft.

Is the Chinese buildup aimed specifically at India? Not at all; the Lanzhou Military Region prioritizes security in the Xinjiang Uygur Autonomous Region, that is, suppressing so-called secessionist movements among the Uighurs, safeguarding the energy facilities in the Tarim basin, and preventing a spillover of extremism and violence from central Asia. The 13 Group Army, of Chengdu, has as its primary task supporting the People's Armed Police Force controlling Tibet and monitoring the porous and unstable boundary with Myanmar. The Su-27 aircraft are also usable as a second-tier strike force in case of an armed conflict with Taiwan. Yet, the modernizations in the two military regions do take India into account as a potential challenger. The point of departure remains the so-called principle of active defense under high-tech conditions. This implies that the PLA should be able to intervene in neighboring countries whenever China's sovereignty is in danger. The main difference with earlier decades is that military units are no longer devoted to a specific threat in a specific area. Instead, they are intended to be able to deploy quickly in many places, inside and outside the People's Republic, and to deal with various conventional and nonconventional challenges. "We don't have the luxury anymore of having to address one single enemy," a Chinese military expert has summarized, explaining, "but for the troops in Chengdu and Lanzhou, a potential war with India is still central in our military planning and scenarios." Consequently, although India is not the sole target, the maintenance of a capacity of four hundred thousand soldiers with a strong presence of offensive arms systems at a short distance from the Indian border remains an important source of conventional deterrence.

"They Shall Not Pass" is the motto of the 2nd Mountain Division, one of the army units that has been watching China for almost half a century. Yet, even more so than the PLA, the capacity of the Indian armed forces is severely overstretched. With an alarming proliferation of armed resistance in the northeast, an expansion of the Naxalite uprising in the east of the subcontinent, and unstable states all along the border, units like the 2nd Mountain Division are struggling to counter these perils. The Eastern and Northern commands, responsible for securing the border with China, shifted most of their capacity to contain the insurgency in Kashmir and the rebellious northeast. Under the Calcutta-based Eastern Command, the army has three corps at its disposal, but they are all greatly depleted.

After the increasing activity of small Chinese units at the end of 2007, the defense minister, the national security adviser, and the chiefs of the Eastern and Northern commands agreed to augment the army's strength at the border. This meeting also followed a strategic reassessment of China's capabilities that brought the preparation period for a potential Chinese assault from six months to only a few weeks. In December 2007, the 27th Mountain Division, from the 33rd Corps, was relocated to its home base in Kalimpong after being deployed for more than ten years in Kashmir. Located near the strategically important junction of Bhutan, India, and China, this move sought to address the mounting presence of Chinese soldiers in this area. General C. K. Saboo, the corps commander, subsequently reported that more "sophisticated weapons with a range of up to 100 km or more" would be deployed in his area. He stated that "105mm field guns and howitzers and 155mm Bofors howitzers are already deployed on the border," and, "these guns are fitted with additional facilities like laser and radar jamming systems. These guns can penetrate up to 30 km inside China."[7] Reportedly, the minister also approved plans to revamp the 4 Corps, based in Tezpur, and the 2 Corps, based in Dimapur. In 2007, the Indo-Tibetan Border Police, authorized to monitor the LAC, increased its manpower, with twenty new battalions, and commissioned six new sectoral headquarters.

The Indian air force has followed this trend. The Eastern Air Command saw an impressive boost of its capability. The command's main responsibility is to deliver offensive air support to counter insurgency operations and covers the eastern states that border the countries of Bangladesh, China, and Myanmar. Yet, most modernizations have gone far beyond the capability to deal with domestic rebel movements. The Indian government decided to base squadrons of its most potent fighter jets, the Su-30MKI, in the eastern sector from 2008 onward. These Sukhoi aircraft increase India's preparedness to launch air-denial operations. The crafts have an operational radius of around fifteen hundred kilometers and are equipped with an in-flight refueling facility that extends their radius by another five hundred kilometers. "Buddy-refuelling, an Su-30 tanking up another, gives us the tactical advantage of refuelling in enemy territory," an officer has explained.[8] The first two squadrons, with thirty-six fighters, will be based at Tezpur air base. The shelters and runway of this base were recently renovated.[9] Apart from the Sukhoi, Tezpur will be strengthened with new air-defense systems and advanced combat helicopters better equipped for high-altitude warfare and the lifting of advance landing groups. In addition to Tezpur, the Indian air force is also in the process of upgrading its other air bases in the eastern sector. The runway length at the base in Kalaikunda, in West Bengal state, has been extended to back forward operations in Arunachal.[10] The command has also refurbished its forward air bases at Chabua, Jorhat, and Hashimara air bases.

These measures are targeted specifically against the Chinese buildup of military infrastructure in Tibet and southern China. "We do not see any short-term threat from China on the Arunachal Pradesh border," F. H. Major, the chief of air staff, has asserted, "but in the longer run, the threat cannot be ruled out as the economy of that country is growing as ours."[11] Likewise, Air Marshal P. K. Barbora, chief of the Eastern Air Command, has emphasized, "The perception of east India has changed and our defences are at their peak to thwart any misadventure now, especially after what happened in 1962 . . . In terms of numbers, we cannot match China as their economy is growing more rapidly than ours, but if we talk about specifics in the northeast, we have a deterrent force available and will be well-prepared to cater to any misadventure with the force-multipliers in place."[12]

It is from the military perspective that China's numerous transportation projects in Tibet gain more significance than only as the promotion of commerce. India's security community perceives the new Qinghai-Lhasa railway and the extensions to Nyingchi and Yadong as strategic corridors that will allow the PLA to deploy rapidly all along the border with northeast India.[13] Indian analysts cried foul after China's official news agency, Xinhua, reported that a battalion took the train to Lhasa for the first time, only a few days after an incident at Chumdi Pass.[14] As a consequence of the improved logistical infrastructure in Tibet, the Indian army revised its threat assessments. For a low-level threat, the estimated time to launch an offensive with two battalions decreased from fifteen to seven days. For a medium-level threat, implying an assault of two brigades, it went from thirty days to fifteen days. For a high alert, India now assumes that China is able to mobilize two divisions in twenty days instead of ninety to one hundred eighty days. In addition, the call from corporate actors for new roads along the Chinese border was suddenly joined by the Indian military, claiming that the absence of logistical infrastructure was no longer an obstacle hampering a possible Chinese assault. During a visit to Assam in December 2007, the defense minister acknowledged that his government had to invest in new roads and railways to allow troops to relocate quickly. The Ministry of Defence calculated that India needs to urgently construct seventy-two roads, various bridges, and three new airstrips to address the Chinese challenge. The ministry reportedly summoned the Border Roads Organisation to shift its priority to the northeast.

In sum, the confidence-building measures that have been implemented over the last decade only partially broke the ice between the military forces dispatched along the LAC. The new communication channels and the withdrawal of main military systems from the border area reduced to some extent the risk of tensions escalating into violent clashes. The stabilization of the boundary also allowed the two governments to concentrate their militaries on more pressing challenges. Nonetheless, these improvements did not reach the core of the predicament. The defense of the border decreased in priority, but its need did not disappear. Maintaining the balance of power in the border area remains prominent in both countries' strategizing and is still nourished by frightening reports of small-scale but provocative troop deployments and the construction of new transportation arteries, which can facilitate swift mobilization. The military tit-for-tat game continues as India now seeks to catch up with China on infrastructure and troop deployment. This trust deficit also has its ramifications for the political relationship. As the news media and politicians bring the tensions to the fore, the scope for negotiations on a border settlement is significantly reduced.

CHINA'S INDIAN OCEAN DILEMMA

Converting the Indian Ocean into an Indian Lake—such is the ambition of India's current projection of maritime power. Control over the ocean surrounding the Indian subcontinent runs like a manifest destiny throughout its postcolonial history, starting with Jawaharlal Nehru's remark that "whatever power controls the Indian Ocean has, in the first instance, India's sea-borne trade at her mercy and, in the second, India's very independence itself," and the subsequent claim by then minister of home affairs Sardar Patel that "the geographical position and features of India make it inevitable for India to have a strong navy to guard its long coastline and to keep a constant vigil on the vast expanse of the sea that surrounds us."[15] New Delhi's naval aspirations have been boiling for a long time, but budget constraints and other security priorities kept a lid on them.

Only since the beginning of the new century has India been making headway with its plans to rule the waves. The budget for the navy increased from U.S.$1.3 billion in 2001 to U.S.$2.8 billion in 2008. New Delhi aims for a fleet of 130 military vessels, consisting of three aircraft carrier battle groups, by 2020. In total, the navy has asked for 40 new ships. One of the main stars of this naval system is the *Vikramaditya*, an aircraft carrier worth U.S.$1.6 billion that will be equipped with sixteen MiG-29 multirole fighter aircraft. The navy also plans the commissioning of two to three smaller carriers, each including twelve combat aircraft. Additionally, the government gave the green light for seven new destroyers (P-15 and P-15A Kolkata class), thirteen multirole frigates (P-17 and P-17A Shivalik class, and Talwar-A class), twelve P-28 corvettes, eight mine countermeasures vessels, and several so-called Naval Offshore Patrol Vessels. India continues to invest in the replacement of its submarines; current plans foresee eighteen new diesel and nuclear submarines by 2012.

The modernization of the fleet has been backed up by a significant improvement in onshore infrastructure. The home ports of the Western and Eastern fleets were moved from the congested docks of Mumbai and Visakhapatnam to new bases in Karwar, INS Kadamba, and one other fifty kilometers south of the port of Visakhapatnam, in Rambilli. In 2000, the Indian government approved the opening of the Joint Andaman and Nicobar Command, only a stone's throw away from the Strait of Malacca. At Port Blair the Far Eastern Naval Command is expanding its facilities for both berthing larger vessels and dispatching naval aviation. The navy also beefed up its surveillance capacity. All along the Indian shore, new intelligence installations were erected to reach further into the ocean.

Apart from vessels and infrastructure, naval diplomacy is another element of India's grand maritime strategy. New Delhi has concluded cooperation agreements with all island states in the Indian Ocean. With the Seychelles it inked agreements assuring access to its ports. The Indian navy frequently patrols the country's territorial waters, delivers technical military assistance, and has provided Mauritius with an interceptor patrol boat, helicopters, and a surveillance aircraft. Likewise, the navy assisted Mauritius with the surveying of its exclusive economic zone and furnished the local coast guard with offshore patrol vessels, helicopters, and other equipment. With the Maldives, India signed, in 2006, a memorandum of understanding on defense cooperation. The document addressed intensified joint training and future cooperation in naval surveillance. The Indian defense minister highlighted "the privileged partnership" by handing over a fast patrol boat and a vessel for hydrologic research. Further south, India persuaded Madagascar to open its territory for a new Indian surveillance station to monitor the high seas around the island.

At several points, the Indian navy succeeded in stepping up its soft power by reacting rapidly to a humanitarian crisis. India was one of the first countries to dispatch military support to the states that were hit by the tsunami in 2004. It also reached out to the coastal states of eastern Africa and initiated joint training programs and educational exchanges with the navies of South Africa, Tanzania, Kenya, and Mozambique. In 2004, the navy provided security support for the African summit in Mozambique. "Increasing our influence in the Indian Ocean Region entails more than just showing the flag," a Defence Ministry official has asserted, "it asks for a permanent effort to increase our soft power via comprehensive cooperation with as much as possible countries from the Rim."[16]

India's maritime power advances under the banner of cooperative security. India indeed may be aiming at maritime hegemony in the surrounding ocean, but, if any, this is explained as benevolent hegemony; India assumes the role of gentle policeman, keeping a close eye out for the sake of the whole region. An officer at the planning division has contended, "We have to make our neighbours clear that we are guarding the Indian Ocean as a common good."[17] Such assertions characterize the discourse of the navy's commanders. Chief of naval staff Admiral Sureesh Mehta, for instance, has stressed that "if required in this Indian Ocean region, we will undertake humanitarian missions, stop piracy and gun-running, and all those kind of things."[18]

The aim of maintaining stability in the Indian Ocean penetrates to the core of India's economic interests. More than 95 percent of its exports are shipped through the surrounding waters. Up to 81 percent of the volume of oil that India consumes is provided via the Arabian Sea. India actually drills up to 70 percent of its hydrocarbons in offshore blocks.[19] Since the late 1990s, state-owned energy companies have discovered more promising offshore deposits of gas and oil. Apart from energy, the Indian Ocean is precious for several other assets, like mineral ores and fish. Besides hydrocarbons the Indian Ocean contains several other valuable minerals; titanium, zirconium, and thorium are found in the Gulf of Mannar Gulf and in the Bay of Bengal.[20] Across several millions of square meters, the ocean floor is covered with so-called polymetallic nodules; these volcanic composites hold manganese, iron, and nickel. Several of these areas are commercially exploitable.[21]

More than 16 million Indians live from fishery and its related sectors. Yet, these activities are exposed to various threats. Piracy is a permanent problem in most of the adjacent seas. The naval wing of the Liberation Tigers of Tamil Eelam, a Sri Lankan rebel movement, has frequently hijacked ships for direct material gain, extortion, or to force its political agenda. Such violence significantly imperils New Delhi's plans to develop a new maritime corridor through the straits between its shores and Sri Lanka. In sum, India certainly has plenty of legitimate reasons to develop the military capacity to deal with these numerous threats. As chief of naval staff Admiral Sushil Kumar has claimed, "Economic progress and security stability are two sides of the same coin. India's economic prosperity is linked directly to the maritime dimension of the country's international trade and energy security." India also risked repeatedly falling victim to the spillover of violence from other countries in the Indian Ocean region. In 1988, New Delhi ordered a military intervention in the Maldives to thwart a Pakistan-backed attempt to topple the pro-Indian regime of President Abdul Gayoom. In 1987, a peacekeeping mission was deployed to Sri Lanka.

Nonconventional threats alone, however, do not explain India's naval muscle flexing. The capability of most new arms systems goes far beyond chasing pirates and poachers.[22] Most of the navy's increasing budget has been used to boost India's capacity to deal with threats from other states. The huge amount of money used to purchase and develop submarines clearly indicates that India does not trust the maritime ambitions of other countries. The Scorpène and Amur class subs are capable of evading detection systems of potential rivals, and their firepower is unequalled by that of most other navies in the region. The ATV far exceeds conventional striking power. Its final purpose is to have nuclear-powered submarines, armed with nuclear-tipped cruise or ballistic missiles, to ensure credible second-strike capabilities.[23] The P-15A Kolkata-class destroyers will be armed with sixteen BrahMos cruise missiles, enhancing air-defense and antisubmarine warfare systems. The stealthy P-17 Shivalik frigates are frigates in name only; these ships' firepower equals that of a destroyer and enables them to engage in both defensive and offensive actions.

The ultimate outcome of this modernization is a navy that will be capable of pursuing strategies of both sea denial and limited sea control. Sea denial, blocking other countries' access to strategic lanes of communication, would lead to a situation of parallel deterrence. Thus, India will be able to deter other states with its nuclear force, and, at the same time, it also acquires the capacity to cut their economic lifelines. Sea control goes further, implying India might use the Indian Ocean for various operations, ranging from sea denial to the projection of power into littoral states. The BrahMos cruise missiles, the aircraft carrier groups, the Joint Andaman and Nicobar Command, and the new landing platform docks certainly could fulfill an important role in such operations.

The Indian navy is thus developing the capacity to play the parts of friendly policeman and formidable guardian. Again, the origins of this evolution are found in India's recent military history. Many naval strategists refer to the British Empire's ability to reach the coasts of the Indian subcontinent after establishing maritime hegemony in the Indian Ocean. During the Cold War, New Delhi was forced to look at how the United States took over the role of dominant maritime power in the region; it transformed the islet of Diego Garcia, only fourteen hundred kilometers away from India's shores, into a military bulwark. The base race with the Soviet Union and China also led to similar developments in Sri Lanka, Bangladesh, and the Maldives. In 1971, at the height of India's war with Pakistan over Bangladesh, the U.S. Navy sent an aircraft carrier group to the Bay of Bengal to compel India to pull back. Having learned from this incident, the Indian navy itself successfully dispatched several vessels to the Arabian Sea to caution Pakistan during the Kargil War, in 1999.

India remains concerned about naval intrusion in the Indian Ocean. The *Indian Maritime Doctrine,* issued in 2004, asserts, "All major powers of this century will seek a toehold in the Indian Ocean Region. Thus, Japan, the EU, and China, and a reinvigorated Russia can be expected to show presence in these waters either independently or through politico-security arrangements. There is, moreover, an increasing tendency of extra regional powers of military intervention in littoral countries to contain what they see as a conflict situation."[24] The 2003 annual defense report stressed that "the seas surrounding India have been a theatre of super power rivalry in the past, and continue to be a region of heightened activity from and by extra-regional navies on account of global security concerns."[25]

To what extent is China a focal point of this distrust? Admiral Mehta, appointed as chief of naval staff in 2006, downplayed allegations that India wants to discourage China from building up its military presence in South Asia: "We do not consider China as an adversary at any point of time. We would like to have cooperative relations with it as we do with other countries."[26] Yet, other statements have sounded less reassuring. On Indian television he declared that "China has very extended lines through which its oil has to flow, and they have to ensure that their oil supplies remain unhindered. And therefore as a policy they are doing what they are doing."[27] Nearly in the same breath he emphasized that China "is shaping the maritime battle field in the region. It is making friends at the right places. If you don't have the capability to operate in those waters, for a length of time, then you need friends who will support your cause, when the time comes, so definitely China is doing that, as there are Pakistan, Bangladesh, Myanmar, Sri Lanka and down below Africa. So it is a known fact that we are ringed by states, which may have a favourable disposition towards China." Appraisals like these are also present in the reports of the Ministry of Defence. Its 2006 annual report, for example, stated the ministry will continue to monitor "China's military modernization, including in the maritime sector."[28]

That China is a concern became visible also in the navy's look-east policy. At the beginning of the new century, the Ministry of Defence started to shift its maritime presence from the Arabian Sea to the Bay of Bengal. Beginning in 2000, more and more exercises were carried out in the eastern part of the Indian Ocean and even in the South China Sea. The navy also wants to bring the Eastern Command on a par with its Western counterpart. INS Kadamba and the new base south of Visakhapatnam are expected to become equals.[29] Whereas the Western Naval Command has been reinforced with the delivery of such advanced surface combatants such as Talwar-class frigates and Delhi-class destroyers, the Eastern Command is likely to profit from the new generation of vessels. Its home port will reportedly berth two aircraft carriers, support ships, and new Scorpène submarines. "China has fuel interests of its own as fuel lines from Africa and the Gulf run through these waters, and so they are also building up their Navy," Vice Admiral Raman Suthan, commander of the Eastern Fleet, has claimed, adding, "we keep hearing about China's interest in Coco Island and are wary of its growing interest in the region, and we are keeping a close watch. The naval fleet in east India has long legs and, with the government's emphasis on the look east policy, we are strengthening east now."[30] Ministry of Defence officials also acknowledge that the Far Eastern Command will expand its capability beyond maritime policing, and that India "should maintain control over the Andaman Sea as China's principal maritime gateway."[31] This objective explains the increasing presence of main military systems. The commands' chief, Air Marshal P. P. Rajkumar, disclosed that there are plans to include fighters, bigger ships, and more army troops, and that the facilities on the islands will be developed "in bits and pieces."

India's naval diplomacy seeks to preempt China in dropping its anchor at strategic places. Military exercises and the supply of naval systems create operational compatibility that in turn contributes to privileged partnerships and makes tactical military exchanges with the People's Republic less easy. In 2005, the Indian navy successfully prevented the Seychelles from accepting naval assistance from China, by organizing a high-level visit by naval chief Admiral Arun Prakash and through the donation of the INS *Tarmugli* to the Seychelles Coast Guard. Naval headquarters allegedly considered this gesture so urgent that it ordered the ship pulled from its own fleet barely three years after its commissioning. The stopover of Chinese president Hu Jintao in the Seychelles in 2007 raised eyebrows among many Indian security analysts. The Chinese presence in the Maldives port of Marao, the Sri Lankan harbor of Hambantota, and Myanmar's Coco Islands is watched with great suspicion and is considered one of the drivers of India's naval charm offensive.[32]

Is the Chinese navy in fact trying to strengthen its military presence in the Indian Ocean? Several Indian and Western analysts have hinted that China is providing itself with a chain of naval hubs along the sea lanes of communication.[33] This "string of pearls" strategy would bring the Chinese navy to strategic locations such as Myanmar, Bangladesh, Sri Lanka, the Maldives, the Seychelles, Pakistan, and eastern Africa. Other experts have argued that

Beijing is determined to counterbalance India's naval strength and create the capacity to break through an Indian maritime blockade. The People's Republic certainly has good reason to fret about protecting its economic lifelines in the South Asian seas. Approximately 62 percent of the country's exports and 90 percent of its oil imports are shipped via the Indian Ocean. The ocean also acts as a conveyor belt for other natural resources excavated in China's newfound mining empire in Africa. It has been proved that China tried to obtain a naval base in Sri Lanka's port of Trincomalee in the early 1980s. Currently the PLA sees as its responsibility guarding maritime corridors even if they are far from Chinese shores.

Yet, China's naval presence in South Asia is not as advanced as many observers assume. Since the 1990s, there has been an increase in port calls to Indian Ocean states from an annual average of two between 1995 and 2000 to four between 2001 and 2007.[34] The deployment of three warships in the Gulf of Aden in 2008 was the first and only important naval operation in the Indian Ocean. The mission was part of a multilateral effort to combat piracy and was backed by the UN Security Council. The so-called string of pearls thus far appears to be more a chain of commercial ventures than military stepping-stones. The supposed Chinese intelligence facilities in the Coco Islands turned out to be more media tales than actual projects.[35] Chinese engineers did contribute to the construction of naval bases at Sittwe, Hianggyi, Khaukphyu, Mergui, and Zadetkyi Kyun, and the navy trained Myanmar's naval intelligence officials and assisted Yangon in executing surveys near India's territorial waters; nevertheless, none of the formal agreements related to these ventures included access assurances for the Chinese navy.[36] Moreover, since 2002, the military junta in Myanmar has diligently attempted to move closer to the Indian navy in order to reduce its military dependence on its neighbor to the north. In September 2003, the chief of the Indian navy, Admiral Madhvendra Singh, paid an official visit to Myanmar; this visit coincided with the first joint military exercise. Since 2003, India has been training Myanmar naval officers.[37] The port of Sittwe, in several reports assumed to be a bulwark of the PLA, now rather seems to be flush with Indian businessmen from Calcutta.[38] Interviews with staff from China Harbor Construction Corporation also revealed that no military considerations played a role when it was negotiating with Islamabad for the infrastructure project at Gwadar in 2001.[39] Analysts at the Chinese Academy of Military Sciences stressed that, in a crisis, a naval anchorage such as Gwadar would be too vulnerable faced with India's military dominance in the Arabian Sea and the deployment of medium-range missiles.[40] Likewise, Hutchison Port Holdings, the Hong

Kong–based company that made a bid for the development of a terminal in Colombo, and officials from the Chinese and Sri Lankan foreign ministries deny that the Chinese navy was involved in the preparation of the bid, or that China has plans to dispatch military vessels.[41] Even an official at the Indian Ministry of Defence argued that a Chinese naval presence in Sri Lanka "will never survive a strike by our maritime bombers."

Chinese officers and experts have argued that India should not take its military leadership in the Indian Ocean for granted. At the same time, there have been recent Chinese efforts to develop a blue-water navy. Ever since Admiral Liu Huaqing published his famous roadmap for the Chinese navy, its modernization has been approached from the perspective of an eventual conflict in the Taiwan Strait. This implies, on the one hand, the capacity to launch an amphibious invasion and, on the other, deflection of an American counterstrike. Therefore, the Chinese navy seeks to develop concentric lines of defense. Initially this objective was limited to the South and East China Seas, but in the coming decade it will seek to extend this defensive perimeter far into the Pacific. This explains the presence of, for example, the new Jiang-kai-class frigates and the Luzhou-class destroyers, which possess the capacity for long-distance operations and radar, air defense, command, and communication systems for engaging multiple distant targets on the high seas.

But naval strategies are not static. For example, the Chinese navy reacted to the swift modernization of its Japanese counterpart by strengthening its Northern Fleet. The Southern Fleet was slightly revamped as a response to the increasing capacity of the Vietnamese navy. Recently, civilian and military experts have started to address the Chinese vulnerability in the Indian Ocean.[42] Zhang Yuncheng, for instance, contends that "excessive reliance of China's oil on the Malacca Strait implies that China's energy security is facing a Malacca dilemma. If some accident occurs or if the strait is blocked by foreign powers, China will experience a tremendous energy security problem." However, according to Zhang, such a threat will come not from India but other powers, such as Japan and the United States. This assessment is shared by Zhu Fenggang, who assumes that the United States and Japan might deny access to the strait as a coercive measure against China. Many others have taken these observations as a reason for a mercantilist, or Mahanian, naval policy, which, apart from Taiwan, also takes into account the defense of maritime trade. "We must be prepared as early as possible," Zhang Wenmu has asserted, referring explicitly to the Indian Ocean. He continues, "Ocean power is of permanent importance for the trade of coastal countries . . . Therefore, a modern ocean-going navy is long needed to ensure open sea lanes and potential ocean resources."[43] Hence, the debate on how to protect its maritime supply lines is only starting to take place. Expert discussions on China's maritime security dilemma in the Indian Ocean will, without a doubt, lead to policy choices.

A naval arms race with India is not a likely outcome. Most important, the country's naval power will remain mainly tied up with Taiwan until a settlement with the island is reached. Whereas enhanced capability in the East and South China Seas does not weaken readiness to deal with nearby Taiwan, a shift of attention toward the Indian Ocean would do so and is therefore not an option. Second, there is still a huge difference between a naval deployment in the Eastern and South China Seas, both considered a historical sphere of influence, and one in the Indian Ocean, where, apart from the expedition by Zheng He in the fourteenth century, China does not have any plausible argument to offer its neighbors that area also historically belongs within its maritime area of interest. Even countries like Pakistan, Sri Lanka, Myanmar, and Bangladesh would receive such a move with distrust. Third, it is doubtful that the People's Republic would reduce its vulnerability to an Indian sea-denial operation by sending its fleet westward of the Strait of Malacca. If a major crisis occurred, a Chinese naval counteroffensive would be easy prey, since ships would inevitably have to sail through the narrow strait in Southeast Asia. Moreover, even if the Chinese navy succeeded in overcoming the Eastern Naval Command, India's Western Naval Command would, because of the strategic depth, still be able to block oil supplies from the Persian Gulf for days, weeks, if not months.

In any case, the costs of a Chinese counteroperation would be too high, so it seems more plausible for the People's Republic to try to raise the costs for India to deny access and simultaneously to reduce its dependence on the shipping lanes in the Indian Ocean. Instead of building up a naval presence in South Asia to balance India, it would be easier to deter the country in other ways: along the border, via Pakistan, and so on. In addition, China could diversify its supply lines. One option is the development of the new Silk Road stretching from Shanghai to Rotterdam and the Middle East. Another possibility is a logistical corridor through Pakistan, which would reduce the exposure to risks at sea. Such a connection, in particular a gas corridor to central Asia and the Middle East, may significantly improve China's energy security, but, owing to their limited freight capacity, roads and railways will not offer an alternative for the export and import of other goods. The ultimate alternative to the Indian Ocean would be the Arctic Ocean. If these waters became navigable, China would be able to not only diversify the risks but also reduce the average transportation time to Europe and Western Africa. Since 2000, China has been investing more in scientific research at the North Pole; it has opened a research base, and expeditions north of the Bering Strait have increased in number.

India and China's naval power has always been subordinated to the development of a strong army to deal with the numerous challenges on land. Nowadays, however, the two countries are laying the groundwork for a capable blue-water navy. The plans on the drawing board exhibit aspirations that go much further than the safeguarding of exclusive economic zones or the maintenance of supremacy toward their archrivals Pakistan and Taiwan. In an effort to legitimize these projects, defense analysts refer mainly to the necessity to protect maritime supply lines from perils like piracy and terrorism. Such nonstate challengers cannot justify, however, the purchase of costly offensive systems like destroyers, nuclear-powered submarines, and aircraft carriers. India in particular has invoked for justification the swiftly modernizing Chinese navy and its potential interest in taking a position in the Indian Ocean. In Beijing India has yet to figure prominently in naval strategizing, but as Indian military officers and experts continue to depict the Chinese navy as a nascent threat, a naval race between the two powers may become a self-fulfilling prophecy.

NUCLEAR DETERRENCE

In April 2007, India successfully tested its Agni-III intermediate-range ballistic missile (IRBM). Although this event did not have the direct diplomatic consequences as the nuclear test in 1998, its impact on the Sino-Indian military balance was considerable.[44] This missile was uniquely designed to reach China. India's previous ballistic missiles, the Agni-I and Agni-II, had a rather short action radius and were developed mainly to deter Pakistan. The Agni-III was India's first missile that could reach any part of China's entire territory, and, with its range of between thirty-five hundred kilometers and four thousand kilometers, the People's Republic is also the only nuclear power that would be a relevant target. Although New Delhi has stated that it would not be equipped with nuclear warheads, the missile supports a wide range of warhead configurations, with a total payload ranging from six hundred kilograms to eighteen hundred kilorams.[45] Moreover, despite huge technological constraints, the Defence Research and Development Organisation, the agency charged with the development of India's nuclear arsenal, is continuing work on multiple independently targetable reentry vehicle technology to enable the Agni-III to circumvent Chinese missile defense countermeasures.[46] The fact that construction of this missile type was ordered in 2001, at a time when ties with Beijing were improving, together with the troubled and over-priced development costs, demonstrates that the relevance of nuclear deterrence did not disappear from India's China agenda.[47]

After India reached sufficient nuclear deterrence vis-à-vis Pakistan in the late 1990s, its nuclear aspirations shifted to its northern neighbor. The priority became not to reach an equivalence with China but to bolster a minimal deterrence capability. The People's Republic possesses approximately four hundred nuclear missiles, and many Indian strategists believe that several of them are pointed at their country. In 2002, India's annual defense report claimed that "every major Indian city is within reach of Chinese missiles and this capability is being further augmented to include Submarine Launched Ballistic Missiles (SLBMs). The asymmetry in terms of nuclear force is pronouncedly in favour of China and is likely to get further accentuated as China responds to counter the US missile defence programme." Several studies cast the light of suspicion on China's assumed missile deployment at military bases in Tibet, such as Nagchuka, Tsaidam, Terlingkha, and other nearby places like Kunming and Datong. Analysts have also warned that China will station new short-range missiles on the Tibetan Plateau and that they would be considered tactical, thus lowering the threshold for a nuclear conflict.[48]

On the Chinese side there is confidence its weight will hold, but there are aspects of India's nuclear showing off that raise eyebrows. Beijing is concerned about India's Advanced Air Defence program, which can affect the impact of its older generation of single-warhead IRBMs. It has also hinted that the new missiles could undermine its superiority over Tibet and that its relevance as a buffer will be undermined by India's gradual nuclear buildup.[49] Other Chinese observers highlight the risk that looming nationalism could make India's nuclear deterrence less pragmatic and rational. Finally, there is the consideration that India's improving nuclear power may make it more assertive toward Pakistan and thus disturb Pakistan's role as a counterweight that China has steadily constructed over the past decades.[50]

SIMULTANEOUS TO THE DIPLOMATIC THAW of the last decades, the military interaction between China and India has evolved from a trench warfare to pacification and, since the 1990s, also confidence building. The armed forces of both countries have reduced their presence at the disputed boundary and have engaged in an increasing number of exchanges. The Cold War mentality may be ebbing to some extent; it certainly has not disappeared. An enduring security dilemma propels a military tit-for-tat game.

This situation stems from a rational extrapolation of each other's interests into malevolent intentions. For instance, China has reasonable interests in reducing its exposure to Indian dominance in the Indian Ocean, and thus the latter should anticipate China's attempts to extend its naval strength beyond the Malacca Strait.

That such a negative appraisal receives endorsement over more positive views may be rationally inherent to a security dilemma; it is undoubtedly stimulated by several additional factors. Always in search of more means military establishments naturally tend to emphasize gloomy assessments, and since they still have significant leverage with their governments, appeals are likely to be heard to some extent, and subsequent projects ultimately endorse the arguments of the defense community in the other country. Second, many of the military leaders were trained in scenario writing that sought its inspiration in the hot war of 1962 or in nuclear confrontations. Track dependency remains an important feature of strategic thinking. Third, as demonstrated in earlier chapters, civilian experts on Sino-Indian relations who tend to be more suspicious dominate the news media, especially in India. Moreover, several of these experts are on advisory bodies, such as the influential National Security Council. Finally, apprehension is stoked by external powers, most notably the United States. Although India is still reluctant to team up, America's military appetite for the South Asian juggernaut makes China very uncomfortable.

In their order of security challenges, China and India rank each other far below domestic perils and Taiwan or Pakistan. This means that they take each other into account in their arms-development programs, but it is not a matter of extreme responsiveness in which every slight improvement of one player is directly followed by an adjustment by the other. Maintaining the military balance is more a matter of watching certain general thresholds that, once they have been crossed by the other camp, may lead to some alterations. This is the case with nuclear arms, where no Cold War–like parity is aimed at but rather a minimal deterrence. Nor are both sides looking for military supremacy at the border, but they are seeking rather to develop the capability to react flexibly on a wide range of challenges. China and India are still far from an arms race, but they will not allow each other to leap too far ahead. The security dilemma will impede the two regional powers from moving from confidence building to military cooperation. Even though they face similar challenges in many areas of Asia, self-help will continue to prevail in the development of synergies toward issues like maritime security, terrorism, and instability in neighboring states. The balance of power between China and India differs in the various dimensions of military capability, that is, conventional and nonconventional, but on the whole they are both vulnerable to potential acts of hostility. The situation of multilevel soft deterrence leads to stronger security interdependence and hence a reduced probability of armed conflict. Therefore, for the near future, the security dilemma will not bring peace but it will lead to a precarious form of stability as the costs of war rise significantly on both sides of the Himalayas.

SIX

REGIONAL SECURITY COOPERATION

CHINA AND INDIA HAVE UNLEASHED a diplomatic charm offensive in Asia to satisfy their growing economic needs. Delegations fly back and forth between Asian capitals to broker new trade agreements and business deals. In their wake, Chinese and Indian engineers are laying out the infrastructure necessary to carry the expanding trade flows. The economization of China and India's regional diplomacy has created new security challenges. In many parts of the region their economic ventures have come under threat from organized criminality, terrorism, and domestic instability in partner countries, not least in their immediate neighborhood. In the corridor of states stretching from Pakistan to Myanmar, Chinese and Indian economic interests have been confronted by various security risks. This area, where mainly nontraditional violence draws strong concern from both sides, has for a long time been an arena for Sino-Indian rivalry.[1]

This chapter studies to what extent growing commercial interests in the region will lead to enhanced security cooperation between China and India. My aim is to test empirically whether trade and the increasing interest in a stable neighborhood will mitigate the "protracted contest," as it is described by scholars like John Garver.[2] Will India and China join forces to promote security and to deal with the unrest in neighboring states? Four assumptions are central. First, it is assumed that economic security has become a more important element in China and India's neighborhood policy. Second, as a consequence of their increasing economic interests the two countries have become more confronted by nontraditional security challenges. Third, it is presupposed that this similarly growing exposure has led to more regional security interdependence. Finally, this interdependence can be expected to lead to more security cooperation.

The idea of security interdependence taps into the Copenhagen school of international studies, in particular the two key concepts of regional security complexes and securitization.[3] Defining a regional security complex as a geographically restricted set of states whose security interests are so interlinked that solutions cannot be achieved apart from one another, Barry Buzan approaches Nepal, Bhutan, and Myanmar as insulators and buffer states that separate the two larger East and South Asian regional security complexes, mainly because of a lack of connectedness.[4] Pakistan is perceived as only a part of the South Asian complex. Given the growing logistical links, cross-border commercial activity, trade, investments, and flows of people, threats as well can be expected to travel more easily over short distances. In this regard, consideration is given to what extent a subregional security complex is emerging as a consequence of the similar challenges that Beijing and New Delhi are facing due to increasing connectedness and the growing nontraditional security threats.

This in turn brings us to the pattern of security interdependence. Three types of security complexes can be distinguished. At the negative end lie conflict formations, which are driven by threat perceptions.[5] Security interests are perceived as a zero-sum-game in which self-help and the quest for creating a favorable balance of power are decisive. Cooperation is absent because of the fear of losing influence. This is the setting that bears the most resemblance to the idea of a protracted contest that Garver and most other students of Sino-Indian relations have postulated. Security complexes may also take the shape of security regimes, where the security dilemma is somewhat mitigated and cooperation is possible. At the other end of the spectrum rests the security community in which threat perceptions have completely disappeared.[6]

According to the Copenhagen school, the evolution from conflict formation to other stages depends mainly on the type of securitization.[7] Although security interdependence may have become an urgent reality, it still has to be recognized as such before it can lead to cooperation. On the one hand, *similar* security interests between states do not necessarily have to be approached as *common* interests; on the other, common security interests may be accepted but still not lead to security cooperation because in the hierarchy of security objectives they are still ranked below the wish to maintain diplomatic, military, or economic dominance vis-à-vis another state. In order to assess the prospects for cooperation between China and India in their common neighborhood, the extent to which recent securitization of regional economic interests leads to a desecuritization of their mutual interaction in this area must be measured.

While Ole Wæver rightly stresses that political discourse should be a key focus in such an assessment, this chapter aims at striking a balance between discourse and deeds. In their most primitive form joint security interests could take the shape of a joint willingness to repress low-level risks such as criminality. New Delhi and Beijing could also jointly decide to support local regimes for suppressing armed resistance and rebellion. Yet, the evolution from a conflict setting to enhanced security cooperation needs to go further; the quality of collective regional security efforts should also be assessed by looking at the extent to which India and China are prepared to put pressure on local elites to foster more comprehensive security, that is, an inclusive political transition in which all rival parties are involved, as well as the tackling of economic and political mechanisms at the basis of grievances and violence. In a competitive context where neighboring regimes are considered precious allies, sovereignty tends to be perceived as sacrosanct and above all a comfortable premise for strengthening goodwill and influence among political leaders. In such a situation it is attractive to neglect that those political fiends are often more a part of security problems than of their solution. The quality of cooperation, rather than cooperation as such, will reveal whether China and India succeed in desecuritizing their bilateral relations in regional affairs for the sake of securing their short- and long-term economic interests.

In the following sections, I elucidate how China and India have expanded their influence in their shared neighborhood, how this transformation has rendered them more vulnerable to various nontraditional threats, and to what extent they have grasped these challenges to join forces with regard to regional security issues.

INTERESTS

The grouping of Bhutan, Nepal, Pakistan, and Myanmar is one of the least-developed quarters in Asia, and their trade relations with China and India have remained limited. In 2007, China's trade volume with the subregion amounted to only U.S.$8.1 billion. India's stood at U.S.$4.3 billion. That year, China's investment stock was not more than U.S.$400 million; for India this remained well below U.S.$200 million. Nevertheless, there are still several beckoning opportunities. This market is a perfect fit with the unsophisticated industries in India and China's landlocked provinces. Between 2001 and 2007, Chinese exports to the subregion grew from U.S.$1.3 billion to

U.S.$6.1 billion, with Xinjiang, Yunnan, and Tibet representing 18 percent of this volume. India saw its business expand from U.S.$600 million to U.S.$2.1 billion. The poorly developed states are also a lucrative target for engineering companies. Fazal-ur-Rahman estimated that, in 2006, the total contracted volume of engineering work gained by China in Pakistan alone amounted to U.S.$8.64 billion.[8] By the end of 2007, the accumulated amount of contracts China had signed with Myanmar for labor services reached U.S.$4.7 billion, with a total realized turnover of U.S.$3.1 billion.[9] In Nepal the accumulated value of such contracts surpassed U.S.$1 billion.

Natural resources are another asset in which China and India both take an interest. Chinese and Indian companies are eying oil reserves in Pakistan and Myanmar. In 2007, Zhenhua Oil, a subsidiary of CNPC, signed an agreement with Islamabad to explore reserves in the provinces of Punjab, Northwest Frontier, and Baluchistan. In 2006, CNPC successfully bid for the rights to explore a block in Sindh, eastern Pakistan. All three Chinese oil giants have gained a footing in Myanmar. In October 2004, a consortium led by CNOOC's Myanmar unit, China Huanqiu Contracting and Engineering, started drilling at onshore blocks C-1, C-2, and M, as well as at offshore blocks A-4, M-2, and M-10. In July 2004, Sinopec's Dian-Qian-Gui unit signed a production-sharing contract with Myanmar Oil and Gas Enterprise to look for mineral fuels at Block D in the onshore area of Mahudaung, in Rakhine state. In 2007, CNPC signed production-sharing contracts to explore for oil and gas in three offshore blocks, AD-1, AD-6, and AD-8, off the western Rakhine coast. Regarding India ONGC, GAIL, and Essar have made forays and become involved in blocks A-1 and A-3, also off the Rakhine coast. In September 2007, ONGC signed separate production-sharing contracts for natural gas in three deep-sea blocks, AD-2, AD-3, and AD-9. In 2008, Essar started exploratory drilling for natural gas at an inland block near Sittwe, in Rakhine state.

Myanmar's largely untapped mineral reserves have also attracted the attention of its neighbors. In 2004, China and Myanmar signed a memorandum on cooperation in the exploitation of mineral resources, including copper, nickel, and iron. At the same time, a large-scale mineral exploration project was approved between the China Hainan Jiayi Machine Import and Export Company and Myanmar's Department of Geological Survey and Mineral Exploration, providing for the exploration right for copper and other minerals in Kachin state. China Nonferrous Metal Mining Company got approval to invest U.S.$500 million in nickel-mining operations in Mandalay province. In 2005, an agreement followed with Kingbao Mining for nickel exploration in northwestern Myanmar's Mwetaung region. On a smaller scale, several Indian companies are digging for gold and precious stones, especially near the border with India. Approximately 76 percent of the country's timber production is shipped to China and India. Another commodity of strategic importance is pigeon peas. India relies on Myanmar for half its import of these legumes. Any disruption in the supply could cause severe social difficulties because many Indians spend a significant part of their earnings on the product for their daily patties.[10] In Pakistan, Chinese companies have invested in excavation projects in Baluchistan. In 2003, the Metallurgical Construction Corporation hammered out a concession for copper, gold, and silver mining in Saindak.

Finally, there is the objective to turn the subregion into a transit corridor. For China, securing its commercial links means access to the Indian Ocean from Yunnan via Myanmar and, second, from Xinjiang via Pakistan. India needs to keep an eye on its links between the northeast and Myanmar, as well as those that could be further developed to central Asia via Pakistan. Equally important to the facilitation of cross-border trade is preventing interaction with neighboring countries that could undermine stability and economic development of their fragile peripheral areas. While the people that live in such places might not always feel attached to the political center, the center is more and more interested in the soil they live on. Tibet and Xinjiang, for instance, are of vital importance for supplying natural resources to the factories on the Chinese coast. Xinjiang has promising deposits of oil and natural gas. Since 1999, Chinese geologists have discovered more than six hundred new sites of copper, iron, lead, and zinc deposits on the Tibetan Plateau.[11] India's remote northeast is believed to contain large reserves of fossil fuels, uranium, and various mineral ores. Upstream control in these regions is a prerequisite for national growth and domestic stability.

In recent years, Chinese and Indian economic interests in their neighborhood have expanded significantly. The region has become a direct target for natural resources, and indirectly it is expected to play an important role in the development of domestic peripheral areas. The economization of both countries' relations with their neighbors has resulted in increasing vulnerability. The growing dependence on safe transit and the supply of natural resources means that it will be more difficult to absorb disruptions to which they might become exposed.[12] Although the links with countries like Myanmar and Pakistan remain modest compared to China and India's overall engagement with the global economy, this region has become more important for their economic security.[13]

BELT OF INSECURITY

Given this increasing vulnerability, what are the risks for China and India's economic security? For one thing, they are confronted by the proliferation of criminal activities in the border areas. The porous boundaries with Nepal and Myanmar in particular are a transit zone for smuggling. Most of India and China's drug imports come from Myanmar. The Wa ethnic group, with communities in both Myanmar and China, has developed a certain division of labor where Wa farmers in Myanmar produce poppies and Chinese Wa act as smugglers and furnishers of chemicals to make heroine.[14] Across the border with Yunnan, Manipur, and Mizoram, gangs are involved in the smuggling of rare species of animals, gems, and timber. Brothels and gambling bars have shot out of the ground like mushrooms. India is struggling with criminal activities mainly at its border with Nepal. Armed gangs are active in the trafficking of Nepali women, arms, oil, and drugs. Apart from the dramatic prevalence of AIDS in border areas such as Yunnan or the Indian states of Mizoram, Bihar, and Uttar Pradesh, this has also led to a steady criminalization of border towns, with Indian and Chinese citizens more often falling prey to violence. Since 2006, overseas drug traders have opened new trafficking routes for smuggling narcotics to China through India and Nepal.[15] In some areas, even the security forces face aggression. In February 2008, for example, three Chinese marine police officers were injured in a gunfight with Myanmar drug traffickers on the Mekong River.[16] In 2003, Indian border guards reportedly were so often victim to armed aggression they ceased patrolling in several sections of the border with Myanmar.

The situation is aggravated when criminal activities mingle with armed rebellion. Several areas where China and India look to improve transport infrastructure are affected by rebel movements. In Myanmar China's oil pipeline and road and railway projects run partially through Shan state, a region fragmented into drug empires and ravaged by rival warlords. Two main armed movements, the Shan State Army and the Shan State National Army, are among the most resilient competitors of the military junta. A study by Toshihiro Kudo reveals that most of the current trade links with China have become prone to violence and, further, that the trade flows via the main road from Ruili to Mandalay are monopolized by a branch of the Myanmar military intelligence service.[17] Power struggles between the State Peace and Development Council (SPDC) and rebel groups, as well as internal rivalry between different units of the military, loom large over China's ambition to link the city of Kunming to the Andaman Sea. India's routes are imperiled too.

The Kaladan Project, for connecting the state of Mizoram to the Myanmar port of Sittwe, covers the unstable states of Chin and Arakan, where various armed movements from Myanmar, Bangladesh, and India seek refuge.

The challenges in Pakistan are even more serious. In Baluchistan, where several Chinese projects are located, rebel movements have frequently targeted Chinese workers. In May 2004, three Chinese were killed in Gwadar. In February 2006, three Chinese engineers were shot dead. In July that year, a car bomb targeted a vehicle carrying Chinese mine workers. In South Waziristan, an area near the border with Afghanistan, one Chinese hostage held by Islamic militants was killed while another was freed in a rescue mission by Pakistani forces. In June 23, Islamist hard-liners abducted seven Chinese nationals. A month later, three Chinese nationals were killed in a town near Peshawar, in northwestern Pakistan. The killings were widely seen as revenge for the government's crackdown on religious militants holed up in Islamabad. Islamic radicals have targeted Chinese citizens because they are perceived as an ally of the regime of President Musharraf. States like Baluchistan and Waziristan feel that Chinese investments are benefiting the political elite in Islamabad rather than the local populations. They are also angered by what they see as repression of the Muslim Uighur minority community in China's Xinjiang Uygur Autonomous Region. This violence has caused CNPC to reconsider its exploration activities. Escalating rebellion in Baluchistan risks hampering other companies' exploitation of natural resources. Moreover, Indian and Chinese plans to develop a logistical corridor through this region, to the Indian Ocean and central Asia, respectively, will be thwarted if the new roads and pipelines become a target for insurgents.

In Nepal domestic political violence has affected mainly India's interests. Several opposition groups have targeted India as a new imperialist oppressor. In 2000, a wave of anti-Indian sentiment resulted in attacks on Indian entrepreneurs and led to four deaths. In 2004, after Indian armed forces arrested one of their leaders, Nepalese Maoist factions threatened Indian businessmen in the border areas and forced them to leave within twenty-four hours.[18] They torched Indian oil tankers and opened fire on Indian truckers. In 2005 and 2006, outbursts of anger followed alleged attempts by India to interfere in Nepalese domestic affairs. Again Indian entrepreneurs where threatened with expulsion.[19] In 2006, an Indian national was killed in fights between security forces and Maoists in a Nepalese border town.

While instability threatens interests abroad, domestic security is at risk, too, as violence spills over the border into sensitive regions. The forested mountains near the Indian lowlands or the rocky valleys of the Himalayas are perfect terrain for rebels to shelter themselves or from which to make forays.

Most of the Indian and Chinese people living in these areas are among the poorest of their countries. Often, these groups are banished to the economic and political margins, resulting in frustration, an informal economy prone to criminality, and increasing awareness of local ethnic and religious identities. Several of these isolated regions have stronger cultural and economic links with neighboring states than with the rest of the country.

At the end of 2007, India's northeast counted eleven rebel movements, each with an average of 850 combatants.[20] New Delhi considers them one of the main stumbling blocks to domestic development. Blackmail, looting, popular support among impoverished farmers, and the porous boundary with Nepal, Myanmar, Bhutan, and Bangladesh allow the armed groups to persist in their activities. All are assumed to have training camps and weapons stockpiles in neighboring countries. The Naxalites, an amalgamation of leftist resistance groups, find refuge in Nepal and Bhutan. Indian home minister Shivraj Patil said that, in 2007, ten states and 180 districts in the country were affected by the "Naxalite problem," good for a total of seven hundred violent incidents. The Madheshi resistance in the Terai region in southern Nepal exposes Uttar Pradesh and Bihar to cross-border violence. Combatants of the Janatantrik Terai Mukti Morcha faction often run over the border with India seeking shelter from raids by Nepalese security forces. Indian citizens from Uttar Pradesh are believed to have participated in Terai riots.[21] Because the Madheshi armed rebellion is closely related to property feuds, smuggling, and other criminal activities, the political economy of this Nepalese conflict risks undermining the stability in the fragile Indian border states. Moreover, as the conflict in southern Nepal becomes more and more complicated, with the Madheshis involved in a struggle against Nepalese Maoists and both entities fragmenting internally, violence can further escalate and become uncontrollable.[22] Nepal is also a potential stepping-stone for Islamic terrorists. Several attacks by Pakistani terrorists since the late 1990s have had a connection with Nepal.[23] Nepal has been used as an infiltration route into and from Jammu and Kashmir.[24] New Delhi now also fears that the Islamic communities in southern Nepal may become a means for Pakistani Islamic extremists to target India. Finally, there is Pakistan. Apart from the conflict in Kashmir, where the Pakistani military continues supporting anti-India guerrillas, the Talibanization of the rest of Pakistan is the single-most important source of terrorist attacks in India.

China's security fear of a spillover of violence relates first and foremost to Tibetan refugees. Approximately thirty-five thousand Tibetans live in Bhutan, Myanmar, and Nepal. Beijing's attitude toward these communities is ambivalent. On the one hand there is the opinion that the expulsion of ethnic Tibetans favors the dominance of Han Chinese in the region and rids the People's Republic of a problem. On the other, the concentration of Tibetans in neighboring countries represents a potential bastion of resistance. In the 1960s and 1970s for instance, Tibetans, supported by the United States, launched a guerrilla war from Nepal's Mustang district. China is also concerned that Tibetan emancipation in Nepal may stir unrest within its own borders. Protests in its neighboring countries are seen as a blow to the Chinese government's legitimacy. Beijing wants to make sure that it controls the emerging logistical links with Nepal to avoid emigrated Tibetans' having access to them in China.

Beijing is also concerned that Pakistan could become a sanctuary for Islamist secessionists from Xinjiang. According to the Chinese government, members of the East Turkestan Liberation Organization use Pakistan as a hideaway and for rearming. As border trade with Pakistan expanded, local security services became concerned about the presence of Pakistani citizens connected to Islamist organizations like Tablighi Jamaat and the Jamaat-e-Islami. In 1999, an alleged religious militant from Pakistan was executed. In December 2000, Chinese security forces reportedly arrested over two hundred heavily armed militants near the Karakoram Highway. In addition, in 2003, Pakistanis were arrested in the Kashgar region for selling "illegal" copies of the Koran.[25] In January 2004, China drew up a list of militants reportedly linked to Al Qaeda factions in Pakistan's tribal areas.[26] Beijing has claimed that Muslim separatists in Xinjiang receive training in Pakistan and Kashmir from groups associated with Al Qaeda and afterward return to China, "where they carry out violent attacks on members of China's Han majority."[27] In 2007, Chinese police raided an alleged terrorist camp in a western mountain region near the border with Pakistan and killed eighteen suspects.[28] After retrieving so-called Uighur radicals from as far as Baluchistan, in southern Pakistan, Beijing became increasingly worried about the Talibanization of the Pakistani state and society. China started to fear that, if the political center weakens further, extremist Islamist groups will gain a free hand and form a permanent threat to the development of its far west.[29]

The strip from the Irrawaddy to the Hindu Kush is fraught with peril. Chinese and Indian economic interests have faced various security threats. As mentioned earlier, China and India have similar economic interests, but do these shared interests, together with the increasing risks also outlined in the preceding, also lead to similar security interests? It turns out this is indeed the case. The religious extremism in Pakistan is a main concern for both. In Bhutan, Nepal, and Myanmar, the shared concern is the state's incapacity to control the volatile mixture of criminality, rebellion, and refugees. For both countries, these similar security interests are translated into three shared objectives. First, it is a matter of protecting their citizens or investment projects from becoming a target of xenophobic, frustrated mobs or terrorists. Second, there is the need to watch the intraregional movement of organized crime, terrorism, and rebellion. Third, and this is where the two former aspects come together, China and India need capable and stable states around them to allow economic expansion and the development of their remote, impoverished districts.

China and India share a similar vulnerability that has resulted in similar security interests. The question then arises whether *similar* interests also imply *common* interests. After all, it could be claimed that India's problem with Pakistani terrorists is not China's concern, despite the similarity as a security challenge. It has to be questioned whether security concerns are so closely linked that they can no longer be addressed separately. It goes beyond the scope of this paper to map the complex dynamics of instability in South Asia, but, for example, it is obvious that China and India will not be able to persuade the Pakistani government to end its support to terrorism without working together. Neither will the military junta in Myanmar feel encouraged to invest more in the domestic peace process if one of its neighbors supports the regime whatever position it takes in the process of national reconciliation. It will also be impossible for Beijing and New Delhi to curb the flows of narcotics, refugees, and terrorists without cooperation.

Security interdependence has thus become a pressing reality and resulted in a new subregional security complex. Instead of a cushion between the two East and South Asian security complexes, the increasing permeability of the traditional buffer states has blurred the barrier between the two regional security complexes. China and India must be ever more watchful of the situation in their shared neighborhood to maintain domestic stability. Even from inaccessible states like Bhutan, growing cross-border travel, smuggling, and trade will make it easier for rebels to penetrate onto Chinese or Indian soil. Economic interests have become a catalyst for expanding security interdependence. Myanmar, until recently negligible, has turned into a priority for New Delhi's foreign economic policy, as has Nepal for Beijing. In the past few years, both countries have become besieged by Chinese and Indian traders and investors. These interests go beyond the traditional realist appraisal of scholars like Garver. Neighboring states can no longer be considered solely as devices for old-fashioned balancing strategies as their interior stability in relation to the maintenance of regional balances of power becomes more important. Nevertheless, it remains to be seen whether the new security interdependence will also lead to security cooperation.

SEEKING SECURITY UNDER UNCERTAINTY

Nontraditional threats and transnationalization of informal violence have rendered problematic the conventional realist assumptions about regional security and require a resecuritization of regional policies.[30] Securitization means that security issues become recognized as threats and thus form the starting point for conceiving security policies.[31] The question, though, is whether this resecuritization is taking place. Are India and China's regional threat perceptions and security objectives shifting from counterbalancing each other to tackling nontraditional threats and maintaining economic security, and, consequently, is this evolution allowing them to translate similar security interests into common policies and cooperation? This section assesses whether this resecuritization has occurred, acknowledging that such an evaluation must focus both on political language and policies as variables.[32]

The combat against terrorism has become one of the focal points in Sino-Indian cooperation. In 2002, the two countries initiated a bilateral counterterrorism mechanism that provides for an annual dialogue at the director level. Earlier, this issue was included in a joint security dialogue. In December 2007, India and China launched an unprecedented five-day antiterrorism training exercise in the Chinese province of Yunnan that involved more than two hundred troops. The same year, China, India, and Russia endorsed a joint communiqué on counterterrorism in which they vowed to coordinate action against "any factor that feeds international terrorism, including its financing, illegal drug trafficking and trans-national organized crime." In 2008, at a lecture in Beijing, Prime Minister Manmohan Singh stated that "recent developments in our neighbourhood have brought home to us again the imperative need to collectively fight terrorism and extremism in all its forms." In private talks with his counterpart, Wen Jiabao, Singh particularly stressed the need to exert pressure on the Pakistani government to stop sponsoring Islamist terrorism.[33]

Despite these new initiatives, Sino-Indian cooperation on terrorism tends to be declaratory. The issue appears to be brought to the fore to add relevance to the partnership rather than to developing operational synergies. India, for instance, has complained that the joint mechanism on terrorism lacks substance. According to an Indian official, the Chinese side "was satisfied with having such a dialogue," while New Delhi wanted to use it as a platform for mobilizing China to urge Pakistan to stop supporting terrorists in Kashmir and elsewhere in the region. "We tabled this a couple of times, and the Chinese took note, but no action followed," he explained. Reportedly, both sides have also had discussions on the role of Afghanistan, Nepal, and Bangladesh as incubators of terrorism, but they did not arrive at a common position. For India, the main objective is to raise the problem of neighboring countries' becoming stepping-stones for terrorists higher up on the regional and international agendas, but Beijing, for its part, remains opposed to the internationalization of such problems. "There is no progress on terrorism cooperation," an Indian expert has claimed, "India hoped to find an ally in the Chinese, but China prefers to deal with Pakistan unilaterally to keep extremists out of Xinjiang. While India castigated some neighbouring countries for supporting terrorism, the Chinese will simply not do this." Despite the spectacular picture of the joint exercise in Yunnan, cooperation between the two countries' security forces to combat terrorism has not been explored. There are virtually no links between the intelligence agencies or specialized offices in ministries, and there is no exchange of information.

With regard to cross-border criminality, China and India have agreed to joint efforts to combat the drugs trade. Their agreement on drug-control cooperation, signed in 2000, was aimed specifically at curbing the traffic via Myanmar. Officials have met regularly since the signing. In 2003, China and India held a roundtable with Myanmar, Laos, and Thailand, which resulted in the Chiang Rai Declaration on drugs control.[34] In 2006, the five convened to discuss a joint strategy, including intelligence sharing and training, for fighting the narcotics trade in the Golden Triangle.[35] The two-day meeting was followed by a bilateral one between China and India. Again, at most, such discussions were more about fact-finding than laying the groundwork for joint action. There have been discussions about Myanmar and Afghanistan but not, for example, on the India-Nepal-China connection. While the two countries agree that the drugs trade should be eradicated, they differ on the strategy. China prefers a carrot-and-stick approach, offering alternatives to poppy production for farmers in northern Myanmar while sticking to a relentless crackdown on the traders. India opts for fencing its border and destroying the poppy fields. Similar to their relationship on terrorism, there are no specific programs or exchanges of information. Even on smuggling, the two countries have made little progress beyond putting their intentions on paper. In 2005, for instance, India signaled its frustration over Chinese smugglers' boosting trade in products from endangered species like ivory and Shahtoosh wool, but this fell on deaf ears.

In the long term, a secure environment depends on stable governments rather than stepping in where neighboring states fail. Several conditions are necessary for enhancing political stability. First, it demands a comprehensive rapprochement between the central political elites and political mutineers. Second, the central governments need to raise their legitimacy among the many societal entities. This implies transparent public finance and transparent governance. Notably, these prerequisites are more and more recognized by Chinese and Indian opinion leaders, and the two countries have the leverage to make a difference. But are they prepared to make use of it?

Apart from India's exclusive posture toward Nepal and Bhutan, China and India have traditionally insisted on not interfering in each other's domestic affairs. Historically this principle accorded with the struggle against "imperialist practices." It also served as a diplomatic modus operandi for improving trust and confidence in neighboring states. Beginning in the late 1990s, the primacy of sovereignty became a tool for economic diplomacy. Refraining from touching on delicate political issues facilitated business with many countries, especially when desiring concessions for natural resources or government contracts. Currently, the principle of noninterference is challenged by the regional context, where internal policies can have serious external consequences. China and India thus face a dilemma. Sticking to their traditional standards could aggravate the tensions between their political partners and rival factions. Distancing from them might encourage those same elites to turn to other, foreign friends. The degree to which China and India succeed in arriving at a common position on this challenge is a key determinant in assessing their cooperation in regional security affairs.

With regard to Nepal, India's immediate security concern has always been garnering the support of the Nepalese government in quelling Maoist factions. China's aim has been controlling the flow of Tibetan refugees. Initially, this resulted in diplomatic efforts to stay on good terms with Nepal's king. After 1972, King Birendra succeeded in utilizing his central role in the armed forces and domestic politics to position himself as the diplomatic gatekeeper in Nepal's diplomatic relations with its neighbors. Beijing and India alike sought to curry favor with the royal palace. Birendra's assassination in 2001 required India and China to revise their policies. From the beginning, India was reluctant to cultivate ties with Birendra's successor, his younger brother Gyanendra.[36] In 2002, when Gyanendra sought consultations with New Delhi, the government put off his visit three times, fearing that the king's dismissal of the parliament and prime minister could lead to a total political meltdown.

China saw the tensions between Kathmandu and New Delhi as a chance to gain influence. In July 2002, Gyanendra was invited with all *égards* by Chinese president Jiang Zemin. The meeting resulted in a new trade agreement and the Chinese promise to side with the king's efforts to restore order. As a gesture, China also sent military officers to participate in trainings organized by the Nepalese army. Frustrated over the chilly ties with New Delhi,

Gyanendra tried to force India into a more conciliatory position by hedging toward China and Pakistan. In April 2003, for the first time Nepal forced Tibetan refugees back into Chinese territory rather than allowing them to proceed to India, as it had over the years.[37] In June 2004, following a week-long visit to Beijing, General Pyar Jung Thapa revealed on state radio and television that China would step up its security cooperation with Nepal. The same month, Pakistani prime minister Shaukat Aziz called on Kathmandu and discussed the delivery of defense equipment, military aid, and security cooperation. In February 2005, after seizing absolute power, Gyanendra tried to ward off increased Indian pressure by moving even closer to China. He engineered the closure of the Dalai Lama's representative office in Kathmandu. The government stopped issuing exit permits to new refugees and halted the registration of marriages and births of Tibetans. Nepal also closed down the Tibetan Welfare Office.[38] In March 2005, the king decided to open the Lhasa-Kathmandu Road, which had never been opened after its construction. That same month, after refusing to meet with the Indian ambassador and accepting aid from Pakistan, Gyanendra announced a meeting with Chinese foreign minister Li Zhaoxing, in Kathmandu.[39]

When Chinese prime minister Wen Jiabao visited New Delhi in April 2005, he reportedly assured his Indian interlocutors that China would not take advantage of the flux in Nepal and that it would be prepared to work with India to maintain stability in the country. Nevertheless, the two countries kept to their opposite courses. The Indian government believed that the risk of prolonged anarchy and even a possible Maoist takeover would increase if the king sought to single-handedly take on the Maoists without broad political support. Therefore, its policy was to avoid legitimating the new monarch by keeping its contacts with the regime low profile and trying to strengthen its relations with other political entities, such as the democratic parties. India also decided to temporarily halt arms supplies.

China did not share India's views and took for granted that the king's grip on the army was strong enough to suppress Tibetan refugees. Unlike India's soft quarantining, Beijing openly backed Gyanendra and even counteracted India's policies by stepping up military cooperation. In June 2005, it supplied Nepal with five armored personnel carriers. In August, Nepalese foreign minister Ramesh Nath Pandey returned from Beijing with a pledge of U.S.$12 million in budgetary support. In October, China agreed to provide U.S.$1 million in military aid to Nepal, following a visit by the chief of the Royal Nepalese Army. In November, eighteen military trucks loaded with arms crossed the Nepalese border.[40] In December, a high-level delegation from the PLA, led by the deputy commander of the Chengdu Military Re-

gion, General Gui Quanzhi, paid a visit to Nepal. Indian defense minister
Pranab Mukherjee said that the arms supply and military training provided
by China were a "concern."[41]

Only when Gyanendra's position started to weaken due to growing violence, persistent political opposition, American pressure, and the breaking up
of the army as a solid royalist fortress did the Chinese embassy in Kathmandu
gradually start reporting to Beijing that the king may not be able to maintain
his power and that it should not put all its eggs in one basket. A marked
shift came during the visit of State Councilor Tang Jiaxuan in March 2006.
Tang separately called on the leaders of various parties such as Girija Prasad
Koirala, president of the Nepali Congress, Sher Bahadur Deuba, another top
leader of the Nepali Congress, and Communist Party of Nepal leaders Amrit
Kumar Bohara and Bharat Mohan Adhikari. In a speech he clarified that
China hoped "that all constitutional forces in Nepal would come closer in the
best interest of the country and the people."[42] After the parliament scrapped
the major powers of the king in June 2007, China swiftly changed its position and established contacts with all constituents of the antiroyalist Seven
Party Alliance. In November 2006, the vice-minister of the International Department of the Communist Party of China, Liu Hongcai, led a delegation to
meet with all members of the alliance, expressing its "high appreciation of
putting the interests of their country and people first." The Chinese ambassador, Zheng Xianglin, explained that his country would play an active role
in Nepal's peace process. He added that China would not interfere in Nepal's
internal affairs by making comments on the Maoists.[43]

China's diplomatic maneuvering has been to deal with the government of
Nepal irrespective of its format or political base.[44] "Unlike the Indian establishment which talks different to different political parties, China suggested
the Nepali leaders to improve the livelihood of the Nepali people through
maintaining economic development and restoring a sort of permanent peace
in the country."[45] Interviews with Chinese experts and officials have revealed
that China's indifference about who rules stemmed from the belief that whoever was in power would be obliged to foster contacts with China to check
India's dominance.

While China does not openly contest India's political prominence, China's
diplomatic pragmatism has allowed for a gradually changing economic status
quo. Between 2003 and 2007, Nepal's imports from China grew faster than
those from India. China has agreed to provide duty-free access to goods manufactured in Nepal. Nepal has produced a list of 1,550 items for export to the
Chinese market at 0 percent custom tariffs. China has also invested in new
railway connections. It is expected that, by 2010, 2.8 million tons will be car-

ried to and from Tibet via a new railway. An extension of this artery to Nepal, combined with the improvement of the highway, could easily boost annual cross-border freight capacity from thirteen thousand tons to three hundred thousand tons. The Chinese ambassador in Katmandu has indicated that China is also ready to deliver petroleum products to Nepal, thereby undermining India's monopoly as oil supplier. China's expanding connections with local business communities has also strengthened its position within Nepal's civil society. On several occasions business leaders have pleaded for closer contacts with the People's Republic and mentioned China as a tool for pushing for a more favorable trade regime with India. China's posture has also resulted in more soft power. China's ambivalent attitude in contrast to India's meddling in Nepalese politics has strengthened Nepalese perceptions of India as an aggressive, hegemonic power. This has been the case particularly with the Maoist groups; although Beijing has maintained a distance and refrained from developing contacts, it has also never lashed out at them as the Indian government has done continuously.

Historically, Nepal has been considered a buffer state separating China from South Asia. Nepal is now becoming a porous corridor as natural barriers are overcome. More than ever, China and India have a joint interest in maintaining order and stability; yet, the domestic turmoil has been addressed in different ways. New Delhi, still confident of its influential position as a commercial gateway, has sought to defend its security interests by actively interfering in Nepal's political transition. Beijing has been well aware of the fact that regardless of who might rule the country, its leader will try to reduce Nepal's dependence on India. This has given China enough certainty that its security concerns, such as Tibetan refugees, will be taken care of. Consequently, it has taken a more ambivalent attitude vis-à-vis Nepal's political struggles while, at the same time, continuing to alter the economic balance of power. Impeded by distrust, China and India still deal with security challenges unilaterally: China with Tibetan exiles, India with the Maoists and other insurgents in the south of Nepal. The pressure for gaining influence means that the underlying economic and political dynamics of Nepal's continuing disintegration are scarcely addressed, and even less so the challenges that lie ahead.

In connection with Pakistan, the main challenge is responding to the alarming Talibanization of the country.[46] Chinese and Indian officials or experts tend to have comparable interpretations of the domestic instability in Pakistan. They share the observation that political feudalism leads to predatory economic patronage systems and the marginalization of violent regions like Baluchistan. There is also awareness of the omnipotence of the military in politics and key economic branches, with the result that any kind of government will lack a grip on the armed forces and their links with Islamist extremists.[47] None wants to see Pakistan develop into an Islamic state, using religion as the social and political glue to keep the country together. Interviews with Chinese officials have also revealed a rising concern over Pakistan's using Kashmir as a hub for sending out Islamist terrorists all over southern Asia.[48] Two leading experts have even noted that, in the future, radical Tibetan secessionists in India, Nepal, and Pakistan could take the mujahideen as a model for their struggle.[49]

Whereas it does not support India's territorial claims, Beijing moved from overt support of an independent Kashmir to consequent appeals to both sides to face the need for peace and stability above all. In its hierarchy of interests, Beijing still does not want to see India strengthening its grip on Ladakh, but over the past years, the need for stability moved higher up on the agenda. Finally, neither Beijing nor India takes for granted that the end of the military-based regime of President Musharraf and the emergence of a civilian political leadership would improve Pakistan's coherence or lead to a pacification of its several runaway districts. After all, not only the central leadership as such is flawed, it is believed, but also the political, administrative, and economic structures throughout Pakistani society.

Despite the fact that a looming collapse of Pakistan resulted in a convergence of direct security interests, China and India have pursued contradictory policies. While India perceives the Pakistani military establishment as a part of the problem, the Chinese government approaches it as a part of the solution. A Chinese scholar has stressed, "Although we talk to several parties in Pakistan, we cannot deny that the armed forces are likely to remain a pivotal partner for China to defend its security interests in the coming years."[50] A Chinese official has added that, "for the coming period it is impossible that a civilian political government will be able to steer the army's policies in the region. Any government will rely on the army to restore domestic stability."[51] Maintaining Pakistani generals' attention to China's security challenges is seen as a priority, rather than working with the Indian armed forces, which are not even able to safeguard their own borders. China also finds that limiting its relations with the army would benefit the American influence and steer it away from Chinese security objectives.

These pragmatic considerations explain China's continued support of the Pakistani military. It has maintained its traditional supply of all kinds of arms systems. Between 2001 and 2007, it sold hardware for a total of U.S.$5.1 billion.[52] China has on many occasions delivered military aid. Since 2001, the emphasis has gradually moved to the fight against terrorism. In 2004 and

2006, joint antiterrorist exercises were organized. It is reported that the Chinese embassy in Islamabad maintains close links with the Inter-Services Intelligence and other military players in discussing cross-border threats and risks to Chinese citizens in Pakistan.[53] The embassy partly rationalizes China's refusal to facilitate talks between Pakistan and India on the question of Kashmir, despite repeated invitations from New Delhi: Beijing wants to avoid pushing its Pakistani friends to stop its support of terrorism while sitting at the table with Indian interlocutors; it will never humiliate its long-standing partner in front of its archrival.[54] It also clarifies why the Chinese government insists on military protection of its investment projects in Pakistan's volatile districts rather than mitigating local tensions by insisting on more transparency and a fair redistribution of taxes and other incomes.

This does not mean that the People's Republic has bet on one horse. In the run-up to the national elections in 2008, the Chinese embassy in Islamabad established informal contacts with the two main opposition parties, the Pakistan Peoples Party (PPP) and the Pakistan Muslim League.[55] After the parliamentary elections in February 2008, which led to the defeat of President Musharraf, China was one of the first to offer support to the new government. In March 2008 it announced a U.S.$500 million low-interest loan to help ease Pakistan's growing financial problems.[56] Immediately after the appointment of the PPP's Yousuf Raza Gilani as Pakistan's prime minister and Shah Mehmood Quresh as the minister of foreign affairs, they were publically congratulated by their Chinese counterparts.[57] Yet, at the same time, China reaffirmed its privileged relationship with the military. In April 2008, Chinese defense minister Liang Guanglie invited President Musharraf to discuss the expansion of cooperation between the militaries of his country and Pakistan.[58]

China's security interests in Pakistan are served in the same way as those in Nepal: it combines a close military relationship with political ambivalence. Knowledge of the complex nature of the domestic instability in Pakistan has grown, as has China's economic and diplomatic influences. Nonetheless, China is unwilling to side with India on terrorism or to address the root causes of violence and the long-term risk of a collapsing state. In part this is because Beijing is not confident that pressure will help in any case, and partly because it does not want to loose Pakistan as a pawn on the South Asian chessboard.

Violence in Myanmar has become a recurrent topic on the bilateral agenda. In 2003, Indian prime minister Vajpayee reportedly brought the stalled transition in Myanmar to the fore during his visit to China. In 2004, Beijing endorsed India's initiative to work more closely with the SPDC in order to impede cross-border rebel movements. During the crackdown on protests in several Myanmar cities in September 2007, the Chinese and Indian ministers of foreign affairs, Yang Jiechi and Pranab Mukherjee, respectively, clarified their positions in the UN General Assembly. In October that year, the issue was tabled at the trilateral meeting with Russia in Harbin. According to an official of the Indian Ministry of External Affairs, the political transition was also discussed in meetings with diplomats from the Chinese embassy in New Delhi. Yet, the official remarked that these talks did not go not beyond "fact finding and conveying official standpoints. We recognize the importance of the Convention [the National Convention, in which the junta and opposition have to work toward a new constitution], but did not consider ways to stimulate this process."

In terms of public declarations, Chinese and Indian positions have gone through a double convergence. First, Beijing and New Delhi have come to share the idea that the military junta has to commit itself to the seven-step path providing a new constitution and a multiparty democratic general election in 2010.[59] Both states have expressed their support for reconciliation with the main opposition groups, including Aung San Suu Kyi's National League for Democracy. After 2002, Beijing and New Delhi simultaneously became more vociferous. In September 2003, for example, President Hu Jintao made clear that "China hopes Myanmar will remain stable, its ethnic groups will live in harmony, its economy will keep growing and the Myanmar people will live in happiness." The Indian Ministry of Foreign Affairs pleaded for "transition to democracy," which "offers the best possibilities for addressing problems both of political stability and economic development."[60]

Second, they have arrived at the same position with regard to the way the military regime has to be approached.[61] "Quiet diplomacy" is the channel through which the two countries convey their expectations. They also requested the United Nations take the lead in pushing the generals, within a narrow mandate and without intimidating sanctions. The corresponding diplomatic discourse left nothing to the imagination. Chinese politicians have been determined to respect Pauk Paw, the term that expresses the traditional Sino-Burmese friendship: "China opposes outside interference in Myanmar's internal affairs and all must respect Myanmar's sovereignty," President Hu Jintao affirmed at a meeting with Senior General Than Shwe, in April 2005, "China will never change her stand concerning Myanmar . . . China accepts that Myanmar has the right to choose and practise the most suitable system."[62] At a meeting of the Greater Mekong Subregion in July 2005, Prime Minister Wen Jiabao stressed: "China will continue to promote cooperation with Myanmar, no matter how the international situation fluctuates."[63]

When India's External Affairs minister Natwar Singh visited Myanmar, he underlined his country attached "very high priority to its relations with Myanmar as a valuable neighbour and strategic partner" and that national reconciliation could continue with "the objectives set by Myanmar for itself." Likewise, during a recent visit to Myanmar, his successor, Pranab Mukherjee, made clear the country's "hands off" policy on the struggle for restoration of democracy going on in Myanmar. He asserted that India had to deal with governments "as they exist." "We are not interested in exporting our own ideology," the minister stressed, "we are a democracy and we would like democracy to flourish everywhere. But this is for every country to decide for itself." An Indian analyst explained that this convergence in discourse was the result of a rhetorical tit-for-tat approach by the South Block: "While several members of Parliament have kept pushing for a strong line on human rights in Burma, the government carefully adapted its posture to China's attitude." In 2006, China, India, and Russia blocked the proposal to establish a support team of the Office of the High Commissioner for Human Rights that would accompany the follow-up mission of special envoy Paulo Sérgio Pinheiro.

A wide gap remains between discourse and deeds. While China and India were adopting a critical tone and implicitly asking the generals to step aside, behind this rhetorical facade they continued strengthening the junta's position, in disregard of the main political setbacks. Both sides increased their military assistance. China reportedly sold up to fifteen hundred military trucks, jeeps, patrol boats, aircraft, artillery, small arms, and communication systems devices.[64] All this hardware added together amounts to an annual average of more than U.S.\$100 million. India started supplying arms to Myanmar in 2003 and has offered helicopters, tanks, artillery, naval systems, and counterinsurgency training to Myanmar's military.[65] China has maintained close contacts with the military establishment, and India has been catching up. In the late 1990s, India and Myanmar launched Operation Golden Bird. Troops from the two countries chased Indian insurgents on the Mizoram border. In 2005, the Indian army launched operations against such rebel groups as the Karen National Union, Chin National Army, Chin National Front, Karen Freedom Fighters, and the Arakan Liberation Party. This reportedly led to the destruction of twelve camps and the elimination of eighty-two rebels.[66] China and India also continued beefing up the military government's position as economic doorkeeper, despite the fact that corruption and a lack of redistribution of income is one of the main sources of secessionist struggles and political opposition.[67] Chinese and Indian investments in the energy and mining sectors have become one of the main sources of income for the junta. Even though several of the purchased blocks are located in areas with ethnic minorities, these groups do not enjoy any of the benefits. Local communities are often forced out to make room for plants, roads, and dams.

Myanmar has become a focal point in China and India's neighborhood policies. Together with Nepal and Pakistan, the country offers a good example of the diplomatic schizophrenia with which Beijing and New Delhi approach security challenges: beneath the surface of rhetorical convergence, distrust and the fear of losing out inhibit substantial security cooperation.

Thus, despite the growing security interdependence, regional cooperation has remained superficial and unreliable. The declarations of peace remain in sharp contrast to the underlying competition. The security dilemma remains in place, as strategies are driven mainly by self-help and the fear of losing influence to the other. Rather than being mitigated by economic interests and tending toward a substantial resecuritization, commerce seems to add another dimension to the Sino-Indian contest. Sino-Indian relations are situated somewhere between conflict formation and a very loose security regime. While there is some collaboration, it has scarcely penetrated to the core of the security challenges, namely the impunity with which flawed regimes continue undermining stability in their countries. Behind a surface of cooperation, China is gradually altering the economic balance of power in its favor. If it succeeds in further strengthening its economic prowess in countries like Pakistan and undermining India's commercial stronghold in Nepal, it may soon alter the overall balance of power in South Asia.

THIS CHAPTER HAS DEMONSTRATED the increasing importance of China and India's common periphery. For both states, a stable environment has become a precondition for domestic development and maintaining economic growth. While strengthening their economic influence in the neighborhood, China and India have run up against a threefold security challenge: cross-border hostilities, attacks on economic projects abroad, and the risk of extremism affecting frontier regions. Consequently, the traditional fault line between the East and South Asian security complex has blurred. Instead of as buffers, the band of states from Pakistan to Myanmar should be considered as a subregional security complex that increasingly coalesces the two regional complexes.

The second conclusion is that the increasing regional security interdependence has not in fact led to sound security cooperation. Joint efforts have grown in number, but they have been more about process than progress. A primary flaw is that most dialogues remain limited to a routine exchange of official positions instead of an exploration of options for practical cooperation. "Security dialogues have become a goal as such," an Indian official has argued, "instead of tackling real challenges, their main added value is that political leaders can give the impression that they are pursuing a successful foreign policy."[68] Second, if efforts do go beyond talk, the outcomes are highly limited. The attempt to curb the regional drug trade, for instance, has not yielded tangible results.[69] The struggle against terrorism is having no effect because of a total lack of intelligence sharing and diverging approaches vis-à-vis Pakistan as a main sponsor of Islamist extremism. Third, direct bilateral policies toward smaller neighbors are preferred over the more complicated trilateral action. Finally, cooperation is restricted to the turmoil that occurs only at the surface of a much more complicated emergency in which weak states like Pakistan, Myanmar, and Nepal are entangled.

This modest outcome can be attributed to several factors. One might assume that the Chinese and Indian governments lack an understanding of the intricate nature of the insecurity because the economization and corresponding resecuritization of their regional policies are a relatively recent phenomenon. However, statements by political leaders reveal a full understanding that a secure neighborhood requires more than chasing smugglers and rebels. Chinese and Indian officials are well informed about the root causes of instability in states like Pakistan and Myanmar. Moreover, the confrontation with nontraditional security challenges is not especially new. As early as the 1990s, smuggling, the drug trade, and cross-border armed resistance had become a priority on their foreign agendas. Hence, a lack of alertness can be excluded as a possible explanation. Beijing and New Delhi do understand that a secure environment depends to a large extent on successful and legitimate governance.

Another reason for the superficial security approach could be the fact that China and India's strategies to maintain order at home are more about repressing rebellion than tackling the causes of public grievances. Although Beijing's harmonious society policy, India's costly rural-development schemes, and the struggles against red tape display a consensus that stability depends to a large extent on socioeconomic equality and good governance, both states still find that military repression of unrest is crucial for guaranteeing their own domestic development. The two countries thus find themselves in another dilemma. On the one hand, there is the need to promote comprehensive security in their neighborhood, but, on the other hand, the traditional Weberian model of national security is considered still valid for themselves. To the extent that diplomacy is a mirror of domestic politics, championing good governance and inclusive economic development abroad remains unattractive—unattractive, but not necessarily excluded. As shown earlier, China and India reluctantly do criticize governments for a lack of accountability. Beijing has resorted to quite blunt statements vis-à-vis Myanmar; India has used a lot of rhetorical ammunition against Nepal's monarchy. Nonetheless, deeds often have not mirrored the pointed statements. Military support, low-interest credit, economic aid, diplomatic backing—all these tools have been applied to stay on good terms with the local political elites.

Despite facing similar regional security challenges, China and India refrain from cooperation and tend to stick to their business-as-usual approach toward problem states. This cannot be explained by arguments that speak of a lack of understanding and the self-interested preference for a strong state. What is revealed is that the continual backing of predatory regimes and unstable governments stems mainly from the fact that the immediate objective to maintain influence prevails over the necessity of promoting stability for the long haul. The ambition to gain access to local markets and natural resources is a main driving force. Noteworthy is that economic aspirations are not only about absolute gains but also about relative gains. As China and India are the main competitors in the third countries mentioned in this discussion, it is the fear of losing commercial opportunities to the other that explains the problematic regional security cooperation between them. The risk of being cheated is too high. The cases of Pakistan, Myanmar, and Nepal also show that the economization of regional policies has not led to a desecuritization of their interaction in traditional frontline states. Apart from economic interests, both giants continue to watch each other and try to tilt the balance of diplomatic and political influence in their favor.

The emergence of trading states leads to a mitigation of rivalry, or so liberal theory of international relations supposes. The example of Sino-Indian interaction in southern Asia shows that this is not necessarily the case. Despite economic ambitions' resulting in a stronger security interdependence, the conflict setting remains. What is more, the same economic ambitions have added new impetus to the regional struggle for influence and mean that China and India's crooked friends have nothing to fear.

CONCLUSION

BLACK-SUITED BUSINESSMEN cast restless shadows on the glimmering marble of a hotel on the outskirts of New Delhi. At this forum organized by the Associated Chambers of Commerce and Industry of India and sponsored by the city of Shenzhen a few hundred Chinese and Indian traders rummage for rewarding contacts and contracts. This commercial eagerness has become a main catalyst for new forms of cooperation between China and India. Yet, the business networking is in sharp contrast with another kind of industriousness. Far away from New Delhi, in the Brahmaputra valley, everything has been made ready for a complete upgrade of the air force base at Tezpur. Its obsolete MiG-21 jets have been phased out to be replaced by Su-30 fighters in order to step up military deterrence against the same country beckoning to the Indian business leaders in the Méridien Hotel. The Sino-Indian relationship is characterized by a misleading ambivalence that amalgamates liberalist optimism about the opportunities that globalization brings with realist skepticism about the competition that turns out to be inescapable to reap these benefits. Despite increasing cooperation, distrust and rivalry are still prevalent in a way that they will inhibit the development of a solid partnership.

This book began with an examination of whether two emerging trading nations breed a complex interdependence that results in enough positive expectations to neutralize tensions and conflict. Looking back on recent decades, commerce has indeed become one of the main policy objectives of Beijing and New Delhi. Indicators like export figures, inward foreign direct investments, and tariff rates confirm the increasing openness toward the global economy. After a long period of inward-looking economic policies, the late

1970s ushered in a new trend toward liberalization. From then on, China offered without check its vast reservoir of labor to the international market by attracting investments and by developing a strong export-oriented industry. In India the policy reorientation was less drastic. In the 1970s and 1980s, New Delhi pushed through a probusiness strategy and a selective liberalization aimed at attracting technological know-how. Only under the cabinet of Narasimha Rao was the dismantling of trade barriers set in motion. The five-year plans that have followed since the late 1990s have demonstrated India's willingness to emulate China's strong liberalization.

In China as well as in India, measures for a more overt economic policy always followed periods of economic upheaval and concurrent political legitimacy crises. In fact, the moves toward outward-oriented liberalization stemmed from attempts by the central political elites to reinvent themselves. They resorted to international capital as an alternative to their failing policies of plan-led growth. This also explains the coincidence of economic reform and political conservatism. The result of this alteration was a new formula for nationalism. Beijing and New Delhi discarded the initial idea of national unity based on ideological and cultural particularism and replaced it with the promise of common prosperity and economic greatness as the new national "superglue." Networks of patronage via state-owned companies and large amounts of subsidies lost importance and made way for private mobility in a context of more economic opportunities in the secondary and tertiary sectors. Bonds to political parties, such as the Communist Party in China and the National Congress Party in India, remain an important stepping-stone for social promotion, but these political bastions have become more and more parallel with the strong entities of private interest. The central political elites have tried to answer this challenge by making themselves indispensable as legal gatekeepers, guardians of domestic stability, and by providing strategic services like public infrastructure, energy supply, and so forth. Hence, for India and China, the prospect of becoming an affluent and modern trading state formed the driving force of a new episode of nation building and constructive nationalism.

The second assumption was that the two nascent trading nations would attach less importance to the politico-military equation and prefer to foster peace as a precondition for development. Chapter 2 described how bilateral relations evolved from a loose ideological alliance, in a period of realpolitik and deterrence, to an interaction based mainly on shared economic interests. The Five Principles of Peaceful Coexistence clearly reflected the two young states' anxieties over their sovereignty being violated by external powers. Territorial defense stood out as one of the main goals of their foreign policies.

Although this aim was directed primarily toward the two Cold War superpowers, it quickly appeared that their own disputed border would end up as its main subject. The Indo-Chinese War of 1962 revealed the political sensitivity toward external provocations, partly as a consequence of the central elites' difficult quest for a consolidation of its domestic influence. The subsequent period of deterrence had a double function. On the one hand, it allowed Beijing and New Delhi to stabilize the situation, to avoid open war, and to focus on internal power struggles or economic challenges. On the other, fear of external threats was exploited as a lightning rod for public frustration.

In the 1980s, the first steps were taken to demilitarize the border. Confidence-building measures were implemented and political exchanges restarted. Yet, improving relations between Deng Xiaoping and Rajiv Gandhi reflected a reorientation of political attention toward domestic economic reform rather than actual reconciliation. The aim to boost trade and investment made stability along the border more compelling, breeding a sense of *indirect* interdependence that relegated competing territorial claims to a lower rank on the political agenda. In the 1990s, increasing bilateral trade and the expectation for more profits from deepened commercial relations started to strengthen *direct* economic interests.[1] Narasimha Rao and Jiang Zemin lifted political and economic cooperation to a higher level, and, simultaneously, several influential interest groups joined the call for intense cooperation.

The diversifying bonds, evolving from state-centric ties to a proliferation of stakeholders, led to a sense of complex interdependence. Corporate and private contacts began to play an important role in the diplomatic rapprochement.[2] Politicians and business leaders soon floated the idea of Chindia, a complex of two nations in which cooperation thrives on a clear division of labor: India's services and China's industry. The central wisdom in the official discourse became that China and India needed to strengthen their positions in international affairs mainly by tapping the global market opportunities and developing stable and prospering societies.[3] Instead of pursuing relative gains aimed at counterbalancing other powers, domestic resilience became the cornerstone of what was called comprehensive national growth. Moreover, statements by politicians like Manmohan Singh and Wen Jiabao about "making boundaries redundant," increasing connections across the Himalayas, and the demilitarization of the Line of Actual Control also seemed to indicate that the primacy of territorial sovereignty had lost importance and that the desire for the status of trading states indeed leads to cooperation and peace.

Yet, there are four main reasons why these first steps toward a comprehensive partnership between India and China will not succeed. To begin, the

Ricardian miracle will soon turn out to be a mirage. As chapter 3 stressed, a division of labor is not static, and India and China's actual complementarity will disappear once they achieve their economic ambitions. India will become a big challenge to China's position as factory or assembling hall of the world when it achieves the industrialization mapped out in the Tenth and Eleventh Five-Year Plans. China, for its part, will threaten India's position as an emerging IT and services champion. Even when the international economy grows, or, as the traditional argument of liberalist economists formulates it, the cake becomes larger, decreasing labor intensity and overproduction will spur competition for profits and jobs. Beijing and New Delhi's current trade policy, for instance, in regard to trade pacts and logistical connectedness in Asia, has not yet led to intense competition, but they must be considered as bridgeheads for conflicting trade policies. Trade expectations are not reliable as a driver of comprehensive Sino-Indian cooperation. "There is a risk that in the foreseeable future the frozen dispute about the border might be complemented by a hot trade conflict," a senior Chinese diplomat has concluded.[4]

Second, the enthusiasm on the part of political leaders and traders for cooperation is not matched in their respective societies. Suspicion is still a prominent element of public perceptions. The growing bilateral contacts and the euphoric statements by various ministers have not resulted in more positive views. On the contrary, between 2004 and 2007, Indians became significantly less optimistic vis-à-vis China as a trustworthy partner. The Indian parliament has taken a constructive position and allowed recent governments to explore new synergies, but suspicion among parliamentarians has restrained the scope for enhanced talks on the border dispute and further trade liberalization. Experts from both countries have also remained reluctant. They have acknowledged that Sino-Indian relations are improved and that stable relations are necessary for sustaining economic growth, but military intentions, economic competition, and conflicting diplomatic ambitions have also resulted in a plea for prudence and restraint. Moreover, whereas Chinese experts thus far have not paid much attention to India as a potential strategic rival, India's military growth and its regional diplomatic activities are starting to raise concern. Fostering trading states is one thing; creating trading nations is a step further. The lack of public support will make convergence a delicate balancing exercise for the Chinese and Indian governments. Going too far in economic opening up will rouse protectionists and provoke complaints of dumping and unfair competition. While the need for a border demarcation is recognized, the slightest concession could provoke nationalist sentiments. "Standing weak" and "undermining national security" are the kind of criticism that political leaders can expect if they ignore the balance of power in Asia. The political determination may be strong, but the limited support renders their policies vulnerable to setbacks.

Third, trade and mutual economic gains have not neutralized the military security dilemma. Despite twenty years of negotiations at all levels, China and India have not succeeded in reaching a breakthrough on their border dispute. Moreover, while several confidence-building measures have been implemented along the boundary, the trenches are still manned. Frequent incursions into disputed areas and military incidents have sustained armed deterrence. The improvement of military capability that New Delhi and Beijing have undertaken aims at least partly to ward off military aggression. China is becoming increasingly frustrated over India's maritime expansion in the Indian Ocean and its possible impact on its commercial lifelines to Africa and the Middle East. In fact, India appears to be aiming at multilevel deterrence. Apart from a military presence at the border, it also sees the People's Republic as a key target for its naval buildup and a new generation of nuclear missiles. Military power plays have thus not disappeared. That is not to say that a new war is imminent; deterrence will thwart confrontation, but each country is likely to continue to try to alter the balance of power in its favor. Though constrained, this military competition will further complicate the border dispute and lead to more suspicion in regional affairs.

Finally, it cannot be taken for granted that the growing interest in economic security will reduce rivalry between China and India in their neighborhood. There is a strong case for regional security cooperation as China and India confront similar challenges: cross-border hostilities, assaults on economic projects abroad, and the risk of extremism affecting frontier regions. For both countries, a stable environment has become more important for domestic development and protecting commercial ventures abroad. Again, distrust is inhibiting translation of this security interdependence into sound synergies. The fear of losing influence or missing economic opportunities still means that regional security cooperation is limited to a few defective agreements to deal with smugglers and terrorists, and that the causes of instability in neighboring states are hardly addressed. Persistent economic competition and diplomatic rivalry cause Beijing and New Delhi to deal with challenges in a unilateral way, leading to cozying up to friendly but flawed political regimes. In sum, the enduring rivalry for regional power means that instability is temporarily suppressed rather than that China and India contribute to a long-term solution.

Hence, economic drivers are too weak to reverse threat perceptions, and the sense of security interdependence is not strong enough to temper the race for regional influence. *In the short term, we will therefore observe a continuation of the great power contest.* At the same time, whereas trade has been in the background during recent decades, economic ambitions will now assume the fore as key determinants of the intensity and character of conflict.

The ambition to tap the international market will lead to fiercer economic rivalry and more aggressive regional diplomacy. While China has not been impressed by India's slow industrial growth, this contempt may soon give way to trepidation. If New Delhi makes headway with its plans in the next few years, these policies might come too early for China to absorb the harsher competition. For the long haul, increasing domestic consumption, innovation, and slower demographic growth could permit China to let a part of its production capacity move to India or to compensate for losses in third export markets with domestic demand. Rapid industrial development in its southern neighbor, however, would come too early for digesting the consequences without experiencing serious social and political consequences. In that event, the rush for natural resources and consumer markets would become relentless and lead New Delhi and Beijing to woo whichever state with whatever means at their disposal. This would in turn allow the many crooked governments in the neighborhood to pursue their divide-and-rule politics with even more vigor, hold off the needed internal reforms, further imperil regional stability, and increase the chance of serious interference and rivalry in the case of a power vacuum developing in such states.

On the other hand, the case for commerce as a source of national prosperity and unity could weaken if wealth does not trickle down fast enough. What if New Delhi is not capable of implementing its reforms to absorb the enormous glut of new members of the labor market? What if employment does not rise rapidly enough to relieve the demographic pressure in the countryside and in the large cities? What if the states in the Hindu belt or in the northeast continue to lag behind? The success of regionalist, leftist, and ethnocentric parties at the expense of the traditional political center on the one hand and disappointing economic performances on the other tend to be mutually reinforcing. Political fragmentation leads to poor implementation of new economic policies and vice versa. For the political center, which faces elections at the state or national levels nearly every year, economic restructuring forms a huge electoral burden in the short term. If it also becomes disillusioned with the benefits of constructive nationalism in the longer term, it is not unthinkable that the BJP and the Congress Party could slip back into their old habits of negative nationalism. This might result in growing domestic conflict, but another option would be to find an external scapegoat. At that point negative public attitudes and skeptical reports from the experts could lead the government to reverse its pro-China stand and commence rhetorical confrontation and military power plays.

Hence, economic interdependence as the raison d'être of strategic cooperation can be nullified by too much appetite for trade as well as by public disappointment in its benefits. There are two additional complicating factors. A changed Chinese perception of India could also lead to deterioration. Although Indian citizens and experts in particular tend to see China as a main challenger, China does not count India among its main competitors. But such opinions are susceptible to change. The security community in Beijing has become alarmed by India's military buildup in the Indian Ocean. India's overtures to Myanmar, central Asia, and to Japan and Taiwan have raised eyebrows among many officials and advisers. The nuclear deal between India and the United States is widely perceived in Beijing as a potential stepping-stone to future rallying against China.

China will gradually come to take India more seriously as a challenger and also consequently modify its policies. Moreover, by adapting its self-perception partially to the hostile attitudes in India, China might also adjust its policies in the direction of these negative views and lay more emphasis on military deterrence and diplomatic counterbalancing.

The evolution of capabilities, too, will affect the partnership between both states. Bit by bit, China is eating into India's traditional sphere of influence. Given its limited financial means, New Delhi is no match for China's economic charm offensive and will have to keep an eye on its neighbor's ongoing alteration of the regional economic balance of power. As a consequence of the growing commercial ties, new transport infrastructure, investments, and aid packages, Beijing is pulling states like Nepal out of India's sphere of influence. By cultivating political goodwill and closer relations with local political leaders, governments will be able to reduce their dependence on India, and this in turn will permit China to go further in developing diplomatic synergies and even enhanced military collaboration. As India becomes conscious of this creeping revision of the regional power equilibrium, it could become even more willing to resort to old-fashioned power plays, in which it compensates for its limited economic influence with military diplomacy or pragmatic alliances with other powers, such as Japan and Russia. Such policies might lead to the emergence of an Asian "concert of power" that aims at a certain degree of diplomatic predictability while curbing one another's influence. Such a concert may foster new checks and balances that would enhance regional stability, but it would remain precarious, especially because of domestic uncertainty and disquieting nationalism: "Any plan conceived in moderation must fail when the circumstances are set in extremes."[5]

Commerce and conquest are not mutually exclusive. It is an illusion to believe that economic interdependence has replaced the traditional designs of military deterrence and competition for regional influence. The growing interest in commerce has in fact fueled power plays. In the end trading states remain conquering states.

NOTES

INTRODUCTION.
SINO-INDIAN RIVALRY IN AN ERA OF GLOBALIZATION

1. I.e., of a total labor force of 1.3 billion, up to 655 million persons are employed in agriculture.

2. I.e., GDP per capita PPP (UNDP, *Human Development Report* [Houndmills, Basingstoke, U.K.: Palgrave Macmillan, 2008], 232–33).

3. The figures are 35 percent for China, 80 percent for India (ibid., 239).

4. The total greenfield FDI in manufacturing projects grew by 3 percent between 2004 and 2006, compared to 189 percent between 2002 and 2004 (UNCTAD, *World Investment Report 2007* [New York: United Nations, 2007], 211).

5. Garver, *Protracted Contest*.

6. Garver, "Security Dilemma in Sino-Indian Relations."

7. Sachdeva, "Attitude towards China's Growing Influence in Central Asia."

8. Dixit, *India-Pakistan in War and Peace*; Paul, *India-Pakistan Conflict*.

9. Dabhade and Pant, "Coping with Challenges to Sovereignty."

10. Lall, "Indo-Myanmar Relations in the Era of Pipeline Diplomacy."

11. Ren, "Bushi di er renqi nei de Yinmei guanxi jiqi zouxiang"; Guo, "Xiao Bushi zhengfu dui Hua zhengce zouxiang jiqi dui Zhongmei anquan guanxi de yingxiang"; Song, "Shixi Yinri guanxi jiqi dui Zhongyin guanxi de yingxiang"; Zhao, "Zhong E Yin zhanlue guanxi de zhengce yiyi yu fazhan qianjing."

12. See, for example, Wang Long, "Yindu haiyang zhanlue ji dui Zhongyin guanxi de yingxiang" (India's Ocean Strategy and Its Implications for Sino-Indian Relations), *Nanya yanjiu jikan*, no. 2 (2005): 113–220; Li Bing, "Yindu de haishang zhanlue tongdao sixiang yu zhengce" (India's Strategic Maritime Passage: Thinking and Policy), *Nanya yanjiu*, no. 2 (2006): 16–21.

13. Jairam Ramesh, *Making Sense of Chindia: Reflections on China and India* (New Delhi: India Research Press, 2005), 51.

14. Cheng Ruisheng, "Trend of India's Diplomatic Strategy," *China International Studies*, no. 3 (April 2008): 20–40.

15. Ren Jia, "Zhongguo yu Yindu jingmao guanxi de fazhan ji qianjing" (China-India Trade and Economic Relations: Development and Prospects), *Nanya yanjiu*, no. 2 (2005): 15–19; Wang Jiqiong, "Zhongyin guanxi zai quanqiuhua jiasu shiqi de xinfazhan" (Sino-Indian Relations in an Era of Globalization), *Nanya yanjiu jikan*, no. 3 (2006): 51–57.

16. Abraham and Van Hove, "Rise of China"; Asher and Sen, *India–East Asia Integration*; Bhattacharyay and De, "Promotion of Trade and Investment between People's Republic of China and India"; T. N. Srinivasan, "China and India: Economic Performance, Competition and Cooperation," *Journal of Asian Economics* 15, no. 2 (2004): 613–36; Wu and Zhou, "Changing Bilateral Trade between China and India"; Yang, "Zhongyin fangzhipin fuzhuang maoyi hezuo qianjing."

17. Ray and De, *India and China in an Era of Globalisation*.

18. Kang, "Getting Asia Wrong," 83.

19. On foreign policy analysis, see Valerie Hudson, "Foreign Policy Analysis: Actor-Specific Theory and the Ground of International Relations," *Foreign Policy Analysis* 1, no. 1 (2005): 1–30; Michael Clarke, "The Foreign Policy System: A Framework for Analysis," in *Understanding Foreign Policy: The Foreign Policy Systems Approach*, ed. Michael Clarke and Brian White, 27–59 (Cheltenham, U.K.: Elgar, 1989); Douglas Foyle, "Foreign Policy Analysis and Globalization: Public Opinion, World Opinion, and the Individual," *International Studies Review* 5, no. 2 (2003): 155–202.

20. Richard Snyder et al., *Foreign Policy Decision Making: An Approach to the Study of International Politics* (New York: Palgrave Macmillan, 2003), 53.

21. "L'effet naturel du commerce est de porter à la paix. Deux nations qui négocient ensemble se rendent réciproquement dépendantes: si l'une a intérêt d'acheter, l'autre a intérêt de vendre; et toutes les unions sont fondées sur des besoins mutuels" (Montesquieu, *L'Esprit des lois* [1748], part 4, book 20, chap. 2).

22. Singh adds that greater trilateral economic interaction is vital ("Manmohan Calls for a Trilateral Framework on Economic Front," *Hindu*, January 26, 2007).

23. Li Xing, "Hu: China, India True Friends," *China Daily*, November 23, 2006.

24. Robert Gilpin, *The Challenge of Global Capitalism* (Princeton, N.J.: Princeton University Press, 2000); Michael Gerace, *Military Conflict, Power and Trade* (London: Cass, 2004).

25. Stephen Walt, "The Enduring Relevance of the Realist Tradition," in *Political Science: The State of the Discipline*, ed. Ira Katznelson and Helen Milner (New York: Norton, 2002); Robert Gilpin, *War and Change in World Politics* (Cambridge: Cambridge University Press, 1981); Randall Schweller, "Bandwagoning for Profit: Bringing the Revisionist State Back In," *International Security* 19, no. 1 (1994): 72–107.

26. Chen, "Nationalism, Internationalism and Chinese Foreign Policy," 42.

27. Rosecrance, *Rise of the Trading State*, 33–34.

28. Deutsch, *Political Community and the North Atlantic Area*, 8.

29. Keohane and Nye, *Power and Interdependence*, 43.

30. M. K. Narayanan, "India-China May Sign Border Pact," *Gulf News*, April 11, 2005; and P. K. Vasudeva, "Mountains of Peace," *Tribune*, July 22, 2005. Robert O. Keohane and Joseph S. Nye are the most prominent scholarly examples of this thesis; see Keohane and Nye, *Power and Interdependence*.

31. Philip Cerny, "The New Security Dilemma: Divisibility, Defection and Disorder in the Global Era," *Review of International Studies* 26, no. 4 (2000): 623–46.

32. Good governance here should be interpreted in the sense of the Chinese concept of "harmonious growth," i.e., maintaining domestic stability by keeping economic liberalization up to par with the advancement of political reform, the strengthening of the rule of law, and the promotion of social security and justice.

ONE. EMERGING TRADING STATES

1. Robert W. Cox, "Towards a Post-Hegemonic Conceptualization of World Order," in *Governance without Government: Order and Change in World Politics*, ed. James N. Rosenau and Ernst-Otto Czempiel (Cambridge: Cambridge University Press, 1992), 144.

2. Government of India, Planning Commission, *Industrial Policy Resolution* (New Delhi: Planning Commission, 1948), article 8.

3. Kothari, "Congress 'System' in India"; Rajni Kothari, "Continuity and Change in the Party System," in Sheth, *Citizens and Parties*.

4. Brecher, *Nehru*, 117–27.

5. Government of India, Planning Commission, *Industrial Policy Resolution*, article 8.

6. Mao Zedong, "Don't Hit Out in All Directions" (part of a speech delivered at the Third Plenary Session of the Seventh Meeting of the Central Committee of the Chinese Communist Party, Beijing), in *Selected Works of Mao Zedong*, ed. Central Committee of the Chinese Communist Party (Beijing: Foreign Languages Press, 1971), 5:214.

7. Government of India, Planning Commission, *Industrial Policy Resolution* (New Delhi: Planning Commission, 1951), article 8.

8. Griffin, *Alternative Strategies for Economic Development*; Brass, *Politics of India since Independence*, 249.

9. Government of India, Planning Commission, *Industrial Policy Resolution* (New Delhi: Planning Commission, 1956), article 5.

10. Mao Zedong, "Strive to Build a Great Socialist Country" (opening address at the First Session of the First National People's Congress, Beijing), in *Selected Works of Mao Zedong*, 5:464.

11. Government of India, Planning Commission, *Industrial Policy Resolution*, article 7.

12. Tomlinson, *Economy of Modern India*, 201.

13. Government of India, Planning Commission, *Industrial Policy Resolution*, article 8.

14. Karunaratine, "Failure of the Community Development Programme in India."

15. Erdman, *Swatantra Party and Indian Conservatism*.

16. Denoon, "Cycles in Indian Economic Liberalization."

17. Srivastava, *Lal Bahadur Shastri*, 210.

18. Hankla, *Party Linkages and Economic Policy*.

19. Jagdish N. Bhagwati and T. N. Srinivasan, *Foreign Trade Regimes and Economic Development: India* (Cambridge, Mass.: NBER, 1975).

20. Frankel, *India's Political Economy*, 124–30.

21. Hankla, *Party Linkages and Economic Policy*, 8.

22. Joshi and Little, *India*.

23. Hankla, *Party Linkages and Economic Policy*, 9.

24. Frankel, *India's Political Economy*, 136.

25. Kohli, *Democracy and Discontent*, 219.

26. Krishna, *Postcolonial Insecurities*, 24.

27. Jonathan Spence, *Mao Zedong* (New York: Viking, 1999), 200.

28. Weil, *Red Cat, White Cat*, 293.

29. With Stalin's death, for example, Mao lost his most important ally. As tensions mounted in the time of his successor, Nikita Khrushchev, the USSR decided, in 1969, to suspend all economic and technological support to China.

30. Dennis J. Blasko, "Always Faithful: The PLA from 1949 to 1989," in Graff and Higham, *Military History of China*, 254–56.

31. Mao launched the Cultural Revolution fearing that the revolutionary zeal of his communist movement was in decline. Supported by the newly formed Red Guards, he began a nationwide purge to rid the party of capitalists and revisionists.

32. William Wei, "'Political Power Grows Out of the Barrel of a Gun': Mao and the Red Army," in Graff and Highham, *Military History of China*; Scobell, *China's Use of Military Force*, 94–144.

33. Weil, *Red Cat, White Cat*, 290.

34. Deng was originally purged during the first years of the Cultural Revolution. In 1973 he was reinstated but purged again, in 1976, by the Gang of Four.

35. Deng Xiaoping, "We Should Take a Longer-Range View in Developing Sino-Japanese Relations" (excerpt from a talk with Prime Minister Yasuhiro Nakasone of Japan, March 25, 1984, Beijing; available online at http://web.peopledaily.cn/english/dengxp/vol3/text/c1190.html).

36. Frank, *Indira*.

37. Schaffer and Hemani, "India," 144–45.

38. Kohli, "Politics of Economic Liberalization in India," 328.

39. Jeffrey, *What's Happening to India?*; Nirvikar Singh, "Cultural Conflict in India: Punjab and Kashmir," in Crawford and Lipschutz, *Myth of Ethnic Conflict*, 320–52.

40. Kohli, *Politics of Economic Growth in India*.

41. Rodrik and Subramanian, *From "Hindu Growth" to Productivity Surge*, 4.

42. Sen Gupta, *Rajiv Gandhi*, 150–51.

43. Rajiv Gandhi, "Foreword."

44. Denoon, "Cycles in Indian Economic Liberalization," 51.

45. Deng Xiaoping, "Be Realistic and Look to the Future" (main points of a speech at a meeting of the Industrial Decision Drafting Committee, August 20, 1963, Beijing; available online at http://web.peopledaily.com.cn/english/dengxp/vol1/text/a1420.html).

46. On the decentralization of economic policy making, see Goodman and Segal, *China Deconstructs*; Zhao and Zhang, "Decentralization Reforms and Regionalism in China"; Oksenberg and Tong, "Evolution of Central-Provincial Fiscal Relations in China"; Cheung, Chung, and Lin, *Provincial Strategies of Economic Reform in Post-Mao China*. On the consequences of this devolution, see Poncet, "Fragmented China."

47. On the political devices for economic guidance, see Lardy, *Foreign Trade and Economic Reform in China*; Naughton, *Growing Out of the Plan*; Gao, *China's Economic Reform*.

48. See, for example, Lardy, *Agriculture in China's Modern Economic Development*.

49. Swaine and Tellis, *Interpreting China's Grand Strategy*, chap. 4.

50. Chan, Tracy, and Zhu, *China's Export Miracle*, chaps. 1–3.

51. Surjit S. Bhalla, *Chinese Mercantilism: Currency Wars and How the East Was Lost* (New Delhi: ICRIER, 1998), 4–12; Albert Keidel, *China's Currency: Not the Problem*, Carnegie Endowment for International Peace, Policy Brief 39 (Washington, D.C., 2005) (www.carnegieendowment.org/publications/index.cfm?fa=view&id=17041&prog=zch).

52. Deng Xiaoping, "Adhere to the Principle 'To Each According to His Work'" (from a talk given March 28, 1978; available online at http://web.peopledaily.com.cn/english/dengxp/vol2/text/b1180.html).

53. Ahluwalia and Little, *India's Economic Reforms and Development*.

54. Varshney, "Mass Politics or Elite Politics?"

55. Interview with P. V. Narasimha Rao, *Walk the Talk*, NDTV, May 11, 2004 (www.indianexpress.com/full_story.php?content_id=16723).

56. Mustapha Kamal Pasha, "Liberalization, State Patronage, and the 'New Inequality' in South Asia," *Perspectives on Global Development and Technology* 16, no. 1 (2000): 81.

57. Metcalf and Metcalf, *Concise History of India*, 281.

58. "Delhi's Fried Chicken Blues," *Asia Week*, November 24, 2005.

59. Ashok Malik, "The BJP, the RSS Family and Globalization in India," *Harvard Asia Quarterly* 7, no. 1 (2003) (www.asiaquarterly.com/content/view/131/40).

60. Ghuman, "Public Enterprises in India," 228.

61. Montek Singh Ahluwalia, "Privatization: From Policy Formulation to Implementation—The View from the Inside" (Fifth Annual Fellow's Lecture, Center for the

Advanced Study of India, University of Pennsylvania, April 17, 2002); this was elaborated in a slightly different form in Montek Singh Ahluwalia, "Economic Reforms in India Since 1991."

62. Schaffer and Hemani, "India," 146.

63. Jenkins, "Labor Policy and the Second Generation of Economic Reform in India."

64. This was the view of Balraj Madhok, a retired politician described as an "old-style Hindu nationalist" who "was Vajpayee's political mentor in the 1950s and 1960s" ("Master of Ambiguity," *Financial Times*, April 2, 2004).

65. Shahid K. Abbas, "10th Plan Okayed; PM for Tough Reforms for 8% Growth," *Rediff*, October 5, 2002.

66. Jenkins, "Labor Policy and the Second Generation of Economic Reform in India."

67. Government of India, Department of Industrial Policy and Promotion, *The Industrial Infrastructure Upgradation Scheme* (New Delhi: Department of Industrial Policy and Promotion, 2005).

68. C. P. Chandrasekhar, "The Verdict and the Way Ahead," *Frontline*, June 18, 2004.

69. United Progressive Alliance, *Common Minimum Programme* (New Delhi: United Progressive Alliance, 2004).

70. Gucharan Das, "The India Model," *Foreign Affairs* 85, no. 1 (2006): 85.

71. Manmohan Singh, "Onward India," *Wall Street Journal*, January 26, 2006.

72. Government of India, Department of Industrial Policy and Promotion, *Foreign Direct Investment Policy, April 2006* (New Delhi: Ministry of Commerce and Industry, 2006).

73. "Full Text of Hu Jintao's Speech at 2005 Fortune Global Forum," *People's Daily*, May 17, 2005.

74. "President Hu Preaches Morality to the Chinese," *China Daily*, March 16, 2006.

75. For the official estimates, see "China Expects Higher Urban Employment Rate," Xinhua, March 6, 2005; "China Faces Uphill Task on Job Creation," *China Daily*, February 20, 2006.

76. These conditions concerned, e.g., higher capitalization requirements for alien companies.

77. UNCTAD, *Handbook of Statistics*, 2006, http://stats.unctad.org/Handbook/TableViewer/dimView.aspx.

78. UNCTAD, *FDI Interactive Database*, 2008, http://stats.unctad.org/Handbook/TableViewer/dimView.aspx.

79. Kalpana Kochhar et al., *India's Pattern of Development: What Happened, What Follows?* NBER Working Papers (Cambridge, Mass.: National Bureau of Economic Research, 2006).

80. Das, "India Model," 2–16.

81. Varshney, "Why Have Poor Democracies Not Eliminated Poverty?" 735–36.

82. Montek Singh Ahluwalia, "Understanding India's Reform Trajectory," 270.

83. Antonio Gramsci, "The Intellectuals," in *Selections from the Prison Notebooks* (London: Lawrence and Wishart, 1971), 184.

84. Rao and Singh, *Political Economy of India's Federal System and Its Reform*, 4–8.

85. Chen, "Nationalism, Internationalism and Chinese Foreign Policy," 47.

86. Bharatiya Janata Party, *An Agenda for Development, Good Governance, Peace, and Harmony* (www.bjp.org/content/view/765/428).

87. "Atal's Picture-Perfect Hindutva," *India Telegraph*, January 1, 2003.

88. "The Man Behind 'India Shining' Slogan," *Rediff*, April 2, 2004.

89. Chen, "Nationalism, Internationalism and Chinese Foreign Policy," 52.

90. Robert Cox, "Towards a Post-Hegemonic Conceptualization of World Order: Reflections on the Relevancy of Ibn Khaldun," in Rosenau and Czempiel, *Governance Without Government*, 143–44.

91. Andreas Pickel, "False Oppositions: Reconceptualizing Economic Nationalism in a Globalizing World," in Helleiner and Pickel, *Economic Nationalism in a Globalizing World*, 11–14.

TWO. THE EVOLUTION OF SINO-INDIAN RELATIONS

1. "Greater Tri-lateral Economic Interaction Vital: Manmohan," *Hindu*, January 26, 2007.

2. "Hu Makes Five-Point Proposal on Sino-Indian Relations," *People's Daily*, November 23, 2006.

3. Rosecrance, *Rise of the Trading State*, xi.

4. Daniel Deudney and G. John Ikenberry, "Realism, Structural Liberalism, and the Western Order," in Kapstein and Mastanduno, *Unipolar Politics*.

5. Haas, *Uniting of Europe*.

6. Keohane and Nye, *Power and Interdependence*, 20–25.

7. Benjamin Cohen, *Crossing Frontiers*, 47.

8. Mao Zedong, "Our Great Victory in the War to Resist U.S. Aggression," in *Selected Works of Mao Zedong*, ed. Central Committee of the Chinese Communist Party (Beijing: Foreign Languages Press, 1971).

9. Tanham, *Indian Strategic Thought*, 32.

10. Deshingkar, "India-China Relations."

11. Camilleri, *Chinese Foreign Policy*, 6.

12. Ibid., 7.

13. Nanda, *Indian Foreign Policy*, 87–99.

14. Zhou Enlai was foreign minister until 1958. Only in the early 1970s did Zhou's influence begin to increase substantially.

15. Jonathan Spence, *Mao Zedong* (New York: Viking, 1999), 225. See also Terrill, *New Chinese Empire and What It Means for the United States*.

16. Camilleri, *Chinese Foreign Policy*, 52. See also WTO, *Statistics Database*, 2006 (www.wto.org/english/res_e/statis_e/statis_e.htm).

17. Baldev Raj Nayar, *India's Quest for Technological Independence*, 2 vols. (New Delhi: Lancers, 1983), 1:2.

18. Nehru, for instance, mediated between China and the Allied forces during the Korean War (1950–1953).

19. Gopal, *Jawaharlal Nehru*, 2:138–75, 227–43.

20. Brecher, *Nehru*, 256.

21. Ibid., 202.

22. Giri Deshingkar, "The Nehru Years Revisited," in Tan Chung, *Across the Himalayan Gap*.

23. Krishna Nehru Hutheesingh, *Nehru's Letters to His Sister* (London: Faber and Faber, 1963), 95.

24. Li Lianqing, "Zhou Enlai's Diplomatic Policy and the Five Principles of Peaceful Co-existence," in *Thoughts on International Strategy by the PRC Founders*, 109–23 (Beijing: Central Historical Documents Press, 1993); Li Xiangqian, "From 'Intermediate Zone' to 'the Third World,'" ibid., 198–214.

25. Yun-yuan Yang, "Controversies over Tibet."

26. Maxwell, *India's China War*, 115.

27. Well known is the example of intelligence chief B. N. Mullik, who supported religious resistance in Tibet and deployed agents behind the disputed border even before conflict broke out. See Hoffmann, "Rethinking the Linkage between Tibet and the China-India Border Conflict."

28. Maxwell, "India's Forward Policy," 105.

29. Mehra, "India's Border Dispute with China," 162.

30. Maxwell, "India's Forward Policy," 157–63.

31. Brecher, "Non-Alignment Under Stress"; Edwardes, "Illusion and Reality in India's Foreign Policy," 48.

32. Quoted in Edwardes, "Illusion and Reality in India's Foreign Policy," 49.

33. The sudden death of Shastri led the Indian government to place the project on the back burner again.

34. On the 1965 war, see Ganguly, *Origins of War in South Asia*, 34–52; Gulati, *Pakistan's Downfall in Kashmir*, 21–56; Dixit, *India-Pakistan in War and Peace*, 307–27; Ganguly, *Unending Conflict*, 15–51; Ashok Kapur, "Major Powers and the Persistence of the India-Pakistan Conflict," in Paul, *India-Pakistan Conflict*, 131–55.

35. Surjit Mansingh, *India's Search for Power*.

36. Garver, *Protracted Contest*, 193.

37. Choudhury, *India, Pakistan, Bangladesh, and the Major Powers*, 184; Garver, *Protracted Contest*, 195–97.

38. On the 1971 war, see Ganguly, *Origins of War in South Asia*, 53–81; Sisson and Rose, *War and Secession*, 111–253; Ganguly, *Unending Conflict*, 51–79.

39. On China's involvement, see Sisson and Rose, *War and Secession*, 246–53; Garver, *Protracted Contest*, 207–15.

40. Indira Gandhi, "India and the World," 77.

41. Frankel, *India's Political Economy*, 527–28.

42. Kreisberg, "India After Indira," 885.

43. Mancall, *China at the Center*, 437.

44. Garver, "Indian Factor in Recent Sino-Soviet Relations," 67.

45. Thomas, *Indian Security Policy*, 7.

46. Baral, Mohapatra, and Mishra, "Rajiv Gandhi's China Diplomacy," 260.

47. Deng Xiaoping, "Promote the Friendship between China and India and Increase South-South Cooperation" (excerpt from a talk with a delegation from the Indian Council for Social Sciences Research, October 22, 1982; available online at http://web.peopledaily.com.cn/english/dengxp/vol3/text/c1060.html).

48. Baral, Mohapatra, and Mishra, "Rajiv Gandhi's China Diplomacy," 260.

49. This concerned the so-called Sumdorong Chu incident.

50. Deng Xiaoping, "A New International Order Should Be Established with the Five Principles of Peaceful Coexistence as Norms" (excerpt from a talk with Prime Minister Rajiv Gandhi of India, December 21, 1988; available online at http://web.peopledaily.com.cn/english/dengxp/vol3/text/c1060.html).

51. Wen Jun, "National Economic Security and Its Implications for China," *Xin Hua wen zhai* 10, no. 2 (1999): 45–48.

52. Speech by Prime Minister Narasimha Rao at Beijing University, September 9, 1993 (available online at http://ignca.nic.in/ks_41006.htm).

53. Mohan, *Crossing the Rubicon.*

54. Gujral, *Foreign Policy for India*, 241.

55. On these reforms, see B. Bhattacharya, "India's Foreign Economic Policy: Evolving Context and Tasks"; Kishan Rana, "Promoting India's Economic Objectives Abroad: The Main Task Ahead"; P. M. S. Malik, "The Changing Face of India's Economic Diplomacy," all of which are found in Lalit Mansingh, *Indian Foreign Policy*, 209–47. See also Rana, "Economic Diplomacy in India."

56. Johnston, "Is China a Status Quo Power?" 13.

57. Li Qinggong and Wei Wei, "New Security Concept," *Jiefangjun bao*, December 24, 1997.

58. Michael D. Swaine, "Chinese Decision Making Regarding Taiwan, 1979–2000," in Lampton, *Making of Chinese Foreign Security Policy in the Era of Reform*, 289–337.

59. On Chinese decision making during the crisis, see Andrew Scobell, "Show of Force: Chinese Soldiers, Statesmen, and the 1995–1996 Taiwan Strait Crisis," *Political Science Quarterly* 115, no. 2 (2000): 227–46; You Ji, "Changing Leadership Consensus: The Domestic Context of War Games," in *Across the Taiwan Strait*, ed. Suisheng Zhao, 77–99 (New York: Routledge, 1999).

60. Brahma Chellaney, "India and China: Giants' Smiles Mask Tension," *International Herald Tribune*, November 28, 1996.

61. Gujral, *Foreign Policy for India*, 250.

62. A meticulously written analysis of the development of India's nuclear program can be found in Perkovich, *India's Nuclear Bomb.*

63. Sidhu, *Evolution of India's Nuclear Doctrine*, 11–14.

64. BJP, *For a Strong and Prosperous India* (New Delhi: BJP, 1996) (www.bjp.org/content/blogcategory/97/428).

65. Atal Bihari Vajpayee, *I Dream of a Strong and Prosperous India* (New Delhi: BJP, February 1996) (www.bjp.org/leader/idream.htm); T. V. Paul, "The Systemic Bases

of India's Challenge to the Global Nuclear Order," *Non-Proliferation Review* 6, no. 1 (fall 1998): 1–11.

66. See the BJP 1998 Election Manifesto at www.bjp.org/content/view/2626/428/.

67. See, for example, "China Being Offered Access to US Missile Knowhow," *Hindustan Times*, March 19, 1998; and "US 'Helps' Prevent Sale of Chinese N-Material to Iran," *Hindustan Times*, March 15, 1998.

68. On China's role in Pakistan's nuclear program, see T. V. Paul, "The Causes and Consequences of China-Pakistani Nuclear/Missile Cooperation," in Dittmer, *South Asia's Nuclear Security Dilemma*, 175–89.

69. XII Lok Sabha Debates, Session II, May 29, 1998, http://parliamentofindia.nic.in/ls/lsdeb/ls12/ses2/c290598.htm.

70. K. Subrahmanyam, "A Credible Deterrent," *Times of India*, June 6, 1998, 13.

71. Government of India, Ministry of Defence, *Annual Report 1996–1997* (New Delhi: Ministry of Defence, 1996), 6.

72. Perkovich, *India's Nuclear Bomb*, 384–85; K. Subrahmanyam, "Nuclear Defence Philosophy," *Times of India*, November 8, 1996.

73. K. Subrahmanyam, "Nuclear India in Global Politics," *Strategic Digest* 28, no. 12 (December 1998): 18.

74. Perkovich, *India's Nuclear Bomb*, 440–41

75. A. G. Noorani, "The Meaning of George Fernandes," *Frontline* 16, no. 22 (1999) (www.hinduonnet.com/fline/fl1622/16221030.htm). See also, on George Fernandes (www.outlookindia.com/author.asp?name=George+Fernandes).

76. On this argument, see Zhang Ming, *China's Changing Nuclear Posture*; Garver, "Restoration of Sino-Indian Comity Following India's Nuclear Tests."

77. Garver, "Restoration of Sino-Indian Comity Following India's Nuclear Tests."

78. Sutter, *China's Rise in Asia*, 242–44.

79. "Newsmaker: Jaswant Singh," June 11, 1998, *Online NewsHour* (www.pbs.org/newshour/bb/asia/jan-june98/india_6–11.html).

80. Raja Mohan, "India, China Set to Begin Dialogue," *Hindu*, February 24, 1999.

81. Cheng Ruisheng, "Sino-Indian Relations After India's Nuclear Tests" (paper presented at the UNESCO, LNCV, and USPID conference on the Nuclearization of South Asia, Como, May 20–22, 1999, http://lxmi.mi.infn.it/~landnet/NSA/cheng.pdf).

82. On China's posture during the Kargil conflict, see Garver, "China's Kashmir Policies."

83. Tang Jiaxung, "Pakistan Counterparts Discuss Kashmir," Xinhua, June 11, 1999.

84. "If Removal of Quantitative Restrictions Has Adverse Impact, We'll Counter It Through the Weapon of Tariff," *Rediff*, March 31, 2000.

85. John Cherian, "A Momentous Change," *Frontline* 19, no. 24 (2006) (www.hinduonnet.com/fline/fl1924/stories/20021206006001900.htm).

86. See, for instance, Surjit Mansingh, *India-China Relations in the Context of Vajpayee's 2003 Visit*, Sigur Center Asia Papers (Washington, D.C.: Sigur Center for Asian Studies, George Washington University, 2004).

87. People's Republic of China, Ministry of Foreign Affairs, *Declaration on Principles for Relations and Comprehensive Cooperation between the People's Republic of China and the Republic of India*, Beijing, June 25, 2003.

88. Qin Jize, "Border Row on Agenda for Wen's India Visit," *China Daily*, May 5, 2005.

89. BJP, *Vision Document 2004* (New Delhi: BJP, 2004), 14.

90. Congress Party, *Security, Defence and Foreign Policy*.

91. At the time, a Chinese strategic dialogue was already in place with Japan. The same year saw an upsurge of such dialogues, as Beijing started them with the EU, France, Russia, Pakistan, and the United States.

92. Government of India, Ministry of External Affairs, *Joint Declaration by the Republic of India and the People's Republic of China*, New Delhi, November 21, 2006, http://meaindia.nic.in/declarestatement/2006/11/21jd01.htm.

93. Ambarish Mukherjee and Moumita Bakshi, "Destination China for India Inc," *Hindu Business Line*, April 15, 2005.

94. "China, India Move Closer in Trade," *Asia Times*, February 11, 2005.

95. "Tata Sons Looking to Grow in China," *Hindu Business Line*, August 30, 2005.

96. People's Republic of China, Ministry of Foreign Affairs, *7th Session of China-India Joint Group on Economic, Trade, Science and Technology Cooperation Held in New Delhi*, March 23, 2006 (www.fmprc.gov.cn/eng/wjb/zwjg/zwbd/t241923.htm).

97. Wang Xu, "China, India Urged to Step Up Co-operation," *China Daily*, November 2, 2006.

98. S. D. Naik, "India-China: Path-Breaking Initiatives," *Hindu Business Line*, July 2, 2003.

99. "China, India Move Closer in Trade," *Asia Times*, February 11, 2005.

100. Confederation of Indian Industry, *Complementing Competencies* (New Delhi: Confederation of Indian Industry, 2006) (www.mycii.org/library/digital_collection.htm).

101. "China Asks India to Take Action to Boost Sino-Indian Trade to $100 Billion by 2015," *India Daily*, May 14, 2006.

102. Siddharth Srivastava, "India Cannot Afford to Snub China," *Asia Times*, November 24, 2006.

103. P. V. Indiresan, "The Kunming Initiative," *Frontline* 17, no. 7 (2000) (www.hinduonnet.com/fline/fl1707/17070980.htm). Yunnan created a special department for nurturing ties with neighboring countries, the Yunnan Provincial Council for Promoting Trade with Foreign Countries.

104. "Assam Chief Minister for Reopening Stilwell Road," *Narinjara News*, November 17, 2006; Amit Baruah, "Northeast as a Trade Hub," *Hindu*, September 20, 2004; "Northeast India Hopes to Reopen Stilwell Road for Trade," *People's Daily*, January 8, 2006.

105. On the economic links between India's northeast and China's southern provinces, see Bhattacharyay and De, "Promotion of Trade and Investment between People's Republic of China and India."

106. "North East CMs Demand Better Infrastructure," *Assam Tribune*, December 10, 2005; "Duliajan College Holds Debate on Reopening of Stilwell Road," *Assam Tribune*, December 8, 2006.

107. Nirupama Subramanian, "Yunnan Looks to Enhance Ties with India," *Hindu*, June 18, 2005.

108. "Trade Fair Venue Shifted to Salt Lake," *Hindu Business Line*, January 18, 2007.

109. "IEF Mission," *Tribune of India*, March 3, 2004.

110. Government of Sikkim, Department of Commerce and Industries, *Nathula Trade Prospects, Potentials and Opportunities* (Gangtok: Department of Commerce and Industries, 2006).

111. "Fair Venue Shifted to Salt Lake," *Hindu Business Line*, January 18, 2007; see also "Hunan Province of China and West Bengal Will Soon Enter into a Trade Alliance," *India Daily*, May 29, 2006.

112. "Bengal Plans Complex for Chinese Investors at Haldia," *Hindu Business Line*, September 4, 2006.

113. Other Indian states were Kerala (2002), Punjab (2003, later canceled), Tamil Nadu (2006), and Haryana (2006). Government of Gujarat, Industrial Extension Bureau, "Brief Report on Visit of Government of Gujarat Delegation to Singapore and China" (www.indextb.com/pdf/si-ch-del06.pdf).

114. Luo and Zhao, "Yindu dui Hua Zhengce de tiaozheng yu Zhongyin guanxi de weilai zouxiang," 18.

115. "The Mother of All FTA's," *Asia Times*, March 31, 2005.

116. P. Suryanarayana, "India, China Discuss Economic Ties," *Hindu*, March 25, 2005.

117. *Report of the India-China Joint Study Group on Comprehensive Trade and Economic Cooperation*, April 2005, 70–89 (www.hinduonnet.com/thehindu/nic/0041/report.pdf).

118. Mahendra P. Lama, "India-China Border Trade through Nathu La in Sikkim: Potentials and Challenges," in Ray and De, *India and China in an Era of Globalisation*, 183.

119. Quoted in Amit Baruah, "Nathu La Beckons," *Frontline* 23, no. 4 (2006) (www.hinduonnet.com/fline/fl2314/stories/20060728002603600.htm).

120. Sujan Dutta, "Nathu-La Wider Road Reply to Beijing," *Calcutta Telegraph*, November 21, 2006.

121. "India-China Trade to Gear Up," *People's Daily*, August 5, 2005.

122. The road will link from Jammu and Kashmir, Himachal Pradesh, Uttaranchal, Sikkim to Arunachal Pradesh. "Govt to Build Road Along Sino-Indian Border," *Assam Tribune*, March 20, 2006.

123. "After Nathu La, Stilwell Road Might Be Next," *Times of India*, August 22, 2006.

124. "China, India Sign Energy Agreement," *China Daily*, January 13, 2006.

125. "India, China on Path of Nuke Cooperation," *Rediff*, November 21, 2006.

126. Pandian, "Political Economy of Trans-Pakistan Gas Pipeline Project."

127. Ping Yin, "Russia-China-India Pipeline Being Discussed," *China Daily*, December 7, 2006.

128. Siddharth Varadarajan, "New Delhi, Beijing Talk Nuclear for the First Time," *Hindu*, November 22, 2006.

129. People's Republic of China, Ministry of Foreign Affairs, *Joint Statement First China-India Financial Dialogue*, New Delhi, April 7, 2006 (www.fmprc.gov.cn/eng/wjb/zzjg/yzs/gjlb/2681/2683/t247651.htm).

130. Philip R. Lane and Sergio L. Schmukler, *The International Financial Integration of China and India*, CEPR Discussion Papers, no. 5852 (London: Centre for Economic Policy Research, 2006).

131. P. S. Suryanarayana, "India, China to Act in Concert on WTO Issues," *Hindu*, June 26, 2003.

132. "China, India and Pakistan Stall WTO Talks on Textile Quotas," *Daily Times*, November 26, 2005.

133. Dev Chatterjee, "India, China to Take On West at WTO," *Indian Express*, November 24, 2006.

134. "China, India Team Up to Study WTO Affairs," *People's Daily*, May 13, 2002.

135. "Zhu Okays Infosys Office in Shanghai," *Tribune*, January 17, 2002.

136. Anil K. Joseph, "China, India to Cooperate in New Round of WTO Talks," *Rediff*, June 22, 2003; Zhao Gancheng, "Wending Zhongyin guanxi yu chuangzao zhanlue jiyu chuyi," 18.

THREE. RICARDO'S REALITY

1. Kamal Nath, "India, China Economic Ties Poised to Grow" (statement at the World Economic Forum, Davos, Switzerland, January 27, 2005).

2. United Nations Population Division, *World Population Prospects: The 2006 Revision Population Database*, http://esa.un.org/unpp/p2k0data.asp.

3. On China, see Jinjun Xue and Wei Zhong, "Unemployment, Poverty and Income Disparity in Urban China," *Asian Economic Journal* 17, no. 3 (2003): 383–405; John Knight and Jinjun Xue, "How High Is Urban Unemployment in China?" *Journal of Chinese Economic and Business Studies* 4, no. 2 (2004): 91–107; Simon Appleton et al., "Labor Retrenchment in China: Determinants and Consequences," *China Economic Review* 13, no 2 (2002): 252–75; John Giles et al., "What Is China's True Unemployment Rate?" (paper presented at the Institute for Population and Labor Economics, Chinese Academy of Social Sciences, Beijing, October 2004). On India, see T. N. Srinivasan, "Employment and Unemployment since the Early Seventies" (working paper, no. 306, Stanford Center for International Development, Stanford University, 2006); Government of India, National Sample Survey Organisation, *Employment and Unemployment Situation, 2004–2005* (New Delhi: Ministry of Statistics and Programme Implementation, 2005), part 1, p. iii; World Bank, *World Development Indicators 2005* (Washington, D.C.: World Bank, 2005), table 2.5.

4. Labor force statistics drawn from World Bank, *World Development Indicators 2005*, table 2.2, which indicates 61.4 million unemployed in China and 38.4 million unemployed in India.

5. FAO, *Compendium of Food and Agriculture Indicators 2005* (Rome: FAO, 2006).

6. On the Chinese estimates, see "Fears of High Jobless Rate in 2007," *China Daily*, December 20, 2007; for India, see National Sample Survey Organisation, *Employment and Unemployment Situation*, part 1, p. iii.

7. On jobless growth, see Ricardo J. Caballero and Mohamad L. Hammour, *Jobless Growth: Appropriability, Factor Substitution, and Unemployment*, NBER Working Papers, no. 6221 (Cambridge, Mass.: National Bureau of Economic Research, 1997). For India, see Bhattacharya and Sakthivel, *Economic Reforms and Jobless Growth in India in the 1990s*. For China, see Tan Wei, "Where Are the Jobs?" *Beijing Review* 32 (2006) (www.undprcc.lk/rdhr2006/G2235H835352H/INTHE-NEWS/1122_Beijing_Review.pdf).

8. Barry Bosworth and Susan M. Collins, "Accounting for Growth: Comparing China and India," *Journal of Economic Perspectives* 22, no. 1 (winter 2008): 45–66.

9. Barry Eichengreen, *Global Imbalances and the Lessons of Bretton Woods*, NBER Working Papers, no. 10497 (Cambridge, Mass.: National Bureau of Economic Research, 2004).

10. Ma Kai, "The 11th Five-Year Plan: Targets, Paths and Policy Orientation" (statement to the National Development and Reform Commission, Beijing, March 19, 2006), http://en.ndrc.gov.cn/newsrelease/t20060323_63813.htm.

11. Government of India, Planning Commission, *Tenth Five Year Plan, 2002–2007* (New Delhi: Planning Commission, 2002), 665.

12. Ibid.

13. Ibid., 666.

14. Kumar, *Towards an Employment-Oriented Export Strategy*, 10.

15. Chetan Ahya and Mihir Sheth, "Excess Liquidity Stock Shrinking Rapidly," Morgan Stanley, January 4, 2006 (www.morganstanley.com/views/gef/archive/2006/20060104-Wed.html).

16. Figures are drawn from "Emerging-Market Indicators," *Economist*, November 18, 2006.

17. European Central Bank, *The Accumulation of Foreign Reserves* (Frankfurt am Main: European Central Bank, 2006); Albert Keidel, *China's Currency: Not the Problem*, Carnegie Endowment for International Peace, Policy Brief 39 (Washington, D.C., 2005).

18. See U.S. Treasury (www.ustreas.gov/tic/mfh.txt).

19. The variation depends on the extent to which round-tripping is taken into account. Figures are drawn from the UNCTAD FDI database (www.unctad.org/Templates/Page.asp?intItemID=1923). On round-tripping, see Geng Xiao, *People's Republic of China's Round-Tripping FDI: Scale, Causes and Implications* (Tokyo: Asian Development Bank Institute, 2004).

20. "Chidambaram Pitches for Larger U.S. FDI Inflows," *Hindu*, March 4, 2006.

21. S. P. Gupta, ed., *Report of the Committee on India Vision 2020* (New Delhi: Planning Commission, Government of India, 2002), 27.

22. "Annual FDI to China Expected to Reach US$100 Billion," *People's Daily*, January 2, 2003.

23. Planning Commission, *Tenth Five Year Plan*, 667.

24. The export complementarity ratio measures the extent to which the composition of exports of two reporters differs. A completely divergent export composition (ratio = 1) means high complementarity and consequently lower competition; a ratio of 0 means no complementarity. Figures are drawn from the WTO trade statistics for 2006.

25. Qureshi and Wan, *Trade Expansion of China and India*, 13.

26. Planning Commission, *Tenth Five Year Plan*, 667.

27. See www.emergingtextiles.com.

28. "China's Export Engine," *Washington Post*, September 13, 2006; Ashok Dasgupta, "Outlays Up for Social Sector Programmes," *Hindu*, March 1, 2006.

29. Government of India, Department of Information Technology, *Draft Paper on National Electronics/IT Hardware Manufacturing Policy* (New Delhi: Department of Information Technology, 2003).

30. Government of India, Department of Heavy Industry, *Indian Machine Tools Industry* (New Delhi: Department of Heavy Industry, 2006), http://dhi.nic.in/MACHINE%20TOOLS%20INDUSTRY.pdf.

31. Kumar, *Towards an Employment-Oriented Export Strategy*, 17.

32. See www.china.org.cn/english/BAT/188506.htm.

33. "Major High-Tech Projects Planned for 2006–2010," *China Daily*, March 6, 2006.

34. RNCOS, *China Software: World Class Low Cost Manufacturing* (Delhi: RNCOS Industry Research, September 2008); Savio S. Chan, *IT Outsourcing in China: How China's Five Emerging Drivers Are Changing the Technology Landscape and IT Industry* (New Delhi: Outsourcing Institute, 2005).

35. Government of India, Ministry of Commerce, *Foreign Trade Policy, 2004–2009* (New Delhi: Ministry of Commerce, 2004); see also "Govt Aims to Double India's Share in World Farm Trade, *Hindu*, February 16, 2006.

36. "China Faces Overproduction in 11 Sectors," *People's Daily*, December 18, 2005.

37. Figures are drawn from UNCTAD, *World Investment Report 2007* (New York: United Nations, 2007), annex 1.1.2, p. 265.

38. Ibid.

39. Eugen von Keller and Wei Zho, *From Middle Kingdom to Global Market: Expansion Strategies and Success Factors for China's Emerging Multinationals* (Shanghai: Roland Berger Strategy Consultants, 2003); Friedrich Wu, "The Globalization of Corporate China," *NBR Analysis* 16, no. 3 (December 2005): 5–29; Andreas Lunding, *China's Champions in Waiting* (Frankfurt am Main: Deutsche Bank, 2006).

40. *BP Statistical Review of World Energy 2006* (London: British Petroleum, 2006).

41. Ibid.

42. Energy Information Administration, *International Energy Outlook 2006* (Washington, D.C.: EIA, 2006), 210.

43. Streifel, *Impact of China and India on Global Commodity Markets*; International Tropical Timber Organization, *Annual Review and Assessment of the World Timber Situation, 2005* (Yokohama: ITTO, 2005), 29.

44. Figures calculated based on *BP Statistical Review of World Energy 2006*.

45. Ibid.

46. USGS, *2005 Minerals Yearbook* (Washington, D.C.: U.S. Geological Survey, 2007), various chaps.

47. Planning Commission, *Tenth Five Year Plan*, chap 7.3: 759–800.

48. "PM Asks Scientists to Develop Alternative Sources of Energy," *Hindustan Times*, January 3, 2007.

49. "China to Pour One Trillion Yuan into Development of Oil Alternative," *People's Daily*, December 15, 2006.

50. "China, India Not a Case of the Tortoise and the Hare," *People's Daily*, October 12, 2006.

51. *Report of the India-China Joint Study Group on Comprehensive Trade and Economic Cooperation*, April 2005, 20 (www.hinduonnet.com/thehindu/nic/0041/report.pdf).

52. "India and China Not Rivals: Singh," *People's Daily*, December 12, 2005.

53. Wu and Zhou, "Changing Bilateral Trade between China and India," 517; Qureshi and Wan, *Trade Expansion of China and India*.

54. Daniel H. Rosen, Scott Rozelle, and Jikun Huang, *Roots of Competitiveness: China's Evolving Agriculture Interests* (Washington, D.C.: Institute for International Economics, 2004); Thomas I. Wahl, "China as a Horticultural Competitor," *Good Fruit Grower*, January 2006, 28–29.

55. Wu Yongnian, "Yindu jingji minzu zhuyi de yuanqi, yingxiang ji Zhongguo de duice," 59.

56. "India-China FTA Will Not Work, Says Kamal Nath," *Deccan Herald*, July 15, 2005.

57. V. Sridhar, "Free Trade Fears," *Frontline* 22, no. 10 (2005) (www.hinduonnet.com/fline/fl2210/stories/20050520002709800.htm).

58. Ibid.

59. "Industry, Govt Not Ready for China FTA," *Central Chronicle*, November 18, 2006.

60. "Industry and Govt Not Yet Ready for FTA with China," *Zee News*, November 17, 2006; Zhang Jin, "Economist Maps Out Hopes for Trade," *China Daily*, April 8, 2004.

61. Charlotte Windle, "China Faces Indian Dumping Allegations," *BBC World*, July 31, 2006.

62. Monica Gupta, "Auto Parts Sector Up Against 'Dumping' from China," *Business Standard*, October 4, 2006.

63. Bhattacharya and Bhattacharyay, *Free Trade Agreement between People's Republic of China and India*, 8.

64. Aditi Roy Ghatak, "Finite Ores, Implications for Mineral Policy," *Hindu*, September 13, 2005; "Exporting Iron Ore Is Against National Interests: Tata Steel MD," *Hindu Business Line*, August 17, 2005.

65. "Chinese Importers Boycott Indian Iron Ore," *People's Daily*, March 9, 2007.

66. J. S. Metcalfe and I. Steedman, "A Note on the Gain from Trade," in *Fundamental Issues in Trade Theory*, ed. Ian Steedman (New York: Macmillan, 1979); Bayne and Woolcock, *New Economic Diplomacy*.

67. Michel Kostecki and Olivier Naray, *Commercial Diplomacy and International Business*, Discussion Paper in Diplomacy, no. 107 (The Hague: Netherlands Institute of International Relations Clingendael, 2007).

68. Jacob Viner, *The Customs Union Issue* (New York: Carnegie Endowment for International Peace, 1950).

69. Goyal and Joshi, "Bilateralism and Free Trade"; Luis Abugattas Majluf, *Swimming in the Spaghetti Bowl: Challenges for Developing Countries in the "New Regionalism,"* Policy Issues in International Trade and Commodities Study Series, no. 27 (New York: United Nations, 2004); Maurice Schiff and L. Alan Winters, *Regional Integration and Development* (Washington, D.C.: World Bank, 2003); Lahiri, *Regionalism and Globalization*; Edward D. Mansfield and Helen V. Milner, eds., *The Political Economy of Regionalism* (New York: Columbia University Press, 1997); Paul Krugman, *Geography and Trade* (Cambridge, Mass.: MIT Press, 1991).

70. Jo-Ann Crawford and Sam Laird, "Regional Trade Agreements and the WTO," *North American Journal of Economics and Finance* 12, no. 2 (2001): 193–205.

71. On the motivations, see, for instance, Asher and Sen, *India–East Asia Integration*; Wu and Chen, "Prospects for Regional Economic Integration between China and the Five Central Asian Countries"; Kumar, Sen, and Asher, *India-ASEAN Economic Relations*; Srinivasan and Tendulkar, *Reintegrating India with the World Economy*; Sheng, *China-ASEAN Free Trade Area*. On the policies, see Y. Yonding, "Regional Integration from a Chinese Perspective," in *Regional Integration in East Asia from the Viewpoint of Spatial Economics*, ed. Masahisa Fujita (New York: Palgrave Macmillan, 2007); Rahul Sen, "New Regionalism in Asia"; Roland-Holst and Weiss, "People's Republic of China and Its Neighbours"; Chaturvedi, *Trade Facilitation Measures in South Asian FTAs*; Mehta and Narayanan, *India's Regional Trading Arrangements*. On the impact on regional integration, see Men, "Construction of the China-ASEAN Free Trade Area"; Abraham and Van Hove, "Rise of China"; Marion Wang, "Greater China"; Wang Jiangyu, *China's Regional Trade Agreement (RTA) Approach*.

72. Low, "Multilateralism, Regionalism, Bilateral and Cross Regional Free Trade Arrangements."

73. Association of Southeast Asian Nations, *ASEAN Statistics*, table 2 (www.ASEANsec.org/13100.htm).

74. Ibid., table 5.

75. Suparna Karmakar, *India-ASEAN Cooperation in Services: An Overview*, Indian Council for Research on International Economic Relations Working Papers, no. 176 (New Delhi: Indian Council for Research on International Economic Relations, 2005).

76. The three were Thailand, in 1985, Singapore, in 1986, and Malaysia, in 1988.

77. Michael Richardson, "Asian Leaders Cautious on Forging New Regional Partnerships," *International Herald Tribune*, November 27, 2000.

78. As of January 2004, China imposes no tariffs on exports of most goods from these three states. Beijing also established a China-ASEAN Cooperation Fund to finance projects, which should enable Cambodia, Laos, and Myanmar to ameliorate their investment climates.

79. Sheng, *China-ASEAN Free Trade Area*, 6; Alice D. Ba, "China-ASEAN Relations: The Significance of an ASEAN-China Free Trade Area," in Cheng, deLisle, and Brown, *China under Hu Jintao*, 311–48.

80. Sheng, *China-ASEAN Free Trade Area*, 19.

81. Zhao, "Model of Decentralized Development"; "China and ASEAN Share Broad Prospects in Cooperation: Interview with Vice Minister of Foreign Trade Long Yongtu," *People's Daily*, April 26, 2002.

82. "China-ASEAN FTA Agreement Benefits China's Textile Export," Xinhua, January 20, 2006.

83. Zha, Daojiong, *The Politics of China-ASEAN Economic Relations: Assessing the Move Towards an FTA*, IUJ Research Institute Working Papers 2002-3 (Niigata, Japan: International University of Japan, 2003).

84. On India's economic interests, see Yahya Faizal, "India and Southeast Asia: Revisited," *Contemporary Southeast Asia* 25, no. 1 (2003): 79–106; Rajesh Mehta, *Potential of India's Bilateral Free Trade Arrangements: A Case Study of India and Thailand*, RIS Discussion Papers, no. 24 (New Delhi: RIS, 2002).

85. "China's ASEAN Entry to Hit India Hard," *Financial Express*, October 26, 2006. See also Amita Batra, *Asian Economic Integration: Asean+3+1 or Asian+1s?* Indian Council for Research on International Economic Relations Working Papers, no. 186 (New Delhi: Indian Council for Research on International Economic Relations, 2006), 21–27.

86. Government of India, Ministry of External Affairs, *ASEAN-India Relations* (New Delhi: Ministry of External Affairs, 2006), 2, http://meaindia.nic.in/onmouse/ASEAN%20-India.pdf.

87. S. Majumder, "Doha Talks Failure: Giving the India-ASEAN FTA a New Thrust," *Hindu Business Line*, August 24, 2006.

88. Amiti Sen, "Hurdles Galore on Road to FTA with ASEAN," *Economic Times*, January 29, 2007.

89. "New Rules for ASEAN FTA in July," *Financial Express*, June 11, 2005

90. Majumder, "Doha Talks Failure."

91. Includes Bangladesh, Bhutan, India, Myanmar, Nepal, Sri Lanka, and Thailand. Yahya, "BIMSTEC and Emerging Patterns of Asian Regional and Interregional Cooperation."

92. "India Set to Get Access to Bimstec Markets," *Business Standard India*, June 23, 2005.

93. UN Comtrade database, http://comtrade.un.org/db/, and World Bank Country Files: Bhutan (devdata.worldbank.org/AAG/btn_aag.pdf) and Nepal (devdata.worldbank.org/AAG/npl_aag.pdf).

94. "Agreement on Trade, Commerce and Transit between the Government of the Republic of India and the Royal Government of Bhutan," July 28, 2006, http://commerce.nic.in/bhutan.pdf; "Indo-Nepal Treaty of Trade," March 2002, http://commerce.nic.in/trade/nepal.pdf.

95. Muherji, Jayawardhana, and Kelegama, *Indo–Sri Lanka Free Trade Agreement*.

96. Subhashini Abeysinghe, *CEPA with India: Opportunities for Trade and Investment* (Colombo: Sri Lanka Chamber of Commerce, 2004) (www.chamber.lk/in-pages/informationbank/CEPA%20with%20India.pdf).

97. Taneja, *Indo–Sri Lanka Trade in Services*.

98. Suteethorn, *Economic Cooperation between Thailand and India and Its Implication on the Asian Community*.

99. Government of India, Department of Commerce, "Comprehensive Economic Cooperation Agreement between the Republic of India and the Republic of Singapore" (New Delhi: Department of Commerce, 2003).

100. Mehta, *Economic Co-operation between India and Singapore*, 38–39.

101. "Malaysia in Talks with India on FTA," *Hindu Business Line*, September 28, 2004.

102. I define central Asia as the grouping of Afghanistan, Iran, Kazakhstan, Kyrgyzstan, Tajikistan, Turkmenistan, and Uzbekistan.

103. The SCO member states are China, Kazakhstan, Kyrgyzstan, Russia, Tajikistan, and Uzbekistan.

104. Sheives, "China Turns West."

105. Niklas Swanström, "China and Central Asia: A New Great Game or Traditional Vassal Relations?" *Journal of Contemporary China* 14, no. 45 (2005): 76–81.

106. Sheives, "China Turns West," 206–9.

107. Gurudas Das, "Border Trade in India's North-East" (paper presented at the ICSSR seminar "Challenges of Development in North-East India," Shillong, October 21, 2003), 7.

108. Government of India, Planning Commission, *The Report of the Working Group on Roads for the Eleventh Five Year Plan* (New Delhi: Planning Commission, 2007).

109. Jonathan Holslag, "Myanmar in the Frontline" (briefing paper, ESISC, Brussels, January 29, 2006).

110. "Hope Floats for Mizo Waterway," *Calcutta Telegraph*, February 2, 2007.

111. Amit Baruah, "'Important Milestone' Says Jaswant," *Hindu*, February 14, 2001.

112. "Projects with Neighbouring Countries: Unstarred Question No. 3637," Lok Sabha, April 24, 2003 (www.meaindia.nic.in/parliament/rs/2003/04/24rapr3637.htm); "Mizoram to Become Corridor to the East," *Aizwal*, March 12, 2007.

113. *People's Daily*, January 5, 2002.

114. Ravi Dhami, "Mahendranagar-Tanakpur Road Construction to Start Soon," *Himalayan Times*, May 3, 2007; Atul Aneja, "The Politics of Trade Routes," *Hindu*, April 30, 2007.

115. Santanu Sanyal, "Indo-Nepal Trade via Birgunj ICD from Feb 1," *Hindu Business Line*, January 5, 2005.

116. "Tibet's New Railway to Extend to China-Nepal Border," Xinhua, August 27, 2006.

117. "Rasuwagadhi Road to Enhance Nepal-China Trade Ties," interview with Chinese ambassador to Nepal, Sun Heping, Kantipur, May 24, 2004.

118. Garver, "Development of China's Overland Transportation Links with Central, South-west and South Asia," 11.

119. "New Railway Linking China, Europe to Be Built," Xinhua, March 13, 2004.

120. Fazal-ur-Rahman, "Prospects of Pakistan Becoming a Trade and Energy Corridor for China," Strategic Studies 27, no. 2 (2007) (www.issi.org.pk/journal/2007_files/no_2/article/a3.htm).

121. Government of Pakistan, Board of Investment, "Gwadar: Historical Perspective" (www.gwadarnews.com/gwadar-port.asp).

122. "Widening of Karakoram Highway Project Inaugurated in Pakistan," Lahore Times, February 17, 2008.

123. Syed Fazl-e-Haider, "China-Pakistan Rail Link on Horizon," Asia Times, February 24, 2007.

124. C. Raja Mohan, "India, Iran Unveil Road Diplomacy," Hindu, January 26, 2003.

125. De, "Cooperation in the Regional Transportation Infrastructure Sector in South Asia."

126. RIS, Restoring Afghanistan-Pakistan-India-Bangladesh-Myanmar (APIBM) Corridor: Towards a New Silk Road in Asia, RIS Policy Briefs, no. 30 (New Delhi: RIS, March 2007).

127. See, for example, Rahul Singh, "India to Counter Chinese Presence in Myanmar," Hindustan Times, April 15, 2007; Kudo, Myanmar's Economic Relations with China, 9–10.

128. Quoted in Singh, "India to Counter Chinese Presence in Myanmar."

129. Interviews with Indian Ministry of External Affairs officials, Delhi, January 2007.

130. Sudha Ramachandran, "India's Rail-Building Challenge," Asia Times, January 3, 2007.

131. Tara Dahal, "Nepal as a Transit State: Emerging Possibilities" (working paper, Institute of Foreign Affairs, Kathmandu, 2006); Prakash S. Raj, "Nepal as a Transit Point" (working paper, Institute of Foreign Affairs, Kathmandu, 2005).

132. Interview with Indian Border Roads Organisation official, Tezpur, January 12, 2007.

133. Ibid.

134. For an economic profile of India's northeastern states, see Murayama, Inoue, and Hazarika, Sub-Regional Relations in Eastern South Asia. On the Chinese province of Yunnan, see Asian Development Bank, The Mekong Region: Economic Overview (Manila: ADB, 2002); Hong Kong Trade Development Council, Market Profile of Yunnan Province (www.accci.com.au/keycity/yunnan.htm).

135. Das and Purkayastha, Border Trade.

136. See, for instance, Andrews-Speed, Liao, and Dannreuther, Strategic Implications of China's Energy Needs; Ebel, China's Energy Future; Downs, China's Quest for

Energy Security; Cordesman and Al-Rodhan, *Global Oil Market*; Bahgat, "Pipeline Diplomacy"; Lall, "Indo-Myanmar Relations in the Era of Pipeline Diplomacy"; Lord, *Imperfect Competition and International Commodity Trade*; Mohammed Ahrari, *Dynamics of Oil Diplomacy*; Tang, *With the Grain or Against the Grain?*; Tanvi Madan, *Brookings Foreign Policy Studies Energy Security Series: India* (Washington, D.C.: Brookings Institution, 2006); Jakobson and Zha, "China and the Worldwide Search for Oil Security."

137. Zha Daojiong, "China's Energy Security: Domestic and International Issues," *Survival* 48, no. 1 (2006): 186.

138. Madan, *India*, 27.

139. This paragraph is based on Jonathan Holslag, "China's Resource and Energy Policy in Sub-Saharan Africa" (report for the Development Committee of the European Parliament, Brussels, 2007), 11–12.

140. Zhao Huaxin, "China Names Key Industries for Absolute State Control," *China Daily*, December 19, 2006. See also "China to Speed Up Fostering Multinational Mining Groups," *People's Daily*, October 29, 2004.

141. Zhao, *Reform of China's Energy Institutions and Policies*; "China to Foster Mineral Conglomerates to Boost Yield," *China Mining*, December 27, 2006.

142. People's Republic of China, Ministry of Commerce, *China Nonferrous Metal Mining (Group) Co., Ltd.: Group Profile*, November 16, 2006.

143. Damian Brett and Magnus Ericsson, "Chinese Expansion to Create New Global Mining Companies," *Commodities Now*, October 2006.

144. David Brooks, "Chinese Group, Global Alumina Ink Offtake Pact," *American Metal Market*, May 18, 2005.

145. Minmetals, "CMN Organisational Structure," October 2006 (www.cmnltd. com:8080/CmnltdWeb/2zzjg.jsp).

146. Minmetals, "Minmetals and Exim Bank Seal Credit Line," November 15, 2005 (www.minmetals.com/english/new1212/news/newsxq/200512150178.htm).

147. Despite these efforts, Chinese mining and oil companies remain modest international players. In 2006, UNCTAD ranked only one Chinese enterprise among the world's twenty largest mining transnational corporations. Two firms made the oil top twenty, but their assets are minor compared to those of the six largest international players (UNCTAD, *World Investment Report 2006* [New York: United Nations, 2006], 123).

148. Interview with Indian mining expert, Delhi, December 6, 2007.

149. "India, China Plans for Oil Sector Cooperation at Early Stage, *India Daily*, August 26, 2005.

150. "China, India Sign Five Memoranda on Energy Cooperation," *People's Daily*, January 13, 2006.

151. Balaji Reddy, "India Calls for Asian Gas Grid Connecting India, China, Japan to Gas Producing Areas of Asia," *India Daily*, February 15, 2005.

152. "ONGC, Sinopec Acquire Columbia's Omimex," *Financial Express*, September 21, 2006.

153. See, for instance Nandakumar, "Sino-Indian Cooperation in the Search for Overseas Petroleum Resources."

154. Watkins, "China-Myanmar Oil Pipeline Funded."

155. Robert Axelrod, *The Complexity of Cooperation: Agent-Based Models of Competition and Collaboration* (Princeton, N.J.: Princeton University Press, 1997).

156. Lall, "Indo-Myanmar Relations in the Era of Pipeline Diplomacy," 437–39.

FOUR. SHIFTING PERCEPTIONS

1.   Putnam, "Diplomacy and Domestic Politics."

2.   Deutsch, *Political Community and the North Atlantic Area*.

3.   James Rosenau, "Citizenship in a Global Changing Order," in Rosenau and Czempiel, *Governance Without Government*, 272–94; Doyle, *Ways of War and Peace*; Albert et al., *Identities, Borders, Orders*.

4.   Chicago Council on Global Affairs, *The United States and the Rise of China and India* (Chicago: Chicago Council on Global Affairs, 2006).

5.   Pew Global Attitudes Project, *Global Unease With Major World Powers* (Washington, D.C.: Pew Research Center, 2002).

6.   Marshall M. Bouton et al., *Global Views 2006* (Chicago: Chicago Council on Global Affairs, 2006).

7.   National Democratic Alliance, *An Agenda for a Proud, Prosperous India* (New Delhi: National Democratic Alliance, 2003).

8.   National Democratic Alliance, *An Agenda for Development, Good Governance, Peace, and Harmony* (New Delhi: National Democratic Alliance, 2004). See also the BJP's *Vision Document 2004*, available at www.bjp.org/Press/mar_3104a.htm.

9.   Indian National Congress, *Election Manifesto for the 1999 Lok Sabha Elections* (New Delhi: Indian National Congress, 1999).

10. Communist Party of India, *Manifesto for the 14th Lok Sabha Elections, 2004* (New Delhi: Communist Party of India, 2004), 11.

11. Communist Party of India, *Programme* (New Delhi: Communist Party of India, 2006) (www.cpim.org); M. K. Pandhe, "Indian TU Delegation in China," *People's Democracy* 28, no. 44 (2004): 65–72.

12. "Chinese Intrusion 'Insulting and Shameful,'" *UNI* (New Delhi), July 27, 2003.

13. "Chidambaram Indulging in Double Speak, Says Vaiko," *Hindu*, April 17, 2006.

14. I am considering here the questions raised in the Lok Sabha.

15. Question numbers 368, 193, 265, 497, 2002, 2003, 2430, 2878, 3479, 4124.

16. Government of India, Lok Sabha Secretariat, *Third Report of the Standing Committee on External Affairs* (New Delhi: Lok Sabha Secretariat, December 2004), recommendation 10, sect. 415; idem, *Second Report of the Standing Committee on External Affairs* (New Delhi: Lok Sabha Secretariat, April 2000), sect. 60.

17. Government of India, Lok Sabha Secretariat, *Action Taken on the Recommendations Contained in the Thirteenth Report on Demands for Grants* (New Delhi: Lok

Sabha Secretariat, March 2003), 27; idem, *Fifth Report of the Standing Committee on External Affairs* (New Delhi: Lok Sabha Secretariat, March 2005), recommendation 3, sect. 22.

18. Government of India, Lok Sabha Secretariat, *Third Report* (December 2004), sect. 68.

19. Government of India, Lok Sabha Secretariat, *Sixth Report of the Standing Committee on External Affairs* (New Delhi: Lok Sabha Secretariat, August 2001), sect. 13.

20. Government of India, Lok Sabha Secretariat, *Seventh Report of the Standing Committee on External Affairs* (New Delhi: Lok Sabha Secretariat, April 2005), sect. 65.

21. Partially quoted from "Arunachal an Integral Part of India, Says Pranab," *Rediff,* November 9, 2006. See also "Arunachal Issue Not Debatable," *Times of India,* November 24, 2006.

22. Rajya Sabha, uncorrected debate, March 6, 2007, http://164.100.24.167/rsdebate/deb_ndx/210/06032007/1to2.htm.

23. Indian experts: Ajit Kumar Doval (senior fellow at the Institute of Peace and Conflict Studies [IPCS] and former head of the Intelligence Bureau); Arvind Virmani (member of the JEG, adviser to the Planning Commission, and director of the Indian Council for Research on International Economic Relations [ICRIER]); B. G. Verghese (senior fellow at the Centre for Policy Research [CPR] and member of Indian dialogue groups with Bangladesh, Nepal, Pakistan, and China); Brahma Chellaney (member of the prime minister's Policy Advisory Group and former adviser to India's National Security Council); Lalit Mansingh (senior fellow at the IPCS and former foreign secretary); Nagesh Kumar (member of the JEG and director of the Research and Information System for the Non-Aligned and Other Developing Countries [RIS]); Nimmi Kurian (research professor at the CPR); Phunchok Stobdan (senior fellow at the Institute for Defence Studies and Analyses [IDSA] and former director of the National Security Council); Rajiv Kumar (director and chief executive of ICRIER); Shankar Acharya (member of the Prime Minister's Economic Advisory Council and honorary professor at ICRIER); Sujit Dutta (senior fellow at the IDSA and member of the India-China Eminent Persons' Group). Chinese experts: Lan Jianxue (senior fellow at the Chinese Academy of Social Sciences [CASS]); Ma Jiali (senior researcher at the China Institutes of Contemporary International Relations [CICIR]); Sun Peijun (member of the JEG and CASS, president of the Chinese Association of South Asian Studies); Sun Shihai (professor at CASS and frequent consultant to the Chinese government); Wan Dehai (senior fellow at the Institute of South Asian Research, Chengdu University); Wang Hongwei (professor in South Asian studies at CASS); Zha Daojiong (professor at Renmin University and adviser to China's ministries of Commerce and Foreign Affairs); Zhang Wenmu (senior fellow at CICIR); Zhang Yunling (member of the JEG and director of the Institute of Asia-Pacific Studies at CASS); Zheng Ruixiang (senior researcher at the China Institute of International Studies [CIIS]).

24. "China, India Gingerly Try to Mend Ties," *India Times*, May 25, 2003.

25. "India, China Reopen Historic Border Pass After 44 Years," *VOA News* (Delhi), July 6, 2006.

26. Rajeev Sharma, "Chinese Envoy's Remark Unwarranted," *Tribune* (Chandigarh), November 19, 2006.

27. Brahma Chellaney, "Look East, at Japan, Not China," *Asian Age*, August 17, 2007.

28. Sujit Dutta, "Much Hype, Small Gains," *Rediff*, July 3, 2001.

29. Ma, "Yindu zhanlue diwei tuxian."

30. Ma, "Yindu xingshi de huigu yi zhanwang"; Ma, *Guanzhu Yindu*. See also Wang Hongwei, "Tancheng duihua shi yi zeng xin"; Wang Hongwei, "Zhongyin guanxi jinru mulin youhao xinshiqi."

31. Jabin Jacob, *Report of the IPCS-KAF Trilateral Dialogue Conference between India, China and Germany* (New Delhi: Konrad Adenauer Foundation, March 13, 2007), 5.

32. "Sino-Indian Ties Enter New Stage," *People's Daily*, June 23, 2003; Sun Shihai, "Dui Zhongyin jianli huxin guanxi de jidian sikao."

33. Ma, "Yindu zhanlue diwei tuxian," 23.

34. "53 Years of Sino-Indian Relations: Background Report," Xinhua, June 23, 2003 (www.chinaembassy.org.in/eng/sgxw/hjwl/Indian%20PM%20Visit/t61582.htm).

35. Sheela Bhatt, "China and India Are Seeking Each Other Out," *Rediff*, December 19, 2006.

36. Antoaneta Bezlova, "India, China Make Things Move," Inter Press Service, October 8, 2006; "CCTV, 53 Years of Sino-Indian Relations."

37. Arvind Virmani, *A Tripolar Century: USA, China and India*, Indian Council for Research on International Economic Relations Working Papers, no. 160 (New Delhi: Indian Council for Research on International Economic Relations, 2003), 12; Nagesh Kumar, ed., *Towards an Asian Economic Community: Vision of a New Asia* (New Delhi: RIS, 2005).

38. B. G. Verghese, "Land Bridges in Inner Asia," *Business Standard* (New Delhi), July 12, 2003.

39. Jaideep Saikia and Wang Hongwei, "Giants at Peace: India and China," *Swords and Ploughshares* 15, no. 3 (2005): 14–16; "China Reasserts Claim to Area Bordering Tibet," *India Times*, November 15, 2006.

40. Zhang Wenmu, "Yindu de diyuan zhanlue yu Zhongguo Xizang wenti"; Zhang Wenmu, "Shijie diyuan zhengzhi tixi you Yindu weilai anquan."

41. "Return Tawang to China to Resolve Boundary Dispute," *Rediff*, March 7, 2007.

42. Brahma Chellaney, "Tibet is the Key," *Deccan Chronicle*, November 18, 2006.

43. Sharma, "Chinese Envoy's Remark Unwarranted."

44. Phunchok Stobdan, "Central Asia and India's Security," *Strategic Analysis* 28, no. 1 (2004): 54–83.

45. Brahma Chellaney, "China's Unprincipled Principles," *Asian Age*, June 20, 2007.

46. Dutta, "Much Hype, Small Gains."

47. Jo Johnson and Richard McGregor, "Old Grievances Bedevil Efforts to Reach Across the Himalayas," *Financial Times*, November 20, 2006.

48. Nagesh Kumar, "Moving Towards a Strategic Partnership," *Financial Express*, April 12, 2004.

49. Virmani, *Tripolar Century*.

50. "Our Eastern Door," *Imphal Free Press*, October 19, 2004.

51. Jabin T. Jacob, "India-China Relations: Current Developments; Report of the IPCS Seminar Held on 26 March 2004," no. 1352 (New Delhi: Institute of Peace and Conflict Studies, April 1, 2004).

52. Vivek Raghuvanshi, "4-Nation Naval Exercise May Presage New Alliance," *Defence News*, July 23, 2007.

53. Chellaney, "Look East, at Japan, Not China."

54. Steven R. Weisman, "Dissenting on Atomic Deal," *New York Times*, March 3, 2006.

55. Nimmi Kurian, "Prospects for Sino-Indian Trans-border Economic Linkages," *International Studies* 42, nos. 3–4 (2005): 295–306.

56. Dan Blumenthal and Joseph Lin, "Oil Obsession: Energy Appetite Fuels Beijing's Plans to Protect Vital Sea Lines," *Armed Forces Journal*, June 2006. See also Jun Niu and Lan Jianxue, "Zhongmei guanxi yu dongya heping" (Sino-U.S. Relations and Peace in East Asia) in *Dongya heping yu anquan* (Peace and Security in East Asia), ed. Yan Xuetong and Jin Dexiang, 28–73 (Beijing: Shishi chubanshe, 2005).

57. Ma Jiali, "Emerging Sino-Indian Relations," *Contemporary International Relations*, May–June 2007, 43–49; see also Zhang Wenmu, "Zhongguo nengyuan anquan yu zhen che xuan zhe."

58. Zhang Yunling, "Zonghe anquan guan ji dui wo guo anquan de sikao"; Xu Binglan, "Emerging Asia Looking for Bigger Role," *China Daily*, April 22, 2005.

59. "A Friendship That Spans Generations," *Beijing Review*, June 8, 2006.

60. Saikia and Wang, "Giants at Peace"; Zhang Wenmu, "Zhongguo nengyuan anquan yu zhen che xuan zhe"; "Likely Sino-Indian FTA Conducive to Nation," *People's Daily*, June 25, 2004; Wang Hongwei, "Sino-Indian Economic and Scientific Cooperation Promising," 45; Sun Peijun and Hua Biyun, "Yindu de jingji gaige."

61. Ashish Gupta, "An Idea Before Its Time," *Business Today*, April 15, 2005.

62. Indrajit Basu, "China Willing, India Shy," *Asia Times*, April 14, 2005; see also Paranjoy Guha Thakurta, "China Could Overtake US's India Trade," *Asia Times*, March 15, 2006.

63. On average, one per twenty-four thousand.

64. Quoted in Basu, "China Willing, India Shy."

65. Larson, *Origins of Containment*.

FIVE. THE MILITARY SECURITY DILEMMA

1. Mansingh, "India-China Relations in the Post–Cold War Era," 269; Zheng, "Shifting Obstacles in Sino-Indian Relations," 66.

2. Chien-Peng Chung, *Domestic Politics, International Bargaining and China's Territorial Disputes*, 122–67.

3. "Chinese Intrusion into Arunachal Pradesh: New Delhi Takes Up Matter with Beijing," *Hindu*, July 28, 2003.

4. Ibid.

5. Interview with expert, CASS, Beijing, December 7, 2007.

6. "Sukhoi Base in the East to Counter China," *Times of India*, September 28, 2007; Deng Guilin, "Air Force in Tibet Sets Up a Comprehensive Logistics Support System," *Jiefangjun bao*, July 17, 2007.

7. "Trade at Nathu La Amidst Guns and Roses," *Himalayan Review*, June 11, 2007.

8. Vishnu Makhijani, "Indian Air Force Enhances Strategic Reach Against China," IANS, September 30, 2007.

9. "Sukhoi Base in the East to Counter China."

10. Majumdar, Bappa (2007), China in mind, India to boost eastern air power, *Straits Times*, 8 August 2007.

11. No short-term threat from China on Arunachal border, *Rediff*, 20 November 2006.

12. Bappa Majumdar, "China in Mind, India to Boost Eastern Air Power," *Straits Times*, August 8, 2007.

13. "The Dragon Has Now Got Wings," *Indian Express*, January 6, 2008.

14. "Qinghai-Tibet Railway Not Just a Big Deal for Chinese," Xinhua, July 2, 2006.

15. Nehru, *Discovery of India*, 536; Sardar Patel, November 20, 1948, quoted in Scott, "India's Grand Strategy for the Indian Ocean," 203.

16. Interviews with official, Ministry of Defence, New Delhi, January 17, 2008.

17. Ibid.

18. P. S. Suryanarayana, "No Evil Design Behind Proactive Naval Exercises: Admiral Mehta," *Hindu*, May 21, 2007.

19. Ministry of Petroleum and Natural Gas, http://petroleum.nic.in/petroleum/ps-body.jsp.

20. United Nations Division for Ocean Affairs and the Law of the Sea, Office of Legal Affairs, and the International Seabed Authority, *Marine Mineral Resources: Scientific Advances and Economic Perspectives* (New York: United Nations, 2004), 37–38.

21. Ibid., 59.

22. K. R. Singh, *Maritime Security for India: New Challenges and Responses* (New Delhi: New Century, 2008), 58–114.

23. "N-Submarine May Be Operational by 2012," *India Times*, March 11, 2007.

24. Government of India, Integrated Headquarters, Ministry of Defence (Navy), *Indian Maritime Doctrine* (New Delhi: Ministry of Defence, April 25, 2004).

25. Ibid., 9.

26. Atul Aneja, "India Wants Cooperative Ties with China: Navy Chief," *Hindu*, January 11, 2007.

27. "India Not Competing with China: Navy Chief," *NDTV*, December 26, 2007.

28. Singh, *Maritime Security for India*, 13.

29. Interview with official, Ministry of Defence, Navy, New Delhi, January 18, 2008.

30. "India Upping Antennae in Bay of Bengal to Counter China," *ZeeNews*, November 14, 2007.

31. Ibid.

32. Interviews with an expert at the IDSA and an official of the Ministry of Foreign Affairs, New Delhi, January 16 and 18, 2008.

33. Walgreen, "China in the Indian Ocean Region"; Vijay Sakhuja, "Strategic Shift in Chinese Naval Strategy in Indian Ocean," no. 1899 (New Delhi: Institute of Peace and Conflict Studies, December 6, 2005); Lee, "China's Expanding Maritime Ambitions in the Western Pacific and the Indian Ocean."

34. People's Republic of China, State Council Information Office, *White Paper on National Defense* (Beijing: State Council Information Office, 2002–2008).

35. Andrew Selth, "Chinese Whispers: The Great Coco Island Mystery," *Irrawaddy* 15, no. 1 (2007) (www.irrawaddy.org/article.php?art_id=6640).

36. Interviews with official, Ministry of Defense, Bangkok, November 14, 2007; Ministry of Foreign Affairs, New Delhi, January 18, 2007.

37. Jonathan Holslag, "Myanmar in the Frontline" (briefing paper, ESISC, Brussels, January 29, 2006), 8.

38. Interviews with official, Ministry of Defense, Bangkok, November 14, 2007; Institute of Security and International Studies, Bangkok, November 15, 2007.

39. Telephone interviews with expert, Institute of Strategic Studies, Islamabad, January 3, 2008; European official, Brussels, December 22, 2007.

40. Interview with expert, CASS, Beijing, December 7, 2007.

41. Arindam Hazare, "Colombo Port Adds to India's China Woes," *Rediff*, October 29, 2007.

42. Interviews with expert, CASS, Beijing, December 7, 2007, and CICIR, Beijing, December 8, 2007; see also Zheng, "Assessing the Question of India's Rise."

43. Zhang Wenmu, "Sea Power and China's Strategic Choices," *China Security* 2, no. 2 (2006): 22. See also Zhang Wenmu, "Shijie diyuan zhengzhi tixi you Yindu weilai anquan," 49; Xu, "Maritime Geostrategy and the Development of the Chinese Navy in the Early 21st Century."

44. Sanjay Badri Maharaj and Arun Vishwakarma, "Evaluating India's Land-Based Missile Deterrent," *Indian Defence Review* 19, no. 4 (2004) (www.bharat-rakshak.com/SRR/Volume13/sanjay.html); Rajain, *Nuclear Deterrence in Southern Asia*.

45. Arun Vishwakarma, "Strategic Missiles," *India Defence Review* 22, no. 1 (2007) (www.bharat-rakshak.com/MISSILES/Images/Indian_Long_Range_StrategicMissiles_-Agni-III_r11.pdf).

46. Vishwakarma, "Strategic Missiles."

47. Rahul Bedi, "India Holds Back from Test Firing Agni III," *Jane's Defence Weekly*, May 23, 2006; Vishal Thapar, "Agni-III Raring to Go, Government Not Keen," CNN-IBN, May 15, 2006; Varun Sahni, "India and Missile Acquisition: Push and Pull Factors," *South Asian Survey* 11, no. 2 (2004): 287–99.

48. Neha Kumar, "India Ballistic Missile Defence Capabilities and Future Threats" (New Delhi: ICPS, 2007).

49. "India Needs to Eliminate Anxiety About China," *People's Daily*, June 9, 2001.

50. Zhang Ming, *China's Changing Nuclear Posture*, 46–47.

SIX. REGIONAL SECURITY COOPERATION

1. John Garver, "Sino-Indian Rivalry in Nepal: The Question of Arms Sales to Nepal," *Asian Survey* 31, no. 10 (1991): 956–75; Kant, "Nepal's China Policy"; Khadka, "Chinese Foreign Policy toward Nepal in the Cold War Period"; Lok Raj Baral, "Nepal's Security Policy and South Asian Regionalism"; Rabindra Mishra, "India's Role in Nepal's Maoist Insurgency," *Asian Survey* 44, no. 5 (2004): 627–46; Padmaja Murthy, "India and Nepal"; Maung Maung, "Sino-Burma Boundary Settlement"; C. P. FitzGerald, *China and Southeast Asia since 1945* (London: Longman, 1973), 54–62; Haacke, Myanmar's Foreign Policy, 16; Egreteau, *Wooing the Generals*. See also Rajain, *Nuclear Deterrence in Southern Asia*; Dittmer, *South Asia's Nuclear Security Dilemma*.

2. Garver, *Protracted Contest*.

3. See, for instance, Buzan, Wæver, and de Wilde, *Security*; Rick Fawn and Jeremy Larkins, eds., *International Society After the Cold War: Anarchy and Order Reconsidered* (London: Macmillan, 1996); Buzan and Wæver, *Regions and Powers*; Holger Stritzel, "Towards a Theory of Securitization," *European Journal of International Relations* 13, no. 3 (2007): 357.

4. Buzan and Wæver, *Regions and Powers*, 93–124.

5. Buzan, Wæver, and de Wilde, *Security*, 12; Robert Jervis, *Perception and Misperception in International Politics* (Princeton, N.J.: Princeton University Press, 1976).

6. Buzan, Wæver, and de Wilde, *Security*, 12; Deutsch et al., *Political Community and the North Atlantic Area*.

7. Ole Wæver, "Securitization and Desecuritization," in *On Security*, ed. Ronnie D. Lipschutz (New York: Columbia University Press, 1995); Stritzel, "Towards a Theory of Securitization."

8. "Enhanced Economic Cooperation to Promote Sino-Pakistani Ties," *People's Daily*, November 23, 2006.

9. Yan Liang, "China-Myanmar Economic Ties Make New Progress," Xinhua, December 9, 2007.

10. Interview with Chinese diplomat in Delhi, January 17, 2008. See also UN Comtrade statistical database 2008, http://comtrade.un.org/db/.

11. "Huge Mineral Resources Found on Qinghai-Tibet Plateau," Xinhua, February 13, 2007.

12. Keohane and Nye, *Power and Interdependence*, 10–11; Kenneth N. Waltz, *Theory of International Politics* (New York: Random House, 1979), 140. Vulnerability is

defined as the costs of changed transactions once remedial measures have been taken.

13. Roy and Banerjee, *Understanding India's Economic Security*.

14. Interview with Ministry of Foreign Affairs official, Bangkok, November 20, 2007.

15. "Worsening Drug Trafficking Poses New Challenge to China," *China Daily*, February 14, 2007.

16. "Chinese Marine Police Hurt in Myanmar Shootout," *Straits Times*, February 25, 2008.

17. Kudo, *Myanmar's Economic Relations with China*.

18. "Maoist Threat Forces Indians Out of Nepal," *Hindu Times*, April 7, 2005.

19. "Anti-India Sentiment Sweeps Nepal," *Hindu*, April 24, 2006.

20. Rand global terrorism database; Memorial Institute for the Prevention of Terrorism Knowledge Base.

21. Krishna Hari Pushkar, "India's Neighbourhood Intervention in Madhesh," *Nepal Monitor*, February 14, 2008; Sanjaya Dhakal, "Terror in Terai: Missing Seriousness," *Nepali Times*, January 10, 2007.

22. Ajit Kumar Singh, *India-Nepal: Subversion without Borders* (New Delhi: Institute for Conflict Management, 2006); Prashant Jha, "Open Border, Closed Minds," *Nepali Times*, October 5–11, 2007.

23. "Pak's Nepal Embassy a Hub for ISI Activities," *Daily Excelsior*, January 9, 2002.

24. "Ultras Surrender after Getting Trained in Pak," *Tribune*, June 28, 2006.

25. Hayder Mili, "Xinjiang: An Emerging Narco-Islamist Corridor?" *Terrorism Monitor* 3 (April 21, 2005).

26. "China Admits to Terrorist Camps in Pakistan," *Indian Express*, April 19, 2007.

27. John Pomfret, "Asian Leaders Target Muslim Extremists," *Washington Post*, June 16, 2001.

28. "China Forces Raid Terrorist Camp near Pakistan," Associated Press, January 8, 2007.

29. Ziad Haider, "Sino-Pakistan Relations and Xinjiang's Uighurs: Politics, Trade, and Islam along the Karakoram Highway," *Asian Survey* 45, no. 4 (2005): 522–45; M. Ehsan Ahrari, "China, Pakistan, and the 'Taliban Syndrome.'"

30. Robert O. Keohane, "The Globalization of Informal Violence, Theories of World Politics, and the 'Liberalism of Fear,'" *Dialogue IO* 1 (2002): 29–43.

31. Wæver, "Securitization and Desecuritization."

32. Stritzel, "Towards a Theory of Securitization." See also Thierry Balzacq, "The Three Faces of Securitization: Political Agency, Audience and Context," *European Journal of International Relations* 11, no. 2 (2005): 171–201.

33. E-mail interview with Indian expert at the IDSA, February 15, 2008.

34. "China, India, Laos, Myanmar, Thailand Pledge Joint Efforts on Drug Control," Xinhua, July 24, 2003.

35. "Five-Nation Meet to Firm Up Drug Control Strategies," *Tribune*, January 11, 2006.

36. Subhash Kapila, "India's Strategically Unwise Nepal Policy," *Hindu Times*, September 1, 2005.

37. Dabhade and Pant, "Coping with Challenges to Sovereignty."

38. Ibid., 166.

39. "Nepal Monarchy Showing Signs of Weakness in the Middle of Drifting into Directionless Foreign Policy," *India Daily*, April 1, 2005.

40. "Chinese 'Deliver Arms to Nepal,'" BBC News, November 25, 2005.

41. "Chinese Security Deployed in Nepal after Tibet Unrest," AFP, March 15, 2008.

42. "China in Favour of Unity among Constitutional Forces: Tang," *Nepal News*, March 17, 2006.

43. "China Not Shunning Maoists in Nepal," *Himalayan Times*, June 21, 2007.

44. "Yafei Tells PM China Is Ready to Support Nepal," *Nepal News*, March 3, 2008.

45. "Nepal: No Dictates from China, Only Suggestions!" *Nepal Telegraph*, May 12, 2007.

46. Garver, "China's Kashmir Policies"; C. Raja Mohan, "Ladakh: Gateway to Central Asia," *Hindu*, August 23, 2004; Rajeev Ranjan Chaturvedy, *Chinese Strategy in the High Himalayas*, IDSA Strategic Comments (New Delhi: Institute for Defence Studies and Analyses, November 21, 2006); Mohan Malik, "The China Factor in the India-Pakistan Conflict," *Parameters*, spring 2003, 35–50; Tarique Niazi, *China, Pakistan, and Terrorism*, FPIF Commentary (Washington, D.C.: Foreign Policy in Focus, July 16, 2007).

47. Zhang Minqiu, *Zhongyin guanxi yanjiu*; Zhang Guihong, "Sino-Indian Security Relations."

48. Interviews with two Chinese Ministry of Commerce officials, Beijing, December 19, 2007. See also Ma Jiali, "Yinba guanxi huinuan de beihou" (Behind the Indo-Pakistani Thaw), *Xiandai guoji guanxi* 2 (February 2004): 43–44; Liu, "Yinba guanxi huanhe"; Wang Dong, "Yinba guanxi de bianhua yu Keshimier wenti."

49. E-mail interview with scholar at Fudan University, Shanghai, and the CICIR, Beijing, March 12, 2008.

50. E-mail interview with scholar at CASS, Beijing, April 1, 2008.

51. Interview with Chinese diplomat, New Delhi, January 17, 2008.

52. This is a conservative figure; see International Monetary Fund, Statistics Department, Direction of Trade Statistics, 2008 (www.imfstatistics.org/DOT).

53. Interview with expert at the CIIS, Brussels, April 27, 2008.

54. Ibid.

55. Ibid.

56. "China Announces U.S.$500 Million Aid to Pakistan," *Nation*, November 13, 2008.

57. "Chinese FM Felicitates Qureshi," *Pakistan Times*, April 2, 2008.

58. "China, Pakistan Vow to Boost Military Cooperation," *Pakistan Times*, April 3, 2008.

59. Department of Public Information, News and Media Division, *Speed Up Myanmar Reconciliation Process, Urges Secretary-General* (New York: United Nations, October 5, 2007).

60. *Statement on Myanmar at the United Nations Security Council Open Briefing, by H. E. Ambassador Wang Guangya, Permanent Representative of the People's Republic of China to the UN*, October 5, 2007 (www.china-un.org/eng/hyyfy/t369705.htm).

61. Lin, "Miandian guonei zhengzhi he guoji guanxi xianzhuang."

62. "Senior General Than Shwe and President Mr Hu Jintao Hold Talks," *New Light of Myanmar*, April 27, 2005.

63. "Prime Minister Wen Jiabao Meets Soe Win," Ministry of Commerce, Beijing, July 9, 2005.

64. Jonathan Holslag, "Myanmar in the Frontline" (briefing paper, ESISC, Brussels, January 29, 2006), 8.

65. Ibid. See also Brian McCartan, "Myanmar Deal Right Neighborly of India," *Asia Times*, January 11, 2008.

66. Zou Keyuan, "China's Possible Role in Myanmar's National Reconciliation," *Copenhagen Journal of Asian Studies* 17, no. 1 (2003): 59–77.

67. Kudo, *Myanmar's Economic Relations with China*.

68. Interview with Indian diplomat, Singapore, January 24, 2008.

69. Ibid.; interview with expert at the Institute of Security and International Studies, Bangkok, November 21, 2007.

CONCLUSION

1. A discussion about the relevance of trade expectations can be found in Copeland, "Economic Interdependence and War," 4–41.

2. Keohane and Nye, *Power and Interdependence*, 22–36.

3. Rosecrance, *Rise of the Trading State*, 9.

4. Interview with Ministry of Foreign Affairs official, Beijing, June 26, 2008.

5. Von Metternich, Klemens, *Metternich: The Autobiography, 1773–1815* (London: Ravenhall, 2005), 139.

BIBLIOGRAPHY

Abraham, Filip, and Jan Van Hove. "The Rise of China: Prospects of Regional Trade Policy." *Review of World Economics* 141, no. 3 (2005): 486–509.

Acharya, Amitav. *Constructing a Security Community in Southeast Asia.* London: Routledge, 2001.

Adeney, Katharine, and Marie Lall. "Institutional Attempts to Build a 'National' Identity in India." *India Review* 4, nos. 3–4 (2005): 258–86.

Ahluwalia, Isher Judge, and I. M. D. Little, eds. *India's Economic Reforms and Development: Essays for Manmohan Singh.* New Delhi: Oxford University Press, 1998.

Ahluwalia, Montek Singh. "Economic Reforms in India Since 1991: Has Gradualism Worked?" *Journal of Economic Perspectives* 16, no. 3 (2002): 67–88.

——. "Understanding India's Reform Trajectory: Past Trends and Future Challenges." *India Review* 3, no. 4 (2004): 269–77.

Ahrari, M. Ehsan. "China, Pakistan, and the 'Taliban Syndrome.'" *Asian Survey* 40, no. 4 (2000): 658–71.

Ahrari, Mohammed E. *Dynamics of Oil Diplomacy: Conflict and Consensus.* New York: Arno Press, 1980.

Albert, Mathias, et al. *Identities, Borders, Orders: Rethinking International Relations Theory.* Minneapolis: University of Minnesota Press, 2001.

Andrews-Speed, Philip, Xuanli Liao, and Roland Dannreuther. *The Strategic Implications of China's Energy Needs.* Adelphi Papers 346. Oxford: Oxford University Press, 2002.

Asher, Mukul G., and Rahul Sen. *India–East Asia Integration: A Win-Win for Asia.* RIS Discussion Papers 91. New Delhi: RIS, 2005.

Bahgat, Gawdat. "Pipeline Diplomacy: The Geopolitics of the Caspian Sea Region." *International Studies Perspectives* 3, no. 3 (2002): 310–28.

Baral, J. K., J. K. Mohapatra, and S. P. Mishra. "Rajiv Gandhi's China Diplomacy: Dynamics and Problems." *International Studies* 26, no. 3 (1989): 257–70.

Baral, Lok Raj. "Nepal's Security Policy and South Asian Regionalism." *Asian Survey* 26, no. 11 (1986): 1207–19.

Bates, Robert. "Area Studies and the Discipline: A Useful Controversy?" *Political Science and Politics* 30, no. 2 (1997): 166–69.

Bayne, Nicholas, and Stephen Woolcock, eds. *The New Economic Diplomacy: Decision-Making and Negotiation in International Economic Relations.* London: Ashgate, 2003.

Beeson, Mark, ed. *Contemporary Southeast Asia: Regional Dynamics, National Differences.* New York: Palgrave Macmillan, 2004.

Bhattacharya, B. B., and S. Sakthivel. *Economic Reforms and Jobless Growth in India in the 1990s.* New Delhi: Institute of Economic Growth, 2005.

Bhattacharya, Swapan K., and Biswa N. Bhattacharyay. *Free Trade Agreement between People's Republic of China and India: Likely Impact and Its Implications to Asian Economic Community.* ADB Institute Discussion Papers, no. 59. Tokyo: Asian Development Bank Institute, 2006.

Bhattacharyay, Biswa, and Prabir De. "Promotion of Trade and Investment between People's Republic of China and India: Toward a Regional Perspective." *Asian Development Review* 22, no. 1 (2005): 45–70.

BJP. *BJP Election Manifesto 1998.* New Delhi: BJP, 1998 (www.bjp.org/content/view/2626/428).

——. *For a Strong and Prosperous India.* New Delhi: BJP, 1996 (www.bjp.org/content/blogcategory/97/428).

——. *Vision Document 2004.* New Delhi: BJP, 2004.

Brass, Paul. *The Politics of India since Independence.* Cambridge: Cambridge University Press, 1990.

Brecher, Michael. *Nehru: A Political Biography.* Oxford: Oxford University Press, 1959.

——. "Non-Alignment Under Stress: The West and the India-China Border War." *Pacific Affairs* 52, no. 4 (1979): 612–30.

Buzan, Barry. "Security Architecture in Asia: The Interplay of Regional and Global Levels." *Pacific Review* 16, no. 2 (2003): 143–73.

Buzan, Barry, and Ole Wæver. *Regions and Powers: The Structure of International Security.* Cambridge: Cambridge University Press, 2003.

Buzan, Barry, Ole Wæver, and Jaap de Wilde. *Security: A New Framework for Analysis.* London: Lynne Rienner, 1997.

Camilleri, Joseph A. *Chinese Foreign Policy: The Maoist Era and Its Aftermath.* Oxford: Robertson, 1980.

Chan, Thomas, Noel Tracy, and Zhu Wenhui. *China's Export Miracle: Origins, Results, and Prospects.* London: Macmillan, 1999.

Chaturvedi, Sachin. *Trade Facilitation Measures in South Asian FTAs: An Overview of Initiatives and Policy Approaches.* RIS Working Papers 118. New Delhi: RIS, 2006.

Chen Zhimin. "Nationalism, Internationalism and Chinese Foreign Policy." *Journal of Contemporary China* 14, no. 42 (2005): 35–53.

Cheng, Tun-jen, Jacques deLisle, and Deborah Brown, eds. *China under Hu Jintao: Opportunities, Dangers and Dilemmas.* Singapore: World Scientific, 2006.

Cheung, Peter T. Y., Jae Ho Chung, and Zhimin Lin, eds. *Provincial Strategies of Economic Reform in Post-Mao China: Leadership, Politics, and Implementation.* Armonk, N.Y.: M. E. Sharpe, 1998.

Choudhury, G. W. *India, Pakistan, Bangladesh, and the Major Powers: Politics of a Divided Subcontinent.* New York: Free Press, 1975.

Chung, Chien-peng. *Domestic Politics, International Bargaining and China's Territorial Disputes.* London: Routledge, 2004.

Chung, Tan, ed. *Across the Himalayan Gap: An Indian Quest for Understanding China.* New Delhi: Vedam, 1998.

Cohen, Benjamin. *Crossing Frontiers: Explorations in International Political Economy.* Boulder, Colo.: Westview Press, 1991.

Cohen, Stephen Philip. *India: Emerging Power.* Washington, D.C.: Brookings Institution Press, 2001.

Congress Party. *Security, Defence and Foreign Policy.* New Delhi: Congress Party, 2004 (www.congresssandesh.com/manifesto-2004/17.html).

Copeland, David S. "Economic Interdependence and War." *International Security* 20, no. 4 (1996): 4–41.

Cordesman, Anthony H., and Khalid R. Al-Rodhan. *The Global Oil Market: Risks and Uncertainties.* Washington, D.C.: Center for Strategic and International Studies, 2006.

Crawford, Beverly, and Ronnie D. Lipschutz, eds. *The Myth of "Ethnic Conflict": Politics, Economics, and "Cultural" Violence.* Berkeley: University of California Press, 1998.

Crawford, Neta. "The Passion of World Politics." *International Security* 24, no. 2 (2000): 116–56.

Dabhade, Manish, and Harsh Pant. "Coping with Challenges to Sovereignty: Sino-Indian Rivalry and Nepal's Foreign Policy." *Contemporary South Asia* 13, no. 2 (2004): 157–69.

Das, Gurudas, N. Bijoy Singh, and C. J. Thomas, eds. *Indo-Myanmar Border Trade: Status, Problems and Potential.* New Delhi: Akansha, 2005.

Das, Gurudas, and R. K. Purkayastha, eds. *Border Trade: North-East India and Neighbouring Countries.* New Delhi: Akansha, 2002.

De, Prabir. "Cooperation in the Regional Transportation Infrastructure Sector in South Asia." *Contemporary South Asia* 14, no. 3 (2005): 267–88.

Denoon, David B. "Cycles in Indian Economic Liberalization, 1966–1996." *Comparative Politics* 31, no. 1 (1998): 43–60.

Deshingkar, Giri. "India-China Relations: The Nehru Years." *China Report* 27, no. 1 (1991): 96–100.

Deutsch, Karl, et al. *Political Community and the North Atlantic Area.* Princeton, N.J.: Princeton University Press, 1957.

Dittmer, Lowell, ed. *South Asia's Nuclear Security Dilemma: India, Pakistan, and China*. New Delhi: Pentagon Press, 2005.

Dixit, J. N. *India-Pakistan in War and Peace*. New York: Routledge, 2002.

Dossani, Rafiq, and Srinidhi Vijaykumar. *Indian Federalism and the Conduct of Foreign Policy in Border States*. Stanford, Calif.: Stanford University, Shorenstein APARC, 2005.

Downs, Erica Strecker. *China's Quest for Energy Security*. Arlington, Va.: Rand, 2000.

Doyle, Michael W. *Ways of War and Peace: Realism, Liberalism, and Socialism*. New York: Norton, 1997.

Ebel, Robert E. *China's Energy Future: The Middle Kingdom Seeks Its Place in the Sun*. Washington, D.C.: Center for Strategic and International Studies, 2005.

Edelstein, David M. "Managing Uncertainty: Beliefs About the Intentions of Great Powers." *Security Studies* 12, no. 1 (2002): 1–40.

Edwardes, Michael. "Illusion and Reality in India's Foreign Policy." *International Affairs* 41, no. 1 (1965): 48–58.

Egreteau, Renaud. *Wooing the Generals: India's New Burma Policy*. New Delhi: Authorspress, 2003.

Erdman, Howard L. *The Swatantra Party and Indian Conservatism*. Cambridge: Cambridge University Press, 1967.

Frank, Katherine. *Indira: The Life of Indira Nehru Gandhi*. Boston: Houghton Mifflin, 2002.

Frankel, Francine. *India's Political Economy, 1947–1977*. Princeton, N.J.: Princeton University Press, 1978.

Gandhi, Indira. "India and the World." *Foreign Affairs* 51, no. 1 (1972): 65–77.

Gandhi, Rajiv. "Foreword." In *7th Five Year Plan*. New Delhi: Planning Commission, 1985.

Ganguly, Sumit. *The Origins of War in South Asia: Indo-Pakistani Conflicts since 1947*. Boulder, Colo.: Westview Press, 1986.

——. *Unending Conflict: India-Pakistan Tensions since 1947*. New York: Columbia University Press, 2002.

Gao Shangquan. *China's Economic Reform*. London: Macmillan, 1996.

Garver, John W. "China's Kashmir Policies." *India Review* 3, no. 1 (2004): 1–24.

——. "Development of China's Overland Transportation Links with Central, South-west and South Asia." *China Quarterly* 185, no. 1 (2006): 1–22.

——. "The Indian Factor in Recent Sino-Soviet Relations." *China Quarterly* 125 (1991): 55–85.

——. *Protracted Contest: Sino-Indian Rivalry in the Twentieth Century*. Oxford: Oxford University Press, 2001.

——. "The Restoration of Sino-Indian Comity Following India's Nuclear Tests." *China Quarterly* 168, no. 4 (2001): 865–89.

——. "The Security Dilemma in Sino-Indian Relations." *India Review* 1, no. 4 (2002): 1–38.

Ghosh, Partha S. "Foreign Policy and Electoral Politics in India: Inconsequential Connection." *Asian Survey* 34, no. 9 (1994): 807–17.

Ghuman, B. S. "Public Enterprises in India: Phases of Reform in the 1990s." *Asian Journal of Public Administration* 21, no. 2 (1999): 220–33.

Goodman, David S. G., and Gerald Segal, eds. *China Deconstructs: Politics, Trade and Regionalism*. New York: Routledge, 1995.

Gopal, Sarvepalli. *Jawaharlal Nehru: A Biography*. 3 vols. Oxford: Oxford University Press, 1974.

Government of India, Ministry of External Affairs. *Report of the India-China Joint Study Group on Comprehensive Trade and Economic Cooperation*. New Delhi: Ministry of External Affairs, April 2005.

Goyal, Sanjeev, and Sumit Joshi. "Bilateralism and Free Trade." *International Economic Review* 47, no. 3 (2006): 749–78.

Graff, David A., and Robin Higham, eds. *A Military History of China*. Boulder, Colo.: Westview Press, 2002.

Griffin, Keith. *Alternative Strategies for Economic Development*. London: Macmillan, 1989.

Grover, V. K. "India: The Need for a Post Cold War Foreign Policy." *India Quarterly* 57, no. 1 (2001): 171–76.

Gujral, L. K. *A Foreign Policy for India*. New Delhi: External Publicity Division, Ministry of External Affairs, Government of India, 1998.

Gulati, M. N. *Pakistan's Downfall in Kashmir: The Three Indo-Pak Wars*. Delhi: Manas, 2001.

Guo Zhengyuan. "Xiao Bushi zhengfu dui Hua zhengce zouxiang jiqi dui Zhongmei anquan guanxi de yingxiang" (The Orientation of the Bush Administration's China Policy and Its Impact on Sino-U.S. Security Relations). *Heping yu fazhan* 8, no. 3 (2001): 31–38.

Haacke, Jürgen. *Myanmar's Foreign Policy: Domestic Influences and International Implications*. Adelphi Papers 381. London: International Institute for Strategic Studies, 2006.

Haas, Ernst B. *The Uniting of Europe: Political, Social, and Economic Forces, 1950–1957*. Stanford, Calif.: Stanford University Press, 1958.

Hankla, Charles R. *Party Linkages and Economic Policy: An Examination of Indira Gandhi's India*. Atlanta: Georgia State University, 2005.

Heath, Oliver. "Party Systems, Political Cleavages and Electoral Volatility in India: A State-Wise Analysis." *Electoral Studies* 24, no. 2 (2005): 177–99.

Helleiner, Eric, and Andreas Pickel, eds. *Economic Nationalism in a Globalizing World*. Ithaca, N.Y.: Cornell University Press, 2005.

Hoffmann, Steven. "Rethinking the Linkage between Tibet and the China-India Border Conflict: A Realist Approach." *Cold War Studies* 27, no. 1 (2006): 75–100.

Jakobson, Linda, and Zha Daojiong. "China and the Worldwide Search for Oil Security." *Asia-Pacific Review* 13, no. 2 (2006): 60–73.

Jayasuriya, Kanishka, ed. *Asian Regional Governance: Crisis and Change*. London: Routledge, 2004.

Jeffrey, Robin. *What's Happening to India? Punjab, Ethnic Conflict, Mrs. Gandhi's Death, and the Test for Federalism*. New York: Holmes and Meier, 1986.

Jenkins, Rob. "India's States and the Making of Foreign Economic Policy: The Limits of the Constituent Diplomacy Paradigm." *Journal of Federalism* 33, no. 4 (2003): 63–82.

——. "Labor Policy and the Second Generation of Economic Reform in India." *The Politics of India's Next Generation of Economic Reforms*, special issue, *India Review* 3, no. 2 (2004).

Johnston, Alastair Iain. "Is China a Status Quo Power?" *International Security* 27, no. 4 (2003): 5–56.

Joshi, Vijay, and I. M. D. Little. *India: Macroeconomics and Political Economy, 1964–1991*. Washington, D.C.: World Bank, 1994.

Kang, David C. "Getting Asia Wrong." *International Security* 27, no. 4 (2003): 57–85.

——. "Hierarchy, Balancing and Empirical Relations." *International Security* 28, no. 3 (2004): 165–80.

Kant, Rama. "Nepal's China Policy." *China Report* 30, no. 2 (1994): 161–73.

Kapstein, Ethan B., and Michael Mastanduno, eds. *Unipolar Politics: Realism and State Strategies After the Cold War*. New York: Columbia University Press, 1999.

Karunaratine, Gregory. "The Failure of the Community Development Programme in India." *Community Development Journal* 11, no. 1 (1976): 95–119.

Katzenstein, Peter J. "Regionalism in Comparative Perspective." *Cooperation and Conflict* 31, no. 2 (1996): 123–59.

Keohane, Robert O., and Joseph S. Nye. *Power and Interdependence: World Politics in Transition*. Boston: Little, Brown, 1977.

Kerr, David. "Greater China and East Asian Integration: Regionalism and Rivalry." *East Asia* 21, no. 1 (2004): 75–92.

Khadka, Narayan. "Chinese Foreign Policy toward Nepal in the Cold War Period." *China Report* 35, no. 1 (1999): 61–81.

Kohli, Atul. *Democracy and Discontent: India's Growing Crisis of Governability*. New York: Cambridge University Press, 1990.

——. *Politics of Economic Growth in India, 1980–2005*. Princeton, N.J.: Princeton University Press, 2005.

——. "Politics of Economic Liberalization in India." *World Development* 17, no. 3 (1989): 305–28.

Kothari, Rajni. "The Congress 'System' in India." *Asian Survey* 4, no. 2 (1964): 1161–73.

Kreisberg, Paul. "India After Indira." *Foreign Affairs* 61, no. 4 (1985) (www.foreignaffairs.com/articles/39634/paul-h-kreisberg/india-after-indira).

Krishna, Sankaran. *Postcolonial Insecurities: India, Sri Lanka, and the Question of Nationhood*. Minneapolis: University of Minnesota Press, 1999.

Kudo, Toshihiro. *Myanmar's Economic Relations with China: Can China Support the Myanmar Economy?* Institute of Developing Economies Discussion Papers, no. 66. Chiba, Japan: Institute of Developing Economies, 2006.

Kumar, Nagesh, et al. *Towards an Employment-Oriented Export Strategy: Some Explorations*. New Delhi: Research and Information System for Developing Countries, 2006.

Kumar, Nagesh, Rahul Sen, and Mukul Asher, eds. *India-ASEAN Economic Relations: Meeting the Challenges of Globalization*. New Delhi: RIS, 2006.

Kurian, Nimmi. *Emerging China and India's Policy Options*. New Delhi: Lancers, 2006.

Lahiri, Sajal, ed. *Regionalism and Globalization: Theory and Practice*. London: Routledge, 2001.

Lake, David A., and Patrick M. Morgan. *Regional Orders: Building Security in a New World*. University Park: Penn State Press, 1997.

Lall, Marie. "Indo-Myanmar Relations in the Era of Pipeline Diplomacy." *Contemporary Southeast Asia* 28, no. 3 (2006): 424–46.

Lampton, David M., ed. *The Making of Chinese Foreign and Security Policy in the Era of Reform*. Stanford, Calif.: Stanford University Press, 2001.

Lardy, Nicolas R. *Agriculture in China's Modern Economic Development*. Cambridge: Cambridge University Press, 1983.

——. *Foreign Trade and Economic Reform in China, 1978–1990*. Cambridge: Cambridge University Press, 1992.

Larson, Deborah Welch. *Origins of Containment: A Psychological Explanation*. Princeton, N.J.: Princeton University Press, 1989.

Lee Jae-Hyung. "China's Expanding Maritime Ambitions in the Western Pacific and the Indian Ocean." *Contemporary Southeast Asia* 24, no. 3 (2002): 553–54.

Lim, Robyn. *The Geopolitics of East Asia: The Search for Equilibrium*. New York: Routledge 2003.

Lin, Xixing. "Miandian guonei zhengzhi he guoji guanxi xianzhuang" (The Present Situation of Myanmar's Internal Politics and International Relations). *Dongnanya yanjiu*, March 2004, 8–17.

Liu, Yi. "Yinba guanxi huanhe: Yuanyin yu qushi" (Indo-Pakistani Rapprochement: Reasons and Trends). *Dangdai Ya Tai* 3 (March 2004): 29–33.

Lord, Montague J. *Imperfect Competition and International Commodity Trade: Theory, Dynamics, and Policy Modelling*. Oxford: Oxford University Press, 1991.

Low, L. "Multilateralism, Regionalism, Bilateral and Cross-Regional Free Trade Arrangements: All Paved with Good Intentions for ASEAN?" *Asian Economic Journal* 17, no. 1 (2003): 65–86.

Luo, Xongfei and Zhao Jian. "Yindu dui Hua zhengce de tiaozheng yu Zhongyin guanxi de weilai zouxiang" (India's Policy Adjustment Toward China and Tendency of China-India Relations). *Nanya yanjiu* 2 (2003): 25–29.

Ma, Jiali. *Guanzhu Yindu: Jueqi zhong de daguo* (Focus on India: Emerging Power). Tianjin: Renmin chubanshe, 2002.

——. "Yindu xingshi de huigu yu zhanwang" (India: Review and Forecast). *Xiandai guoji guanxi* 2 (2001): 54–58.

——. "Yindu zhanlue diwei tuxian" (India's Elevating Strategic Position). *Heping yu fazhan* 7, no. 4 (2000): 9–16.

Mancall, Mark. *China at the Center: 300 Years of Foreign Policy*. New York: Free Press, 1986.

Mansingh, Lalit. *Indian Foreign Policy: Agenda for the 21st Century.* Vol. 1. New Delhi: Foreign Service Institute, 1997.

Mansingh, Surjit. "India-China Relations in the Post–Cold War Era." *Asian Survey* 24, no. 3 (1994): 285–300.

———. *India's Search for Power: Indira Gandhi's Foreign Policy, 1966–1982.* New Delhi: Sage, 1985.

Maung Maung. "The Sino-Burma Boundary Settlement." *Asian Survey* 1, no. 1 (1961): 38–43.

Maxwell, Neville. *India's China War.* London: Cape, 1970.

———. "India's Forward Policy." *China Quarterly* 45 (1970): 157–63.

Mehra, Parshotam. "India's Border Dispute with China: Revisiting Nehru's Approach." *International Studies* 42, nos. 3–4 (2005): 357–65.

Mehta, Rajesh. *Economic Co-operation between India and Singapore: A Feasibility Study.* RIS Discussion Papers 41. New Delhi: RIS, 2003.

Mehta, Rajesh, and S. Narayanan. *India's Regional Trading Arrangements.* RIS Working Papers 114. New Delhi: RIS, 2005.

Men, Jing. "The Construction of the China-ASEAN Free Trade Area: A Study of China's Active Involvement." *Global Society* 21, no. 2 (2006): 249–68.

Metcalf, Barbara D., and Thomas R. Metcalf. *A Concise History of India.* Cambridge: Cambridge University Press, 2002.

Mohan, Raja C. *Crossing the Rubicon: The Shaping of India's New Foreign Policy.* New Delhi: Viking, 2003.

Mukherji, Indra Nath, Tilana Jayawardhana, and Saman Kelegama. *Indo–Sri Lanka Free Trade Agreement: An Assessment of Potential and Impact.* Islamabad: South Asia Network of Economic Research Institutes, 2004.

Murayama, Mayumi, Kyoko Inoue, and Sanjoy Hazarika. *Sub-Regional Relations in Eastern South Asia: With Special Focus on India's North Eastern Region.* Joint Research Program Series, no.133. Chiba, Japan: Institute of Developing Economies, 2005.

Murthy, Padmaja. "India and Nepal: Security and Economic Dimensions." *Strategic Analysis* 28, no. 9 (1999): 1531–47.

Nanda, B. R., ed. *Indian Foreign Policy: The Nehru Years.* Honolulu: University of Hawai'i Press, 1976.

Nandakumar, J. "Sino-Indian Cooperation in the Search for Overseas Petroleum Resources: Prospects and Implications for India." *International Journal of Energy Sector Management* 1, no. 1 (2007): 84–95.

Naughton, Barry. *Growing Out of the Plan: Chinese Economic Reform, 1978–1993.* Cambridge: Cambridge University Press, 1995.

Nayar, Baldev Raj, and T. V. Paul. *India in the World Order: Searching for Major-Power Status.* Cambridge: Cambridge University Press, 2003.

Nehru, Jawaharlal. *The Discovery of India.* Oxford: Oxford University Press, 1956.

Oksenberg, Michel, and James Tong. "The Evolution of Central-Provincial Fiscal Relations in China, 1971–1984." *China Quarterly* 125 (1991): 1–32.

Panda, Pramoda Kumar. *Making of India's Foreign Policy: Prime Ministers and Wars.* New Delhi: Raj, 2003.

Pandian, S. "The Political Economy of Trans-Pakistan Gas Pipeline Project: Assessing the Political and Economic Risks for India." *Energy Policy* 33, no. 5 (2005): 659–70.

Paranjpe, Shrikant. *Parliament and the Making of Indian Foreign Policy.* Pune: University of Pune, 1997.

Paul, T. V., ed. *The India-Pakistan Conflict: An Enduring Rivalry.* Cambridge: Cambridge University Press, 2005.

——. "Soft Balancing in the Age of U.S. Primacy." *International Security* 30, no. 1 (2005): 46–71.

Payne, Anthony, ed. *The New Regional Politics of Development.* New York: Palgrave Macmillan, 2004.

Pempel, T. J., ed. *Remapping East Asia: The Construction of a Region.* Ithaca, N.Y.: Cornell University Press, 2005.

Perkovich, George. *India's Nuclear Bomb: The Impact on Global Proliferation.* Berkeley: University of California Press, 1999.

——. "Is India a Major Power?" *Washington Quarterly* 27, no. 1 (2003): 129–44.

Poncet, Sandra. "A Fragmented China: Measure and Determinants of Chinese Domestic Market Disintegration." *Review of International Economics* 13, no. 3 (2005): 409–30.

Poon, Jess P. H. "Regionalism in the Asia Pacific: Is Geography Destiny?" *Area* 33, no. 3 (2001): 252–60.

Putnam, Robert D. "Diplomacy and Domestic Politics: The Logic of Two-Level Games." *International Organization* 42, no. 3 (1998): 427–60.

Qureshi, Mahvash Saeed, and Guanghua Wan. *Trade Expansion of China and India: Threat or Opportunity?* Helsinki: World Institute for Development Economics Research, 2008.

Rai, Ajai K. "Diplomacy and the News Media: A Comment on the Indian Experience." *Strategic Analysis* 27, no. 1 (2003): 21–40.

Rajain, Arpit. *Nuclear Deterrence in Southern Asia: China, India and Pakistan.* New Delhi: Sage, 2005.

Rana, Kishan S. "Economic Diplomacy in India: A Practitioner's Perspective." *International Studies Perspectives* 5, no. 1 (2004): 66–70.

——. "Inside the Indian Foreign Service." *Foreign Service Journal* 80, no. 3 (2003): 28–36.

Rao, M. Govinda, and Nirvikar Singh. *The Political Economy of India's Federal System and Its Reform.* Santa Cruz: University of California, 2004.

Ray, Jayanta Kumar, and Prabir De, eds. *India and China in an Era of Globalisation: Essays on Economic Cooperation.* New Delhi: Bookwell, 2005.

Ren, Fei. "Bushi di er renqi nei de Yinmei guanxi jiqi zouxiang" (India-U.S. Relations in President Bush's Second Term). *Nanya yanjiu* 2 (2005): 26–30.

Rodrik, Dani, and Arvind Subramanian. *From "Hindu Growth" to Productivity Surge: The Mystery of the Indian Growth Transition.* IMF Working Papers. Washington, D.C.: IMF, 2004.

Roland-Holst, David, and John Weiss. "People's Republic of China and Its Neighbours: Evidence on Regional Trade and Investment Effects." *Asian Pacific Economic Literature* 19, no. 2 (2005): 18–35.

Rosecrance, Richard. *The Rise of the Trading State: Commerce and Conquest in the Modern World.* New York: Basic Books, 1986.

Rosenau, James N., and Ernst-Otto Czempiel, eds. *Governance Without Government: Order and Change in World Politics.* Cambridge: Cambridge University Press, 1992.

Ross, Robert. "The Geography of the Peace: East Asia in the Twenty-first Century." *International Security* 23, no. 4 (1999): 81–118.

Roy, Jayanta, and Pritam Banerjee. *Understanding India's Economic Security.* New Delhi: Confederation of Indian Industry, 2007.

Sachdeva, Gulshan. "Attitude towards China's Growing Influence in Central Asia." *China and Eurasia Forum Quarterly* 4, no. 3 (2006): 224–59.

Schaffer, T., and S. A. Hemani. "India: A Fragmented Democracy." *Washington Quarterly* 4 (1999): 143–50.

Schiff, Maurice, and L. Alan Winters. *Regional Integration and Development.* Washington, D.C.: International Bank for Reconstruction and Development / World Bank, 2003.

Schulz, Michael, Fredrik Söderbaum, and Joakim Öjendal, eds. *Regionalization in a Globalizing World.* London: Zed, 2001.

Scobell, Andrew. *China's Use of Military Force.* Cambridge: Cambridge University Press, 2003.

Scott, David. "India's Grand Strategy for the Indian Ocean: Mahanian Visions." *Asia-Pacific Review* 13, no. 2 (2006): 192–211.

Sen, Rahul. "New Regionalism in Asia: A Comparative Analysis of Emerging Regional and Bilateral Trading Agreements Involving ASEAN, China and India." *Journal of World Trade* 40, no. 4 (2006): 553–96.

Sen Gupta, Bhabani. *Rajiv Gandhi: A Politcal Study.* Delhi: Konark, 1989.

Sharma, S. R. *Foundations of Indian Foreign Policy.* New Delhi: Omsons, 2002.

Sheives, Kevin. "China Turns West: Beijing's Contemporary Strategy towards Central Asia." *Pacific Affairs* 79, no. 2 (2006): 205–35.

Sheng Lijun. *China-ASEAN Free Trade Area: Origins, Developments and Strategic Motivations.* ISEAS Working Papers: International Politics and Security Issues Series, no. 1 (2003). Singapore: Institute of Southeast Asian Studies, 2003.

Sheth, D. L., ed. *Citizens and Parties: Aspects of Competitive Politics in India.* New Delhi: Allied Publishers, 1975.

Shivam, Ravinder K. *India's Foreign Policy: Nehru to Vajpayee.* New Delhi: Commonwealth, 2001.

Sidhu, W. P. S. *The Evolution of India's Nuclear Doctrine.* New Delhi: Centre for Policy Research, 2004.

Sisson, Richard, and Leo E. Rose. *War and Secession: Pakistan, India, and the Creation of Bangladesh*. Berkeley: University of California Press, 1990.

Smith, David. *The Dragon and the Elephant: China, India and the New World Order*. London: Profile, 2007.

Song, Zhihui. "Shixi Yinri guanxi jiqi dui Zhongyin guanxi de yingxiang" (An Analysis of the Impact of India-Japan Relations on Sino-Indian Relations). *Nanya yanjiu jikan* 2 (February 2006): 70–74.

Srinivasan, T. N., and Suresh D. Tendulkar. *Reintegrating India with the World Economy*. New Delhi: Oxford University Press, 2003.

Srivastava, C. P. *Lal Bahadur Shastri: A Life of Truth in Politics*. New Delhi: Oxford University Press, 1995.

Streifel, Shane. *Impact of China and India on Global Commodity Markets*. Washington, D.C.: World Bank, 2006.

Sun, Peijun and Hua Biyun. "Yindu de jingji gaige: Chengjiu, wenti yu zhanwang" (India's Economic Reform: Achievements, Problems, and Prospects). *Nanya yanjiu* 1 (2003): 23–31.

Sun, Shihai. "Dui Zhongyin jianli huxin guanxi de jidian sikao" (Some Reflections on China and India Building Relations of Mutual Trust). *Nanya yanjiu* 2 (2003): 3–7.

Suteethorn, Chularat. *Economic Cooperation between Thailand and India and Its Implication on the Asian Community*. Chiba, Japan: Institute of Developing Economies, 2005.

Sutter, Robert G. *China's Rise in Asia: Promises and Perils*. Oxford: Rowman and Littlefield, 2005.

Swaine, Michael D., and Ashley J. Tellis. *Interpreting China's Grand Strategy: Past, Present, and Future*. Santa Monica, Calif.: Rand, 2000.

Talbott, Strobe. *Engaging India: Diplomacy, Democracy, and the Bomb*. Washington, D.C.: Brookings Institution Press, 2004.

Taneja, Nisha, et al. *Indo–Sri Lanka Trade in Services: FTA II and Beyond*. New Delhi: Indian Council for Research on International Economic Relations, 2004.

Tang, James. *With the Grain or Against the Grain? Energy Security and Chinese Foreign Policy in the Hu Jintao Era*. Washington, D.C.: Brookings Institution, 2006.

Tanham, George K. *Indian Strategic Thought: An Interpretive Essay*. Santa Monica, Calif.: Rand, 1992.

Terrill, Ross. *The New Chinese Empire and What It Means for the United States*. New York: Basic Books, 2003.

Thomas, Raju G. C. *Indian Security Policy*. Princeton, N.J.: Princeton University Press, 1986.

Tomlinson, B. R. *The Economy of Modern India*. Cambridge: Cambridge University Press, 1993.

Varma, Seema. *Foreign Policy of India*. New Delhi: Mohit, 2004.

Varshney, Ashutosh. "Mass Politics or Elite Politics? India's Economic Reforms in Comparative Perspective." In *India in the Era of Economic Reforms*, edited by Jeffrey

D. Sachs, Ashutosh Varshney, and Nirupam Bajpai, 222–60. New Delhi: Oxford University Press, 1999.

———. "Why Have Poor Democracies Not Eliminated Poverty?" *Asian Survey* 40, no. 4 (2000): 718–36.

Walgreen, David. "China in the Indian Ocean Region: Lessons in PRC Grand Strategy." *Comparative Strategy* 25, no. 1 (2006): 55–73.

Wang, Jiangyu. *China's Regional Trade Agreement (RTA) Approach: The Law, the Geopolitics, and the Impact on the Multilateral Trading System.* Hong Kong: Chinese University of Hong Kong, 2004.

Wang, Marion. "Greater China: Powerhouse of East Asian Regional Cooperation." *East Asia* 21, no. 4 (2004): 38–63.

Wang, Dong. "Yinba guanxi de bianhua yu Keshimier wenti" (Change in Indo-Pakistani Relations and the Kashmir Issue). *Nanya yanjiu jikan* 2 (February 2004): 18–24.

Wang, Hongwei. "Sino-Indian Economic and Scientific Cooperation Promising." *Beijing Review*, March 7, 2002.

———. "Tancheng duihua shi yi zeng xin" (Frank Dialogue, Dispelling Doubts, Increasing Trust). *Nanya yanjiu* 1 (1999): 14–17.

———. "Zhongyin guanxi jinru mulin youhao xinshiqi" (Sino-Indian Relations Have Entered a New Era of Friendship and Good Neighborliness). *Nanya yanjiu* 75, no. 2 (2003): 8–14.

Watkins, Eric. "China-Myanmar Oil Pipeline Funded: Gas Line Planned." *Oil and Gas Journal*, November 20, 2008 (www.ogj.com/display_article/346003/7/ONART/none/Trasp/1/Myanmar-awards-China-pipeline-rights).

Weil, Robert. *Red Cat, White Cat: The Contradictions of Market Socialism.* New York: Review Press, 1996.

Wendt, Alexander. *Social Theory of International Politics.* Cambridge: Cambridge University Press, 1999.

Winters, L. Alan, and Shahid Yusuf, eds. *Dancing with Giants: China, India, and the Global Economy.* Washington, D.C.: International Bank for Reconstruction and Development/World Bank, 2007.

Wu, H. L., and C. H. Chen. "The Prospects for Regional Economic Integration between China and the Five Central Asian Countries." *Europe-Asia Studies* 56, no. 7 (2004): 1059–80.

Wu, Yanrui, and Zhanyue Zhou. "Changing Bilateral Trade between China and India." *Journal of Asian Economics* 17, no. 3 (2006): 509–18.

Wu, Yongnian. "Yindu jingji minzu zhuyi de yuanqi, yingxiang ji Zhongguo de duice" (India's Economic Nationalism: Roots, Impact, and Countermeasures China Should Take). *Nanya yanjiu jikan* 3 (March 2007): 6–11.

Xu, Qi. "Maritime Geostrategy and the Development of the Chinese Navy in the Early 21st Century." *Naval War College Review* 59, no. 4 (2004): 46–67.

Yahya, Faizal. "BIMSTEC and Emerging Patterns of Asian Regional and Interregional Cooperation." *Australian Journal of Political Science* 40, no. 3 (2005): 391–410.

——. "India and Southeast Asia: Revisited." *Contemporary Southeast Asia* 25, no. 1 (2003): 85–108.

Yang, Yun-yuan. "Controversies over Tibet: China versus India, 1947–49." *China Quarterly*, no. 111 (1987): 407–20.

Yang, Mei. "Zhongyin fangzhipin fuzhuang maoyi hezuo qianjing" (Prospects of Sino-Indian Textile and Clothing Trade). *Nanya yanjiu jikan* 2 (February 2007): 54–60.

Zhang, Ming. *China's Changing Nuclear Posture: Reactions to the South Asian Nuclear Tests*. Washington, D.C.: Carnegie Endowment for International Peace, 1999.

——. *The Restoration of Sino-Indian Comity Following India's Nuclear Tests*. Washington, D.C.: Carnegie Endowment for International Peace, 1999.

Zhang, Guihong. "Sino-Indian Security Relations: Bilateral Issues, External Factors and Regional Implications." *South Asian Survey* 12, no. 1 (2005): 61–74.

Zhang, Minqiu, ed. *Zhongyin guanxi yanjiu (1947–2003)* (Sino-Indian Relations [1947–2003]). Beijing: Beijing daxue chubanshe, 2004.

Zhang, Wenmu. "Shijie diyuan zhengzhi tixi you Yindu weilai anquan" (The Global Geopolitical System and India's Future Security). *Zhanlue yu guanli* 3 (March 2001): 43–52.

——. "Yindu de diyuan zhanlue yu Zhongguo Xizang wenti" (India's Geostrategy and the Issue of Chinese Tibet). *Zhanlue yu guanli* 2 (February 1998): 24–31.

——. "Zhongguo nengyuan anquan yu zhen che xuan zhe" (The Energy Security of China and Policy Options). *Shijie jinji yu zhenzhi* 6, no. 5 (2003): 11–18.

Zhang, Yunling. "Zonghe anquan guan ji dui wo guo anquan de sikao" (The Concept of Comprehensive Security and Reflections on China's Security). *Dangdai Ya Tai* 1 (January 2000): 1–16.

Zhao, Guangzhi. "A Model of Decentralized Development: Border Trade and Economic Development in Yunnan." *Journal of China Studies and International Affairs* 32, no. 10 (1996): 85–108.

Zhao, Jimin. *Reform of China's Energy Institutions and Policies: Historical Evolution and Current Challenges*. Belfer Center for Science and International Affairs Discussion Papers 2001-20. Cambridge, Mass.: Energy Technology Innovation Project, Kennedy School of Government, Harvard University, 2001.

Zhao, X. B., and L. Zhang. "Decentralization Reforms and Regionalism in China: A Review." *International Regional Science Review* 22, no. 3 (1999): 251–81.

Zhao, Gansheng. "Wending Zhongyin guanxi yu chuangzao zhanlue jiyu chuyi" (How to Stabilize China-India Relations and Create a Strategic Opportunity). *Nanya yanjiu* 2 (February 2003): 2–8.

——. "Zhong E Yin zhanlue guanxi de zhengce yiyi yu fazhan qianjing" (China-Russia-India Strategic Relations: Policy Implications and Prospects for Development). *Nanya yanjiu* 2 (2005): 3–8.

Zheng, Ruixiang. "Assessing the Question of India's Rise." *Guoji wenti yanjiu* 1 (2006): 37–42.

——. "Shifting Obstacles in Sino-Indian Relations." *Pacific Review* 6, no. 1 (1993): 63–70.

INDEX

Praise for *Falling Upward*

"Richard Rohr has been a mentor to so many of us over the years, teaching us new ways to read Scripture, giving us tools to better understand ourselves, showing us new approaches to prayer and suffering, and even helping us see and practice a new kind of seeing. Now, in *Falling Upward*, Richard offers a simple but deeply helpful framework for seeing the whole spiritual life—one that will help both beginners on the path as they look ahead and long-term pilgrims as they look back over their journey so far." —Brian McLaren, author of *Faith After Doubt* and *Do I Stay Christian?* (brianmclaren.net)

"The value of this book lies in the way Richard Rohr shares his own aging process with us in ways that help us be less afraid of seeing and accepting how we are growing older day by day. Without sugar coating the challenging aspects of growing older, Rohr invites us to look closer, to sit with what is happening to us as we age. As we do so, the value and gift of aging begin to come into view. We begin to see that, as we grow older, we are being awakened to deep, simple, and mysterious things we simply could not see when we were younger. The value of this book lies in the clarity with which it invites us to see the value of our own experience of aging as the way God is moving us from doing to being, from achieving to appreciating, from planning and plotting to trusting the strange process in which, as we diminish, we strangely expand and grow in all sorts of ways we cannot and do not need to explain to anyone, including ourselves. This freedom from the need to explain, this humble realization of what we cannot explain, is itself one of the unexpected blessings of aging this book invites us to explore. It sounds too good to be true, but we can begin to realize the timeless wisdom of the elders is sweetly and gently welling up in our own mind and heart." —Jim Finley, retreat leader, Merton scholar, and author of *The Healing Path*

"This is Richard Rohr at his vintage best: prophetic, pastoral, practical. A book I will gratefully share with my children and grandchildren." —Cynthia Bourgeault, Episcopal priest, retreat leader, and the author of *Mystical Courage* and *The Corner of Fourth and Nondual*

"*Falling Upward* is a book of liberation. It calls forth the promise within us and frees us to follow it into wider dimensions of our spiritual authenticity. This 'second half of life' need not wait till our middle years. It emerges whenever we are ready and able to expand beyond the structures and strictures of our chosen path and sink or soar into the mysteries to which it pointed. Then the promise unfolds—in terms of what we discover we are and the timescapes we inhabit, as well as the gifts we can offer the world. With Richard Rohr as a guide, the spunk and spank of his language and his exhilarating insights, this mystery can become as real and immediate as your hand on the doorknob." —Joanna Macy, author *World as Lover, World as Self*

"Father Richard Rohr has gathered innumerable luminous jewels of wisdom during a lifetime of wrestling with self, soul, God, the church, the ancient sacred stories of initiation and its modern realities, and the wilder and darker dimensions of the human psyche. *Falling Upward* is a great and gracious gift for all of us longing for lanterns on the perilous path to psychospiritual maturity, a path that reveals secrets of personal destiny only after falling into the swamps of failure, woundedness, and personal demons. An uncommon, true elder in these fractured times, Richard Rohr shows us the way into the rarely reached second half of life and the encounter with our souls—our authentic and unique way of participating in and joyously contributing to our miraculous world." —Bill Plotkin, PhD, author of *The Journey of Soul Initiation*, *Soulcraft*, and *Nature and the Human Soul*

"In *Falling Upward*, Fr. Richard Rohr's wisdom illuminates the purpose and direction of our life journey. It turns out that our souls are engaged in a sacred dance that leads 'beyond the strong opinions, needs, preferences, and demands of the first half of life' toward the True Self and the 'serene discipleship' of the second half of life." —The Rev. Dr. Barbara A. Holmes, author of *Joy Unspeakable*, *Crisis Contemplation*, and *Race and the Cosmos*

FALLING UPWARD

A Spirituality for the Two Halves of Life

Revised and Updated

Richard Rohr

Foreword by Brené Brown

JB JOSSEY-BASS™

A Wiley Brand

Published by John Wiley & Sons, Inc., Hoboken, New Jersey.
Published simultaneously in Canada and the United Kingdom.

ISBNs: 9781394185696 (Hardback), 9781394185719 (ePDF), 9781394185702 (ePub)

CONTENTS

The greatest and most important problems of life are fundamentally insoluble.... They can never be solved, but only outgrown.
—CARL JUNG

 First there is the fall, and then we recover from the fall. Both are the mercy of God!
—LADY JULIAN OF NORWICH

To the Franciscan friars, my brothers, who trained me so well in the skills and spirituality of the first half of life that they also gave me the grounding, the space, the call, and the inevitability of a further and fantastic journey.

NOSTOS AND ALGA: RETURNING HOME IN THE SECOND HALF OF LIFE

BY BRENÉ BROWN

For many of us, the word "homesick" often conjures up images of a child's fleeting sadness or their temporary yearning for home and family. In today's culture, the emotion itself is often dismissed and trivialized as a juvenile feeling that we should be able to quickly shake off—it's a fuzzy overnight-camp feeling, not a fierce emotional experience that is key to the human experience and central to our hardwired need for a sense of place and belonging. As I find myself grabbing Fr. Richard Rohr's hand for guidance during what feels like the most important and rockiest life transition yet—the transformation from the first half of life to the second half of life—I am drawn to exploring the contours of homesickness to better understand why I can't shake this unyielding longing for a home that exists only inside me.

As a researcher who studies emotion, I've found that the fuzzy overnight-camp feeling has an important history that oddly follows the first-to-second-half-of-life transformation. For many years, homesickness was considered a serious medical condition that sometimes resulted in death. In the late 1600s, Swiss medical student Johannes Hofer coined the medical term "nostalgia" to capture the homesickness he witnessed in patients who were living far from home. These patients were so overcome with the need to return that they stopped functioning and sometimes died. He created the term by combining the Greek words *nostos* (homecoming) and *alga* (pain). In many wars across history, including the US Civil War and the French Revolution, homesickness and nostalgia were seen as threats to soldiers' physical and mental health. Strict restrictions were placed on music or songs that could incite the grief, desperation, and longing associated with homesickness.

So, what happened? Did adults just stop feeling homesick? Susan Matt, Presidential Distinguished Professor of History at Weber State University and author of *Homesickness: An American History,* explains:

> In a society that values independence, ambition, and optimism, many adults feel compelled to repress their homesickness. Mobility is regarded as a time-honored American tradition, moving on a painless and natural activity. Those who feel grief at parting hide the emotion, believing it to be a sign of immaturity, maladjustment, and weakness. Instead of displaying homesickness, Americans express hopefulness and cheerfulness, two character attributes much valued in American society. Trepidations about breaking home ties must be subordinated to sunny hopes for the future. Homesickness must be repressed.[1]

Fr. Richard might say that homesickness became problematic for first-half-of-life ambitions so we pathologized and infantilized those who experienced it.

While research and history have taught me about the power of homesickness, it's my intimate relationship with homesickness that fills me with a sense of reverence, awe, and respect for the emotion. As a child, the happiest place on earth for me was my grandmother's house. She was my person, and I was her person. There was a lot of turmoil in my house growing up and there was a lot of trauma in my grandmother's life, so we were for each other everything that was good about the world. We played cards, watched *Hee Haw,* and went to see movies that my parents wouldn't let me see. *Smokey and the Bandit* was our favorite. I loved defying my parents, and she loved Burt Reynolds. It was win-win. I lived for those hot summer weeks with her in San Antonio.

Yet every year I got desperately homesick after four or five days. I came to know and hate that feeling. I could sense it coming on—creeping into my mind and sliding across my shoulders and down my arms until the sorrow reached my hands and I would find myself emotionally reaching for my parents. Even as a child, I recognized homesickness as both an emotion and a physical yearning—a desperate grasping at something that was completely out of reach. Homesickness was and is such a strange sadness. It takes the shape of low-grade grief one minute and restless desperation the next. It can crash down on us like a wave and steal our breath. Then, out of nowhere and without notice, it can pull back and we can ride the calm — for a little while.

After my grandmother died, I experienced an even more complex side of the emotion. I learned what it means to be homesick for a place that no longer exists. I still frequently make the trip from Houston to San Antonio, and for the first ten years after her death, I couldn't even look at the road sign for the exit to her street. Yes, I missed her, but I also missed that sense of place. Even today, I would give anything to sit with her in the backyard under the pecan tree, listening to the call of the mourning dove or the chirping of the cicadas — nature sounds that are nostalgic for many of us, yet sounds that I'm absolutely convinced are exclusive to Me-Ma's backyard.

A couple of years ago, my mom was diagnosed with rapid-onset dementia. As my sisters and I care for her, I'm forced to navigate a swirl of many emotions, including my old companion homesickness. It's been many decades since I've snuggled into my mother's lap, but, until very recently, I always found shelter in our shared memories. That soothing place is gone. I'm desperately homesick for that place.

I had not thought a lot about the role homesickness has played in my life until I reread *Falling Upward*. The first time I read about the transition from the first half of life and the embrace of the second half of life, I was way too deep in my own first-half-of-life energy to think the second half would ever be for me. But now, thanks to this book, I'm gaining an understanding of this transition and why my spiritual homesickness is more than emotional pain — it's a spiritual yearning.

Spiritual homesickness has been a constant in my life. It was not an everyday experience, but a predictable and always reoccurring desperation to find a sense of sacredness within me, not outside of me: my soul, my home, God in me. It was homesickness for a place that exists only inside me.

Through my thirties and forties, I would occasionally succumb to the yearning, drop everything, and run as fast as I could to *visit* the home within me. The door to my internal spiritual home would be one simple experience, one encounter with a thin place — maybe sitting in my car listening to Loretta Lynn sing "How Great Thou Art," or an afternoon swim with God in Lake Travis, or one night praying the Daily Examen. But then, after that visit, I would leave and go back to my first-half-of-life world. I'd describe this first-half-of-life spirituality as the ebb and flow of *nostos* and *alga*, homecoming and pain.

Over the past two years, I've found that I'm more spiritually homesick than not. Spiritual homesickness has become an almost daily dulling grief. It's not depression or exhaustion. It's an uncomfortable knowing that I'm coming to the end of one thing and the beginning of the next. I'm leaving and arriving. There's fear, but there's also joyful anticipation.

Today, when I return home to the place in me where God dwells, I'm no longer interested in making it a quick visit so I can run back to the world of "what other people think" and "what I can get done." Today, I can barely be dragged out of the house. I'm drawn to different conversations and deeper connections. I want this sacred space to be my home, not somewhere I visit to buttress my "real life" that's on the outside of my connection with God. I'm starting to wonder if my *alga*, my pain, is fueled by my separation from God and from my True Self.

When it comes to the end of one thing and the beginning of another, Fr. Richard writes that good spiritual directors should be talking to us openly about death. Let me assure you, based on this requirement, Fr. Richard is a very good and tenacious spiritual director. I hold his words and ideas close to my heart because he has walked with me through many fires and never pulled any punches. Based on this book, I think Fr. Richard might tell me that I'm experiencing the death of visiting God and the birth of living with God and through God.

Don't get me wrong—leaving the first half of life is scary. Most of us have the first-half-of-life hustle down. The thing is, I'm just never, ever homesick for the first half of my life when I walk away from it. I'm fearful about leaving the rules I understand and the markers for success that I've established for my life. But I don't miss it. Maybe I'm not homesick for the first half of life because it's really never been my true home.

To Fr. Richard: Thank you for your oversized heart, your always curious mind, and those outstretched hands that so many of us reach out to hold, squeeze, and occasionally high-five.

A journey into the second half of our lives awaits us all. Not everybody goes there, even though all of us get older, and some of us get older than others. A "further journey" is a well-kept secret, for some reason. Many people do not even know there is one. There are too few who are aware of it, tell us about it, or know that it is different from the journey of the first half of life. So, why should I try to light up the path a little? Why should I presume that I have anything to say here, and why should I write to people who are still on their first journey—and happily so?

I am driven to write because after over fifty years as a Franciscan teacher, working in many settings, religions, countries, and institutions, I find that many, if not most, people and institutions remain stymied in the preoccupations of the first half of life. By that, I mean that most people's concerns remain those of establishing their personal (or superior) identity, creating various boundary markers for themselves, seeking security, and perhaps linking to what seem like significant people or projects. These tasks are good to some degree and even necessary. We are all trying to find what the Greek philosopher Archimedes (c. 287–c. 212 BCE) called *a lever and a place to stand* so that we can move the world just a little bit. The world would be much worse off if we did not do this first and important task.

But, in my opinion, this first-half-of-life task is no more than finding the starting gate. It is merely the warm-up act, not the full journey. It is the raft but not the shore. If you realize that there is a further journey, you might do the warm-up act quite differently, which would better prepare you for what follows. People at any age must know about the whole arc of their life and where it is tending and leading.

We know about this further journey from the clear and inviting voices of others who have been there, from the sacred and secular texts that invite us there, from our own observations of people who have entered this new territory, and also, sadly, from those who never seem to move on. The further journey usually appears like a seductive invitation and a kind of promise or hope. We are summoned to it, not commanded to go, perhaps because each of us has to go on this path freely, with all the messy and raw material of our own unique lives. But we don't have to do it, nor do we have to do it alone. There *are* guideposts, some common patterns, utterly new kinds of goals, a few warnings, and even personal guides on this further journey. I hope I can serve you in offering a bit of each of these in this book.

All these sources and resources give me the courage and the desire to try to map the terrain of this further journey, along with the terrain of the first journey, but most especially the needed crossover points. As you will see from the chapter titles, I consider the usual crossover points to be a kind of "necessary suffering," stumbling over stumbling stones, and lots of shadowboxing, but often just a gnawing desire for *ourselves,* for something more, or what I will call "homesickness."

I am trusting that you will see the truth of this map, yet it is the kind of soul truth that we only know "through a glass darkly" (1 Corinthians 13:12) — and through a glass brightly at the same time. Yet any glass through which we see is always made of human hands, like mine. All spiritual language is, by necessity, metaphor and symbol. The Light comes from elsewhere, yet it is necessarily reflected through those of us still walking on the journey ourselves. As Desmond Tutu (1931–2021) told me on a trip to Cape Town, "We are only the light bulbs, Richard, and our job is just to remain screwed in!"

I believe that God gives us our soul, our deepest identity, our True Self,[1] our unique blueprint, at our own "immaculate conception." Our unique little bit of heaven is installed by the Manufacturer within the product, at the beginning! We are given a span of years to discover it, to choose it, and to live our own destiny to the full. If we do not, our True Self will never be offered again, in our own unique form — which is perhaps why almost all religious traditions present the matter with utterly charged words like "heaven" and "hell."

Our soul's discovery is absolutely crucial, momentous, and of pressing importance for each of us and for the world. We do not "make" or "create" our souls; we just "grow" them up. We are the clumsy stewards of our own souls. We are charged to awaken, and much of the work of spirituality is learning how to stay out of the way of this rather natural growing and awakening. We need to *unlearn* a lot, it seems, to get back to that foundational life which is "hidden in God" (Colossians 3:3). Yes, transformation is often more about unlearning than learning, which is why the religious traditions call it "conversion" or "repentance."

For me, no poet stated this quite so perfectly as the literally *inimitable* Gerard Manley Hopkins (1844–1889) in his John Duns Scotus–inspired poem "As Kingfishers Catch Fire."[2]

Each mortal thing does one thing and the same:
Deals out that being indoors each one dwells;
Selves—goes itself; *myself* it speaks and spells,
Crying *What I do is me: for that I came.*

All we can give back and all God wants from any of us is to humbly and proudly return the product that we have been given—which is ourselves! If I am to believe the saints and mystics, this finished product is more valuable to God than it seemingly is to us. Whatever this Mystery is, we are definitely in on the deal. True religion is always a deep intuition that we are already *participating* in something very good, in spite of our best efforts to deny it or avoid it. In fact, the best of modern theology is revealing a strong turn toward participation, as opposed to religion as mere observation, affirmation, moralism, or group belonging. There is nothing to join, only something to recognize, suffer, and enjoy as a *participant*. We are already in the *eternal flow* that Christians would call the divine life of the Trinity.

Whether we find our True Self depends in large part on the moments of time we are each allotted and the moments of freedom that we each receive and choose during that time. Life is indeed "momentous," created by accumulated moments in which the deeper "I" is slowly revealed if we are ready to see it. Holding our *inner blueprint*, which is a good description of our soul, and returning it humbly to the world and to God by love and service is indeed of ultimate concern. Each thing and every person must act out its nature fully, at whatever cost. It is our life's purpose and the deepest meaning of "natural law." We are here to give back fully and freely what was first given to us, but now writ personally—by us! It is probably the most courageous and free act we will ever perform—and it takes both halves of our life to do it fully. The first half of life is discovering the script, and the second half is actually writing it and owning it.

So, get ready for a great adventure, the one for which you were really born. If we never get to our little bit of heaven, our life does not make much sense, and we have created our own "hell." So, get ready for some new freedom, some dangerous permission, some hope from nowhere, some unexpected happiness, some stumbling stones, some radical grace, and some new and pressing responsibility for yourself and for our suffering world.

*What is a normal goal to a young person
becomes a neurotic hindrance in old age.*
—CARL JUNG

 No wise person ever wanted to be younger.
—JONATHAN SWIFT

There is much evidence on several levels that there are at least two major tasks to human life. The first task is to build a strong "container" or identity; the second is to find the contents that the container was meant to hold. The first task we take for granted as the very purpose of life, which does not mean we do it well. The second task, I am told, is more encountered than sought; few arrive at it with much preplanning, purpose, or passion. So, you might wonder if there is much point in providing a guide to the territory ahead of time. Yet that is exactly why we must. It is vitally important to know what is coming and being offered to all of us.

We are a "first-half-of-life culture," largely concerned about *surviving successfully*. Probably most cultures and individuals across history have been situated in the first half of their own development up to now, because it is all they had time for. We all try to do what seems like the task that life first hands us: establishing an identity, a home, relationships, friends, community, and security, and building a proper platform for our only life.

But it takes us much longer to discover "the task within the task," as I like to call it: *what we are really doing when we are doing what we are doing.* Two people can have the same job description, yet one is holding a subtle or not-so-subtle life energy (*eros*) in doing their job, while another is holding a subtle or not-so-subtle negative energy (*thanatos*) while doing the exact same job. Most of us are somewhere in between, I suppose.

We actually respond to one another's energy more than to people's exact words or actions. In any situation, our taking or giving of energy is what we are actually doing. Everybody can feel, suffer, or enjoy the difference, but few can exactly say what it is that is happening. Why do we feel drawn or repelled? What we all desire and need from one another, of course, is that life energy called *eros*! It always draws, creates, and connects things.

This is surely what Jesus meant when he said that you could only tell a good tree from a bad one "by its fruits" (Matthew 7:20). Inside of life energy, a group or family will be productive and energetic. Inside of death energy, there will be gossip, cynicism, and mistrust hiding behind every interaction. Yet we usually cannot precisely put our finger on what is happening. That is second-half-of-life wisdom, or what Paul calls "the discerning of spirits" (1 Corinthians 12:10). Perhaps this book can be a school for such discernment and wisdom. That is surely my hope.

It is when we begin to pay attention and seek integrity precisely in *the task within the task* that we begin to move from the first to the second half of our lives. Integrity largely has to do with purifying our intentions and a growing honesty about our actual motives. It is hard work. Most often, we don't pay attention to that inner task until we have had some kind of fall or failure in our outer tasks. This pattern is invariably true for reasons I have yet to fathom.

Life, if we are honest about it, is made up of many failings and fallings amidst all our hopeful growing and achieving. Those failings and fallings must be there for a purpose, a purpose that neither culture nor church has fully understood. Most of us find all failure bewildering, but it does not have to be. My observations tell me that if we can clarify the common *sequencing, staging,* and *direction of life's arc* a bit more, many practical questions and dilemmas will be resolved. That doesn't mean we can avoid the journey itself. Each of us still has to walk it for ourselves before we get the big picture of human life.

Maybe we should just call this book *Tips for the Road,* a sort of roadside assistance program. Or perhaps it is like a medical brochure that describes the possible symptoms of a future heart attack. Reading it when you're well might feel like a waste of time, but it could make the difference between life and death if a heart attack actually happens. My assumption is that the second half of your own life *will* happen, although I hope it is not a heart attack (unless you understand "heart attack" symbolically, of course!).

When I state that you will enter the second half of life, I don't mean it in a strictly chronological way. Some young people, especially those who have learned from early suffering, are already there, and some older folks are still quite childish. If you are still in the first half of your life, chronologically or spiritually, I would hope that this book will offer you some good guidance, warnings, limits, permissions, and lots of possibilities. If you are in the second half of life already, I hope that this book will at least assure you that you are not crazy — and also give you some hearty bread for your whole journey.

None of us go into our spiritual maturity completely of our own accord or by a totally free choice. We are led by *Mystery*, which religious people rightly call grace. Most of us have to be cajoled or seduced into it, or we fall into it by some kind of "transgression," believe it or not, like Jacob finding his birthright through cunning, and Esau losing his by failure (see Genesis 27). Those who walk the full and entire journey are considered "called" or "chosen" in the Bible, perhaps "fated" or "destined" in world mythology and literature, but always they are the ones who have heard some deep invitation to "something more" and set out to find it by both grace and daring. Most get little reassurance from others or even have full confidence that they are totally right. Setting out is always a leap of faith, a risk in the deepest sense of the term, and yet an adventure too.

The familiar and the habitual are so falsely reassuring, and most of us make our homes there permanently. The new is always by definition unfamiliar and untested, so God, life, destiny, and suffering have to give us a push — usually a big one — or we will not go. Someone has to make clear to us that homes are not meant to be lived in, but only to be moved out from.

Most of us are never told that we can set out from the known and the familiar to take on a further journey. Our institutions and our expectations, including our churches, are almost entirely configured to encourage, support, reward, and validate the tasks of the first half of life. This is shocking and disappointing, but I think it is true. We are more struggling to survive than to thrive, more just "getting through" or trying to get to the top than finding out what is really at the top or was already at the bottom. Thomas Merton (1915–1968), the American monk, pointed out that we may spend our whole life climbing the ladder of success, only to find, when we get to the top, that our ladder is leaning against the wrong wall.

Most of us in the first half of life suspect that all is not fully functional, and we are probably right! We were just told to build a nice basement and some kind of foundation for our house, but we were not given any plans or even a hint that we also needed to build an actual "living" room upstairs, let alone a nutritious kitchen or an erotic bedroom, and much less our own chapel. So many, if not most, of us settle for the brick and mortar of first-stage survival and never get to what I will be calling "the unified field" of life itself. As Bill Plotkin, a wise guide, puts it, many of us learn to do our "survival dance," but we never get to our actual "sacred dance."[1]

THE WAY UP AND THE WAY DOWN

The soul has many secrets. They are only revealed to those who want them and are never forced upon us. One of the best-kept secrets, and yet one hidden in plain sight, is that *the way up is the way down*—or, if you prefer, *the way down is the way up*. This pattern is obvious in all of nature, from the very change of seasons and substances on this earth to the six hundred million tons of hydrogen that the sun burns every day to light and warm our earth and even to the metabolic laws of dieting or fasting. The down-up pattern is constant in mythology too, in stories like that of Persephone, who must descend into the underworld and marry Hades for spring to be reborn.

In legends and literature, the sacrifice of something to achieve something else is almost the only pattern. Dr. Faust has to sell his soul to the devil to achieve power and knowledge. Sleeping Beauty must sleep for a hundred years before she can receive the prince's kiss. In Scripture, we see that the wrestling and wounding of Jacob are necessary for Jacob to become Israel (Genesis 32:24–32), and the death and resurrection of Jesus are necessary to create Christianity. The loss and renewal pattern is so constant and ubiquitous that it should hardly be called a secret at all.

Yet it is still a secret, probably because we do not *want* to see it. We do not want to embark on a further journey if it feels like going down, especially after we have put so much sound and fury into going up. This is surely the first and primary reason why many people never get to the fullness of their own lives. The supposed achievements of the first half of life have to fall apart and show themselves to be wanting in some way, or we will not move further. Why would we?

Normally, a job, fortune, or reputation has to be lost, a death has to be suffered, a house has to be flooded, or a disease has to be endured. The pattern, in fact, is so clear that we have to work rather hard, or be intellectually lazy, to miss the continual lesson. This, of course, was the major insight by Scott Peck (1936–2005) in his best-selling book, *The Road Less Traveled*. He once told me personally that he felt most Western people were just spiritually lazy. And when we are lazy, we stay on the path we are already on, even if it is going nowhere. It is the spiritual equivalent of the second law of thermodynamics: everything winds down unless some outside force winds it back up. True spirituality could be called the "outside force," although surprisingly it is found "inside," but we will get to that later.

Some kind of falling, what I will soon call "necessary suffering," is programmed into the journey. All the sources seem to say it, starting with Adam and Eve and all they represent. Yes, they "sinned" and were cast out of the Garden of Eden, but from those very acts came consciousness, conscience, and their own further journey. But it all started with transgression. Only people unfamiliar with sacred story are surprised that they ate the apple. As soon as God told them specifically not to, you know they will! It creates the whole story line inside of which we can find ourselves.

It is not that suffering or failure *might* happen, or that it will only happen to you if you are bad (which is what religious people often think), or that it will happen to the unfortunate, or to a few in other places, or that you can somehow by cleverness or righteousness avoid it. No, it *will* happen, and happen to you! Losing, failing, falling, sin, and the suffering that comes from those experiences—all of this is a necessary and even good part of the human journey. As my favorite mystic, Lady Julian of Norwich (1342–1416), put it in her Middle English, "Sin is behovely!"

You cannot avoid sin or mistakes anyway (see Romans 5:12), but if you try too fervently, it often creates even worse problems. Jesus loves to tell stories like those of the tax collector and the Pharisee (Luke 18:9–14) and the famous one about the prodigal son (Luke 15:11–32), in which one character does life totally right and is, in fact, wrong, while the other, who does it totally wrong, ends up God's beloved! Now deal with that!

Jesus also tells us that there are two groups who are very good at trying to deny or avoid this humiliating surprise: *those who are very "rich" and those who are very "religious."* These two groups have very different plans for themselves, as they try to totally steer their own ships with well-chosen itineraries. They follow two different ways of going "up" and avoiding all "down."

Such a down-and-then-up perspective does not fit into our Western philosophy of progress, nor into our desire for upward mobility, nor into our religious notions of perfection or holiness. "Let's hope it is *not* true, at least for me," we all say. Yet the Perennial Tradition, sometimes called the wisdom tradition, says that it is and will always be true. St. Augustine (354–430) called it the passing-over mystery (or the "paschal mystery," from the Hebrew word for Passover, *Pesach*).

Today, we might use a variety of metaphors: reversing engines, a change in game plan, a falling off the very wagon that we constructed. No one would choose such upheaval consciously. We must somehow "fall" into it. Those who are too carefully engineering their own superiority systems will usually not allow it at all. It is much more *done to us* than anything we do ourselves, and sometimes nonreligious people are more open to this change in strategy than are religious folks who have their private salvation project all worked out. This is how I would interpret Jesus' enigmatic words, "The children of this world are wiser in their ways than the children of light" (Luke 16:8). I have met too many rigid and angry old Christians and clergy to deny this sad truth, but it seems to be true in all religions until and unless they lead to the actual transformation of persons.

In this book, I would like to describe how this message of falling down and moving up is, in fact, the most counter-intuitive message in most of the world's religions, including, and most especially, Christianity. *We grow spiritually much more by doing it wrong than by doing it right.* That might just be the central message of how spiritual growth happens, yet nothing in us wants to believe it. I actually think it is the only workable meaning of any remaining notion of "original sin." There seems to have been a fly in the ointment from the beginning, but the key is recognizing and dealing with the fly rather than needing to throw out the whole ointment!

If there is such a thing as human perfection, it seems to emerge precisely from how we handle the imperfection that is everywhere, especially our own. What a clever place for God to hide holiness, so that only the humble and earnest will find it! A "perfect" person ends up being one who can consciously forgive and include imperfection rather than one who thinks he or she is totally above and beyond imperfection. It becomes rather obvious once you say it out loud. In fact, I would say that *the demand for the perfect is the greatest enemy of the good.* Perfection is a mathematical or divine concept, while goodness is a beautiful human concept that includes us all.

By denying their pain and avoiding the necessary falling, many have kept themselves from their own spiritual depths—and therefore have been kept from their own spiritual heights. First-half-of-life religion is almost always about various types of purity codes or "thou shalt nots" to keep us *up, clear, clean, and together*, like good Boy and Girl Scouts. A certain kind of "purity" and self-discipline is also "behovely," at least for a while in the first half of life, as the Hebrew Torah brilliantly presents. I was a good Star Scout myself and a Catholic altar boy who rode my bike to serve the 6 A.M. mass when I was merely ten years old. I hope you are as impressed as I was with myself.

Because none of us desire, seek, or even suspect a downward path to growth through imperfection, we have to get the message with the authority of a "divine revelation." So, Jesus makes it into a central axiom: The "last" really do have a head start in moving toward "first," and those who spend too much time trying to be "first" will never get there. Jesus says this clearly in several places and in numerous parables, although those of us still on the first journey just cannot hear this. It has been considered mere religious fluff, as most of Western history has made rather clear.

Our resistance to the message is so great that it could be called outright denial, even among sincere Christians. *The human ego prefers anything, just about anything, to falling or changing or dying.* The ego is that part of us that loves the status quo, even when it is not working. It attaches to past and present and fears the future.

When we are in the first half of life, we cannot see any kind of failing or dying as even possible, much less as necessary or good. (Those who have *never* gone up, like the poor and the marginalized, may actually have a spiritual head start, according to Jesus.) Normally, we need a few good successes to give us some ego structure and self-confidence, and to get us going. God mercifully hides thoughts of dying from the young, but unfortunately we then hide it from ourselves till the later years finally force it into our consciousness. Ernest Becker (1924–1974) wrote some years ago that it is not love but "the denial of death"[2] that might well make the world go round. What if he is right?

Some have called this principle of going down to go up a "spirituality of imperfection" or "the way of the wound." It has been affirmed in Christianity by St. Thérèse of Lisieux (1873–1897) as her Little Way, by St. Francis of Assisi (1181–1226) as the way of poverty, and by Alcoholics Anonymous as the necessary first step. The Apostle Paul taught this unwelcome message with his enigmatic, "It is when I am weak that I am strong" (2 Corinthians 12:10). Of course, in saying that, he was merely building on what he called the "folly" of the crucifixion of Jesus—a tragic and absurd dying that became resurrection itself.

Like skaters, we move forward by actually moving from side to side. I found this phenomenon to be core and central in my research on male initiation,[3] and now we are finding it mirrored rather clearly in the whole universe, especially in physics and biology, which reveal one huge pattern of entropy: constant loss and renewal, death and transformation, the changing of forms and forces. Some even see it in terms of "chaos theory": the exceptions are the only rule and then they create new rules. Scary, isn't it?

Denial of the pattern seems to be a kind of practical daily atheism or chosen ignorance among many believers and clergy. Many have opted for the soft religion of easy ego consolations, the human growth model, or the "prosperity Gospel" that has become so common in Western Christianity and in all the areas we spiritually colonize. We do grow and increase, but by a far different path than the ego would ever imagine. Only the soul knows and understands.

What I hope to do in this book, without a lot of need to convince anybody, is to make *the sequencing, the tasks, and the direction* of the two halves of life clear. Then you will be ready to draw your own conclusions. That is why I have called it "falling upward." Those who are ready will see that this message is self-evident: Those who have gone "down" are the only ones who understand "up." Those who have somehow fallen, and fallen well, are the only ones who can go up and not misuse "up." I also want to describe what "up" in the second half of life will look like—and could look like! And, most especially, I want to explore how we transition from one to the other—*and how it is not by our own willpower or moral perfection.* It will be nothing like what we might have imagined beforehand, and we can't engineer it by ourselves. It is done unto us.

One more warning, if that is the right word: You will not know for sure that this message is true until you are on the "up" side. You will never imagine it to be true until you have gone through the "down" yourself and come out on the other side in larger form. You must be pressured "from on high," by fate, circumstance, love, or God, because nothing in you wants to believe it or wants to go through it. Falling upward is a "secret" of the soul, known not by thinking about it or proving it but only by risking it (at least once) and by allowing yourself to be led (at least once). Those who have allowed it know it is true, but only after the fact.

This is probably why Jesus praised faith and trust even more than love. It takes a foundational trust to fall or to fail—and not to fall apart. Faith alone holds you while you stand waiting, hoping, and trusting. Then, and only then, will deeper love happen. It's no surprise at all that in English (and, I am told, in other languages as well) we speak of "falling" in love. I think it is the only way to get there. None would go freely if we knew ahead of time what love is going to ask of us. Very human faith lays the utterly needed foundation for the ongoing discovery of love. Have no doubt, though: *Great love is always a discovery, a revelation, a wonderful surprise, a falling into "something" much bigger and deeper that is literally beyond you and larger than you.*

Jesus tells the disciples as they descend from the mountain of transfiguration, "Do not talk about these things until the Human One is risen from the dead" (by which he means until you are on the other side of loss and renewal). If you try to assert wisdom before people have themselves walked it, be prepared for much resistance, denial, push back, and verbal debate. As the text in Mark continues, "the disciples continued to discuss among themselves what 'rising from the dead' might even mean" (Mark 9:9–10). You cannot imagine a new space fully until you have been taken there. I make this point strongly to help you understand why almost all spiritual teachers tell you to "believe" or "trust" or "hold on." *They are not just telling you to believe silly or irrational things.* They are telling you to hold on until you can go on the further journey for yourself, and they are telling you that the whole spiritual journey is, in fact, for real—which you cannot possibly know yet.

The language of the first half of life and the language of the second half of life are almost two different vocabularies, known only to those who have been in both of them. The advantage of those on the further journey is that they can still remember and respect the first language and task. *They have transcended but also included all that went before.* In fact, if you cannot include and integrate the wisdom of the first half of life, I doubt if you have moved to the second. Never throw out the baby with the bathwater. People who know how to creatively break the rules also know why the rules were there in the first place. They are not merely iconoclasts or rebels.

I have often thought that this is the symbolic meaning of Moses breaking the first tablets of the law, only to go back up the mountain and have them redone (Exodus 32:19–34; 34:1–10) by Yahweh. The second set of tablets emerges after a face-to-face encounter with God, which changes everything. Your first understanding of law must fail you and disappoint you. Only after breaking the first tablets of the law is Moses a real leader and prophet. Only afterward does he see God's glory (Exodus 33:18–23), and only afterward does his face "shine" (Exodus 34:29–35). It might just be the difference between the two halves of life!

A common quote on the Internet today states much the same thing: "Learn and obey the rules very well so you will know how to break them properly." Such discrimination between means and goals is almost the litmus test of whether you are moving in the right direction, and all the world religions at the mature levels will say similar things. For some reason, religious people tend to confuse the means with the actual goal. In the beginning, you tend to think that God really cares about your exact posture, the exact day of the week for public prayer, the authorship and wordings of your prayers, and other such things. Once your life has become a constant communion, you know that all the techniques, formulas, sacraments, and practices were just a dress rehearsal for the real thing—life itself—which can actually become a constant intentional prayer. Your conscious and loving existence gives glory to God.

All this talk of the first and second half of life, of the languages of each, of falling down to go up is not new. It has been embodied for centuries in mythic tales of men and women who found themselves on the further journey. We will now take a closer look at one of the most famous.

A FOUNDING MYTH

Western rationalism no longer understands myths and their importance, although almost all historic cultures did.[4] We are the obvious exception, as we have replaced these effective and healing story lines with ineffective, cruel, and disorienting narratives like communism, fascism, terrorism, mass production, and its counterpart, consumerism. In other words, we all have our de facto worldviews that determine what is important and what is not important to us. They usually have a symbolic story to hold them together, such as that of "Honest Abe" chopping wood in Kentucky and educating himself in Illinois. "Myths" like this become a standing and effective metaphor for the American worldview of self-determination, hard work, and achievement. Whether they are exact historical truth is not even important.

Such myths proceed from the deep and collective unconscious of humanity. Our myths are stories or images that are not always true in particular but entirely true in general. They are usually not historical fact, but invariably they are spiritual genius. They hold life and death, the explainable and the unexplainable together as one. They hold together the paradoxes that the rational mind cannot process by itself. As good poetry does, myths make unclear and confused emotions brilliantly clear and life-changing.

Myths are true basically because they work. A sacred myth keeps a people healthy, happy, and whole—even inside their pain. They give deep meaning, and pull us into "deep time" (which encompasses all time, past and future, geological and cosmological, not just our little time or culture). Such stories are the very food of the soul, and they are what we are trying to get back to when we start fairy tales with phrases like, "Once upon a time" or, "Long ago, in a faraway land." Catholics used to say at the end of their Latin prayers, *Per omnia saecula saeculorum*, which is loosely translated as "through all the ages of ages." Somehow, deep time orients the psyche, gives ultimate perspective, realigns us, grounds us, and thus heals us. We belong to a Mystery far grander than our little selves and our little time. Great storytellers and spiritual teachers always know this.

Remember, the opposite of rational is not always irrational. It can also be *transrational*, or bigger than the rational mind can process. Things like love, death, suffering, God, and infinity are transrational experiences. Both myth and mature religion understand this. The transrational has the capacity to keep us inside an open system and a larger horizon so that the soul, the heart, and the mind do not close down inside of small and constricted space. The merely rational mind is invariably dualistic. It divides the field of almost every moment between what it can presently understand and what it then deems "wrong" or untrue.[5] Because the rational mind cannot process love or suffering, for example, it tends to avoid them, deny them, or blame somebody for them, when in fact they are the greatest spiritual teachers of all, if we but allow them. Our loss of mythic consciousness has not served the last few centuries well, as we have seen the growth of rigid fundamentalism in all the world religions. Now we get trapped in destructive and "invisible" myths because we do not have the eyes to see how great healing myths function.

The Odyssey

The story of Odysseus is a classic transrational myth, one that many would say sets the bar and direction for all later Western storytelling. We all have our own little "odysseys," but the word came from the name of one man, who fought, sailed, and lived a classic pattern of human, tragic, and heroic life many centuries ago.

In Homer's tale *The Odyssey,* written around 700 BCE, we follow the awesome and adventurous journey of the hero Odysseus as he journeys home from the Trojan war. Rowing his boat past seductive sirens (with detours because of a cyclops and the lotus eaters), on through the straits of Scylla and Charybdis, and through the consolations and confusions of both Circe and Calypso, Odysseus tries to get back home. Through trial, guile, error, and ecstasy, chased by gods and monsters, Odysseus finally returns home to his island, Ithaca, and to reunion with his beloved wife, Penelope; his old, dear father, Laertes; his longing son, Telemachus; and even his dying dog, Argos. Great and good stuff!

Accustomed as we are to our normal mythical story line, we rightly expect a "happily ever after" ending to Odysseus' tale. For most readers, that is all, in fact, they need, want, or remember from the story. Odysseus did return, reclaim his home, and reunite with his wife, son, and father. But there is more! In the final two chapters, after what seems like a glorious and appropriate ending, Homer announces and calls Odysseus to *a new and second journey* that is barely talked about, yet somehow Homer deemed it absolutely necessary to his character's life.

Instead of settling into quiet later years, Odysseus knows that he must heed the prophecy he has already received, *but half forgotten*, from the blind seer Teiresias and leave home once again. It is his fate and required by the gods. This new journey has no detailed description, only a few very telling images. I wonder, in 700 BCE, before we began to fully understand and speak about the second-half-of-life journey, whether Homer simply intuited that there had to be *something more*, as Greek literature often did.

"Then came also the ghost of Theban Teiresias, with his golden sceptre in his hand. . . . 'When you get home you will take your revenge on these suitors [of your wife]; and after you have killed them by force or fraud in your own house, you must take a well-made oar and carry it on and on, till you come to a country where the people have never heard of the sea and do not even mix salt with their food, nor do they know anything about ships, and oars that are as the wings of a ship. I will give you this certain token which cannot escape your notice. A wayfarer will meet you and will say [your oar] must be a winnowing shovel that you have got upon your shoulder; on [hearing] this you must fix the oar in the ground and sacrifice a ram, a bull, and a boar to Neptune. Then go home and offer hecatombs [one hundred cattle] to the gods in heaven one after the other. As for yourself, death shall come to you from the sea, and your life shall ebb away very gently when you are full of years and peace of mind, and your people shall bless you. All that I have said will come true.'" [6]

Teiresias' prophecy, which Odysseus half heard earlier in the story, seems to be an omen of what will happen to all of us. Here is my summary of the key points for our purposes, which I hope you will find very telling:

1.   Odysseus receives this prophecy at the point in his story when he is traveling through Hades, the kingdom of the dead, and thus "at the bottom," as it were. It is often when the ego is most deconstructed that we can hear things anew and begin some honest reconstruction, even if it is only half heard and halfhearted.

2.   Teiresias is holding a "golden sceptre" when he gives Odysseus the message. I would interpret that as a symbol that the message is coming from a divine source, an authority from without and beyond, unsolicited or unsought, and maybe even unwanted by Odysseus himself. Often, it takes outer authority to send us on the path toward our own inner authority.

3.   After all his attempts to return there, Odysseus is fated again to leave Ithaca, which is an island, and go to the "mainland" for a further journey. He

is reuniting his small "island" with the big picture, as it were. For me, this is what makes something inherently religious: Whatever reconnects (*re-ligio*) our parts to the Whole is an experience of God, whether we call it "religious" or not. He is also reconnecting his outer journey to the "inland," or his interior world, which is much of the task of the second half of life. What brilliant metaphors!

4. He is to carry the oar, which was his "delivery system" as one who journeyed by ship in his first half of life. But a wayfarer he meets far from the ocean will see it instead as a winnowing shovel, a tool for separating grain from chaff! When he meets this wayfarer, this is the sign that he has reached the end of his further journey, and he is to plant the oar in the ground at that spot and leave it there (much as young men bury their childhood toys at a male initiation rite today). Only then can he finally return home. The first world of occupation and productivity must now find its full purpose.

5. Then he is to sacrifice to the god Neptune, who has been on his trail throughout the first journey. The language of offering sacrifice is rather universal in ancient myths. It must have been recognized that, to go forward, there is always something that must be released, moved beyond, given up, or "forgiven" to enter the larger picture of the "gods."

6. He is to sacrifice three specific things: a wild bull, a breeding boar, and a battering ram. I doubt whether we could come up with three more graphic images of untrained or immature male energy. We cannot walk the second journey with first-journey tools. We need a whole new tool kit.

7. After this further journey, he is to return home to Ithaca, to prepare a solemn sacrifice "to all the gods in heaven." In human language, he is finally living inside the big and true picture. In Christian language, he is finally connected to the larger Reign of God.

8. Only after this further journey and its sacrifices can Odysseus say that he will live happily with his people around him, until he sinks under the comfortable burden of years, and "his life will ebb away very gently" from the sea. Death is largely a threat to those who have not yet lived their life. Odysseus has lived the journeys of both halves of life and is ready to freely and finally let go.

Talk about the wisdom of the deep unconscious! God did not need to wait until we organized human spiritual intuitions into formal religions. The Spirit has been hovering over our chaos since the beginning, according to the second verse of the Bible (Genesis 1:2), and over all creation since the beginning of time (Romans 1:20). Homer was not just a "pagan" Greek, and we are not necessarily wiser because we live twenty-seven hundred years later.

Now, put this powerful myth in the back of your mind as we dive into this exciting exploration of the further journey. It can operate as a sort of blueprint for what I want to address. Just remember this much consciously: *The whole story is set in the matrix of seeking to find home and then to return there, thus refining and defining what home really is.* Home is both the beginning and the end. Home is not a sentimental concept at all, but an inner compass and a North Star at the same time. It is a metaphor for the soul.

CHAPTER 1

THE TWO HALVES
OF LIFE

 We cannot live the afternoon of life according to the program of life's morning; for what was great in the morning will be little at evening, and what in the morning was true will at evening have become a lie.
—CARL JUNG, 2014 / TAYLOR & FRANCIS.

As I began to explore in the Introduction, the task of the first half of life is to create a proper *container* for one's life and answer the first essential questions: "What makes me significant?" "How can I support myself?" and "Who will go with me?" The task of the second half of life is, quite simply, to find the actual *contents* that this container was meant to hold and deliver. As Mary Oliver (1935–2019) put it, "What is it you plan to do with your one wild and precious life?"[1] In other words, the container is not an end in itself, but exists for the sake of our deeper and fullest life, which we largely do not know about ourselves. Far too many people just keep doing repair work on the container itself and never "throw their nets into the deep" (Luke 5:4) to bring in the huge catch that awaits them.

Problematically, the first task invests so much of our blood, sweat, eggs and sperm, tears and years that we often cannot imagine there is a second task or that anything more could be expected of us. "The old wineskins are good enough," we say (see Luke 5:37–39), even though, according to Jesus, they often cannot hold the new wine. As Jesus assures us, if we do not get some new wineskins, the wine and the wineskin will both be lost. The second half of life can hold some new wine because, by then, there should be some strong wineskins, some tested ways of holding our lives together. But that normally means that the container itself has to stretch, die in its present form, or even replace itself with something better. This is the big "rub," as they say, but also the very source of our midlife excitement and discovery.

Various traditions have used many metaphors to make this differentiation clear: beginners and proficients, novices and initiated, milk and meat, letter and spirit, juniors and seniors, baptized and confirmed, apprentice and master, morning and evening, "Peter, when you were young . . . Peter, when you are old" (see John 21:18). Only when we have begun to live in the second half of life can we see the difference between the two. Yet the two halves are *cumulative and sequential, and both are very necessary*. We cannot do a nonstop flight to the second half of life by reading lots of books about it, including this one. Grace must and will edge us forward. "God has no grandchildren. God only has children," as some have said. Each generation has to make its own discoveries of Spirit for itself. If not, we just react to the previous generation—and often overreact. Or we conform and often overconform. Neither is a positive or creative way to move forward.

No pope, Bible quote, psychological technique, religious formula, book, or guru can do your journey for you. If you try to skip the first journey, you will never see its real necessity and also its limitations. You will never know why this first container *must* fail you, experience the wonderful fullness of the second half of the journey, and discover the relationship between the two. Such is the unreality of many people who "never grow up" or who remain narcissistic into their old age. This is not a small number of people in our world today.

"Juniors" on the first part of the journey invariably think that true elders are naïve, simplistic, "out of it," or just superfluous. They cannot understand what they have not yet experienced. They are totally involved in their first task and cannot see beyond it. Conversely, if a person has transcended and included the previous stages, they will always have a patient understanding of the juniors and can be patient and helpful to them somewhat naturally (although not without trial and effort). That is precisely what makes such people elders! *Higher stages always empathetically include the lower, or they are not higher stages.*

Almost all cultures, and even most of religious history, have been invested in the creation and maintenance of first-half-of-life issues: the big three concerns of identity, security, and sexuality and gender. They don't just preoccupy us; they totally take over. That is where history has focused up to now. In fact, most generations have seen boundary marking and protecting those boundaries as their primary and sometimes only tasks in life. Most of history has been about the forging of structures of security and appropriate loyalty symbols to announce and defend one's personal identity, one's group, and one's gender issues and identity. Now, we seem to live in a time when more and more people are asking, "Is that all there is?"

In our formative years, we are so self-preoccupied that we are both overly defensive and overly offensive at the same time, with little time left for simply living, pure friendship, useless beauty, or moments of communion with nature or anything else. Yet that kind of ego structuring is exactly what a young person needs, by and large, to get through the first twenty years or so. It's also what tribes need to survive. Maybe it is what humanity needed to get started. "Good fences make good neighbors,"[2] Robert Frost (1874–1963) wrote, but he also presumed that we don't just build fences. We eventually need to cross beyond them as well to actually meet the neighbor.

So, we need boundaries, identity, safety, and some degree of order and consistency to get started, personally and culturally. We also need to feel "special"; we need our "narcissistic fix." By that, I mean we all need some successes, response, and positive feedback early in life, or we will spend the rest of our lives demanding it, or bemoaning its lack, from others. There is a good and needed "narcissism," if you want to call it that. We have to first have an ego structure to then let go of it and move beyond it. Responding to John the Baptist's hard-line approach, Jesus maintains both sides of this equation when he says, "No man born of woman is greater than John the Baptizer, yet the least who enters the reign of heaven is greater than he is" (Matthew 11:11). Is that double-talk? No, it is second-half-of-life talk.

Basically, if you get mirrored well early in life, you do not have to spend the rest of your life looking in Narcissus' mirror or begging for the attention of others. You have already been "attended to" and now feel basically good—and always will. If you were properly mirrored when you were young, you are now free to mirror others and see yourself—honestly and helpfully. I can see why a number of saints spoke of prayer itself as simply receiving the ever-benevolent gaze of God, returning it in kind, mutually gazing, and finally recognizing that it is one single gaze received and bounced back. The Hindus call this exciting mutual beholding *darshan*. I will say more about this mirroring toward the end of the book.

Once you have your narcissistic fix, you have no real need to protect your identity, defend it, prove it, or assert it. It just is, and it is more than enough. This is what we actually mean by "salvation," especially when we get our narcissistic fix all the way from the Top. When we get our "Who am I?" question right, all the "What should I do?" questions tend to take care of themselves. The very fact that so many religious people have to so vigorously prove and defend their salvation theories makes me seriously doubt whether they have experienced divine mirroring at any great depth.

In the first half of life, success, security, and containment—"looking good" to ourselves and others—are almost the only questions. They are the early stages in Maslow's "hierarchy of needs."[3] In a culture like ours that is still preoccupied with security issues, enormously high military budgets are never seriously questioned by Congress or the people, while appropriations reflecting later stages in the hierarchy of needs—like those for education, health care for the poor, and the arts—are quickly cut, if even considered. The message is clear: We are largely an adolescent culture. Religions, similarly, *need* to make truth claims that are absolutely absolute, and we want them for just that—because they are absolute! This feels right and necessary at this early stage, despite any talk of biblical "faith" or trust, which can only be comprehended later.

We all want and need various certitudes, constants, and insurance policies at every stage of life. *But we have to be careful, or they totally take over and become all-controlling needs, keeping us from further growth.* Thus the most common one-liner in the Bible is, "Do not be afraid"; in fact, someone counted and found that it occurs 365 times—once for each day of the year! If we do not move beyond our early motivations of personal security, reproduction, and survival (the fear-based preoccupations of the "lizard brain"), we will never proceed beyond the lower stages of human or spiritual development. Many church sermons I have heard never seem to move beyond this first level of development—and do not even challenge it. In fact, to challenge it is considered heretical, dangerous, or ill advised.

The very unfortunate result of this preoccupation with order, control, safety, pleasure, and certitude is that a high percentage of people never get to the contents of their own lives! Human life is about more than building boundaries, protecting identities, creating tribes, and teaching impulse control. As Jesus said, "Do not worry about what you will eat or what you will wear." He then asks, "Is life not so much more than food? Is life not so much more than clothing?" (Matthew 6:25). "What will it profit you if you gain the whole world and lose your very soul?" (Matthew 16:26).

There is too much defensive behavior — and therefore too much offensive behavior — in the first half of life to get to the really substantial questions, which are what drive us forward on the further journey. Human maturity is neither offensive nor defensive; it is finally able to accept that reality *is what it is*. Ken Keyes Jr. (1921–1995) so wisely wrote, "You make yourself and others suffer just as much when you take offense as when you give offense."[4] The offended ones feel the need to offend those whom they think have offended them, creating defensiveness on the part of the presumed offenders, which often becomes a new offensive — ad infinitum. There seems to be no way out of this self-defeating and violent ping-pong game — except growing up spiritually. The True Self, you see, is very hard to offend!

STEPS AND STAGES

It was Carl Jung (1875–1961) who first popularized the phrase "the two halves of life" to describe these two major tangents and tasks, yet many other teachers have recognized that there are clear stages and steps to human and spiritual maturation. Process language is not new; it has just used different images.

There are the foundational journey of Abraham and Sarah; the Exodus of Moses; Mohammed's several key flights; Jesus' four kinds of soil; images of the Way of the Cross on the walls of churches; John of the Ladder; the recurring schemas of Sts. Bonaventure, John of the Cross, and Teresa of Ávila; and, in the modern era, Jean Piaget, James Fowler, Lawrence Kohlberg, Clare Graves, Jean Gebser, Abraham Maslow, Erik Erikson, Ken Wilber, Carol Gilligan, Daniel Levinson, Bill Plotkin, and the entire world of Spiral Dynamics. They all affirm that growth and development have a direction and are not a static "grit your teeth and bear it." *Unless you can chart and encourage both movement and direction, you have no way to name maturity or immaturity.* Most of these teachers, each in their own way, seem to coalesce around two key insights that continue to show themselves in almost every one of these constructs.

First, you can only see and understand the earlier stages from the wider perspective of the later stages. This is why mature societies were meant to be led by elders, seniors, saints, and "the initiated." They alone are in a position to be true leaders in a society, or certainly in any spiritual organization. Without them, "the blind lead the blind" (Matthew 15:14), which is typified by phenomena like violent gangs of youth or suicide bombers.

Those who are not true leaders or elders will just affirm people at their own immature level, and of course immature people will love them and elect them for being equally immature. You can fill in the names here with your own political disaster story. But just remember: There is a symbiosis between immature groups and immature leaders, which is why both Plato and Jefferson believed democracy was not really the best form of government. It is just the safest. A truly wise monarch would probably be the most effective at getting things done. (Don't send hate letters, please!)

If you have, in fact, deepened and grown "in wisdom, age, and grace" (Luke 2:52), you are able to be patient, inclusive, and understanding of all the previous stages. That is what I mean by my frequent use of the phrase "transcend and include." That is the infallible sign that you are enlightened, psychologically mature, or a truly adult believer. The "adepts" in all religions are always forgiving, compassionate, and radically inclusive. They do not create enemies, and they move beyond the boundaries of their own "starter group" while still honoring them and making use of them.

Jesus the Jew criticizes his own religion the most, yet never leaves it! Mature people are not either-or thinkers, but they bathe in the ocean of both-and. (Think of Mahatma Gandhi, Anne Frank, Martin Luther King Jr., Mother Teresa, Nelson Mandela, and the like.) These enlightened people tend to grease the wheels of religious evolution. As Albert Einstein (1879–1955) is purported to have said, no problem can be solved by the same level of consciousness that created it. God moves humanity and religion forward by the regular appearance of such whole and holy people.

The second insight about steps and stages is that from your own level of development, you can only stretch yourself to comprehend people just a bit beyond yourself. Some theorists say you cannot stretch more than one step above your own level of consciousness, and that is on a good day! Because of this limitation, those at deeper (or "higher") levels beyond you invariably appear wrong, sinful, heretical, dangerous, or even worthy of elimination. How else can we explain the consistent killing of prophets; the marginalization of truly holy people as naïve; and the rather consistent racism, self-protectiveness, and warlike attitudes of people who think of themselves as civilized? You can be "civilized" and still be judging from the fully egocentric position of an early level of development. In fact, one of the best covers for very narcissistic people is to be polite, smiling, and thoroughly civilized. Hitler loved animals and classical music, I am told.

If change and growth are not *programmed into* your spirituality, if there are not serious warnings about the blinding nature of fear and fanaticism, your religion will *always* end up worshiping the status quo and protecting your present ego position and personal advantage—as if it were God! Although Jesus' first preached message is clearly "change!"—as in Mark 1:15 and Matthew 4:17, where he told his listeners to "repent," which literally means to "change your mind"—it did not strongly influence Christian history.

This resistance to change is so common, in fact, that it is almost what we expect from religious people, who tend to love the past more than the future or the present. All we can conclude is that much of organized religion is itself living inside of first-half-of-life issues, which usually coincides with where most people are in any culture. We all receive and pass on what our people are prepared to hear, and most people are not "early adopters." Yet even the intelligence of animals is determined by their ability to change and adjust their behavior in response to new circumstances. Those who do not, become extinct.

This pattern of resistance is so clear and even so defeating for Jesus that he makes what sounds like one of his most unkind statements: "Do not give to dogs what is holy or throw your pearls before swine. They will trample them, and then they will turn on you and tear you to pieces" (Matthew 7:6). We can save ourselves a lot of distress and accusation by knowing when, where, to whom, and how to talk about spiritually mature things. We had best offer what each one is ready to hear, and perhaps only stretch them a bit! Ken Wilber says that most of us are only willing to call 5 percent of our present information into question at any one point—and again, that is on a very good day. I guess prophets are those who do not care whether we are ready to hear their message. They say it because it has to be said and because it is true.

If there is no wise authority capable of protecting them and validating them, most prophetic or wise people and all early adopters are almost always "torn to pieces." Their wisdom sounds like dangerous foolishness, like most of Jesus' Sermon on the Mount does to Christians, like Gandhi to Great Britain, like Martin Luther King Jr. to white America, like Nelson Mandela to Dutch Reformed South Africa, like Harriet Tubman to the Daughters of the American Revolution, and like American nuns to the Catholic patriarchy.

OF GOD AND RELIGION

Theologically and objectively speaking, we are already in union with God. But it is very hard for people to believe or experience this when they have no positive sense of identity, little courage yet, no strong boundaries to contain Mystery, and little inner religious experience at any depth. Thus, the first journey is always about externals, formulas, superficial emotions, flags and badges, correct rituals, Bible quotes, and special clothing, all of which largely substitute for actual spirituality (see Matthew 23:13–32). Yet they are all used and needed to create the container. Yes, it is largely style and sentiment instead of real substance, but even that is probably necessary. Just don't give your life for mere style and sentiment. Pope John XXIII's motto (possibly originating with Augustine) might be heard here: "In essentials unity, in nonessentials liberty, and in all things, charity."[5] That is second-half-of-life, hard-won wisdom.

In the first half of our lives, we have no container for such awesome content, no wineskins that are prepared to hold such utterly intoxicating wine. You see, *authentic God experience always "burns" us yet does not destroy us* (see Exodus 3:2–3), just as the burning bush did to Moses. But most of us are not prepared for such burning, nor are we even told to expect it. The Islamic mystics seem to be the most honest here, as we see in the ecstatic and erotic poetry of Rumi, Kabir, and Hafiz. By definition, authentic God experience is always "too much"! It consoles our True Self only after it has devastated our false self. We must begin to be honest about this instead of dishing out fast-food religion.[6]

Early stage religion is largely preparing us for the immense gift of this burning, this inner experience of God, as though creating a proper stable into which the Christ can be born. Unfortunately, most people get so preoccupied with their stable, and whether their stable is better than your stable, or whether their stable is the only "one, holy, catholic, and apostolic" stable, that they never get to the birth of God in the soul. There is no indication in the text that Jesus demanded ideal stable conditions. In fact, we could say that the specific mentioning of his birth in a "manger" is making the exact opposite point. Animals, at least, had room for him, while there was "no room for him in the inn" (Luke 2:7) where humans stayed.

As a priest for over half a century, I have found that much of the spiritual and pastoral work of churches is often ineffective at the levels of real transformation. Instead, it calls forth immense passivity and even many passive-aggressive responses. As a preacher, I find that I am forced to dumb down the material in order to interest a Sunday crowd that does not expect or even want any real challenge; nor do people exhibit much spiritual or intellectual curiosity. "Just repeat what I expect to hear, Father, and maybe a joke or two!"

As a spiritual director, I find that most people facing the important transformative issues of social injustice, divorce, failure, gender identity, an inner life of prayer, or any radical reading of the Gospel are usually bored and limited by the typical Sunday church agenda. And these are good people! But they keep on doing their own kind of survival dance because no one has told them about their sacred dance. Of course, clergy cannot talk about a further journey if they have not gone on it themselves.

In short, we have not found a way to do the age-appropriate tasks of the two halves of life, and both groups are losing out. The juniors are made to think that the container is all there is and all they should expect — or, worse, that they are mature and home free because they believe a few right things or perform some right rituals. The would-be maturing believer is not challenged to any adult faith or service to the world, much less mystical union. Everyone ends up in a muddled middle, where "the best lack all conviction, while the worst are full of passionate intensity," as William Butler Yeats (1865–1939) put it.[7] I am convinced that much of this pastoral and practical confusion has emerged because we have not clarified the real differences, the needs, and the somewhat conflicting challenges of the two halves of our own lives. So, let's try.

CHAPTER 2

THE HERO'S JOURNEY

 We have only to follow the thread of the hero-path. Where we had thought to find an abomination, we shall find a god; where we had thought to slay another, we shall slay ourselves; where we had thought to travel outward, we shall come to the center of our own existence; where we had thought to be alone, we shall be with all the world.

—JOSEPH CAMPBELL, *1956 / PRINCETON UNIVERSITY PRESS.*

If we look at the world's mythologies in any of the modern collections, we will invariably see what Joseph Campbell calls the "monomyth of the hero" repeated in various forms for both men and women, but with different symbols.[1] The stages of the hero's journey are a skeleton for what I want to say in this book. In some ways, we are merely going to unpack this classic journey and draw out many of the implications that are even clearer today, both psychologically and spiritually. We are the beneficiaries of spiritual and informational globalization, like never before.

The pattern of the heroic journey is rather consistent and really matches my own research on initiation.[2] Those embarking on this journey invariably go through the following stages in one form or another.

1.   They live in a world that they presently take as given and sufficient. They are often a prince or princess and, if not, sometimes even of divine origin, which of course they always know nothing about. (This amnesia is a giveaway for the core religious problem, as discovering our divine DNA is always the task.) Remember, Odysseus is the king of Ithaca but does not "reign" there until after the second journey.

2.   They have the call or the courage to leave home for an adventure of some type—not really to solve any problem, but just to *go out and beyond*

11

their present comfort zone. For example, the young Siddhartha leaves the walls of the palace, St. Francis goes on pilgrimages to the Muslim world, Queen Esther and Joan of Arc enter the world of battle to protect their peoples, and Odysseus sets out for the Trojan War.

3.   On this journey or adventure, they in fact *find their real problem!* They are almost always "wounded" in some way and encounter a major dilemma, and the whole story largely pivots around the resolution of the trials that result. There is *always* a wounding, and the great epiphany is that the wound becomes the secret key, even "sacred," and a wound that changes them dramatically—which, by the way, is the precise meaning of the wounds of Jesus.

Their world is opened up, the screen becomes much larger, and they do too. Our very word *odyssey* is now used to describe these kinds of discoveries and adventures. Odysseus enters the story as a man alone, weeping on a beach, defeated, with no hope of ever returning home, where he would be a hero. That is his gnawing and unending wound. It is all so unfair, because he was a hero in the Trojan War.

4.   The first task, which the hero thinks is the only task, is only the vehicle and warm-up act to get them to the real task. The hero "falls through" what is merely *their life situation* to discover their *Real Life*, which is always a much deeper river, hidden beneath the appearances. Most people confuse their life situation with their actual life, which is an underlying flow beneath the everyday events. This deeper discovery is largely what religious people mean by "finding their soul."

5.   The hero then returns to where they started and "knows the place for the first time," as T. S. Eliot put it,[3] but now with a gift or "boon" for their people or village. As the last step of Alcoholics Anonymous states, a person must *pass the lessons learned on to others—or there has been no real gift at all.* The hero's journey is always an experience of an excess of life, a surplus of energy, with plenty left over for others. The hero has found *eros,* or life energy, and it is more than enough to undo *thanatos,* the energy of death.

If it is authentic life energy, it is always experienced as a surplus or an abundance of life. The hero is by definition a "generative" person, to use Erik Erikson's fine term, concerned about the next generation and not just themselves. The hero lives in deep time and not just in their own small time.

In fact, I would wonder if anyone could be a hero if they did not live in what many call deep time—that is, past, present, and future all at once.

⁓

Interestingly enough, this classic tradition of a true "hero" is not our present understanding at all. There is little social matrix to our present use of the word. A "hero" now is largely about being bold, muscular, rich, famous, talented, or "fantastic" by oneself, and often *for* oneself, whereas the classic hero is one who "goes the distance," whatever that takes, and then has plenty left over for others. True heroism serves the common good or it is not really heroism at all.

To seek one's own *American Idol* fame, power, salary, or talent might historically have made one famous, or even infamous—but not a hero. To be a celebrity or a mere survivor today is often confused with heroism, which is probably a sign of our actual regression. Merely to survive and preserve our life is a low-level instinct that we share with good little lizards, but it is not heroism in any classic sense. We were meant to thrive and not just survive. We are glad when someone survives, and that surely took some courage and effort. But what are you going to do with your now-resurrected life? That is the heroic question.

The very first sign of a potential hero's journey is that you must leave home, the familiar, which is something that may not always occur to someone in the first half of life. (In fact, many people have not left home by their thirties today, and most never leave the familiar at all!) If you have spent many years building your particular tower of success and self-importance—your "private salvation" project, as Thomas Merton called it[4]—or have successfully constructed your own superior ethnic group, religion, or "house," you won't want to leave it. (Now that many people have second, third, and fourth houses, it makes me wonder how they can ever leave home.)

Once you can get "out of the house," your "castle" and comfort zone, much of the journey has a life—and death—of its own. The crucial thing is to get out and about, into the real and bigger issues. In fact, this was the basic plotline of the founding myth that created the three monotheistic religions, with Yahweh's words to Abraham and Sarah: "Leave your country, your family, and your father's house, and head for the new land that I will show you" (Genesis 12:1). We seem to have an amazing capacity for missing the major point—and our own necessary starting point along with it. We have rather totally turned around our very founding myth! No wonder religion is in trouble.

I wonder whether we no longer have a capacity for that real *obedience* to the gods or sense of destiny, call, and fate that led Odysseus to leave father, wife, and son for a second journey. That is the very same obedience, by the way, that Jesus scandalously talks about in several places, like Luke 14:26 ("If anyone comes to me without leaving their own father and mother, spouse and children, brothers and sisters—yes, and even their own life, they cannot be my disciple"). I always wonder what so-called "family values" Christians do with shocking lines like that. Jesus was not a nuclear-family man at all, by any common definition! What led so many saints to seek the "will of God" first—above their own? What has led so many Peace Corps workers, missionaries, and skilled people to leave their countries for difficult lands and challenges? I would assume it was often a sense of a further journey, an invitation from their soul, or even a deep obedience to God.

Most of the calls of the disciples in the Christian Scriptures are rather clearly invitations to leave "your father and your nets" (Matthew 4:22). When he calls his first disciples, Jesus is talking about further journeys to people who are already happily and religiously settled! He is not talking about joining a new security system, a religious denomination, or even a religious order that pays all your bills. Again, it is very surprising to me that so many Christians who read the Scriptures do not see this. Maybe they cannot answer a second call because they have not yet completed the first task. Unless you build your first house well, you will never leave it. *To build your house well is, ironically, to be nudged beyond its doors.*

Remember, Odysseus did a lot of conquering, Abraham a lot of "possessing," Francis a lot of partying, David and Paul a lot of killing, Magdalene a lot of loving, and all of us a lot of ascending and descending, before being ready to move on to the next stage of the journey. Many of us cannot move ahead because we have not done the first task, learned from the last task, or had any of our present accomplishments acknowledged by others. During my fourteen years as chaplain at the Albuquerque jail, I met so many men who remained stymied forever in a teenage psyche because they had not been able to build their first "house" well—or at all. Nor was there anyone who believed in them. They had usually not been parented well, or had not been given the mirroring that would have secured them within the first half of their lives.

Yes, we are seduced and fall into the second half of our lives, but a part of that movement is precisely that we have finished the first life tasks, at least in part. We can—and will—move forward as soon as we have completed and lived the previous stage. We almost naturally float forward by the quiet movement of grace when the time is right—and the old agenda shows itself to be insufficient, or it even falls apart. All that each of us can do is to live in the *now* that is given. We cannot rush the process. We can only carry out each stage of our lives to the best of our ability—and then we no longer need to do it anymore! Next, let me describe in greater detail how we build that first house.

CHAPTER 3

THE FIRST HALF OF LIFE

 The world is more magical, less predictable, more autonomous, less controllable, more varied, less simple, more infinite, less knowable, more wonderfully troubling than we could have imagined being able to tolerate when we were young.
—JAMES HOLLIS, *2006 / PENGUIN RANDOM HOUSE.*

I cannot think of a culture in human history, before the present postmodern era, that did not value law, tradition, custom, authority, boundaries, and morality of some clear sort. These containers give us the necessary security, continuity, predictability, impulse control, and ego structure that we need before the chaos of real life shows up. Healthily conservative people tend to grow up more naturally and more happily than those who receive only free-form, "build it yourself" worldviews, in my studied opinion.

Here is my conviction: *Without law in some form, and also without butting up against that law, we cannot move forward easily and naturally.* The rebellions of two-year-olds and teenagers are in our hardwiring, and we have to have something hard and half-good to rebel against. We need a worthy opponent against which we test our mettle. As Rainer Maria Rilke (1875–1926) put it, "When we victorious are, it is over small things, and though we won, it leaves us feeling small."[1]

We need a very strong container to hold the contents and contradictions that arrive later in life. We ironically need a very strong ego structure to let go of our ego. We need to struggle with the rules more than a bit before we throw them out. We only internalize values by butting up against external values for a while. All of this builds the strong self that can *positively* obey Jesus—and "die" to itself. In fact, far too many (especially women and disadvantaged people) have lived very warped and defeated lives because they tried to give up a self that was not there yet.

This is an important paradox for most of us, and the two sides of this paradox must be made clear for the very health of individuals, families, and cultures. It is crucial for our own civilization right now. We have too many people on the extremes. Some make a "sacrificial" and heroic life their whole identity and end up making everyone else around them sacrifice so that they can be sacrificial and heroic. Others, in selfish rebellion and without any training in letting go, refuse to sacrifice anything.

Basically, if we stay in the protected first half of life beyond its natural period, we become well-disguised narcissists or adult infants (who are also narcissists!)—both of whom are often thought to be successful "good old boys" by the mainstream culture. No wonder that Bill Plotkin calls us a "patho-adolescent culture."[2]

The first-half-of-life container, nevertheless, is constructed through impulse controls; traditions; group symbols; family loyalties; basic respect for authority; civil and church laws; and a sense of the goodness, value, and special importance of our country, ethnicity, and religion (as, for example, the Jews' sense of their "chosenness"). The educated and sophisticated Western person today has many levers (Archimedes), but almost no solid place on which to stand, with either very weak identities or terribly overstated identities. This tells me we are not doing the first-half-of-life task very well. How can we possibly get to the second?

Most people are trying to build the platform of their lives all by themselves, while working all the new levers at the same time. I think of CEOs, business leaders, soldiers, or parents who have no principled or ethical sense of themselves and end up with some kind of "pick and choose" morality in the pressured moment. This pattern leaves the isolated ego in full control and surely represents the *hubris* that will precede a lot of impending tragedies.

This pattern is probably predictable when we try to live life backward and build ourselves a wonderful superstructure before we have laid any real foundations from culture, religion, or tradition. Frankly, it is much easier to begin rather conservative or traditional. (I know some of us do not want to hear that.)

I think we all need some help from the Perennial Tradition that has held up over time. We cannot each start at zero, entirely on our own. Life is far too short, and there are plenty of mistakes we do not need to make—and some that we *need* to make. We are parts of social and family ecosystems that are rightly structured to keep us from falling but also, more important, to show us *how* to fall and also *how to learn* from that very falling. Think of the stories of the Brothers Grimm, Hans Christian Anderson, or Laura Ingalls Wilder, most of which circle around a dilemma, a problem, a difficulty, a failure, or an evil that begs to be overcome—and always is.

We are not helping our children by always preventing them from what might be necessary falling, because *we learn how to recover from falling by falling!* It is precisely by falling off the bike many times that we eventually learn what the *balance* feels like. The skater pushing both right and left eventually goes where they want to go. People who have never allowed themselves to fall are actually *off balance*, while not realizing it at all. That is why they are so hard to live with. Please think about that for a while.

Law and tradition seem to be necessary in any spiritual system, *both to reveal and to limit our basic egocentricity and to make at least some community, family, and marriage possible.* When we watch ten-year-olds intensely defend the rules of their games, we see what a deep need this is early in life. It structures children's universe and gives them foundational meaning and safety. We cannot flourish early in life inside a totally open field. Children need a good degree of order, predictability, and coherence to grow up well, as Maria Montessori, Rudolf Steiner, and many others have taught. Chaos and chaotic parents will rightly make children cry, withdraw, and rage—both inside and outside.

Cesar Milan, the "dog whisperer," says that dogs cannot be peaceful or teachable if they have no limits set to their freedom and their emotions. They are actually happier and at rest when they live within very clear limits and boundaries, with a "calm and assertive" master. My dog Venus was never happier and more teachable than when I was walking her—but on her leash. Could it be the same for humans at certain stages? I suspect so, although it is humiliating to admit it.

Without laws like the Ten Commandments, our existence here on this earth would be pretty pathetic. What if we could not rely on people to tell us the truth or not to steal from us? What if we were not expected to respect our parents, and we all started out with cynicism and mistrust of all authority? What if the "I love you" between partners was allowed to mean nothing? What if covetousness, which René Girard (1923–2015) called "mimetic rivalry,"[3] was encouraged to grow unstopped, as it is in capitalist countries today? Such shapelessness would be the death of any civilization or any kind of trustworthy or happy world. I wonder: Are we there already?

Without laws, human life would be anarchy and chaos, and that chaos would multiply over the generations, like the confused languages of the Tower of Babel (Genesis 11:1–9). We now need basic parenting classes in junior high schools because so many children have been poorly parented by people who themselves were poorly parented. Far too many people are verbally, physically, sexually, and psychologically abused in our society by people who have no basic relationship skills and no inner discipline.

People who have not been tutored by some "limit situations" in the first half of their life are in no position to parent children; they are usually children themselves. Limit situations, according to the German philosopher Karl Jaspers (1883–1969),[4] are moments, usually accompanied by experiences of dread, responsibility, guilt, or anxiety, in which the human mind confronts its restrictions and boundaries and allows itself to abandon the false securities of this limitedness, move beyond (one hopes in a positive way), and thus enter new realms of self-consciousness. In other words, we ironically need limit situations and boundaries to grow up. A completely open field does not do the job nearly as well or as quickly. Yahweh was creating a good limit situation for Adam and Eve when he told them *not* to eat the apple, fully knowing that they would.

If you want a job done well, on time, with accountability and no excuses, you had best hire someone who has faced a few limit situations. They alone have the discipline, the punctuality, the positive self-image, and the persistence to do a good job. If you want the opposite, hire someone who has been coddled, given "I Am Special" buttons for doing nothing special, had all their bills paid by others, and whose basic egocentricity has never been challenged or undercut. To be honest, this seems to describe much of the workforce and the student body of America. Many of the papers I used to receive in summer graduate courses at major universities were embarrassing to read in terms of both style and content, yet these same "adults" were shocked if they did not get an A. This does not bode well for the future of our country.

CONDITIONAL AND
UNCONDITIONAL LOVE

Over the past century, we have seen millions give themselves to ideologies of communism, fascism, terrorism, and unfettered capitalism (yes, Wall Street is also an embodiment of our ideology!) — often in angry rebellion either against an oppressive container or because they were given no soulful container at all. Like never before, we are now seeing the misplaced anger that was at the bottom of many, if not most, of the social movements of our age. Building on such a negative foundation inevitably produces a negative building.

None of these "isms" ever create a *civilization of love* or even positive energy. They are largely theories in the head that come from the small egoic personality, leaving the soul bereft, starved, and saddened. Without elders, much of our history has been formed by juniors reacting, overreacting, and protecting their own temporary privilege, with no deep-time vision like that attributed to the Iroquois Nation, which considered: What would be good for the next seven generations? Compare that to the modern "Tea Party" movement in America.

For any of you who might think this is just old religious moralizing, I offer the wisdom of Erich Fromm (1900–1980) in his classic book *The Art of Loving*.[5] He stated that the healthiest people he had known, and those who very often grew up in the most natural way, were those who, between their two parents and early authority figures, experienced a combination of unconditional love along with very conditional and demanding love. This seems to be true of so many effective and influential people, like St. Francis, John Muir, Eleanor Roosevelt, and Mother Teresa—and you can add your own. I know my siblings and I received conditional love from our mother and unconditional love from our father. We all admit now that she served us very well later in life, although we sure fought Mom when we were young, and we were glad Daddy was there to balance her out.

I know this is not the current version of what is psychologically "correct," because we all seem to think we need nothing but unconditional love. Any law, correction, rule, or limitation is another word for conditional love. It is interesting to me that very clear passages describing both God's conditional love and also God's unconditional love are found in the same Scriptures, like Deuteronomy and John's Gospel. The only real biblical promise is that *unconditional love will have the last word!*

The most effective organizations, I am told, have both a "good boss" and a "bad boss," who work closely together. One holds us strongly, while the other speaks hard truth to us and sets clear goals and limits for us. Our naïve sense of entitlement and overreaction against all limits to our freedom are not serving us well as parents and marriage partners, not to speak of our needed skills as employees, students, conversationalists, team players, or citizens. It takes the pain of others to produce a humane and just civilization, it seems.

I am convinced that Fromm is wise and correct here, and his wisdom surely matches my own lifetime of observation. It seems we need a foil, a goad, a wall to butt up against to create a proper ego structure and a strong identity. Such a foil is the way we internalize our own deeper values, educate our feeling function, and dethrone our own narcissism. Butting up against limits actually teaches us an awful lot. "I would not have known the meaning of covetousness if the Law had not said, 'You shall not covet,'" wrote Paul in his tour de force *against* the law in his letter to the Romans (7:7)! (For all his possible neuroses, Paul was also a spiritual genius; somehow, it is good to know that neurosis and brilliance can coexist in the same person.)

Those who whine about parents and authority for too long invariably remain or become narcissists themselves. I state this after working with people on many levels, including in the jail, as a counselor, and as a confessor. It has been acceptable for some time in America to remain "wound identified" (that is, using our victimhood as our identity, our ticket to sympathy, and our excuse for not serving), instead of using the wound to "redeem the world," as we see in Jesus and many people who turn their wounds into sacred wounds that liberate both themselves and others.

Oprah would hardly have a TV show if she could not highlight these many amazing people who have turned their wounds into gifts for society, and they are often people who are not overtly religious at all. They often care about others and don't want others to be hurt the way they were. It reminds me of Jesus' story of the two sons, one who said all the right words but never acted on these words, and the other who said the wrong words but in fact "went to work in the vineyard." Jesus said that the person who finally acts and *engages* "does the Father's will," even if they are a tax collector or a prostitute and do not have the right "belief system" (Matthew 21:28–32). *Jesus seems to often find love in people who might not have received much love themselves. Perhaps their deep longing for it became their capacity to both receive it and give it.* This surely matches my own life experience.

HOLDING A CREATIVE TENSION

Mature people invariably thank their harder parent, law-driven church, kick-ass coach, and most demanding professors—but usually years later. This is a clear sign of having transcended—and included. It is what we should expect fifty- to seventy-year-olds to say and what we seldom hear from twenty- to forty-year-olds anymore unless they have grown up quite quickly. Some, of course, have also been wounded quite lethally, as in situations of rape, abuse, or bullying, and it takes them a longer time to heal and grow.

I am trying to place you and then hold you inside of a very creative tension, if you will allow yourself to be held there. I do promise you it is a *creative* tension, because both law and freedom are necessary for spiritual growth, as Paul wrote in Romans and Galatians. He learned this from Jesus, who says seven times in a row, "The Law says . . . but I say" (Matthew 5:21–48), while also assuring us that he has "not come to throw out the law but to bring it to completion" (5:17). Despite having been directly taught to hold this creative tension, rare is the Christian believer who holds it well. We are usually on bended knee before laws or angrily reacting against them—both immature responses.

Actually, I have seen many Jews, Hindus, and Buddhists do it much better, *but very few Christians have been taught how to live both law and freedom at the same time.* Our Western dualistic minds do not process paradoxes very well. Without a contemplative mind, we do not know how to hold creative tensions. We are better at rushing to judgment and demanding a complete resolution to things before we have learned what they have to teach us. This is not the way of wisdom, and it is the way that people operate in the first half of life.

"Primitive" and native societies might well have held this tension better than we do today.[6] There is much evidence that many traditional societies produced healthy psyches and ego structures by doing the first half of life very well, even if they were not as "developed" or individuated as we are. I have seen this myself among indigenous and "undeveloped" peoples in India, the Philippines, and Latin America. They often seem much less neurotic and anxious than we are. They can deal with failure or loss far, far more easily than we can. Any of you who have been in the barrios, favelas, and townships of the world know how often this is true. Owen Barfield (1898–1997) stated that they enjoy a kind of simple but transformative "original participation" with reality and with God.[7]

In the Western world, it seems we cannot build prisons fast enough or have enough recovery groups, therapists, or reparenting classes for all the walking wounded in this very educated, religious, and sophisticated society—which has little respect for limitations and a huge sense of entitlement. How could this happen? How could neuroses and depression be less the exception and more the very norm? Our elderly are seldom elders, it seems to me. When they are true elders, we all fall in love with them.

The presumption has been against law and authority for several centuries now. Tradition or any talk of limits has not been attractive since the protesting Reformation, the unenlightened Enlightenment, or the rise of democracy (all of which were necessary, by the way!). Now, we all start our kids in a kind of free fall and hope that by some good luck or insight they will magically come to wisdom. The ego cannot be allowed to be totally in charge throughout our early years, or it takes over. The entirely open field leaves us the victim of too many options, and the options themselves soon push us around and take control. Law and structure, as fallible as they often are, put up some kind of limits to our infantile grandiosity and prepare us for helpful relationships with the outer world, which has rights too.

FIRST HALF DONE POORLY

I am also deeply aware of the damage that misuse of law, custom, authority, and tradition has done in human history and to personal development. I know the destructive and immature state that mere reliance on structure and authority has engendered. The anger and blindness it often brings is devastating, because it often takes away both a necessary self-confidence and a necessary self-questioning. We see this in our political debates today, in people's lack of basic self-knowledge (too-quick answers keep us from necessary searching), and in scary fundamentalist thinking in all the world religions.

Most wars, genocides, and tragedies in history have been waged by unquestioning followers of dominating leaders. Yet, there is a strange comfort in staying within the confines of such a leader and their ideologies, even if it leads us to do evil. It frees us from the burden of thinking and from personal responsibility. We are also creatures who love the familiar, the habitual, and our own group. We are all tied deeply to our early conditioning, for good and for ill.

Most people will not leave the safety and security of their home base until they have to. Thus the Gospel call, again and again, is to leave home, family, and nets (Mark 1:16–20). Without that necessary separation, order itself, and *my* particular kind of order, will often feel like a kind of "salvation." It has been the most common and bogus substitute for the real liberation offered by mature religion. "Keep the rules, and the rules will keep you!" we were told our first day in the seminary. Franciscans should have known better.

But I am not here to say either-or. I am here to say both-and. It is not just "the exception that proves the rule" but that *somehow the loss or transgression of the rule also proves the importance and purpose of the rule*. We must first eat the fruit of the garden, so we know what it tastes like—and what we are missing if and when we stop eating it. We are perhaps the first generation in history, we postmodern folks, who have the freedom both to know the rules and also to critique the rules at the same time. This is changing everything and evolving consciousness at a rather quick rate.[8]

In the Roman Catholic Church, we are now involved in an enormous example of what some would call "the regressive restoration of persona," a desire to return to the "good old days" when we were supposedly on top, secure, sure of ourselves, and marching together. (I am not persuaded myself, because I lived in those good old days, which were not always so good for a vast majority of people.) We see this especially in young priests, who are seeing the church as their security system and lifelong employer.

Nevertheless, this new tribalism is being found in all the world religions— a desire for rediscovery of one's roots, one's traditions, one's symbols, one's ethnic identity, and one's own unique identity. Some call it the "identity politics" that rules the United States of America. This is understandable in the midst of massive and scary globalization among eight billion people, but it also keeps us trapped at the *bipartisan divide*—and we never achieve the *transpartisan* nature of mature elders. People think that by defeating the other side, they have achieved some high level of truth! It's very sad indeed, but that is as far as the angry or fearful dualistic mind can go.

When some have not been able to do the task of the first half of life well, they go back and try to do it again—and then often overdo it. This pattern is usually an inconsistent mix of old-fashioned styles and symbols with very contemporary ideologies of consumerism, technology, militarism, and individualism. This tends to be these individuals' blind spot, which makes them not true conservatives at all. In fact, neoconservatives are usually intense devotees of modern progress and upward mobility in the system, as we see in most Evangelicals, Mormons, and "traditionalist" Catholics. Only groups that have emphasized actual and costly lifestyle changes for themselves, like the Amish, the Shakers, the Mennonites, Catholic Workers, Poor Clares, and the Quakers, can be called true conservatives.

I saw this pattern in my fourteen years as a jail chaplain. The inmates would invariably be overly religious, highly moralistic, and excessively legalistic (believe it or not!), and many overly intellectualized everything. They would do anything to try to compensate for their dashed hopes and maybe never developed, but publicly humiliated criminal self. Here I was, the Catholic chaplain, and the last thing I sometimes trusted was a lot of "religious" language and Jesus talk. Again, it was a regressive restoration of a failed first half of life. It seldom works long term.

One study pointed out that a strong majority of young men entering seminaries came from single-parent homes, a high percentage having what we would call "father wounds,"[9] which can take the form of an absent, emotionally unavailable, alcoholic, or even abusive father. This overwhelmingly matches my own experience of working in Catholic seminaries, and of men in jail, the military, or any all-male system. Many of these men were formed in postmodern Europe and America, where almost nothing has been stable, constant, or certain since the late 1960s, and even the church was trying to reform itself through the Second Vatican Council.

All has been in flux since about 1968. Then, add to that two decades of nonstop public scandal over the issues of pedophilia and cover-up by the Catholic hierarchy. Such bishops, priests, and seminarians often had no chance to do the task of the first half of life well. It was a movable famine to grow up in, so they backtracked to do what they should have been able to do first—second! They are out of sequence, through no fault of their own. They want a tribe that is both superior and secure—and theirs. Men join a male club like the church to get the male energy they never got as sons, or because they accept the male game of "free enterprise" and social advancement. I have often wondered if I did the same. I hope not.

The result is a generation of seminarians and young clergy who are cognitively rigid and "risk adverse"; who want to circle the wagons around their imagined secure and superior group; who seem preoccupied with the clothing, titles, perks, and externals of religion; and who, frankly, have little use for the world beyond their own control or explanation. Ecumenism, interfaith dialogue, and social justice are dead issues for them. None of us can dialogue with others until we can calmly and confidently hold our own identity. None of us can know much about second-half-of-life spirituality as long as we are still trying to create the family, the parenting, the security, the order, and the pride that we were not given in the first half.

Most of us from my generation cannot go back on this old path, not because it was bad, but *precisely because we already did it and learned from it.* Unfortunately, we have an entire generation of educators, bishops, and political leaders who are still building their personal towers of success and therefore have little ability to elder the young or challenge the beginners. In some ways, they are still beginners themselves. Self-knowledge is dismissed as psychology, love as "feminine softness," and critical thinking as disloyalty, while law, ritual, and priestcraft have become compulsive substitutes for actual divine encounter or honest relationship. This does not bode well for the future of any church or society.

So, let's look at a way through all this because, *spiritually speaking, there are no dead ends.* God will use this too—somehow—and draw all of us toward the Great Life. But there is a way to move ahead more naturally, if we can recognize a common disguise and dead end.

DISCHARGING YOUR LOYAL SOLDIER

In his work at his Animas Institute in Durango, Colorado, Bill Plotkin takes people on long fasts and vision quests in nature. His work offers a very specific and truth-filled plan for moving from what he calls an "egocentric" worldview to a "soul-centric" worldview.[10] Like me, Plotkin is saddened by how much of our world stays at the egocentric first stage of life. His work reveals a historical situation in post–World War II Japan that demonstrates how people could be helped to move from the identity of the first half of life to the growth of the second half. In this situation, some Japanese communities had the savvy to understand that many of their returning soldiers were not fit or prepared to reenter civil or humane society. Their only identity for their formative years had been to be a "loyal soldier" to their country. They needed a broader identity to once again rejoin their communities as useful citizens.[11]

So, these Japanese communities created a communal ritual whereby a soldier was publicly thanked and praised effusively for his service to the people. After this was done at great length, an elder would stand and announce with authority something to this effect: "The war is now over! The community needs you to let go of what has served you and served us well up to now. The community needs you to return as a man, a citizen, and something beyond a soldier." In the men's work, we call this process "discharging your loyal soldier."

This kind of closure is much needed for most of us at the end of all major transitions in life. Because we have lost any sense of the need for such rites of passage, most people have no clear crossover to the second half of their own lives. No one shows us the stunted and limited character of the worldview of the first half of life, so we just continue with more of the same. The Japanese were wise enough to create clear closure, transition, and possible direction. Western people are a *ritually starved* people. In this, our lives are different than most of human history. Even the church's sacraments are overwhelmingly dedicated to keeping us loyally inside the flock and tied to the clergy—loyal soldiers of the church. There is little talk of journeys outward or onward, the kind of journeys Jesus called people to go on.

The state also wants loyal patriots and citizens, not thinkers, critics, or citizens of a larger world. No wonder we have so much depression and addiction, especially among the elderly and also among the churched. Their full life has been truncated with the full cooperation of both church and state.

The loyal soldier is similar to the elder son in Jesus' parable of the prodigal son. His very loyalty to strict meritocracy, to his own entitlement, and to obedience and loyalty to his father, keeps him from the very "celebration" that same father has prepared, even though he begs the son to come to the feast (Luke 15:25–32). We have no indication he ever came! What a judgment this is on first-stage religion, and it comes straight from the boss.

He makes the same point in his story of the Pharisee and the tax collector (Luke 18:9–14), in which one is loyal and observant and deemed wrong by Jesus, while the other has not obeyed the law—yet is deemed "at rights with God." This is classic "reverse theology" meant to subvert our usual merit-badge thinking. Both the elder son and the Pharisee are good loyal religious soldiers, exactly what most of us in the church were told to be, yet Jesus says that both of them missed the major point.

The voice of our loyal soldier gets us through the first half of life safely, teaching us to look both ways before we cross the street, to have enough impulse control to avoid addictions and compulsive emotions, and to learn the sacred "no" to ourselves that gives us dignity, identity, direction, significance, and boundaries. We *must* learn these lessons to get off to a good start. It is far easier to begin life with a conservative worldview and respect for traditions. It gives us an initial sense of "place" and is much more effective in the long run, even if it just gives us a goad to kick against (Acts 26:14). Many of us just fall in love with our first place and position, as an extension of ourselves, and spend our whole life building a white picket fence around it.

Without a loyal soldier protecting us up to age thirty, the world's prisons and psych wards would be even more overcrowded than they are. Testosterone, addiction, ego, promiscuity, and vanity would win out in most of our lives. Without our loyal soldier, we would all be aimless and shapeless, with no home base and no sustained relationships, because there would be no "me" at home to have a relationship with. We'd have lots of levers, but no place to stand.

Paradoxically, our loyal soldier gives us so much security and validation that we may confuse that voice with the very voice of God. *If this inner and critical voice has kept us safe for many years as our inner voice of authority, we may end up not being able to hear the real voice of God.* (Please read that sentence again for maximum effect!) The loyal soldier is the voice of all our early authority figures. Their ability to offer shame, guilt, warnings, boundaries, and self-doubt is the gift that never stops giving, but it is not the "still, small voice" of God (1 Kings 19:12) that *gives us our power instead of always taking our power.*

The loyal soldier cannot get us to the second half of life. They do not even understand it. They have not been there. They can help us get through "hell," with the early decisions that demand black-and-white thinking, but then we have to say goodbye when we move into the subtlety of midlife and later life. The Japanese were correct, as were the Greeks. Odysseus is a loyal soldier for the entire Odyssey, rowing his boat as only a hero can — until the blind prophet tells him there is more and to put down his oar.

If you ever read the *Divine Comedy,* note that Dante lets go of Virgil, who had accompanied him through Hades and Purgatory, knowing that only Beatrice can lead him into Paradise. Virgil is the first-half-of-life man; Beatrice is the second-half-of-life woman.

In the first half of life, we fight the devil and have the illusion and inflation of "winning" now and then. In the second half of life, we always lose because we are invariably fighting God. *The first battles solidify the ego and create a stalwart loyal soldier. The second battles defeat the ego because God always wins.* No wonder so few want to let go of their loyal soldier. No wonder so few have the faith to grow up. The ego hates losing, even to God.

The loyal soldier is largely the same thing that Sigmund Freud (1856–1939) was describing with his concept of the superego, which he said usually substitutes for any real adult formation of conscience. The superego feels like God, because people have had nothing else to guide them. Such a bogus conscience is a terrible substitute for authentic morality. What reveals its bogus character is its major resistance to change and growth and its substituting of small, low-cost moral issues for the real ones that ask *us* to change instead of always trying to change other people. Jesus called it straining out gnats while swallowing camels (Matthew 23:24). It is much more common than I ever imagined, something I didn't learn until I began to serve as a confessor and spiritual director.

There is a deeper voice of God, which we must learn to *hear and obey* in the second half of life. It will sound an awful lot like the voices of risk, of trust, of surrender, of soul, of "common sense," of destiny, of love, of an intimate stranger, of your deepest self, and of soulful "Beatrice." The true faith journey only begins at this point. Up to now, everything is mere preparation. Finally, we have a container strong enough to hold the contents of our real life, which is always filled with contradictions, adventures, and immense challenges. *Psychological wholeness and spiritual holiness never exclude the problem from the solution. If it is wholeness, then it is always paradoxical and holds both the dark and light sides of things.* Wholeness and holiness will always stretch us beyond our small comfort zone. How could they not?

So God, life, and destiny have to loosen the loyal soldier's grasp on our soul, which up to now has felt like the only "me" that we know and the only authority that there is. Our loyal soldier normally begins to be discharged somewhere between the ages of thirty-five and fifty-five, if it happens at all; before that, it is usually mere rebellion or iconoclasm.

To let go of the loyal soldier will be a severe death and an exile from your first base. You will feel similar to Isaiah before he was sent into exile in Babylon: "In the noontime of my life, I was told to depart for the gates of Hades. Surely I am deprived of the rest of my years" (38:10). Discharging your loyal soldier will be necessary to finding authentic inner authority, or what Jeremiah promised as "the law written in your heart" (31:33). First-half-of-life folks will seldom have the courage to go forward at this point unless they have a guide, a friend, a Virgil, a Teiresias, a Beatrice, a soul friend, or a stumbling block to guide them toward the goal. There are few in our religious culture who understand the necessity of a mature internalized conscience, so wise guides are hard to find. You will have many more Aarons building you golden calves than Moseses leading you on any exodus.

Normally, we will not discharge our loyal soldier until they show themselves to be wanting, incapable, or inadequate for the real issues of life — as when we confront love, death, suffering, subtlety, sin, mystery, and so on. It is another form of the falling and dying that I keep talking about. The world mythologies all point to places like Hades, Sheol, hell, purgatory, and the realm of the dead. *Maybe these are not so much the alternative to heaven as the necessary path to heaven.*

Even Jesus, if we are to believe the Apostles, Creed of the church, "descended into hell" before he ascended into heaven. Isn't it strange how we missed that? Every initiation rite I studied worldwide was always about *dying before you die.* When you first discharge your loyal soldier, it will feel like a loss of faith or loss of self. *But it is only the death of the false self and is often the very birth of the soul.* Instead of being ego-driven, you will begin to be soul-drawn. The wisdom and guidance you will need to get you across this chasm will be like Charon ferrying you across the river Styx or Hermes guiding the soul across all scary boundaries. These are your authentic soul friends, and we now sometimes call them spiritual directors or elders. Celtic Christianity called them *anam chara*.

Remember that Hercules, Orpheus, Aeneas, Psyche, and Odysseus all traveled into realms of the dead—and returned! Most mythologies include a descent into the underworld at some point. Jesus, as I noted, also "descended into hell," and only on the third day did he "ascend into heaven." Most of life is lived, as it were, on the first and second days, the threshold days when transformation is happening but we do not know it yet. In men's work, we call this *liminal space.*[12]

St. John of the Cross (1542–1591) taught that God has to work in the soul *in secret* and *in darkness*, because *if we fully knew what was happening and what Mystery/transformation/God/grace will eventually ask of us, we would either try to take charge or stop the whole process.*[13] No one oversees their own demise willingly, even when it is the false self that is dying.

The mystics tell us that God has to undo our illusions secretly, as it were, when we are not watching and not in perfect control. That is perhaps why the best word for God is actually *Mystery*. We move forward in ways that we do not even understand and through the quiet workings of time and grace. When we get there, we are never sure just how it happened, and God does not seem to care who gets the credit, as long as our growth continues. As St. Gregory of Nyssa already said in the fourth century, "Sin happens whenever we refuse to keep growing."[14]

CHAPTER 4

THE TRAGIC SENSE
OF LIFE

 In the deeps are the violence and terror of which psychology has warned us. But if you ride these monsters down, if you drop with them farther over the world's rim, you find what our sciences cannot locate or name, the substrate, the ocean or matrix or ether which buoys the rest, which gives goodness its power for good, and evil its power of evil, the unified field: our complex and inexplicable caring for each other, and for our life together here. This is given. It is not learned.

—ANNIE DILLARD, 1982 / HARPERCOLLINS PUBLISHERS.

The exact phrase, "the tragic sense of life," was first popularized in the early twentieth century by the Spanish philosopher Miguel de Unamuno (1864–1936), who courageously told his European world that they had distorted the meaning of faith by aligning it with the Western philosophy of "progress" rather than with what he saw as rather evident in the Judeo-Christian Scriptures.[1] Jesus and the Hebrew prophets were fully at home with the tragic sense of life, and it made the shape and nature of reality very different for them, for Unamuno, and maybe still for us.

By this clear and honest phrase, I understand Unamuno to mean that life is not, nor ever has been, a straight line forward. According to him, life is characterized much more by exception and disorder than by total or perfect order. Life, as the biblical tradition makes clear, is both loss and renewal, death and resurrection, chaos and healing at the same time. Life seems to be a collision of opposites. Unamuno equates the notion of faith with trust in an underlying life force so strong that it even includes death. Faith also includes reason, but it is a larger category than reason for Unamuno. Truth is not always about pragmatic problem solving and making things "work," but about reconciling contradictions. Just because something might have some dire effects does not mean it is not true or even good. Just because something pleases people does not make it true either. Life is inherently tragic, and that is the truth that only faith, but not our seeming logic, can accept. This is my amateur and very partial summary of the thought of this great Spanish philosopher.

THE "TRAGIC" NATURAL WORLD

In our time, it is quantum physics that shows how true Unamuno's explanation might really be. Most of us were formed by Newtonian worldviews in which everything had a clear cause and equal effect, what might be called an "if-then" worldview. All causality was clear and defined. The truth we are now beginning to respect is that the universe seems to proceed through a web of causes, just as human motivation does, producing ever-increasing diversity, multiplicity, dark holes, dark matter, death and rebirth, loss and renewal in different forms, and yes, even violence: the continual breaking of the rules of "reason" that make wise people look for more all-embracing rules and a larger "logic."

Nature is much more disorder than order, more multiplicity than uniformity, with the greatest disorder being death itself. In the spiritual life, and now in science, we learn much more by honoring and learning from the exceptions than by imposing our previously certain rules to make everything fit. We can now perhaps see what Jesus and Paul both meant by telling us to honor "the least of the brothers and sisters" (Matthew 25:40; 1 Corinthians 12:22–25) and to "clothe them with the greatest care." It is those creatures and those humans who are on the edge of what we have defined as normal, proper, or good who often have the most to teach us. They tend to reveal the shadow and mysterious side of things. Such constant exceptions make us revisit the so-called rule and what we call normal—and recalibrate! The exceptions keep us humble and searching, rather than rushing toward resolution to allay our anxiety.

Our daily experience of this world is almost nothing like Plato's world of universal and perfect forms and ideas. It is always filled with huge diversity and variations on every theme, from neutrino light inside of darkness to male seahorses that bear their young, to the most extraordinary flowers that only open at night for no one to see. Jesus had no trouble with the exceptions, whether they were prostitutes, drunkards, Samaritans, lepers, Gentiles, tax collectors, or wayward sheep. He ate with outsiders regularly, to the chagrin of the church stalwarts, who always love their version of order over any compassion toward the exceptions. Just the existence of a single differently abled person should make us change any of our theories about the necessity of some kind of correct thinking as the definition of "salvation." Yet we have a history of excluding and torturing people who do not "think" right.

I remember the final words of my professor of church history, a very orthodox priest theologian, who said as he walked out of the classroom after our four years of study with him, "Well, after all is said and done, remember that church practice has been more influenced by Plato than by Jesus." We reeled in astonishment, but the four years of history had spoken for themselves. What he meant, of course, was that we invariably prefer the universal synthesis, the answer that settles all the dust and resolves every question—even when it is not entirely true—over the mercy and grace of God.

Jesus did not seem to teach that one size fits all, but instead that his God adjusts to the vagaries and failures of the moment. This ability to adjust to human disorder and failure is named God's providence or compassion. *Every time God forgives us, God is saying that God's own rules do not matter as much as the relationship that God wants to create with us.* Just the Biblical notion of absolute forgiveness, once experienced, should be enough to make us trust, seek, and love God.

But we humans have a hard time with the specific, the concrete, the individual, and the anecdotal story, which hardly ever fits the universal mold. So, we pretend. Maybe that is why we like and need humor, which invariably reveals these inconsistencies. In Franciscan thinking, this specific, individual, concrete thing is always God's work and God's continuing choice, precisely in its uniqueness, not in its uniformity. Scotus called it "thisness." Christians believe that "incarnation" showed itself in one unique, specific person: Jesus. It becomes his pattern too, as he leaves the ninety-nine for the one lost sheep (Matthew 18:12–14). Walter Brueggemann calls this divine pattern of incarnation "the scandal of the particular."[2] Our mind, it seems, is more pleased with universals: never-broken, always-applicable rules and patterns that allow us to predict and control things. This is good for science, but lousy for religion.

The universe story and the human story are a play of forces rational and nonrational, conscious and unconscious; of fate and fortune, nature and nurture. Forces of good and evil play out their tragedies and their graces—leading us to catastrophes, backtracking, mutations, transgressions, regroupings, enmities, failures, mistakes, and impossible dilemmas. (We will get to the good part later!) Did you know that the Greek word for *tragedy* means "goat story"? The Odyssey is a primal goat story, where poor Odysseus keeps going forward and backward, up and down—but mostly down—all the way home to Ithaca.

Each of these experiences is meant to lead us to a new knowledge and a movement "forward" in some sense, yet it is always a humbled knowledge. *Greek hubris was precisely the refusal to be humbled by what should have been humbling.* Notice how no American president can fully admit that his war or his policies were wrong—ever. Popes and clergy have not been known for apologizing. Such pride and delusion formed the core of every Greek tragedy—and became the precise staging for the transformation of Jesus himself into a new kind of life that we call the Risen Christ.

The Gospel was able to accept that life is tragic, but then graciously added that we can survive and will even grow from this tragedy. This is the great turnaround! It all depends on whether we are willing to see down as up. To paraphrase Joseph Campbell, it is where we stumble and fall that we find pure gold. Lady Julian put it even more poetically: "First there is the fall, and then we recover from the fall. Both are the mercy of God!"[3]

We should have been prepared for this pattern, given that the whole drama was set in motion by the "transgression" of Adam and Eve, and then the whole world was redeemed, say many Christians, by an act of violent murder! If God has not learned to draw straight with crooked lines, God is not going to be drawing very many lines at all. *Judeo-Christian salvation history is an integrating, using, and forgiving of this tragic sense of life.* Judeo-Christianity includes the problem inside the solution and as part of the solution. The genius of the biblical revelation is that it refuses to deny the dark side of things, but forgives failure and integrates falling to achieve its only promised wholeness, which is much of the point of this whole book.

Jesus is never upset at sinners (check it out!); he is only upset with people who do not think they are sinners! Jesus was fully at home with this tragic sense of life. He lived and rose inside it. I am now personally convinced that Jesus' ability to find a higher order inside constant disorder is the very heart of his message—and why true Gospel, as rare as it might be, still heals and renews all that it touches.

Jesus found and named the unified field beneath all the contradictions, which Annie Dillard wrote about in the epigraph above. If we do not find that unified field, "our complex and inexplicable caring for each other," or what Buddhists call the Great Compassion, there is no healing to life's inconsistencies and contradictions. *Religion is always about getting us back and down into the unified field, where we started anyway.*

THE GREAT TURNAROUND

In the divine economy of grace, sin and failure become the base metal and raw material for the redemption experience itself. Much of organized religion, however, tends to be peopled by folks who have a mania for some ideal order, which is never true, so they are seldom happy or content. It makes us anal retentive after a while, to use Freud's rude phrase, because we can never be happy with life as it is, always filled with different people, mentally unstable people, people of "other" and "false" religions, irritable people, LGBTQIA+ people, and people with totally different customs and traditions, not to mention *wild* nature, which we have not loved very well up to now. Organized religion has not been known for its inclusiveness or for being very comfortable with diversity. Yet pluriformity, multiplicity, and diversity form the only world there is! It is rather amazing that we can miss, deny, or ignore what is in plain sight everywhere.

Sin and salvation are correlative terms. Salvation is not sin perfectly avoided, as the ego would prefer. In fact, *salvation is sin turned on its head and used in our favor.* That is how transformative divine love is. If this is not the pattern, what hope is there for 99.9 percent of the world? We eventually discover that the same passion which leads us away from God can also lead us back to God and to our true selves. That is one reason I have valued and taught the Enneagram for half a century now.[4] Like few other spiritual tools, it illustrates this transformative truth. Once we see that our "sin" and our gift are two sides of the same coin, we can never forget it. It preserves religion from any arrogance and denial. The only people who do not believe that the Enneagram is true are those who do not understand it or have never used it well.

God seems to be about "turning" our loves around (in Greek, *meta-noia*) and using them toward the Great Love that is their true object. All lesser loves are training wheels, which are good in themselves, but still training wheels. Many of the healing stories in the Christian Scriptures are rather clear illustrations of this message and pattern. Jesus says this specifically of "the woman who was a sinner": "Her sins, her many sins, must have been forgiven her, or she could not have shown such great love" (Luke 7:47). It seems that her false attempts at love became the school and stepping-stones to "such great love."

We clergy have gotten ourselves into the job of "sin management" instead of sin transformation. "If you are not perfect, then *you* are doing something wrong," we have taught people. We have blamed the victim, or have had little pity for victims, while daring to worship a victim image of God. Mistakes are something to be pitied and healed much more than hated, denied, or perfectly avoided. I do not think we should get rid of our sin until we have learned what it has to teach us. Otherwise, it will only return in new forms, as Jesus says of the "unclean spirit" that returns to the house all "swept and tidied" (Luke 11:24–26). Then he rightly and courageously says that "the last state of the house will be worse than the first."

We could say that the tragedy, the "goat stories" of racism, slavery, sexism, the Crusades, the Inquisition, and the two World Wars, all of which emerged in and were tolerated by Christian Europe, are a stunning manifestation of our disillusionment and disgust with ourselves and one another, when we could not make the world right and perfectly ordered, as we were told it should be. We could not love the imperfection within ourselves or the natural world, so how could we possibly build any bridges toward Jews, Muslims, people of color, women, "sinners," or even other Christians? None of them fit into the "order" we had predecided on. We had to kill, force, imprison, torture, and enslave as we pursued our colonization of the rest of the world, along with the planet itself. We did not carry the cross, the tragic sense of life, but we became expert instead at imposing tragedies on others. Forgive my anger, but we must say it.

Philosophers and social engineers have promised us various utopias, with no room for error, but the Hebrew Scriptures, which are full of anecdotes of destiny, failure, sin, and grace, *offer almost no self-evident philosophical or theological conclusions that are always true.*[5] The Pentateuch, the first five books of the Bible, are an amalgam of at least four different sources and theologies (Yahwistic, Eloistic, Deuteronomic, and Priestly). We even have four, often conflicting versions of the life of Jesus in Matthew, Mark, Luke, and John. There is not one clear theology of God, Jesus, or history presented, despite our attempt to pretend there is. The only consistent pattern I can find is that all the books of the Bible seem to agree that *somehow God is with us, and we are not alone.* God and Jesus' only job description is one of constant renewal of bad deals.

The tragic sense of life is ironically not tragic at all, at least in the Big Picture. Living in such deep time, connected to past and future, prepares us for necessary suffering, keeps us from despair about our own failure and loss, and ironically offers us a way through it all. We are merely joining the great parade of humanity that has walked ahead of us and will follow after us. The tragic sense of life is not unbelief, pessimism, fatalism, or cynicism. It is just *ultimate and humiliating realism,* which for some reason demands a lot of forgiveness of almost everything. Faith is simply to trust the real and to trust that God is found within it—even before we change it. This is perhaps our major stumbling stone, the price we must pay to keep the human heart from closing down and to keep the soul open for something more.

CHAPTER 5

STUMBLING OVER THE STUMBLING STONE

 God is both sanctuary and stumbling stone,
Yahweh is a rock that brings Israel down, the
Lord is a trap and snare for the people.
—ISAIAH 8:14

 We would rather be ruined than changed. We
would rather die in our dread than climb the
cross of the moment and let our illusions die.
—W. H. AUDEN

Sooner or later, if you are on any classic "spiritual schedule," some event, person, death, idea, or relationship will enter your life that you simply cannot deal with using your present skill set, your acquired knowledge, or your strong willpower. Spiritually speaking, you will be, you must be, led to the edge of your own private resources. At that point, you will stumble over a necessary stumbling stone, as Isaiah calls it. To state it in our language here, you will and you must "lose" at something. This is the only way that Life-Fate-God-Grace-Mystery can get you to change, let go of your egocentric preoccupations, and go on the further and larger journey. I wish I could say this was not true, but it is darn near absolute in the spiritual literature of the world.

There is no practical or compelling reason to leave our present comfort zone in life. Why should you or would you? Frankly, none of us do unless and until we have to. The invitation probably has to be unexpected and unsought. If we seek spiritual heroism ourselves, the old ego is just back in control under a new name. There would not really be any change at all, but only disguise; just bogus "self-improvement" on our own terms.

Any attempt to engineer or plan our own enlightenment is doomed to failure because it will be ego driven. We will see only what we have already decided to look for, and we cannot see what we are not ready or told to look for.

So, failure and humiliation force us to look where we never would otherwise. What an enigma! Self-help courses of any type, including this one—if it is one, will help only if they teach us to pay attention to life itself. "God comes to you disguised as your life," as I have heard my friend Paula D'Arcy so wisely teach.

So, we *must* stumble and fall, I am sorry to say. And that does not mean *reading about* falling, as you are doing here. We must actually be out of the driver's seat for a while, or we will never learn how to *give up* control to the Real Guide. It is the necessary pattern. This kind of falling is what I mean by *necessary* suffering, which I will describe in the next chapter. It is well dramatized by Paul's fall on the Damascus Road, where he hears the voice ask, "Why are you hurting yourself by kicking against the goad?" (Acts 26:14). The goad or cattle prod is the symbol of both the encouragement forward and our needless resistance to it, which only wounds us further.

It seems that in the spiritual world, we do not really find something until we first lose it, ignore it, miss it, long for it, choose it, and personally find it again—but now on a new level. Three of the parables of Jesus are about losing something, searching for it anew with some effort, finding it, and, in each case, throwing a big party afterward. A sheep, a coin, and a son are all lost and found in Luke 15, followed by the kind of inner celebration that comes with any new "realization" (when something has become *real* for us). Almost every one of Odysseus' encounters coming home from Troy are losses of some type—his men, his control, his power, his time, his memory, his fame, and even the boat itself. Falling, losing, failing, transgression, and sin are the pattern, I am sorry to report. Yet, they all lead toward home.

In the end, we do not so much reclaim what we have lost as discover a significantly new self in and through the process. Until we are led to the limits of our present game plan and find it to be insufficient, we will not search out or find the real source, the deep well, or the constantly flowing stream. Alcoholics Anonymous calls it the Higher Power. Jesus calls this Ultimate Source the "living water" at the bottom of the well when he describes it to the woman who keeps filling and refilling her own little bucket (John 4:10–15).

There must be—and, if we are honest, there always will be—at least *one situation in our lives that we cannot fix, control, explain, change, or even understand.* For Jesus and for his followers, the crucifixion became the dramatic symbol of that necessary and absurd stumbling stone. Yet we have no positive theology of such necessary suffering, for the most part. Many Christians even made the cross into a mechanical "substitutionary atonement theory" to fit into their quid pro quo worldview instead of suffering its inherent tragedy, as Jesus did himself. They still want some kind of order and reason, instead of cosmic significance and soulful seeing.[1]

We, like the ox and Paul, largely still "kick against the goad" instead of listening to and learning from the goads of everyday life. Christians who read such passages were still not able to see that the goads were somehow necessary or even good. Suffering does not solve any problem mechanically as much as it reveals the constant problem that we are to ourselves and opens up new spaces within us for learning and loving. Here, Buddhism was much more observant than Christianity, which made even the suffering of Jesus into God's attempt to solve some cosmic problem — which God had largely created to begin with! The cross solved our problem by first revealing our real problem — our universal pattern of scapegoating and sacrificing others. The cross exposes forever the *scene of our crime*.

In the tale of Odysseus and in other stories from world mythology, the theme of loss and humiliation was constant and unrelenting, variously presented as the dragon, the sea monster, Scylla and Charybdis, an imprisonment, a plague, an illness, a falling into hell, the sirens, a storm, darkness, a shipwreck, the lotus eaters, the state of fatherlessness or orphanhood, homelessness, being stranded on an island, blindness, and often the powerless state of poverty and penury.

Sometimes, it seems that half of the fairy tales of the world are some form of Cinderella, ugly duckling, or poor-child story, telling of the little person who has no power or possessions who ends up being king or queen, prince or princess. We write it off as wishful dreaming, when it is actually the foundational pattern of disguise or amnesia, loss, and recovery. Every Beauty is sleeping, it seems, before they can meet their Prince. The duckling must be "ugly," or there will be no story. The knight errant must be wounded, or he will never even know what the Holy Grail is, much less find it. Jesus must be crucified, or there can be no resurrection. It is written in our hardwiring but can only be heard at the soul level. It will usually be resisted and opposed at the ego level.

My own spiritual father, Francis of Assisi, stated in his *Testament* that when he kissed the leper, "What before had been nauseating to me became sweetness and life."[2] He marks that as the moment of his conversion, the moment when he "left the world." The old game could not, would not work anymore. That seems to have been the defining moment when he tasted his own insufficiency, started drawing from a different and larger source, and found it sufficient—apparently, even more than sufficient. It made him into the classic Christian saint.

The leper was his goad, and he learned not to kick against it, but actually to kiss it. That is the pattern, just as you will sometimes hear from recovering addicts who end up thanking God for their former drinking, gambling, or violence. They invariably say that it was a huge price to pay, but nothing less would have broken down their false self and opened them to love.

I can only think of the many people I met during my fourteen years as a jail chaplain in New Mexico. No one taught them the necessary impulse control and delay of gratification, which is the job of a good parent. With poor identity, weak boundaries, or little inherent sense of their dignity, they allowed themselves to be destroyed—and to destroy others—by drugs, promiscuity, addictive relationships, alcohol, violence, or abuse. Then the enforced and cruel order of the jail was supposed to serve as their reparenting course, but now the lesson was so much harder to learn because of all the inner scarring and resentments toward all authority and toward themselves.

If we do not do the task of the first half of life well, we have almost no ability to rise up from the stumbling stone. We just stay down and defeated, or waste time kicking against the goad. There has been nothing to defeat our "infantile grandiosity," as Dr. Robert Moore (1942–2016) wisely called it.[3] In much of urban and Western civilization today, with no proper tragic sense of life, we try to believe that it is all upward and onward—and by ourselves. It works for so few, and it cannot serve us well in the long run—because it is not true. It is an inherently win-lose game, and more and more people find themselves on the losing side. If the Gospel is indeed gospel ("good news"), then it has to be win-win and a giant victory for both God and us.

Almost all of us end up being casualties of this constantly recurring Greek *hubris*. Some even appear to make it to the "top," but there is usually little recognition of the many shoulders they stood on to move there, the many gratuitous circumstances that made it possible for them to arrive there, and sometimes the necks they have stood on to stay there. Some who get to the top have the savvy to recognize that there is nothing up there that lasts or satisfies. Far too many just stay at the bottom of their own lives and try to overcompensate in all kinds of futile and self-defeating ways.

I am sure many slaveholders in the South were "self-made." Perhaps never in their entire lives did they have to face a situation where they did not "succeed." Such a refusal to fall kept them from awareness, empathy, and even basic human compassion. The price they paid for such succeeding was an inability to allow, join, or enjoy "the general dance." They "gained the whole world, but lost their soul," as Jesus put it (Mark 8:36). They did their survival dance but never got to the sacred dance, which by necessity includes everybody else. If it is a sacred dance, it is always the general dance too.

CHAPTER 6

NECESSARY SUFFERING

 *Anyone who wants to save their life must
lose it. Anyone who loses their life will find it.
What gain is there if you win the whole world
and lose your very self? What can you offer in
exchange for your one life?*
—MATTHEW 16:25–26

*Whoever comes to me and does not hate father
and mother, wife and children, brothers and
sisters, yes, and even life itself, cannot be my
disciple. Whoever does not carry the cross and
follow me cannot be my disciple.*
—LUKE 14:26–27

arl Jung believed that so much unnecessary suffering comes into the
world because people will not accept the "legitimate suffering" that
comes from being human. In fact, he wrote that neurotic behavior is usually
the result of refusing that legitimate suffering![1] Ironically, this refusal of the
necessary pain of being human brings to the person ten times more suffering
in the long run. It is no surprise that the first and always unwelcome message
in male initiation rites is "life is hard." We really are our own worst enemy
when we deny this.

To explain why I begin this chapter on necessary suffering with two
hard-hitting quotes from Jesus of Nazareth, let me share a bit about myself.
I must start with my birth relationship with Catholic Christianity (as I have
been a priest for over fifty years and a Franciscan for sixty), because, in many
ways, it has been the church that has taught me—in ways that it did not
plan—the message of necessary suffering. It taught me by being itself a bearer
of the verbal message, then a holding tank, and finally a living crucible of
necessary (and sometimes unnecessary!) suffering.

A crucible, as you may know, is a vessel that holds molten metal in one
place long enough for it to be purified and clarified. Church membership
requirements, church doctrine, and church morality force almost all issues

47

to an inner boiling point, where you are forced to face important issues at a much deeper level to survive as a Catholic or a Christian, or even as a human. I think this is probably true of any religious community, if it is doing its job. *Before the truth "sets you free," it tends to make you miserable.*

The Christian truth, and Jesus as its spokesman, is the worldview that got me started, that formed me and thrilled me, even though the very tangent that it sent me on made me often critical of much of organized Christianity. In some ways, that is totally as it should be, because I was able to criticize organized religion from within, by its own Scriptures, saints, and sources, and not by merely cultural, unbelieving, or rational criteria. That is probably the only way you can fruitfully criticize anything, it seems to me. You must unlock spiritual things from the inside, not by throwing rocks from outside, which is always too easy and too self-aggrandizing.

Eventually, I found myself held inside Christianity's inherent tensions. Catholicism became, for me, as I think it has for many, *a crucible and thus a unified field*. This is why it is very hard to be a "former" Catholic, once you really get its incarnational and inherently mystical worldview. I here use Einstein's term "unified field" to describe *that single world of elementary forces, principles, and particles that he assumed held together the entire universe of space-time*. Einstein said that he spent his life looking for this unified field.[2]

Although its vision is often timebound and its vocabulary very "in-house" (if you don't use our words and our definitions of those words, many Catholics hardly know how to talk to you), I still find that Big-Picture Catholicism is often precisely that—very "catholic" and all-embracing—with room for head, heart, body, soul, and history. For all its failures, it is no surprise that the Catholic worldview (note that I am not saying the "Roman" worldview) continues to produce Teilhard de Chardins, Mother Teresas, Thomas Mertons, Edith Steins, Cesar Chavezes, Cory Aquinos, Mary Robinsons, Rowan Williamses, Desmond Tutus, and Dorothy Days. I like to call it "incarnational mysticism." Once you get it, there is no going backward, because nothing is any better.

The pedestrian and everyday church has remained a cauldron of transformation for me by holding me inside both the dark and the light side of almost everything and by teaching me nondualistic thinking to survive. It has also shown me that neither I nor the churches themselves really live much of the real Gospel—at least enough to actually change our present lifestyles! It is just too big a message. Refusing to split and deny reality keeps me in regular touch with my own shadow self and much more patient with the rather evident shadow of the church. I see the exact same patterns in every other group, so my home base is as good a place to learn shadowboxing as anywhere else—and often better than most. Intellectual rigor, a social conscience (at least on paper), and a mystical vision are there for the taking. Catholicism is the "one true church" only when it points beyond itself to the "one true Mystery" and offers itself as the training ground for both human liberation and divine union. Many other religious groups do the same, however, and sometimes much better.

ALL CREATION "GROANS" (ROMANS 8:22)

Creation itself, the natural world, already "believes" the Gospel and lives the pattern of death and resurrection, even if unknowingly. The natural world "believes" in necessary suffering as the very cycle of life: just observe the daily dying of the sun so all things on this planet can live, the total change of the seasons and the plants and trees along with them, and the violent world of animal predators and prey. My sweet black Lab Venus once killed a little groundhog and brought it to me, expecting approval. How could she think this was wonderful when I thought it was terrible? She dropped it with disappointment when she saw my eyes. Only the human species absents itself from the agreed-on pattern and the general dance of life and death. What Venus had done would be disastrous only if I want to be perfectly rational and "progressive."

Necessary suffering goes on every day, seemingly without question. When I wrote this in the deserts of Arizona, I read that only one saguaro cactus seed out of a quarter of a million seeds ever makes it to early maturity, much less reaches its full potential. Most of nature seems to totally accept major loss, gross inefficiency, mass extinctions, and short life spans as the price of life at all. Feeling that sadness, and even its full absurdity, ironically pulls us into the general dance, the unified field, and an ironic and deep gratitude for what *is* given—with no necessity and therefore gratuitously. All beauty is gratuitous.

So, whom can we blame when it seems to be taken away? Grace seems to be at the foundation of everything.

This creative tension between wonderful and terrible is named so well by Gerard Manley Hopkins, as only poets can. Even the long title of his poem reveals his acceptance of the ever-changing flow of Heraclites and also his trust in the final outcome: "That Nature Is a Heraclitean Fire and of the Comfort of the Resurrection."

> Flesh fade, and mortal trash
> fall to the residuary worm; world's wildfire, leave but ash:
> In a flash, at a trumpet crash,
> I am all at once what Christ is, since he was what I am, and
> This Jack, joke, poor potsherd, patch, matchwood, immortal diamond,
> Is immortal diamond.[3]

The resolution of earthly embodiment and divinization is *incarnational mysticism*. As has been said many times, there are finally only two subjects in all of literature and poetry: love and death. Only that which is limited—and even dies—grows in value and appreciation; it is the spiritual version of supply and demand. If we lived forever, they say, we would never take life seriously or learn to love *what is*. I think that is probably true. Being held long and hard inside limits and tension, incarnate moments—crucibles for sure—allows us to search for and often find *the reconciling third* or the unified field beneath it all. "What is most personal is most general," in the words of psychologist Carl Rogers (1902–1987).[4]

Reality, creation, nature itself, what I call the "the First Body of Christ," has no choice in the matter of necessary suffering. It lives the message without saying yes or no to it. It holds and resolves all the foundational forces, all the elementary principles and particles within itself—willingly, it seems. This is the universe in its wholeness, the "great nest of being," including even the powerless, invisible, and weak parts that have so little freedom or possibility. The Second Body of Christ, the formal church, always has the freedom to say yes or no. That very freedom allows it to say "no" much of the time, especially to any talk of dying, stumbling, admitting mistakes, or falling. We see this rather clearly in the recent financial and sexual scandals of the church. Yet God seems ready and willing to wait for, and to empower, free will and a free "yes." Love only happens in the realm of freedom.

Yet, I know that I avoid this daily dying too. The church has been for me a broad education and experience in passion, death, and resurrection by forcing me to go deep in one place. It, and the Franciscans, still offer me an accountability community for what I say I believe, which I find is necessary if I am to live with any long-term integrity. The Dalai Lama and Mother Teresa (1910–1997) said the same. Over many years now, the church has given me the tools and the patience that allow me to try to fill what Parker Palmer calls "the tragic gap"[5] as almost nothing else does. Both the church's practice and its Platonic pronouncements *create tragic gaps for any person with an operative head and a beating heart*. But remember, even a little bit of God is well worth loving, and even a little bit of truth and love goes a long way. The church has given me much more than a little bit. Like all limited parents, it has been a "good enough" church and thus has taught me how to see that goodness everywhere, even in other limit situations, as Karl Jaspers called them. But, in the end, "Only God is good," as Jesus said to the rich young man (Mark 10:18).

So, the church is both my greatest intellectual and moral problem and my most consoling home. She is both pathetic whore and frequent bride. There is still a marvelous marriage with such a bride, and whores do occasionally become brides too. In a certain but real sense, the church itself is the next cross that Jesus is crucified on, as we limit, mangle, and try to control the always-too-big message. All the churches seem to crucify Jesus again and again by their inability to receive his whole body, but they often resurrect him too. I am without doubt a microcosm of this universal church.

The church has never persecuted me or limited me in any way — quite the contrary, which is really quite amazing. Maybe that is the only reason I can talk this way — without, I hope, rancor or agenda. She has held me and yet also held me at arm's length, which is more than enough holding. The formal church has always been a halfhearted bride for me, while the Franciscans have been considerably better. The Gospel itself is my full wedding partner. It always tells me the truth and loves me *through things* till I arrive somewhere new, good, and much more spacious.

So, I offer this personal apologia for those of you who perhaps are wondering why I quote Jesus so much. You might be saying, "Does it really matter?" or "Does it have to be in the Bible to be true?" Well, I quote Jesus because I still consider him to be *the* spiritual authority of the Western world, whether we follow him or not. He is always spot-on at the deeper levels and when we understand him in his own explosive context. You do not even need to believe in his divinity to realize that Jesus is seeing at a much higher level than most of us.

For some of you, my quoting Jesus is the only way you will trust me. For others, it gives you more reasons to mistrust me. But I have to take both risks. If I dared to present all these ideas simply as my ideas, or because they match modern psychology or old mythology, I would be dishonest. Jesus for me always clinches the deal, and I sometimes wonder why I did not listen to him in the first place.

Not surprisingly, many of the findings of modern psychology, anthropology, and organizational behavior give us new windows and vocabulary into Jesus' transcendent message. As you can see, I love to make use of these many tools. Let's look at one example of something that surely seems like entirely unnecessary suffering, which Jesus said in a way that many people have not been prepared to hear. Fortunately for us, it is now supported by the findings of modern psychology and the behavioral sciences.

"HATING" FAMILY

Let me address those most problematic lines I quoted at the beginning of this chapter, in which Jesus talks about "hating" mother, father, sister, brother, and family. Everything in us says that he surely cannot mean this, but if we are to move into the second half of life, he is in fact directing us correctly and courageously.

First of all, do you recognize that he is actually undoing the fourth commandment of Moses, which tells us to "honor your father and mother"? This commandment is necessary for the first half of life — and, one hopes it can be possible forever. As we move into the second half of life, however, we are very often at odds with our natural family and the dominant consciousness of our cultures. It is true more often than I would have ever imagined. Many people are kept from mature religion because of the pious, immature, or rigid expectations of their first-half-of-life family. Even Jesus, whose family thought he was "crazy" (Mark 3:21), had to face this dilemma firsthand. The very fact that the evangelist would risk associating the word "crazy" with Jesus shows how Jesus was surely not following the expected and mainline script for his culture or his religion.

One of the major blocks against the second journey is what we would now call the "collective": the crowd, our society, or our extended family. Some call it the crab-bucket syndrome—we try to get out, but the other crabs just keep pulling us back in. What passes for morality or spirituality in the vast majority of people's lives is *the way everybody they grew up with thinks*. Some would call it conditioning or even imprinting. Without very real inner work, most folks never move beyond it. We might get beyond it in a negative sense, by reacting or rebelling against it, but it is much less common to get out of the crab bucket in a positive way. That is what we want here. Jesus uses quite strong words to push us out of the family nest and to name a necessary suffering at the most personal, counterintuitive, and sentimental level possible.

It takes a huge push, much self-doubt, and some degree of separation for people to find their own soul and their own destiny apart from what Mom and Dad always wanted them to be and do. To move beyond family-of-origin stuff, local church stuff, cultural stuff, or flag-and-country stuff is a path that few of us follow positively and with integrity. The pull is just too great, and the loyal soldier fills us with appropriate guilt, shame, and self-doubt, which, as I noted earlier, feels like the very voice of God.

So, Jesus pulls no punches, saying you *must "hate"* your home base in some way and make choices beyond it. I am happy he said this, or I would never have had the courage to believe how it might be true. It takes therapists years to achieve the same result, reestablish appropriate boundaries from wounding parents and early authority figures, and heal the *inappropriate shame* in those who have been wounded. We all must leave home to find the real and larger home, which is so important that I will develop it more fully in the next chapter. The nuclear family has far too often been the enemy of the global family and mature spiritual seeking.

Perhaps it has never struck you how consistently the great religious teachers and founders leave home, go on pilgrimage to far-off places, do a major turnabout, and choose downward mobility; and how often it is their parents, the established religion at that time, spiritual authorities, and often even civil authorities who fight against them. Read the biographies of Hindu sadhus, the Buddha, Ashoka, Abraham, Joseph, Moses, Jesus, Sufi saints, Francis, Clare, and the numerous hermits and pilgrims of Cappadocia, Mt. Athos, and Russia. You will see that this pattern is rather universal. Instead of our "Don't leave home without it" mentality, the spiritual greats' motto seems to be, "Leave home to find it!" Of course, they were never primarily talking just about physical home, but about all the validations, securities, illusions, prejudices, smallness—and hurts too—that home and family always imply.

Of course, to be honest and consistent, we must ask if "church family" is not also a family that we eventually have to "hate" in this very same way and with the same scandal involved as hating the natural family. (I will address this in a later chapter under the rubric of "emerging Christianity.")

I encourage you to reread the epigraphs at the beginning of this chapter. They are pretty strong, almost brutal, by contemporary standards; but they make very clear that there is a necessary suffering that cannot be avoided, which Jesus calls "losing our very life," or losing what I and others call the "false self." Your false self is your role, title, and personal image that is largely a creation of your own mind and attachments. *It will and must die in exact correlation to how much you want the Real.* "How much false self are you willing to shed to find your True Self?" is the lasting question.[6] Such necessary suffering will always feel like dying, which is what good spiritual teachers will tell you very honestly. (Alcoholics Anonymous is notoriously successful here.) If your spiritual guides do not talk to you about dying, they are not good spiritual guides!

Your True Self is who you objectively are from the beginning, in the mind and heart of God, "the face you had before you were born," as the Zen masters say. It is your substantial self, your absolute identity, which can be neither gained nor lost by any technique, group affiliation, morality, or formula whatsoever. The surrendering of your false self—which you have usually taken for your absolute identity yet is merely a relative identity—is the necessary suffering needed to find "the pearl of great price" (Matthew 13:45–46) that is always hidden inside this lovely but passing shell.

CHAPTER 7

HOME AND HOMESICKNESS

Old men ought to be explorers
Here and there does not matter
We must be still and still moving
Into another intensity
For another union, a deeper communion
—T. S. ELIOT, "EAST COKER"

So, now we move toward the goal, the very purpose of human life, "another intensity . . . a deeper communion," as Eliot called it, that which the container is meant to hold, support, and foster. This is not the fingers pointing to the moon, but the moon itself—and now including the dark side of the moon too. The fullness and inner freedom of the second half of life is what Homer seemed unable to describe. Perhaps he was not there himself yet, perhaps too young, yet he intuited its call and necessity. It was too "dark" for him, perhaps, but he did point toward a further journey and only then a truly final journey home. The goal in sacred story is always to come back home—after getting the protagonist to leave home in the first place! A contradiction? A paradox? Yes, but now home has a whole new meaning, never imagined before. As always, it *transcends but includes* our initial experience of home.

The archetypal idea of "home" points in two directions at once. It points backward toward an original hint and taste for union, starting in the body of our mother. We all came from some kind of home, even a bad one, that always plants the foundational seed of a possible and ideal paradise. It also points forward, urging us toward the realization that this hint and taste of union might actually be true. It guides us like an inner compass or a homing device. In Homer's *Odyssey,* it is the same home, the island Ithaca, that is both the beginning and the end of the journey. Carl Jung offered this concise, momentous insight: "Life is a luminous pause between two great mysteries, which themselves are one."[1] That is precisely what I want to show here.

Somehow, the end is in the beginning, and the beginning points toward the end. We are told that even children with a sad or abusive childhood still long for "home" or "Mother" in some idealized form and still yearn to return to it somehow, maybe just to do it right this time. What is going on there? Agreeing with Jung, I believe that the One Great Mystery is revealed at the beginning and forever beckons us forward toward its full realization. Most of us cannot let go of this implanted promise. Some would call this homing device their soul, some would call it the indwelling Holy Spirit, and some might just call it nostalgia or dreamtime. All I know is that it will not be ignored. It calls us both backward and forward, to our foundation and our future, at the same time. It also feels like grace from within us and, at the same time, beyond us. The soul lives in such eternally deep time. Wouldn't it make sense that God would plant in us a desire for what God already wants to give us? I am sure of it.

To understand better, let's look at the telling word *homesick*. This usually connotes something sad or nostalgic, an emptiness that looks either backward or forward for satisfaction. I am going to use it in an entirely different way, because now you are ready for it. I want to propose that we are both sent and drawn by the same force, which is precisely what Christians mean when they say the Cosmic Christ is both alpha and omega. We are both driven and called forward by a kind of deep homesickness, it seems. There is an inherent and *desirous dissatisfaction* that both sends and draws us forward, and it comes from our original and radical union with God. What appears to be past and future is in fact the same home, the same call, and the same God, for whom "a thousand years are like a single day" (Psalm 90:4) and a single day like a thousand years.

In *The Odyssey,* the stirring of longing and dissatisfaction is symbolized by the collapse of Troy and the inability of most of the Greeks to return home. It seems they had forgotten about home, had made home in a foreign land, or were not that determined to return home (which are all excellent descriptions of the typical detours or dead ends on the spiritual journey). Only Odysseus was trying to get home at all costs, and he is the stand-in for what we all must be. Those who do not seek their home are symbolized perhaps by the lotus eaters whom Odysseus encounters, who forgot themselves and lost their own depths and consciousness. It has been said that 90 percent of people seem to live 90 percent of their lives on cruise control, which is to be unconscious.

The Holy Spirit is that aspect of God that works largely from within and "secretly," at "the deepest levels of our desiring," as so many of the mystics have said. That's why the mystical tradition could only resort to subtle metaphors like wind, fire, descending doves, and flowing water to describe the Spirit. More than anything else, the Spirit keeps us connected and safely inside an already existing flow, if we but allow it. We never "create" or earn the Spirit; we discover this inner abiding as we learn to draw upon our deepest inner life. This utterly unified field is always *given*, as Annie Dillard wrote.

I think also of *Steppenwolf* by Herman Hesse (1877–1962), in which he wrote, "We have no one to guide us. Our only guide is our homesickness."[2] Even Dorothy is guided forward to Oz and back to Kansas by her constant love and search for home. It is part of the reason the story has such lasting appeal. On the level of soul, I believe these sources are all correct. Home is another word for the Spirit that we are, our True Self in God. *The self-same moment that we find God in ourselves, we also find ourselves inside God,* and this is the full homecoming, according to Teresa of Ávila.[3] Until then, we are homesick, although today most would probably just call it loneliness, isolation, longing, sadness, restlessness, or even a kind of depression.

The common word for this inner abiding place of the Spirit, which is also a place of longing, has usually been the word *soul*. We have our soul already—we do not "get" it by any purification process or by joining any group or from the hands of a bishop. The end is already planted in us at the beginning, and it gnaws away at us until we get there freely and consciously. The most a bishop or sacrament can do is to "fan [this awareness] into flame" (2 Timothy 1:6), and sometimes it does. But sometimes great love and great suffering are even bigger fans for this much-needed flame.

The good news is that there *is* a guide, a kind of medical advocate, an inner compass—and it resides within each of us, "included inside the box," as the ads always say. As the Scriptures put it, "The love of God has been poured into our hearts through the Holy Spirit that has been given to us" (Romans 5:5). In another place we are promised, "You will not be left orphaned" (John 14:18) without a mother or home. This is probably one of the many reasons the Holy Spirit was usually considered feminine.

This Holy Spirit guiding all of us from home and toward home is also described in John's Gospel as an "advocate" ("a defense attorney," as *paraclete* literally means; John 14:16), who will "teach us" and "remind us," as if some part of us already knew but still needed an inner buzz or alarm clock to wake us up. The Holy Spirit is always entirely *for us,* more than we are for ourselves, it seems. She speaks in our favor against the negative voices that judge and condemn us. This gives us all such hope — now we do not have to do life all by ourselves or even do life perfectly "right." Our life will be *done unto us,* just as happened to Mary (Luke 1:38) — although, on another level, we are doing it too. Both are equally true.

This mystery has been called the *conspiracy* ("co-breathing") of God, and it is still one of the most profound ways to understand what is happening between God and the soul. True spirituality is always a deep "co-operating" (Romans 8:28) between two. True spirituality is a kind of *synergy* in which both parties give and both parties receive to create one shared truth and joy.[4]

The ancients rightly called this internal longing for wholeness "fate" or "destiny," the "inner voice" or the "call of the gods." It has an inevitability, authority, and finality to it, and it was at the heart of almost all mythology. Almost all heroes heard an inner voice that spoke to them. In fact, their heroism was in their ability to hear that voice and to risk following it — wherever! Sadly, such inner comfort is the very thing we lack today at almost all levels. Our problem now is that we seriously doubt that there is any vital reality to the spiritual world, so we hear no life-changing voices. This is true even for many who go to church, temple, or mosque.

For postmodern people, the universe is not inherently enchanted, as it was for the ancients. We have to do all the "enchanting" ourselves. This leaves us alone, confused, and doubtful. There is no meaning already in place for our discovery and enjoyment. We have to create all meaning by ourselves in such an inert and empty world, and most of us do not seem to succeed very well. This is the burden of living in our heady and lonely time, when we think it is all up to us.

The gift of living in our time, however, is that we are more and more discovering that the sciences, particularly physics, astrophysics, anthropology, and biology, are confirming many of the deep intuitions of religion — and at a rather quick pace in recent years. The universe really is "inspirited matter," we now know, not merely inert. Now, we might call it instinct, evolution, nuclear fusion, DNA, hardwiring, the motherboard, healing, growth, or just springtime, but nature clearly continues to renew itself from within.

God seems to have created things that continue to create and recreate themselves from the inside out. It is no longer God's one-time creation *or* evolution; rather, God's form of creation precisely *is* evolution. *Finally, God is allowed to be fully incarnate, which was supposed to be Christianity's big trump card from the beginning!* It has taken us a long time to get here, and dualistic thinkers still cannot jump the hurdle.

Remember Odysseus' oar that an inland wayfarer saw as a winnowing fan? His oar (or occupation) had become a tool for inner work, a means for knowing the difference between wheat and chaff, essentials and nonessentials, which is precisely the turn toward discernment and subtlety that we come to in the second half of life. What a strange but brilliant symbol Homer offers us. It's no surprise that this marks the end of Odysseus' journey. Now he can *go home* because he has, in fact, *come home* to his true and full self. His sailing and rowing days of mere outer performance are over, and he can now rest in the simplicity and ground of his own deeper life. He is free to stop his human *doing* and can at last enjoy his human *being*.

Because important things bear repeating in different forms, let me summarize the direction of my thought here. I am saying that

- We are created with an *inner drive and necessity* that sends all of us looking for our True Self, whether we know it or not. This journey is a spiral and never a straight line.
- We are created with an inner restlessness and call that urges us on to the risks and promises of *a second half to our life*. There is a God-size hole in all of us, waiting to be filled. God creates the very dissatisfaction that only grace and finally divine love can satisfy.
- We dare not try to fill our souls and minds with numbing addictions, diversionary tactics, or mindless distractions. The shape of evil is much more *superficiality* and blindness than the usually listed "hot sins." God hides, and is found, precisely in the *depths* of everything, even and maybe especially in the deep fathoming of our fallings and failures. Sin is to stay on the *surface* of even holy things, like Bible, sacrament, or church.
- If we go to the depths of anything, we will begin to knock upon something substantial, "real," and with a timeless quality to it. We will move from the starter kit of "belief" to an actual inner *knowing*. This is most especially

true if we have ever (1) loved deeply, (2) accompanied someone through the mystery of dying, (3) or stood in genuine life-changing *awe* before mystery, time, or beauty.

- This "something real" is what all the world religions were pointing to when they spoke of heaven, nirvana, bliss, or enlightenment. They were not wrong at all; their only mistake was that they pushed it off into the next world. *If heaven is later, it is because it is first of all now.*
- These events become the pledge, guarantee, hint, and promise of an eternal something. Once we touch upon the Real, there is an inner insistence that the Real, if it is the Real, has to be forever. Call it wishful thinking, if you will, but this insistence has been a constant intuition since the beginnings of humanity. Jesus made it into a promise, as when he tells the Samaritan woman that the spring within her "will well up unto eternal life" (John 4:14). In other words, heaven/union/love now emerge from within us, much more than from a mere belief system or any belonging system, which largely remains on the outside of the self.

And so, like Odysseus, we leave from Ithaca and we come back to Ithaca, but now it is fully home because all is included and nothing wasted or hated; even the dark parts are used in our favor. All is forgiven. What else could homecoming be?! A lesser-known Greek-Egyptian poet, C. P. Cavafy (1863–1933), expressed this understanding most beautifully in a famous poem called "Ithaca":

Ithaca has now given you the beautiful voyage.
Without her, you would never have taken the road.
With the great wisdom you have gained on your voyage,
with so much of your own experience now,
you must finally know what Ithaca really means.[5]

CHAPTER 8

AMNESIA AND THE BIG PICTURE

 God wanted to give human beings their fullness right from the beginning, but they were incapable of receiving it because they were still little children.

— ST. IRENAEUS (125–203), "AGAINST HERESIES"

 It is the whole of nature, extending from the beginning to the end, that constitutes the one image of God Who Is.

— ST. GREGORY OF NYSSA (330–395), "ON THE CREATION OF MAN"

As many others have said in different ways, we all seem to suffer from a tragic case of mistaken identity. Life is a matter of becoming fully and consciously who we already are, but it is a self that we largely do not know. It is as though we are all suffering from a giant case of amnesia. As mentioned before, the protagonists in so many fairy tales are already nobles, royal, daughters and sons of the king, or even the gods. But their identity is hidden from them, and the story line pivots around this discovery. They have to grow up to fathom their own identity. That fathoming is the very purpose of the journey.

It is religion's job to teach us and guide us on this journey to discover our True Self, but it usually makes the mistake of turning this into a worthiness contest of some sort, a private performance, or some kind of religious achievement on our part through our belonging to the right group, practicing the right rituals, or believing the right things. These are just tugboats to get us away from the shore and out into the right sea. They are the oars to get us working and engaged with the Mystery. Never confuse these instruments with your profound "ability to share in the divine nature" itself (2 Peter 1:4). It is the common, and in this case tragic, confusion of the medium with the message or the style with the substance.

It was largely the fathers of the early church, and especially the Eastern Church, who never compromised on what they called *theosis* or "divinization," as we see in the powerful quotes above. There are many more such astounding quotes,[1] but this very memory is also a part of Western amnesia. The Gospel was just too good to be true—for a future-oriented, product-oriented, and win-lose worldview.

Such deep knowing about our true selves is surely what John was pointing to when he wrote, "It is not because you do not know the truth that I am writing to you, but rather *because you know it already!*" (1 John 2:21). Otherwise, he would not have had the self-confidence to write about spiritual things with such authority, nor would I. We are all drawing upon a Larger Source, the unified field, the shared Spirit. I am also relying upon your inner, deep-time *recognition* more than any linear *cognition*. Maybe you have noticed that by now. I hope so. The English poet William Wordsworth (1770–1850) put it so beautifully:

> Our birth is but a sleep and a forgetting:
> The Soul that rises with us, our Life's Star
> Hath had elsewhere its setting,
> And cometh from afar:
> Not in entire forgetfulness,
> And not in utter nakedness,
> But trailing clouds of glory do we come
> From God, who is our home:
> Heaven lies about us in our infancy!
> Shades of the prison-house begin to close
> Upon the growing boy,
> But he beholds the light, and whence it flows,
> He sees it in his joy.[2]

That bit of his larger poem should be enough to make Wordsworth an honorary doctor of the church! Mature religion is always trying to get us out of the closing prison-house of the false self. Many have said before me that spirituality is much more about unlearning than learning, because the "growing boy" is usually growing into major illusions, all of which must be undone to free him from prison and take him back to his beginnings in God. "Unless you change and become like a little child, you will not enter the reign of God," Jesus says (Matthew 18:3). He says this in response to the egotistical and ambitious question of the apostles, who were asking him, "Who is the greatest?"

I have sometimes wondered if we might be surprised and disappointed by what it means that our faith is "built on the faith of the apostles," as we have so proudly sung and proclaimed. They barely ever got the point and seem as thoroughly foolish as we are, but God still used them, because, like all of us, they were little children too. I indeed share in this very faith. We are all and forever beginners in the journey toward God and truth.

"HEAVEN" AND "HELL"

Any discovery or recovery of our divine union has been called "heaven" by most traditions. Its loss has been called "hell." The tragic result of our amnesia is that we cannot imagine that these terms are first of all referring to present experiences. *When we do not know who we are, we push all enlightenment off into a possible future reward-and-punishment system, within which hardly anyone wins.* Only the True Self knows that heaven is now and that its loss is hell—now. The false self makes religion into the old "evacuation plan for heaven," as my friend Brian McLaren puts it.[3] Amnesia has dire consequences. No wonder the Jews say "remember" so much.

A person who has found their True Self has learned how to live in the big picture as a part of deep time and all of history. This change of frame and venue is called living in "the realm of God" by Jesus, and it is indeed a major about-face. This necessitates, of course, that we let go of our own tiny realms, which we normally do not care to do. Life is all about *practicing for heaven.* We practice by choosing union freely—ahead of time—and now. Heaven is the state of union both here and later. *As now, so will it be then.* No one is in heaven unless they want to be, and all are in heaven as soon as they live in union. Everyone is in heaven when they have plenty of room for communion and no need for exclusion. The more room we have to include, the bigger our heaven will be.

Perhaps this is what Jesus means by there being "many rooms in my Father's house" (John 14:2). If you go to heaven alone, wrapped in your private worthiness, it is by definition *not* heaven. If your notion of heaven is based on the exclusion of anybody else, then it is by definition *not* heaven. The more we exclude, the more hellish and lonely our existence always is. How could anyone enjoy the "perfect happiness" of any heaven if they knew their loved ones were not there or were being tortured for all eternity? It would be impossible. Remember our Christian prayer, "on earth as it is heaven." As now, so then; as here, so there. We will all get exactly what we want and ask for. You can't beat that.

If we accept a punitive notion of a god who punishes or even eternally tortures those who do not love "him," then we have an absurd universe where most people on this earth end up being more loving than God! God excludes no one from union but must allow us to exclude ourselves in order for us to maintain our freedom. Our word for that exclusion is hell, and it must be maintained as a logical possibility. There must be the logical possibility of excluding ourselves from union and choosing separation or superiority over community and love. No one is in hell unless they choose a final aloneness and separation. It is all about *desire*, both allowing and drawing from the deepest level of our desiring. It is interesting to me that the official church has never declared a single person to be in hell, not even Judas, Hitler, or Stalin.

Jesus touched and healed anybody who desired it and asked for it. There were no other prerequisites for his healings. Check it out yourself. Why would Jesus' love be so unconditional while he was in this world and suddenly become totally conditional after death? Is it the same Jesus, or does Jesus change his policy after his resurrection? The belief in heaven and hell is meant to maintain freedom on all sides, with God being the freest of all, to forgive and include, to heal and to bless even God's seeming "enemies." How could Jesus ask us to bless, forgive, and heal our enemies, which he clearly does (Matthew 5:43–48), unless God is doing it first and always? Jesus told us to love our enemies because he saw his Father doing it all the time, and all spirituality is merely the "imitation of God" (Ephesians 5:1).

Ken Wilber described the later stages of life well when he wrote that *the classic spiritual journey always begins elitist and ends egalitarian. Always!*[4] We see it in Judaism, starting with the Jews' early elite chosenness and ending in prophets without borders. We see it in the heady new sect of Christianity that soon calls itself "catholic" or universal. We see it in Sufi Islam and Hindu Krishna consciousness, which sees God's joy everywhere. We see it in mystics like William Blake or Lady Julian, who start with a grain of sand or a hazelnut and soon find themselves swimming in infinity. We see it in the Native American sweat lodge, where the participant ends by touching their sweaty body to the earth and saying, "All my relations!" I wish we could expect as much from Catholics when they so frequently "go to communion."

Life moves first toward diversity and then toward union of that very diversity at ever higher levels. It is the old philosophical problem of "the one and the many," which Christianity should have resolved in its belief in God as Trinity. *Up to now, we have been more in love with elitism than with any egalitarianism. We liked being the "one" but just did not know how to include the many in that very One.*

Even Pope John Paul II (1920–2005) said that heaven and hell were primarily eternal states of consciousness more than geographical places of later reward and punishment.[5] We seem to be our own worst enemies, and *we forget or deny things that are just too good to be true.* The ego clearly prefers an economy of merit, where we can divide the world into winners and losers, to any economy of grace, where merit or worthiness loses all meaning.[6] In the first case, at least a few of us "good guys" attain glory. In the second case, all the glory is to God.

The healing of our amnesia, and any entry into heaven, is the rediscovery of the still-enchanted world of a happy child, but it now includes the maturing experiences of love, unique life journeys, all our relations, and just enough failures to keep us honest and grounded. This "second childhood" perhaps needs a personal or practical example, so allow me to share a bit of my own experience in the second half of my own life.

CHAPTER 9

A SECOND SIMPLICITY

 *Beyond rational and critical thinking, we need
to be called again. This can lead to the discovery of a "second naïveté," which is a return
to the joy of our first naïveté, but now totally
new, inclusive, and mature thinking.*
—PAUL RICOEUR

*People are so afraid of being considered
pre-rational that they avoid and deny the
very possibility of the transrational. Others
substitute mere pre-rational emotions for
authentic religious experience, which is always
transrational.*
—KEN WILBER

These quick summaries (not precise quotations) are from two great
thinkers who more or less describe for me what happened on my own
spiritual and intellectual journey. I began as a very conservative pre–Vatican
II Roman Catholic, living in innocent Kansas, pious and law-abiding, buffered
and bounded by my parents' stable marriage and many lovely liturgical
traditions that sanctified my time and space. That was my first wonderful
simplicity. I was a very happy child and young man, and all who knew me
then would agree.

Yet, I grew in my experience and was gradually educated in a much larger
world of the 1960s and 1970s, with degrees in philosophy and theology and a
broad liberal arts education given me by the Franciscans. That education was
a second journey into rational complexity. I left the garden, just as Adam and
Eve had to do, even though my new Scripture awareness made it obvious that
Adam and Eve were probably not historical figures, but important archetypal
symbols. Darn it! My parents back in Kansas were worried: I was heady with
knowledge and "enlightenment" and was surely not in Kansas anymore. I had
passed, like Dorothy, "over the rainbow." It is sad and disconcerting for a

while, outside the garden, and some lovely innocence dies, yet "angels and a flaming sword" prevented my return to the first garden (Genesis 3:24). There was no going back, unfortunately. Life was much easier on the childhood side of the rainbow.

As time passed, I became simultaneously very traditional and very progressive, and I have probably continued to be so to this day. I found a much larger and even happier garden (note the new garden described at the end of the Bible in Revelation 22). I totally believe in Adam and Eve now, but on about ten more levels. (*Literalism is usually the lowest and least level of meaning.*) I have lived much of my subsequent life like a man without a country—and yet a man who could go to any country and be at home. This nowhere land has surprised even me. I no longer fit in with either the mere liberals or the mere conservatives. This was my first strong introduction to paradox, and it took most of midlife to figure out what had happened—and how—and why it *had* to happen.

This "pilgrim's progress" was, for me, sequential, natural, and organic as the circles widened. I was lucky enough to puddle-jump between countries, cultures, and concepts because of my public speaking. Yet the solid ground of the perennial tradition never really shifted. It was only the lens, the criteria, the inner space, and the scope that continued to expand. I was always being moved toward greater differentiation and larger viewpoints, and simultaneously toward a greater inclusivity in my ideas, a deeper understanding of people, and a more honest sense of justice. God always became bigger and led me to bigger places. If God could "include" and allow, then why not I? I did not see many examples of God "smiting" his enemies; in fact, it was usually God's friends who got smited, as Teresa of Ávila supposedly noted! If God asked me to love unconditionally and universally, then it was clear that God operated in the same way.

Soon, there was a much bigger world than the United States and the Roman Catholic Church, which I eventually realized were also paradoxes. The *e pluribus unum* ("out of many, one") on American coinage did not include very "many" of its own people (Blacks, LGBTQIA+, Native Americans, poor folks, and so on). As a Christian, I finally had to be either Roman or catholic, and I continue to choose the catholic end of that spectrum. Either Jesus is the "savior of the world" (John 4:42), or he is not much of a savior at all.

Either America treats the rest of the world democratically, or it does not really believe in democracy at all. That is the way I see it.

But this slow process of transformation and the realizations that came with it were not either-or decisions; they were great big *both-and realizations*. None of it happened without much prayer, self-doubt, study, and conversation, but the journey itself led me to a deepening sense of what the church calls holiness, what Americans call freedom, and what psychology calls wholeness. I could transcend now precisely because I was able to include and broaden. *Paul Ricoeur's first naïveté was the best way to begin the journey, and a second naïveté was the easiest way to continue that same journey* without becoming angry, split, alienated, or ignorant.

I now hope and believe that a kind of second simplicity is the very goal of mature adulthood and mature religion. Although we often used it in a derogatory way, I wonder if this was not our intuition when we spoke of older people as being in a "second childhood." Maybe that is where we are supposed to go? Maybe that is what Wordsworth meant when he wrote, "the child is father of the man"?[1]

My small personal viewpoint as a central reference point for anything, or for rightly judging anything, gradually faded as life went on. The very meaning of the word *universe* is to "turn around one thing." I know *I* am not that one thing. There is either some Big Truth in this universe, or there is no truth that is always reliable. There is, we hope, some pattern behind it all (even if the pattern is exception!), or it begins to be a very incoherent universe, which is what many postmodern people seem to have accepted. I just can't.

Mature religions, and now some scientists, say that we are hardwired for the Big Picture, for transcendence, for ongoing growth, and for union with ourselves and everything else.[2] Either God is for everybody and the divine DNA is somehow in all the creatures, or this God is not God by any common definition—or even much of a god at all. We are driven, kicking and screaming, toward ever higher levels of union and ability to include (to forgive others for being "other"), it seems to me. "Everything that rises must converge," as Teilhard de Chardin put it.[3]

But many get stopped and fixated at lower levels where God seems to torture and exclude forever those people who don't agree with "him" or get "his" name right. *How could anyone possibly feel safe, free, loved, trustful, or invited by such a small God?* Jesus undid this silliness himself when he said, "You, evil as you are, know how to give good things to your children.... If you, then how much more will God!" (Matthew 7:11). The God I have met and been loved by in my life journey is always an experience of "how much more!" If we are created in the image and likeness of God, then whatever good, true, or beautiful things we can say about humanity or creation we can say of God exponentially. God is the beauty of creation and humanity multiplied to the infinite power.

ANXIETY AND DOUBT

For me, this wondrous universe cannot be an incoherent and accidental cosmos, nor can it be grounded in evil, although I admit that this intellectual leap and bias toward beauty is still an act of faith and trust on my part. Yet, this act of faith has also been the common sense and intuition of 99 percent of the people who have ever lived. I further believe that a free and loving God would create things that continue to recreate themselves, exactly as all parents desire for their children. God seems to want *us* to be in on the deal! The Great Work is ours too.

I do, however, hold a certain degree of doubt about the how, if, when, where, and who of it all. Creative doubt keeps me with a perpetual "beginner's mind," which is a wonderful way to keep growing, keep humble, and keep living in happy wonder. Yet it is this very *quiet inner unfolding of things* that seems to create the most doubt and anxiety for many believers. They seem to prefer a "touch of the magic wand" kind of God (Tinker Bell?) to a God who works secretly and humbly and who includes *us* in the process and the conclusion.

This is the only way I can understand why a Christian would think evolution is any kind of faith problem whatsoever. The only price we pay for living in the Big Picture is to hold a bit of doubt and anxiety about the exact how, if, when, where, and who of it all, but never the *that*. Unfortunately, most Christians are not well trained in holding opposites for very long or living with what could be very creative tension.

Basic religious belief is a vote for some *coherence, purpose, benevolence, and direction in the universe*, and I suspect it emerges from all that I discussed in the last chapter about home, soul, and the homing device of Spirit. This belief is perhaps the same act of faith as that of Albert Einstein, who said that whatever reality is, it would show itself to be both simple and beautiful. I agree! *Faith in any religion is always somehow saying that God is one and God is good—and if so, then all of reality must be that simple and beautiful too.* The Hebrew people made it their creed, wrote it on their hearts, and inscribed it on their doorways (Deuteronomy 6:4–5) so that they could not and would not forget it.

I worry about "true believers" who cannot carry any doubt or anxiety at all, as Thomas the Apostle and Mother Teresa learned to do. People who are so certain always seem, like Hamlet's queen, to "protest too much" and try too hard. *To hold the full mystery of life is always to endure its other half*, which is the equal mystery of death and doubt. To know anything fully is always to hold that part of it which is still mysterious and unknowable.

After eighty years, I am still a mystery to myself! Our youthful demand for certainty does eliminate most anxiety on the conscious level, so I can see why many of us stay in such a control tower during the first half of life. *We do not have enough experience of wholeness to include all its parts yet.* First-half-of-life naïveté includes a kind of excitement and happiness that is hard to let go of unless we know there is an even deeper and tested kind of happiness out ahead of us. But we do not know that yet in the early years, which is why those in the second half of life must tell us about it. Without elders, a society perishes socially and spiritually.

First naïveté is the earnest and dangerous innocence we sometimes admire in young zealots, but it is also the reason we do not follow them (if we are smart) and why we should not elect them or follow them as leaders. It is probably necessary to eliminate most doubt when we are young; doing so is a good survival technique. *But such worldviews are not true—and they are not wisdom.* Wisdom happily lives with mystery, doubt, and unknowing and, in such living, ironically resolves that very mystery to some degree. I have never figured out why unknowing becomes another kind of knowing, but it surely seems to be.[4] It takes a lot of learning to finally "learn ignorance" (*docta ignorantia*) as Dionysius, Augustine, Bonaventure, and Nicholas of Cusa all agreed.

I must sadly admit that I am still rather impatient with people who do not see things this way. It it took me a long time to get here myself, so I have

learned to be more patient and compassionate over time. I don't need to push
the river as much now, or own the river, or get everybody in my precise river.
Nor do others have to name the river the same way I do in order for me to
trust them or their goodwill. It takes lots of drowning in our own too-tiny
river to get to this big and good place.

I, like everyone else, have had my many experiences, teachings, and
teachers. As T. S. Eliot put it in the *Four Quartets,*

> We had the experience but missed the meaning,
> And approach to the meaning restores the experience
> In a different form, beyond any meaning
> We can assign to happiness.[5]

I know that Eliot's wording is dense, so it might be worth reading again.
In the second half of life, we are not demanding our American constitutional
right to the pursuit of happiness or that people must have our same experiences.
Rather, *simple meaning now suffices, and that becomes in itself a much deeper
happiness.* As the body cannot live without food, so the soul cannot live
without meaning. Viktor Frankl (1905–1997) described this so well when he
pointed out that some level of meaning was the only thing that kept people
from total despair and suicide during the Holocaust.[6] Humans are creators
of meaning, and finding deep meaning in our experiences is not just another
name for spirituality. It is also the very shape of human happiness.

This new coherence, a unified field inclusive of the paradoxes, is precisely
what gradually characterizes a second-half-of-life person. It feels like a return
to simplicity after having learned from all the complexity. Finally, at last, we
have lived long enough to see that "everything belongs,"[7] even the sad, absurd,
and futile parts.

In the second half of life, we can give our energy to making even the
painful parts and the formally excluded parts belong to the now-unified
field — especially people who are different and those who have never had a
chance. If we have forgiven ourselves for being imperfect and falling, we can
now do it for just about everybody else. If we have *not* done it for ourselves,
we will likely pass on our sadness, absurdity, judgment, and futility to others.
This is the tragic path of the many elderly people who have not become actual
elders, probably because they were never eldered or mentored themselves.

Such people seem to have missed out on the joy and clarity of the first simplicity, perhaps avoided the interim complexity, and finally lost the great freedom and magnanimity of the second simplicity as well. We need to hold together all the stages of life, and for some strange, wonderful reason, it all becomes quite "simple" as we approach our later years.

In fact, if this book is not making it very simple for you, I am doing it wrong or you are receiving it wrong. The great irony is that we must go through a necessary complexity (perhaps another term for necessary suffering) to return to any second simplicity. There is no nonstop flight from first to second naïveté.

CHAPTER 10

A BRIGHT SADNESS

I die by brightness and the Holy Spirit.
—THOMAS MERTON, "THE BLESSED VIRGIN
MARY COMPARED TO A WINDOW"

There is a gravitas in the second half of life, but it is now held up by a much deeper lightness or "okayness." Our mature years are characterized by a kind of bright sadness and a sober happiness, if that makes any sense. I am grabbing for words to describe many wonderful older people I have met. If you have met them, you know for yourself and will find your own words. There is still darkness in the second half of life—in fact, maybe even more. But there is now a changed capacity to hold it creatively and with less anxiety.

It is what John of the Cross called "luminous darkness," and it explains the simultaneous coexistence of deep suffering and intense joy in the saints, which would be impossible for most of us to even imagine. Eastern Orthodoxy believed that if something was authentic religious art, it would always have a bright sadness to it. I think I agree with this, and I am saying the same of life itself.

In this second half of life, we have less and less need or interest in eliminating the negative or fearful, making again those old rash judgments, holding onto old hurts, or feeling any need to punish other people. Our superiority complexes have gradually departed in all directions. We do not fight these things anymore; they have just shown themselves too many times to be useless, ego-based, counterproductive, and often entirely wrong. We learn to positively ignore and withdraw our energy from evil or stupid things rather than fight them directly.

We fight things only when we are directly called and equipped to do so. We all become a well-disguised mirror image of anything that we fight too long or too directly. That which we oppose determines the energy and frames the questions after a while. We lose all our inner freedom.

By the second half of life, we have learned ever so slowly, and with much resistance, that most frontal attacks on evil just produce another kind of evil in ourselves, along with a very inflated self-image to boot. This incites a lot of push-back from those we have attacked. This seems to be one of the last lessons to be learned. Think of the cold Grand Inquisitor in *The Brothers Karamazov,* the monk who tries to eliminate all humor in *The Name of the Rose,* or the frowning Koran burners in Florida. Holier-than-thou people usually end up holier than nobody.

Daily life now requires prayer and discernment more than knee-jerk responses toward either the conservative or liberal end of the spectrum. We have *a spectrum of responses* now, and they are not all predictable, in contrast with most knee-jerk responses. Law is still necessary, of course, but it is not our guiding star, or even close. It has been wrong and cruel too many times.

The Eight Beatitudes speak to us much more than the Ten Commandments now. I had always wondered why people never want to put a stone monument of the Eight Beatitudes on the courthouse lawn. Then I realized that the Eight Beatitudes of Jesus would probably not be very good for any war, any macho worldview, the wealthy, or our consumer economy. Courthouses are good and necessary first-half-of-life institutions. In the second half, we try instead to influence events, work for change, quietly persuade, change our own attitude, pray, or forgive instead of taking things to court.

Life is much more spacious now. The boundaries of the container have been enlarged by the constant addition of new experiences and relationships. We are like an expandable suitcase, and we became so almost without noticing. Now, we are just *here*, and here holds more than enough.

Such "hereness," however, has its own heft, authority, and influence. Just watch true elders sitting in any circle of conversation. They are often defining the center, depth, and circumference of the dialogue just by being there! Most participants do not even know it is happening. When elders speak, they need very few words to make their point. Too many words — the use of which I am surely guilty — are not needed by true elders. Second simplicity has its own kind of brightness and clarity, but much of it is expressed in nonverbal terms and only when really needed. If you talk too much or too loud, you are usually not an elder.

If we know anything at this stage, we know that we are all in this together and that we are all equally naked underneath our clothes. This probably does not feel like a whole lot of knowing, but even this little bit of honesty gives us a strange and restful consolation. When we are young, we define ourselves by differentiating ourselves. Now, we look for the things we all share in common. We find happiness in alikeness, which has become much more obvious to us now, and we do not need to dwell on the differences between people or exaggerate the problems. Creating dramas has become boring.

In the second half of life, it is good just to be a part of the general dance. We do not have to stand out, make defining moves, or be better than anyone else on the dance floor. Life is more *participatory* than assertive, and there is no need for strong or further self-definition. God has taken care of all that, in much better ways than we ever expected. The brightness comes from within now, and it is usually more than enough. The dance has a seriousness to it, but also an unselfconscious freedom of form that makes it bright and shining. Think of two old lovers quietly dancing to a soft clarinet and piano melody of the 1940s, safe and relaxed in one another's arms and unconcerned whether anyone is watching. The dance is completely for its own sake.

At this stage, I no longer have to prove that I or my group is the best, that my ethnicity is superior, that my religion is the only one that God loves, or that my role and place in society deserve superior treatment. I am not preoccupied with collecting more goods and services. Quite simply, my desire and effort — every day — is to pay back, to give back to the world a bit of what I have received. I now realize that I have been gratuitously given *to* — from the universe, from society, and from God. I try now, as St. Elizabeth Ann Seton (1774–1821) supposedly said, to "live simply so others can simply live."[1]

Erik Erikson (1902–1994) called someone at this stage a "generative" person, one who is eager and able to generate life from their own abundance and for the benefit of following generations. Because such people have built a good container, they are able to "contain" more and more truth, more and more neighbors, more and broader vision, and more and more of a mysterious and outpouring God.

Their God is no longer small, punitive, or tribal. They once worshiped their raft; now they love the shore where it has taken them. They once defended signposts; now they have arrived where the signs pointed. They now enjoy the moon itself instead of fighting over whose finger points to it most accurately, quickly, or definitively.

Our growing sense of infinity and spaciousness is no longer found just "out there" but most especially "in here." The inner and the outer have become one. We can trust our inner experience now, because even God has allowed it, used it, received it, and refined it. As St. Augustine dramatically wrote in his *Confessions*,

> You were within, but I was without. You were with me, but I was not with you. So you called, you shouted, you broke through my deafness, you flared, blazed, and banished my blindness, you lavished your fragrance, and I gasped.[2]

It takes such gasping several times in our life to eventually rest in a bright sadness: We are sad because we now hold the pain of the larger world, and we wish everyone enjoyed what we now enjoy; but there is brightness because life is somehow — on some levels — still "very good," just as Genesis promised. Merton again stated this best, as he concluded my favorite of his books: "It does not matter much [now], because no despair of ours can alter the reality of things, or stain the joy of the cosmic dance which is always there. . . . We are [now] invited to forget ourselves on purpose, cast our awful solemnity to the winds, and join in the general dance."[3]

In the second half of life, we do not have strong and final opinions about everything, every event, or most people, as much as we allow things and people to delight us, sadden us, and truly influence us. We no longer need to change or adjust other people to be happy ourselves. Ironically, we are, more than ever before, in a position to change people — but we do not *need to*, and that makes all the difference. We have moved from doing to being to an utterly new kind of doing that flows almost organically, quietly, and by osmosis. Our actions are less compulsive. We do what we are called to do and then try to let go of the consequences. We usually cannot do that very well when we are young.

This is human life in its crowning, and all else has been preparation and prelude for creating such a human work of art. Now, we aid and influence other people simply by being who we are. Human integrity probably influences and moves people from potency to action more than anything else. It always deeply saddens me when old folks are still full of themselves and their absolute opinions about everything. Somehow, they have not taken their needed place in the social fabric. We need their deep and studied passion so much more than their superficial and loudly stated principles. We need their peace more than their anger.

Yes, the second half of life is a certain kind of weight to carry, but no other way of being makes sense or gives us the deep satisfaction our soul now demands and even enjoys. This new and deeper passion is what people mean when they say, "I must do this particular thing or my life will not make sense" or "It is no longer a choice."

Your life and your delivery system are now one, whereas before, your life and your occupation seemed like two different things. Your concern is not so much *to have what you love* anymore, but *to love what you have*—right now. This is a monumental change from the first half of life, so much so that it is almost the litmus test of whether you are in the second half of life at all.

The rules are all different now, and we often see it in older folks' freedom to give things away. Hoarding, possessing, collecting, and impressing others with their things, their house, or their travels are of less and less interest to them. Inner brightness, still holding life's sadness and joy, is its own reward, its own satisfaction, and their best and truest gift to the world. Such elders are the "grand" parents of the world. Children and other adults feel so safe and loved around them, and they themselves feel so needed and helpful to children, teens, and midlife adults. And they are! They are in their natural flow.

Strangely, all of life's problems, dilemmas, and difficulties are now resolved, not by negativity, attack, criticism, force, or logical resolution, but always by falling into a larger "brightness." Hopkins called it "the dearest freshness deep down things."[4] This is the falling upward that we have been waiting for! One of the guiding principles of our Center for Action and Contemplation puts it this way: "The best criticism of the bad is the practice of the better." I learned this from my father St. Francis, who did not concentrate on attacking evil or others, but just spent his life *falling,* and falling many times into the good, the true, and the beautiful. It was the only way he knew how to fall into God.

Such inner brightness ends up being a much better and longer-lasting alternative to evil than any war, anger, violence, or ideology could ever be. All we have to do is meet one such shining person and we know that they are surely the goal of humanity and the delight of God. I hope you are becoming that shining person yourself and that this book is helping you see it, allow it, and trust it. Otherwise, this book too will be just some more words — instead of words becoming flesh. Until it becomes flesh, it cannot shine and shine brightly.

CHAPTER 11

THE SHADOWLANDS

 A light shines on in the darkness, a light that darkness cannot overcome.
—PROLOGUE TO JOHN'S GOSPEL 1:5

 Make friends with your opponent quickly while he is taking you to court, or he will hand you over to the judge, and the judge to the officer, and the officer will throw you into prison. You will not get out until you have paid the last penny.
—MATTHEW 5:25–26

Despite the joys of such "brightness," we must also address more about the paradoxical journey of getting there. By the second half of life, you have been in regular unwelcome contact with your shadow self, which gradually detaches you from your not-so-bright *persona* (meaning "stage mask" in Greek) that you so diligently constructed in the first half of life. Your stage mask is not bad, evil, or necessarily egocentric; it is just not "true." It is manufactured and sustained unconsciously by your mind, but it can and will die, as all fictions must die.

Persona and shadow are correlative terms. *Your shadow is what you refuse to see about yourself and what you do not want others to see.* The more you have cultivated and protected a chosen persona, the more shadow work you will need to do. Be especially careful, therefore, of any idealized role or self-image, like that of minister, mother, doctor, nice person, professor, moral believer, or president of this or that. These are huge personas to live up to, and they trap many people in lifelong delusion. The more you are attached to and unaware of such a protected self-image, the more shadow self you will very likely have. Conversely, the more you live out of your shadow self, the less capable you are of recognizing the persona you are trying to protect and project. It is like a double blindness keeping you from seeing—and being—your best and deepest self. As Jesus put it, "If the lamp within you is, in fact, darkness, what darkness there will be" (Matthew 6:23).

I have prayed for years for one good humiliation a day, and then I must watch my reaction to it. In my position, I have no other way of spotting both my well-denied shadow self and my idealized persona. I am actually surprised there are not more clergy scandals, because "spiritual leader" or "professional religious person" is such a dangerous and ego-inflating self-image. Whenever ministers, or any true believers, are too anti anything, you can be pretty sure there is some shadow material lurking somewhere nearby.

Your persona is what most people want from you and reward you for, and what you choose to identify with, for some reason. As you do your inner work, you will begin to know that your self-*image* is nothing more than just that. It is not worth protecting, promoting, or denying. As Jesus says in the passage above, if you can begin to "make friends" with those who have a challenging message for you, you will usually begin to see some of your own shadow. If you don't, you will miss out on much-needed wisdom and end up "imprisoned" within yourself or taken to "court" by others, and you will undoubtedly have to "pay the last penny" to reorder your life and your relationships. Think of our many politicians and clergy who have fallen into public disgrace following sexual and financial scandals.

The "opponent taking you to court" is, for me, a telling description of what we allow inner story lines to do to us. In ten seconds, we can create an entire and self-justifying scenario of blame, anger, and hurt—toward ourselves or toward another. Jesus is saying, "Don't go there, or the judge, officer, and courtroom will quickly take over and have their way with you." Buddhist nun and writer Pema Chödrön says that once you create a self-justifying story line, your emotional entrapment within it quadruples! She is surely right, yet I still do it every day and become my own worst judge, attorney, and jury within ten seconds of an offending statement.

Your self-image is not substantial or lasting; it is just created out of your own mind, desire, and choice—and everybody else's preferences for you! It floats around in Plato's unreal world of ideas. It is not objective at all but entirely subjective (which does not mean that it does not have real influence). The movement to second-half-of-life wisdom has much to do with necessary shadow work and the emergence of healthy self-critical thinking, which alone allows you to see beyond your own shadow and disguise and to find who you are "hidden with Christ in God," as Paul put it (Colossians 3:3). This self cannot die, always lives, and is your True Self.

As Jesus taught, "You must recognize the plank in your own eye, and only then will you see clearly enough to take the splinter out of your brother or sister's eye" (Matthew 7:5). He also said, "The lamp of the body is the eye" (Luke 11:34). Spiritual maturity is largely a growth in seeing, and full seeing seems to take most of your lifetime, with a huge leap in the final years, months, weeks, and days of life, as any hospice volunteer will tell you. There seems to be a cumulative and exponential growth in seeing in people's last years, at least for those who do their inner work. There is also a cumulative closing down in people who have denied all shadow work and humiliating self-knowledge. The Nuremburg trials showed us Nazi men who killed millions and were still in total denial and maintenance of their moral self-image till the very end. I am sure you know examples of both of these types.

Shadow work is humiliating work, but properly so. If you do not "eat" such humiliations with regularity and make friends with the judges, the courtrooms, and the officers (that is, all those who reveal to you and convict you of your own denied faults) who come into your life, you will surely remain in the first half of life forever. You never get to the second half of life without major shadowboxing. And, I am sorry to report that it continues until the end of life, the only difference being that you are no longer surprised by your surprises or so totally humiliated by your humiliations. You come to expect various forms of halfheartedness, deceit, vanity, or illusions from yourself, but now you see through them, which destroys most of their game and power.

Odysseus had to face his same poor judgment again and again. He and others suffered much because of it, yet he usually seemed to learn from his shadow side too. Some call this pattern the discovery of the "golden shadow," because it carries so much enlightenment for the soul. The general pattern in story and novel is that heroes learn and grow from encountering their shadow, whereas villains never do. Invariably, the movies and novels that are most memorable show real *character development* and growing through shadow work. This inspires us all because it calls us all.

We all identify with our persona so strongly when we are young that we become masters of denial and learn to eliminate or deny anything that doesn't support it. *Neither our persona nor our shadow is evil in itself. Rather, they just allow us to do evil and not know it.* Our shadow self makes us all into hypocrites on some level. Remember, *hypocrite* is a Greek word that simply means "actor," someone playing a role rather than being "real." We are all in one kind of closet or another and are even encouraged by society to play our roles. Usually, everybody else can see your shadow, so it is crucial that you learn what everybody else knows about you—except you!

The saint is precisely one who has no "I" to protect or project. Their "I" is in conscious union with the "I AM" of God, and that is more than enough. Divine union overrides any need for self-hatred or self-rejection. Such people do not need to be perfectly right, and they know they cannot be anyway, so they just try to be in *right relationship*. In other words, they try above all else to be loving. Love holds them tightly and safely and always. Such people have met the enemy and know that the major enemy is "me." But you do not hate "me," either. You just see through and beyond "me." Shadow work literally *saves you from yourself* (your false self), which is the foundational meaning of salvation to begin with.

I am afraid that the closer you get to the Light, the more of your shadow you see. Thus, truly holy people are *always* humble people. Christians could have benefitted greatly if shadow had been distinguished from sin. Sin and shadow are not the same. We were so encouraged to avoid sin that many of us instead avoided facing our shadow. Then we ended up "sinning" even worse—while unaware besides! As Paul taught, "The angels of darkness must disguise themselves as angels of light" (2 Corinthians 11:14). The persona does not choose to see evil in itself, so it always disguises it as good. The shadow self invariably presents itself as something like prudence, common sense, justice, or "I am doing this for your good," when it is actually manifesting fear, control, manipulation, or even vengeance. The name Lucifer literally means the "light bearer." The evil one always makes darkness look like light—and makes light look like darkness.

Invariably, when something upsets you, and you have a strong emotional reaction out of proportion to the moment, your shadow self has just been exposed. So, watch for any overreactions or overdenials. When you notice them, notice also that the cock has just crowed (see Matthew 26:34)! The reason that a mature or saintly person can be so peaceful, so accepting of self and others, is that there is not much hidden shadow self left. (There is always and forever a little more, however! There are no exceptions. Shadow work never stops.) This denied and disguised self takes so much energy (to face, awaken, and transform all aspects of your life) that you have little time to project your fear, anger, or unlived life onto terrorists, Muslims, socialists, liberals, conservatives, or even hate radio.

As the shadows of things continue to show themselves (shadow, even in the physical universe, is created by an admixture of darkness and light), you lose interest in idealizing or idolizing persons or events, especially yourself. You no longer "give away your inner gold" to others. You keep yours, and you let them keep theirs. That does not mean you stop loving other people. In fact, it means you actually start. It does not mean self-hatred or self-doubt, but exactly the opposite, because you finally accept both your gold and your weaknesses as your own — and they no longer cancel one another out. You can finally do the same for others too, and you do not let one or another fault in a person destroy your larger relationship. Here, you understand the absolute importance of contemplative or nondualistic thinking, which I will address in a bit.

The gift of shadowboxing is in the *seeing* of the shadow and its games, which takes away much of the shadow's hidden power. No wonder that Teresa of Ávila wrote that the mansion of true self-knowledge was the necessary first mansion.[1] Once you have faced your own hidden or denied self, there is not much to be anxious about anymore, because there is no fear of exposure — to yourself or others. The game is over — and you are free. You have now become the "holy fool" of legend and story, which Paul seems to say is the final stage (2 Corinthians 11), when there is no longer any persona to protect or project. You finally are who you are and can be who you are, without disguise or fear.

DEPRESSION AND SADNESS

There will always be some degree of sadness, humiliation, and disappointment resulting from shadow work, so it's best to learn to recognize it and not obsess over it. It is the false self that is sad and humbled, because its game is over. Holy sadness is the price your soul pays for opening to the new and the unknown in yourself and in the world. A certain degree of such necessary sadness (another form of necessary suffering!) is important to feel, to accept, and to face.

In my work with men, I have found that in many men this inability or refusal to feel their deep sadness takes the form of aimless anger.[2] The only way to get to the bottom of their anger is to face the ocean of sadness underneath it. Men are not free to cry, so they just transmute their tears into anger, and sometimes it pools up in their soul in the form of real depression. Men are actually encouraged to deny their shadow self in any competitive society, so we end up with a lot of sad and angry old men. Men are capable of so much more, if they will only do some shadowboxing.

But let me distinguish good and necessary sadness from some forms of depression. *Many depressed people are people who have never taken any risks, never moved outside their comfort zone, never faced necessary suffering, and so their unconscious knows that they have never lived—or loved!* It is not the same as necessary sadness, although it can serve that function. I am afraid that a large percentage of people in their later years are merely depressed or angry. What an unfortunate way to live one's final years.

One of the great surprises is that humans come to full consciousness precisely by shadowboxing, facing their own contradictions, and making friends with their own mistakes and failings. People who have had no inner struggles are invariably both superficial and uninteresting. We tend to endure them more than communicate with them, because they have little to communicate. Shadow work is almost another name for falling upward. Lady Julian put it best of all: "First there is the fall, and then we recover from the fall. Both are the mercy of God!"

CHAPTER 12

NEW PROBLEMS
AND NEW DIRECTIONS

"My Father's sun shines on the good and the bad, his rain falls on the just and the unjust. Jesus said,"
—MATTHEW 5:45

If you are on course at all, your world should grow much larger in the second half of life. But, in yet another paradox, your circle of real confidants and truly close friends will normally grow smaller—and also more intimate. You are no longer surprised or angered when most people—and even most institutions—are doing first-half-of-life tasks. In fact, that is what most groups, institutions, and young people are programmed to do. Don't hate them for it.

Institutions must, by necessity, be concerned with membership requirements, policies, procedures, protocols, and precedents. If they are working organizations, they need to have very clear criteria for hiring and firing, for supervision and management, and have rules for promotion and salaries. They have to be seriously concerned about lawsuits and litigation. We would resent them even more if they did not do these things well, but *these are nevertheless ego needs and not soul needs.* That is our common dilemma, and it is not easily resolved. But it can be a very creative tension.

We avoid this necessary and creative tension when we try to resolve and end it with old shibboleths like "In the real world . . ." or "The bottom line is. . . ." Much of the Gospel has been avoided by such easy dismissals of soul wisdom, which is initially seldom practical, efficient, or revenue-generating. *The bottom line of the Gospel is that most of us have to hit some kind of bottom before we even start the real spiritual journey.* Up to that point, it is mostly religion. At the bottom, there is little time or interest in being totally practical, efficient, or revenue generating. We just want to breathe fresh air. The true Gospel is always fresh air and spacious breathing room.

So, our question now becomes, "How can I honor the legitimate needs of the first half of life while creating space, vision, time, and grace for the second?" *The holding of this tension is the very shape of wisdom.* Only hermits and some retired people can almost totally forget the first and devote themselves to the second, but even they must eat, drink, and find housing and clothing! The human art form is in uniting fruitful activity with a contemplative stance—not one or the other, but always both at the same time.[1]

Groups of any kind have to be concerned with such practical things, which is exactly why we will become impatient with such institutions, including the church, as we grow older and wiser. The implications are staggering. Historically, in the Catholic and Orthodox traditions, some just went off to the side and became monks or nuns, but now, even religious life suffers from the same institutionalization and is not always a satellite of freedom or the wisdom school that it was meant to be. We have been "churchified," I am afraid.

It is very rare to really absorb the Gospel or wisdom thinking in the first half of life, so we settle for "answers" and organizations and build the whole structure around such *non-answer answers.* We cannot turn the other cheek if we are American, nor can we have Eucharistic table fellowship with non-Catholics if we are Catholic. We end up denying the first and deeper river for the sake of the small river that everybody happens to be floating on. In fact, we just try to improve the barges, boats, and bridges on this small upper river so that people can float more comfortably.

In preparing for a 2011 release, the Catholic Church expended huge amounts of effort and time changing words in the liturgy to be more "faithful" to the "definitive Latin text" (which Jesus never spoke and was actually the language of his oppressors), while the world was facing unparalleled disasters at every level. The sanctuary is the only world where the clergy still have a bit of control, it seems. So, again, the meticulous navigating of our small river surpasses ever diving into the Big River.

It makes me wonder if Jesus' first definition of church as "two or three gathered in my name" is not still the best way to avoid these sorts of illusions (Matthew 18:20). So many people I know who are doing truly helpful and healing ministry find their primary support from a couple of enlightened friends—and only secondarily, if at all, from the larger organization. Larger institutions might well provide the skeleton, but the muscle, meat, and miracles invariably happen at the local level.

The ego—and most institutions—demand a tit-for-tat universe, while the soul swims in a sea of abundance, grace, and freedom, which cannot always be organized. Remember, in the Gospel, at the end of the day, the employer pays those who worked part of a day just as much as those who worked the whole day (Matthew 20:1–16). This does not compute except at the level of soul. Soulful people temper our tantrums by their calm, lessen our urgency by their peace, and exhibit a world of options and alternatives when all the conversation turns into dualistic bickering.

Soulful people are the salt, yeast, and light needed to grow groups up (Matthew 5:13–16, 13:33). Note that Jesus does not demand that we be the whole meal, the full loaf, or the illuminated city itself. Instead, we are to be the quiet undertow and overglow that makes all of these happen. This is why all institutions need second-half-of-life people in their ranks. Just "two or three" in each organization are enough to keep them from total self-interest.

If there are not a few soulful people in each group, we can be sure that those who come at the end of the day, who are at the back of the line, or who live on the edge of what we call normal will never get paid. Sadly, that seems to be the direction of both our politics and our churches. So, we have to prepare and equip the two or three second-half-of-lifers in how to stay in there with mostly first-half-of-lifers! That is surely what Jesus meant when he said that disciples must "carry the cross" (Luke 14:27).

When I state that almost all groups and institutions are first-half-of-life structures, this is not to discourage you but, in fact, just the opposite. I state it first of all because it is true, but also to keep you from being depressed or losing all hope by having false expectations. Don't expect or demand from groups what they usually cannot give. Doing so will make you needlessly angry and reactionary. *They must and will be concerned* with identity, boundaries, self-maintenance, self-perpetuation, and self-congratulation. This is their nature and purpose. The most you can hope for is a few enlightened leaders and policies to appear now and then from among those "two or three gathered in my name."

In your second half of life, you can actually bless others in what they feel they must do, allow them to do what they must do, and challenge them if they are hurting themselves or others—but you can no longer join them in the first half of life. You can belong to such institutions for all the good that they do, but you no longer put all your eggs in that one basket. This will keep you and others from unnecessary frustration and anger, and from knocking on doors that cannot be opened from the other side. In short, this is what I mean by "emerging Christianity."[2]

Even Jesus said that it would be a waste of time to throw our seeds on the busy footpath, the rocky soil, or among the thorns. He told us we should wait for receptive soil (Matthew 13:4–9). I call such people multipliers, contemplatives, or change agents. Today, I often find this receptive soil more outside of churches than within, many of which have lost that necessary "beginner's mind," both as groups and as individuals. Yet, Jesus predicted it himself: "The children of this world are often more clever than the children of light" (Luke 16:8), which is probably why he made the sinner, the outsider, the Gentile, the Samaritan, the woman, the Roman centurion, the poor person, and the leper the heroes of his stories.

With so many good and sincere people in their ranks, the only way we can explain why the religions formed in the name of Moses, Jesus, and Mohammed became groups that defined themselves by exclusion and "againstness" is that history up to now has largely been asking first-half-of-life questions. It is always interesting to me that the power of the "keys" that Jesus gave to Peter both to "bind and to loose" (Matthew 16:19) is invariably used to bind and so seldom used to loose—unless it is to the church institution's advantage. Then, when I remember that the first half of life defines itself by "no" and the second half of life by "yes," I can understand. I am grateful that Jesus himself was a teacher from the second half of life, who, according to Paul, "always said yes" (2 Corinthians 1:19–20).

LONELINESS AND SOLITUDE

There is a certain real loneliness if you say yes and all your old friends are saying no. So, be prepared when your old groups, friendships, and even churches no longer fully speak to you the way they used to. I promise you that those confusing feelings are far outdistanced by a new ability to be alone — and to be happy alone. One of the great surprises at this point is that you find that *the cure for your loneliness is actually solitude!* Who would have imagined that to be the case?

I wrote this during my Lenten hermitage, where I was alone for most of forty days. I could not be happier, more united with everybody else, prayerfully united with the tragic sense of life on this planet, and yet totally "productive" too. Most cannot imagine this, I guess, but it is a different level and a different quality of productivity. Once a person moves to deep time, they are utterly one with the whole communion of saints and sinners, past and future. (By the way, I think that is a good way to understand reincarnation!) In deep time, everybody matters, has influence, and is even somehow "present" and not just past.

Basically, the first half of life is writing the text, and the second half is writing the commentary on that text. We all tend to move toward a happy and needed introversion as we get older. Such introversion is necessary to unpack all that life has given us and taken from us. We engage in what is now a necessary and somewhat natural contemplation. We should not be surprised that most older people do not choose loud music, needless diversions, or large crowds. We move toward understimulation if we are on the schedule of soul. Life has stimulated us enough, and now we have to process it and integrate it, however unconsciously. Silence and poetry start being our more natural voice and our more beautiful ear at this stage.[3] Much of life starts becoming highly symbolic and "connecting," and little things become significant metaphors for everything else. Silence is the only language spacious enough to include everything and to keep us from slipping back into dualistic judgments and divisive words.

Poets like Gerard Manley Hopkins, Mary Oliver, David Whyte, Denise Levertov, Naomi Shihab Nye, Rainer Maria Rilke, and T. S. Eliot now name your own inner experience, even if you have never read poetry before. Mystics like Rumi, Hafiz, Kabir, John of the Cross, Thérèse of Lisieux, Baal Shem Tov, Lady Julian of Norwich, and Rabia will speak to you perhaps more than people from your own tradition — whereas before you did not know, or did not care, what they were talking about. Like Jesus, you may soon feel as though you have "nowhere to lay your head" (Matthew 8:20), while a whole set of new heads are now making sense to you! This is true politically too. In fact, if your politics do not become more compassionate and inclusive, I doubt whether you are on the second journey.

This is initially quite scary, but the issue is no longer "Are they in my group, my country, my political party, my social class?" but "Have they 'passed over' to the Big Picture?" Members of this new "nongroup group" can talk to one another rather easily, it seems. What some now call "emerging Christianity" or "the emerging church" is not something you join, establish, or invent. You just name it, and then you see it everywhere—already in place! Such nongroup groups, the "two or three" gathered in deeper truth, create a whole new level of affiliation, dialogue, and friendship, even though they can still enjoy being among their old friends too, as long as they do not talk about anything serious, political, or religious.

A kind of *double belonging* is characteristic of people at this stage. No one group meets all of their needs, desires, and visions. I bet that if you've lasted this long with this book, you yourself are a "double belonger," maybe even a triple or more! Colonized people, oppressed people, and every kind of minority have had to learn several levels of belonging to survive and get through the day. For us more comfortable folks it is still a stretch, but finally a stretch that many are making, perhaps without even realizing it.

BOTH-AND THINKING

What this illustrates, of course, is a newly discovered capacity for what many religions have called "nondualistic thinking" or both-and thinking.[4] It is almost the benchmark of our growth into the second half of life. Calmer and more contemplative seeing does not appear suddenly, but grows almost unconsciously over many years of conflict, confusion, healing, broadening, loving, and forgiving reality. It emerges gradually as we learn to "incorporate the negative," learn from what we used to exclude, or, as Jesus put it, forgive our enemies, both within and without.

We no longer need to divide the field of every moment between up and down, totally right or totally wrong, "with me" or "against me." It just *is. This calm allows us to confront what must be confronted with even greater clarity and incisiveness.* This stance is not passivity at all. It is, in fact, the essential link between true contemplation and skillful action. The big difference is that our small and petty self is out of the way, and if God wants to use us, which God always does, God's chances are far better now!

Dualistic thinking is the well-practiced pattern of knowing most things by comparison. And, for some reason, once you compare or label things (that is, judge), you almost always conclude that one is good and the other is less good or even bad. Don't take my word for it; just notice your own thoughts and reactions. You will see that you will move almost automatically into a pattern of up or down, in or out, "for me" or "against me," right or wrong, black or white, good or bad. It is the basic reason why the "stinking thinking" of racism, sexism, classism, homophobia, religious imperialism, and prejudice of all kinds is so hard to overcome and has lasted so long—even among nice people!

At the risk of being too cleverly alliterative (though it may help you remember), here is the normal sequencing of the dualistic mind: *it compares, it competes, it conflicts, it conspires, it condemns, it cancels out any contrary evidence, and it then crucifies with impunity.* You can call it the seven Cs of delusion and the source of most violence, which is invariably *sacralized* as good and necessary to "make the world safe for democracy" or to "save souls for heaven."

Nondualistic or contemplative thinking was put off or fully denied in the first half of life for the sake of quickly drawn ego boundaries and clear goals, which created a nice, clean *provisional personality.* Dualistic thinking works only for a while to get us started, but if we are honest, it stops being helpful in most real-life situations. It is fine for teenagers to really think that there is some moral or "supernatural" superiority to their chosen baseball team, their army, their ethnic group, or even their religion. But we hope they learn that such polarity thinking is just an agreed-upon game by the second half of life. Our frame should grow larger as we move toward the Big Picture in which one God creates all and loves all: both Red Sox and Yankees, Blacks and whites, Palestinians and Jews, Americans and Afghanis.

The trouble is that a lot of people don't get there. We are often so attached to our frame, game, or raft that it becomes a substitute for objective truth, because it is all we have! Inside such entrapment, most people do not see things as they *are;* rather, they see things as *they* are. In my experience, this is most of the world, unless people have done their inner work, or least some shadow work, and thereby entered into wisdom or nondualistic thinking. Through centuries of meticulous and utterly honest self-observation, Buddhism has helped people see this in themselves probably better than most of the world religions. Jesus saw it, but we did not see him very well.

In the first half of life, the negative, the mysterious, the scary, and the problematic are always exported elsewhere. Doing so gives us a quick and firm ego structure that works for a while. But such splitting *is not an objective statement of truth!* It is just helpful for our private purposes. Eventually, this overcompensation in one direction must be resolved and balanced. This integration, or "forgiveness of everything," as I like to call it, is the very name of growth, maturity, and holiness.

In the second half of life, all that we avoided for the sake of a manufactured ego ideal starts coming back as a true friend and teacher. Doers become thinkers, feelers become doers, thinkers become feelers, extroverts become introverts, visionaries become practical, and the practical ones long for vision. We all go toward the very places we avoided for the last forty years, and our friends are amazed. Now, we begin to understand why Jesus is always welcoming the outsider, the foreigner, the sinner, the wounded one. He was a second-half-of-life man who has had the unenviable task of trying to teach and be understood by a largely first-half-of-life history, church, and culture.

Listen to his dangerous and inclusionary thinking: "My Father's sun shines on the good and the bad, his rain falls on the just and the unjust" (Matthew 5:45). "Don't pull out the weeds or you might pull out the wheat along with it. Let the weeds and the wheat both grow together until the harvest" (Matthew 13:29–30). If I had presented such fuzzy thinking in my moral theology class, I would have gotten an F!

Jesus, I am convinced, was the first nondualistic religious thinker in the West (there were philosophers like Heraclitus), but his teachings were quickly filtered through Greek dualistic logic. Nondualistic wisdom is just not helpful when we are trying to form a strong group, clarify first principles, or demonstrate that our idea is superior to others' ideas. At that stage, real wisdom appears to be pious and dangerous poetry—and, at that necessary early stage, such warnings are probably right! But that is also why clergy and spiritual teachers need to be second-half-of-life people, and why so many of us have mangled, manipulated, and minimized the brilliance of Jesus when we heard him in our early stage of development.

So, we need first to clarify before we can subtly discriminate. Dualistic thinking gets us in the right ball park ("You cannot serve both God and mammon"), but nondualistic wisdom, or what many of us call *contemplation*, is necessary once we actually get in the right field. "Now that I have chosen to serve God, what does that really mean?" Nondualistic thinking presumes that we have first mastered dualistic clarity, but also that we have found it *insufficient* for the really big issues like love, suffering, death, God, and any notion of infinity. In short, we need *both*.

Unless we let the truth of life teach us on its own terms, unless we develop some concrete practice for recognizing and overcoming our dualistic mind, we will remain in the first half of life forever, as most of humanity has up to now. In the first half of life, we cannot work with the imperfect, nor can we accept the tragic sense of life, which finally means that we cannot love anything or anyone at any depth. Nothing is going to change in history as long as most people are merely dualistic, either-or thinkers. Such splitting and denying leaves us at the level of mere information, data, facts, and endlessly arguing about the same. "My facts are better than your facts," we yell at ever higher volume and with ever stronger ego attachment.

Wisdom was distinguished from mere knowledge by Isaiah (11:2), by Paul (1 Corinthians 12:8–9), and by Scholastic philosophy, which spoke of analytic intelligence and intuitive or "connatural" intelligence ("like knows like") as two very different levels of consciousness. We live in a time when we are finally free to appreciate how right they all were.

Now, much of modern science recognizes the very real coherence between the seer and what is seen or even can be seen. *Wisdom seeing has always sought to change the seer first and then knows that what is seen will largely take care of itself*. It is almost that simple, and it is always that hard.

Whole people see and create wholeness wherever they go. Split people see and create splits in everything and everybody. By the second half of our lives, we are meant to see in wholes and no longer just in parts. Yet, we get to the whole by falling *down* into the messy parts—so many times, in fact, that we long and thirst for the wholeness and fullness of all things, including ourselves. I promise you, this unified field is the only and lasting meaning of *up*.

CHAPTER 13

FALLING UPWARD

> How surely gravity's law,
> strong as an ocean current,
> takes hold of even the smallest thing
> and pulls it toward the heart of the world. . . .
> This is what the things can teach us:
> to fall,
> patiently to trust our heaviness.
>
> —RAINER MARIA RILKE, *2001 /*
> *NORTHWESTERN UNIVERSITY PRESS.*

Most of us tend to think of the second half of life as largely about getting old, dealing with health issues, and letting go of our physical life, but the whole thesis of this book is exactly the opposite. What looks like falling can largely be experienced as falling upward and onward, into a broader and deeper world where the soul has found its fullness, is finally connected to the whole, and lives inside the Big Picture.

It is not a loss but somehow a gain, not losing but actually winning. You probably must have met at least one true elder to imagine that this could be true. I have met enough radiant people in my life to know that it is fairly common. They have come to their human fullness, often against all odds, and usually by suffering personally or vicariously. As Jesus describes such people, "from their breasts flow fountains of living water" (John 7:38). These are the models and goals for our humanity, much more than the celebrities and politicos on whom we focus so much today.

I once watched a documentary on the life of Helen Keller (1880–1968), who was blind and deaf. She seemed to have leaped into the second half of life in the chronological first half of her life, once she discovered her depths and despite her severe limitations. She lived an entire life of rather amazing happiness and generativity for others. She was convinced that life was about service to others and not about protecting or lamenting her supposedly handicapped body.

That seems to be the great difference between transformed and nontransformed people. Great people come to serve, not to be served. It is the twelfth and final—and necessary—step of the inspired Twelve Steps of Alcoholics Anonymous. *Until and unless we give our life away to others, we do not seem to have it ourselves at any deep level.* Good parents always learn that. Many of the happiest, most generous and focused people I know are young mothers. This is another one of those utter paradoxes! We seem to be "mirrored" into life by the response, love, and needed challenge of others. Thank God Anne Sullivan (1866–1936) knew how to beautifully mirror Helen Keller, at great, loving cost to herself. We all need at least one such mirror if we are to thrive.

MIRRORING

Somewhere in my late forties, I realized that many people loved and admired me for who I was not, and many people also resented or rejected me for who I was not. Conversely, many loved me for who I really was, warts and all, and *this was the only love that ever redeemed me.* Many others rightly criticized me for who I really was and revealed to me my shadow, which was always painful but often very helpful. In all cases, it became apparent that their responses said much more about *them* and the good or bad quality of their own mirroring than about me at all!

Beauty or ugliness really *is*, first of all, in the eye of the beholder. Good people will mirror goodness in us, which is why we love them so much. Not-so-mature people will mirror their own unlived and confused life onto us, which is why they confuse and confound us so much and why they are hard to love.

At any rate, it is only those who respond to *the real you, good or bad,* that help you in the long run. Much of the work of midlife is learning to tell the difference between people who are still dealing with *their issues through you* and those who are really dealing with *you as you really are.* As an older man who also carries the priest title of "Father," I find that I am often carrying people's "daddy" projections, both for good and for ill. It is a double-edged sword, because I can be used to heal them very easily, and I can be allowed to hurt them very easily. But, in a certain real sense, it is not about *me* at all, but about me as their mirror, reflection, and projection.

By the second half of life, we learn to tell the difference between who we really are and how others can mirror that or not. This will keep us from taking either insults or praise too seriously. I doubt whether this kind of calm discrimination and detachment is possible much before our midfifties at the earliest. How desperately we need true elders in our world to clean up our seeing and stop the revolving hall of mirrors in its tracks.

We all take what we need, get what we want, and reject what we shouldn't from one another. Don't accept your first responses at face value. The only final and meaningful question is, "Is it true?" not, "Who said it?" "When and where did they say it?" "Does the Bible or the pope or my president say it?" or "Do I like it?" The only meaningful, helpful, and humble question is, "Is it objectively true?"

In the second half of life, we gradually step out of this hall of revolving and self-reflecting mirrors. We can usually do this well only if we have *one true mirror ourselves,* at least one loving, honest friend to ground us, which might even be the utterly accepting gaze of the Friend. But, by all means, we must find at least one true mirror that reveals our inner, deepest, and, yes, divine image. This is why intimate moments are often mirroring moments of beautiful mutual receptivity and why such intimacy heals us so deeply. Thinking we can truthfully mirror ourselves is a first-half-of-life illusion. Mature spirituality has invariably insisted on soul friends, gurus, confessors, mentors, masters, and spiritual directors for individuals, and prophets and truth speakers for groups and institutions.

My Franciscan sister St. Clare of Assisi (1194–1253) seemed to find the mirror to be her most frequent and helpful image for what she saw happening in the spiritual life. She loved to advise her sisters to variously "Place yourself before the mirror,"[1] and "Look upon the mirror [of perfect love] each day."[2] She clearly understood that *spiritual gifts are always reflected gifts.* Clare predated the "self psychology" of Heinz Kohut (1913–1981) and our present knowledge of mirror neurons by eight centuries. *Mystics often intuit and live what scientists later prove to be true.*

We really do find ourselves through one another's eyes. Only when that has been done truthfully can we mirror others with freedom, truth, and compassion. Jesus himself predated Clare by twelve centuries when he said, "The lamp of the body is the eye. If your eye is healthy, your whole body will be filled with light" (Matthew 6:22). It is all a matter of learning how to see, and it takes much of our life to learn to see well and truthfully.

In the second half of life, people have less power to infatuate us, but they also have much less power to control us or hurt us. It is the freedom of the second half to *not* need. Both the ecstatic mirroring of my youth and the mature and honest mirroring of my adulthood have held up what I needed to see and could see at the time. They have prepared me for the fully compassionate and Divine Mirror, who has always shown me to myself in times and ways that I could handle and enjoy. I fell many times, relationally, professionally, emotionally, and physically in my life, but there was always a trampoline effect that allowed me to finally fall upward. No falling down was final, but actually contributed to the bounce!

God knows that all of us will fall somehow. Those events that lead us to catastrophize out of all proportion must be business as usual for God—at least eight billion times a day. Like good spiritual directors do, God must say after each failure of ours, "Oh, here is a great opportunity! Let's see how we can work with this." After our ego-inflating successes, God surely says, "Well, nothing new or good is going to happen here!"

Failure and suffering are the great equalizers and levelers among humans. Success is just the opposite. Communities and commitment can form around suffering much more than around how wonderful or superior we are. Just compare the real commitment to one another, to the world, and to truth in "happy, clappy religion" with the deep solidarity of families at the time of a tragic death or among hospice workers and their clients. There is a strange and even wonderful communion in real human pain—actually, much more than in joy, which is too often manufactured and passing. In one sense, pain's effects are not passing, and pain is less commonly manufactured. Thus, it is a more honest doorway into lasting communion than even happiness.

The genius of the Gospel was that it included the problem inside the solution. The falling became the standing. The stumbling became the finding. The dying became the rising. The raft became the shore. The small self cannot see this very easily, because it doubts itself too much, is still too fragile, and is caught up in the tragedy of it all. It has not lived long enough to see the big patterns. No wonder so many of our young commit suicide. This is exactly why we need elders and those who can mirror life truthfully and foundationally for the young. Intimate I-Thou relationships[3] are the greatest mirrors of all, so we dare not avoid them, but for the young they have perhaps not yet taken place at any depth, so young people are always very fragile.

Many of us discover in times of such falling the Great Divine Gaze, the ultimate I-Thou relationship, which is always compassionate and embracing or it would not be divine. Like any true mirror, the gaze of God receives us exactly as we are, without judgment or distortion, subtraction or addition. Such *perfect receiving* is what transforms us. Being totally received as we truly are is what we wait and long for all our lives. All we can do is receive and return the loving gaze of God every day, and afterward we will be internally free and deeply happy at the same time. The One who knows all has no trouble including, accepting, and forgiving all. Soon, we who are gazed upon so perfectly can pass on the same accepting gaze to all others who need it. There is no longer any question of whether someone deserves it. What we received was totally undeserved itself.

Just remember this: No one can keep you from the second half of your own life except yourself. Nothing can inhibit your second journey except your own lack of courage, patience, and imagination. Your second journey is all yours to walk or to avoid. My conviction is that some falling apart of the first journey is necessary for this to happen, so do not waste a moment of time lamenting poor parenting, lost job, failed relationship, physical challenge, gender identity, economic poverty, or even the tragedy of any kind of abuse. *Pain is part of the deal.* If you don't walk into the second half of your own life, it is *you* who do not want it. God will always give you exactly what you truly want and desire. So, make sure you desire: desire deeply, desire yourself, desire God, and desire everything good, true, and beautiful.

All the emptying out is only for the sake of a Great Outpouring.

God, like nature, abhors all vacuums and rushes to fill them.

Basically, the first half of life is writing the text, and the second half is writing the commentary on that text.
—RICHARD ROHR

I'm very happy that I was inspired to write *Falling Upward* because it's had far more response from the contemporary world than I ever expected. I'm even happier twelve years later than I was when I first wrote it because I've seen the response to it. I don't think it's the most important of my books, but, for some reason, it has currency in the present worldview. I think that's because, as I wrote in the book, America is a first-half-of-life culture. Almost all organized religion is as well, until it reaches the mystical level and "un-organizes" itself.

Until then, it's about externals—making a pilgrimage, fasting, genuflecting, making the sign of the cross—all of which are lovely, but they don't necessarily touch the essence. A lot of people don't sense this, which is most unfortunate. They haven't reached the point of midlife malaise, where a part of them says, "Is this all there is? Is this the best I can do? There must be *more* than getting a job and having children." It becomes that practical. We normally have to do those big, practical things first—family and finance—and then, when we stop obsessing about those, we face the malaise, the loneliness, and the necessary disorientation of the transition.

TRANSITIONING INTO THE SECOND HALF OF LIFE

The transition from the first half to the second half of life happens multiple times. That doesn't mean there isn't one big transition. Some door might well open after a death in the family or of someone we love, or the loss of a major job. I think of it like being shot with a shotgun: We keep getting different wounds in different parts of our body. More often than not, it's many little moments of enlightenment, normally between ages forty and fifty-five. But there certainly are people who shift to the second half of life through one big transition.

One transitional situation of which I'm most aware, through counseling people, is the death of their child. People *never* seem to recover. It's unthinkable. It's an absurd world. So, sometimes, a one-time blow takes people into a dark night of sorts. And, *if* they come out of it, many people just turn bitter and closed. Others come out of it and find themselves *naturally* attracted to second-half-of-life values.

PARADOX

The first half of life refuses paradox. It wants clarity. It wants order and explanation. People in the first half of life, when faced with paradox, will say strongly that it's "just fuzzy thinking," the refusal to accept logic. It's rather hard to invite Silicon Valley minds into the mystical because they say, "We trust science. What do we do with paradox? We can't build a car with paradox." So, there has to be a radical acceptance of the world of mystery, the world of mythology. The reason Protestants have so much trouble with the Bible is because they were not given an understanding of paradox, mythology, or how literature works—which is by illusion, symbol, and story. Jesus *only* taught in parables. That's a strong statement, but it makes us realize he was a very different kind of teacher than most teachers in America. Maybe in other countries—for example, Ireland, with its culture of storytelling—it was different. But in America, we don't tend to grow up with storytelling teachers.

Paradox looks like fuzzy thinking, but it's really nuanced, insightful thinking. It likes to see the shadow side of everything, including capitalism, America, the church, ourselves, our marriages. Each of those is a separate conversion, another blow. "Why am I still loving my partner after they've hurt me so much and they're not that wonderful all the time? Yet something in me has decided to love them." That is when you have moved into paradox. You live with paradox much more than you realize. If you have persisted in love of anything or anybody over a long period, you already think in paradox. *You live in paradox.*

Even with precious little children, you probably have seen some little things about them and say, "I wish they weren't that way." But it doesn't matter. Your love overrides your judgments if you're contemplative—by which I mean being reflective. If, instead, you remain in the driven, utilitarian mind, even though you are thinking in paradox, you won't recognize you're in the second half of life. Your love won't override your judgments. You won't realize that every time you love and forgive your partner, or you accept the things you'd really prefer to change in your children, that's a paradox. You need to bring love and forgiveness to yourself without it just being softness. This is about a virtue, not just defaulting to laziness that makes it easy to let yourself off the hook.

You must have done a bit of staring, gazing, and silence, where you just stand and gaze at the absurdity of it all. I recently spoke with a friend about gazing, and I compared it to glancing and glaring. Glancing is quick, nonreflective looking. For example, it's looking at the untrimmed trees along the highway and briefly wondering why they haven't been trimmed. Glaring is looking at them with disgust, with cynical disdain: "Isn't that stupid? Why wouldn't somebody fix that?" So, contemplation can't be glancing, and it can't be glaring; it has to be looking at something until it becomes beautiful. That's contemplation. When you stop needing the trees to be trimmed, when you can be happy with them as they are, you're in the early stages of contemplation.

You see why, for a perfectionist like me, contemplation is necessary to be happy. Perfectionists — and most people, if we're honest — are cutting everything down to size, glancing and glaring, so you don't have to gaze, to worship. Contemplation is allowing the gazing to emerge. At one point, St. Francis said, "Everything is to be adored." When you can move to the point of surrender to this, acceptance of it in its imperfect state, that's adoration. It's like that line in the traditional Anglican wedding ceremony, when the man says to his wife, "I thee worship" — right after speaking of her body. That is daring language to use, publicly saying, "I'm going to worship her body." Then she says it to him too: "I thee worship." That is adoration. That is gazing.

NEAR-DEATH EXPERIENCES

Over the last few years, I've had many health challenges, which some of my friends have called near-death experiences. First, I honestly think they weren't that dramatic, as in, "Wow, I'm going to die tomorrow." I've had so many scares with cancer, and they came in little doses, where I'd be able to say, "Okay, I'm going to die. It might be soon." I'm not aware of my near-death experiences dramatically changing me, but they gave me an overall awareness of the transitory nature of everything. I started seeing everything as dying, and myself along with it. I wasn't focused just on, "I'm going to die," but also, "That tree is going to die. In twenty years, that tree is going to die. In five years, this highway will need total repair." I started seeing the transitory nature of everything. That's why these new TV shows on the universe that show how time is actually about the movement of orbits and cycles, of turning around the sun, are so compelling. We call it time, but it's just movement. Everything is in motion. We call it a day. It means one turn around the axis of the Earth. So, I'd like to state that time is movement, and everything is dying. Everything is moving, all the time.

Now, a lot of people don't come to that realization, don't surrender to the transitory nature of everything, except by the shock of their own death or the shock of their partner's death—or particularly their child's death, which to a parent is just the most cruel, illogical, absurd, and unfair thing possible. I had parents in the New Jerusalem community in Cincinnati who, once they lost a child, were different people. They had different personalities. They were more "sober." I also think, if they'd reflected upon it, they'd have realized they were much less afraid of their own death because of their Christian belief that they would get to see their child again. They had this desire to be reunited with their little one. They had surrendered to the transitory nature of everything.

SUFFERING AND SIN

At this point in the second half of my life, drawing closer to my death, I still don't like suffering. Who does? But, because I haven't suffered like the people in war-torn Ukraine or in drought-ridden Africa suffer, I feel my suffering isn't worthy of the word. If I'm honest, my suffering is mostly discomfort, and who has a right to call that suffering? As a "rich" American, with top-quality healthcare, I've gone to doctors a lot in the last five years, and they always offered a new treatment or pill. It was always an *inconvenience* to go to the doctor again, but to someone who is truly suffering, to someone who is afraid, do I have *anything* to say? How dare you, Richard.

I'm rather strong, I think, in my writings and preaching about the necessity of suffering, the *potential* goodness of suffering, but I do feel phony in stating it with such conviction because I have personally not suffered that much. I have faced illness, absurdity, and my own contradictions, but this is not *big* suffering.

When I think about the necessity and nature of suffering, it makes me think about the nature of sin. For many people, sin and suffering seem to be related. I wrote a short book titled *What Do We Do with Evil?* that looks at sin. The word "sin" is used so much, in both the Hebrew and Christian Scriptures. It's never going to go away. We need to find some good ways to explain it. Even the Greek word used in the Christian Scriptures for sin, *hamartia*, means "missing the mark." That's very different than what I was taught by the Irish nuns in Catholic school, who said sin was "offending God." It was very much the pre-Vatican II message. We really felt like we were hurting God, and when Jesus was whipped on Good Friday, *we* were the ones whipping him.

Organized religion — and I don't think this is an overstatement — controls people by knowing how to blame and shame. If we took away blame and shame, Hinduism, Judaism, Christianity, and Islam wouldn't have much power to hold groups together. That doesn't mean it's *only* about shame. There is some desire to please God, to do the good thing, to be virtuous, to be loving. But when we consider the concept of sin, let's concentrate on the word "illusion" instead of "offending God." Thinking about sin as offending God is an entirely egocentric definition of love, power, and God, whereby we are protecting ourselves so we are in control. We call it patriotism or loyalty or faithfulness. Sin always has a very seemingly heroic definition, like hoarding money for the sake of it, then calling it prudence or common sense. These are self-serving illusions, which can only be held strongly by the individual if they reach a level of validation from the whole culture.

That's why I believe sin is, first of all, a collective illusion. America as a whole has to agree that capitalism is the best. Then it's very easy to believe that illusion because "this many people couldn't be wrong." Here's another one: "America's wars are good wars. We don't fight bad wars." That's why Vietnam was such a disillusioning event for America: We found ourselves fighting a war that was not good at all. The 1960s were the beginnings — and I mean only the beginnings — of facing our illusions, especially racism, militarism, and capitalism.

Sin is the individual buying into what is almost *always* a corporate illusion first. Once you move beyond that corporate level of idolatry, which is the real hiding place of sin and evil, you necessarily become critical of culture and not just critical of the individual. Maybe it takes a few more years of maturity, but you start getting to a place where you aren't worshipful of culture. Almost all countries are worshipful of culture: "This is the way we do it," whatever *it* is. This is what we all agree upon regarding militarism, or capitalism, or what our religion *should* be. Notice in the teaching of Jesus how much he mocked the Pharisees, who were always quoting tradition. Jesus had little respect for that. He knew that "This is the way we do it as Jews" was a hiding place for illusion. Challenging a corporate illusion is the basis of recognizing that justice is a higher level of love.

Now, I'm not concerned here about the sentimental meaning of love (getting people to like us), but a corporate meaning of love. For example, I have a natural sympathy for anybody who suffers injustice and is powerless. This moves me toward a corporate analysis: I care about other people, not just my group and not just myself. After a few more years, we even become inclusive of others and other groups. We stretch our understanding and our experience of corporate love. It keeps moving in outer circles until we even love those who are *not* our group and love those who have *oppressed* our group. Each is a step away from egocentricity as the reference point. When we stop using ourselves as the reference point for *anything*, that would be total freedom.

SEEDS OF TRANSCENDENCE

Notice (or recall) the moments when you experience transcendence in the first half of life: situations where the second half of life plants seeds in your soul, drops breadcrumbs for you to follow. When I worked at the Acoma Pueblo in New Mexico in 1968–1969, it was delightful for me to live in a non-capitalistic village. People's primary concern was not making money or collecting status symbols. Their houses always looked shabby. They drove their cars until they wore out. (They've become much more capitalistic since then.) When I left, they gave me a carload of Acoma pottery. Even in those days, each piece of pottery was worth $400 or $500, but they just gave me the pots without any question. They were just so friendly and so sweet.

After this experience, I went back to the seminary and said, "I'm not sure we have it." We American Franciscans lived in beautiful buildings — not luxurious, but architecturally and artistically filled with art, with symmetry. To see people who didn't idealize all that was very freeing. My next assignment was in a Black parish in a poor part of Dayton, Ohio. I just felt so at home with the community because I saw many of the same characteristics as the Native people, because they weren't allowed to profit from the capitalist culture.

I loved both of my first assignments because people could love one another and could love reality much more naturally than we white, male priests could. You might have heard the quote, which is not original to me, "We're supposed to love people and use things, not use people and love things." The people of the Acoma Pueblo and the Black parish in Dayton loved people and used things. In many ways, they were already moving into the second half of life. So, I didn't take capitalism as an absolute — that all giving deserves the right to take back: the exchange culture in which you and I live. There were people in both places who gave much more readily than I do, without having the right to take.

A CALL TO CONTEMPLATION

As you come to the end of reading *Falling Upward*, I encourage you to focus primarily on a call to *being* rather than a call to action. Learn how to live in a relaxed, peaceful way in this nondual world of mystery. Then, eventually, God will place something on your doorstep that can then move you into action. My friend Elias and I went down to El Paso, Texas. Rather naturally, over the course of a week, we befriended two families, whom we invited to come to Albuquerque. It wasn't heroic anymore. It wasn't an exception. It was, "This is the way we operate now." It demonstrated my natural compassion and empathy for other groups, and particularly for those oppressed by my own country or my own church.

This is true of the Center for Action and Contemplation as well. A lot of people who come to us are still in that nesting period of young life, where it's soaking into their being. Their compassion toward the immigrant is natural, organic, and real. They are willing to put themselves out for immigrants and LGBTQIA+ people because our churches have so persecuted them. Our country has persecuted immigrants, so we're trying to make up for it. That's an empathy that grows on us naturally as we embrace second-half-of-life values.

The reason I use the word "contemplation" so much is that, if you don't change your being and your basic stance in how you contemplate (the Latin means the way you stare at reality), your "doing" will always be artificial, halfhearted, and phony. So give yourself a while for the scene to change. Allow for this change to be "done unto you."

Richard Rohr
Spring 2023

A MEDITATION ON A POEM BY THOMAS MERTON

Thomas Merton, the Cistercian monk who died tragically in 1968, has been a primary teacher and inspiration to me since I first read his book *The Sign of Jonas* in a high school seminary library soon after it was written in 1958. I saw Merton once, for just a moment, as he walked in front of me while I was visiting the monastery with my parents in early June of 1961, the day I had graduated from high school in Cincinnati. Little did I think he would soon die, or did I imagine the ongoing influence he would have on so many people around the world—and on me.

I believe Thomas Merton was probably the most significant American Catholic of the twentieth century, along with Dorothy Day. His whole life was a parable and a paradox, like all of ours, but he had an uncanny ability to describe his inner life with God for the rest of us. His best-selling *Seven Storey Mountain* is a first-half-of-life statement, which has never gone out of print since 1948. It is brilliant in its passion, poetry, discovery, and newly found ecstasy, yet it is still rather dualistic. The following poem, "When in the Soul of the Serene Disciple," written ten years later, shows all the signs of a man in an early second half of life, although he was only in his midforties. I offer it as an appropriate closing for our journey together. The freedom illustrated here might be exactly where the further journey is going to lead you. I hope so.

When in the Soul of the Serene Disciple

When in the soul of the serene disciple
With no more Fathers to imitate
Poverty is a success,
It is a small thing to say the roof is gone:
He has not even a house.

Stars, as well as friends,
Are angry with the noble ruin.
Saints depart in several directions.

Be still:
There is no longer any need of comment.
It was a lucky wind
That blew away his halo with his cares,
A lucky sea that drowned his reputation.

Here you will find
Neither a proverb nor a memorandum.
There are no ways,
No methods to admire
Where poverty is no achievement.
His God lives in his emptiness like an affliction.

What choice remains?
Well, to be ordinary is not a choice:
It is the usual freedom
Of men without visions.[1]

   This poem has spoken to me from the first time I read it, while experiencing my first full hermitage at Gethsemani, Merton's Kentucky monastery, during the Easter season in 1985. I offer it to you as a simple meditation that you can return to again and again to summarize where this journey has led us.

When in the soul of the serene disciple

   At the soul level, and with the peacefulness of time,

With no more Fathers to imitate

   When you have moved beyond the "authoritative," the collective, and the imitative, and you have to be your True Self,

Poverty is a success,
It is a small thing to say the roof is gone:
He has not even a house.

> *When you have made it all the way to the bottom of who you think you are*
> *or need to be, when your humiliating shadow work never stops, when your*
> *securities and protective boundaries mean less and less, and when your*
> *"salvation project" has failed you,*

Stars, as well as friends,
Are angry with the noble ruin,
Saints depart in several directions.

> *When you have faced the hurt and the immense self-doubt brought on by*
> *good people, family, and even friends who do not understand you, who*
> *criticize you, or who even delight at your wrongness,*

Be still:
There is no longer any need of comment.

> *The inner life of quiet, solitude, and contemplation is the only way to find*
> *your ground and purpose now. Go nowhere else for sustenance.*

It was a lucky wind
That blew away his halo with his cares,
A lucky sea that drowned his reputation.

> *This is the necessary stumbling stone that makes you loosen your grip on*
> *the first half of life and takes away any remaining superior self-image.*
> *(Merton is calling this crossover point "lucky" and surely sees it as part of*
> *the necessary and good suffering that the soul needs in order to mature.)*

Here you will find
Neither a proverb nor a memorandum.
There are no ways,
No methods to admire

> *Don't look forward or backward in your mind for explanations or*
> *consolations. Don't try to hide behind any secret, special way that you*
> *have practiced and now can recommend to all! (As we preachy types*
> *always feel we must do.) There are few certitudes now, just naked faith.*

Where poverty is no achievement.
His God lives in his emptiness like an affliction.

> *This is nothing you have come to or crawled down to by effort or insight. You were taken there, and your "there" is precisely nothing. (That is, it is "everything," but not what you expected everything to be!) This kind of God is almost a disappointment, at least to those who were in any way "using" God up to now. There is nothing to claim anymore. God is not a possession of any type, not for your own ego, morality, superiority, or for control of the data. This is the "nada" of John of the Cross and the mystics, and this is Jesus on the cross. Yet, it is a peaceful nothingness and a luminous darkness, while still an "affliction."*

What choice remains?
Well, to be ordinary is not a choice:
It is the usual freedom
Of [people] without [their] visions.

> *In the second half of the spiritual life, you are not making choices as much as you are being guided, taught, and led—which leads to "choiceless choices." These are the things you* cannot <u>not</u> *do because of what you have become, things you do not* need *to do because they are just not yours to do, and things you absolutely* must *do because they are your destiny and your deepest desire. Your driving motives are no longer money, success, or the approval of others. You have found your sacred dance.*

> *Now, your only specialness is in being absolutely ordinary and even "choiceless," beyond the strong opinions, needs, preferences, and demands of the first half of life. You do not need your "visions" anymore; you are happily participating in God's vision for you.*

> *With that, the wonderful dreaming and the dreamer that you were in your early years have morphed into Someone Else's dream for you. You move from the driver's seat to being a happy passenger, one who is still allowed to make helpful suggestions to the Driver. You are henceforth "a serene disciple," living in your own unique soul as never before, yet paradoxically living within the mind and heart of God, and taking your place in the great and general dance.*

Amen, Alleluia!

Bible versions: I studied from the *Jerusalem Bible*, I have made use of the *New American Bible*, and I often read *The Message* to get a new slant on a passage, but the edited form I use is often my own translation or a combination of the above.

Foreword
1. Susan J. Matt, *Homesickness: An American History* (New York: Oxford University Press, 2011), 252.

The Invitation to a Further Journey
1. I am taking the liberty of capitalizing the term "True Self" throughout this book so you will know that I am not referring to the small self or psychological self, but the larger and foundational self that we are in God.

2. John Duns Scotus (1266–1308) was the Franciscan philosopher who most influenced Thomas Merton, Gerard Manley Hopkins, and all of us who love his subtle arguments for divine freedom, a Cosmic Christ, a nonviolent theology of redemption, and, in this poem, his wonderful doctrine of "thisness." For Scotus, God does not create categories, classes, genuses, or species, but only unique and chosen individuals. Everything is a unique "this"! See Mary Beth Ingham, *Scotus for Dunces: An Introduction to the Subtle Doctor* (St. Bonaventure NY: St. Bonaventure University, 2003). Poem: Gerard Manley Hopkins, "As Kingfishers Catch Fire," *Poems and Prose* (New York: Penguin, 1984), 51.

Introduction
1. Bill Plotkin, *Soulcraft: Crossing into the Mysteries of Nature and Psyche* (Novato, CA: New World Library, 2003), 85.

2. Ernest Becker, *The Denial of Death* (New York: Free Press, 1973).

3. Richard Rohr, *Adam's Return: The Five Promises of Male Initiation* (New York: Crossroad, 2004).

4. Karen Armstrong, *A Short History of Myth* (Edinburgh: Canongate, 2006).

5. Richard Rohr, *The Naked Now: Learning to See as the Mystics See* (New York: Crossroad, 2009).

6. *The Odyssey*, trans. Samuel Butler (Lawrence, KS: Digireads.com Publishing, 2009).

Chapter 1: The Two Halves of Life

1. Mary Oliver, "The Summer Day," *New and Selected Poems* (Boston: Beacon, 1992), 94.

2. Robert Frost, "Mending Wall," *The Poetry of Robert Frost*, ed. Edward Connery Lathem (New York: Henry Holt, 1969), 33.

3. Abraham H. Maslow, "A Theory of Human Motivation," *Psychological Review*, 1943, developed and revised in many of his later books.

4. Ken Keyes, Jr., *Handbook to Higher Consciousness* (Coos Bay, OR: Living Love Center, 1975), 166.

5. Pope John Paul XXIII, *Ad Petri Cathedram*, Encyclical on Truth, Unity, and Peace in a Spirit of Charity, June 29, 1959, 72. See https://w2.vatican.va/content/john-xxiii/en/encyclicals/documents/hf_j-xxiii_enc_29061959_ad-petri.html.

6. Ken Wilber, *One Taste: Daily Reflections on Integral Spirituality* (Boston: Shambhala, 2000), 25–258. Although Wilber develops his distinction between the "translative" and the truly "transformative" functions of religion in several places, this is one of the most succinct summaries. Religion must "devastate" before it consoles.

7. W. B. Yeats, "The Second Coming," *The Collected Poems of W. B. Yeats* (New York: Scribner, 1996), 187.

Chapter 2: The Hero's Journey

1. Joseph Campbell, *The Hero with a Thousand Faces* (Princeton, NJ: Princeton University Press, 1973).

2. Richard Rohr, *Adam's Return.*

3. T. S. Eliot, "Little Gidding," *Four Quartets* (New York: Harcourt, Brace, & World, 1971), 145.

4. Thomas Merton, *No Man Is an Island* (New York: Houghton Mifflin, 1955), xii.

Chapter 3: The First Half of Life

1. "The Visionary," *Rainer Maria Rilke: Selected Poems*, trans. Albert Ernest Flemming (New York: Routledge, 2011), 72.

2. Bill Plotkin, *Nature and the Human Soul: Cultivating Wholeness and Community in a Fragmented World* (Novato, CA: New World Library, 2008), 8.

3. "What It Is," *Mimetic Theory*, https://mimetictheory.com/what-it-is-2/.

4. Thomas Fuchs, Christoph Mundt, and Thiemo Breyer, eds., *Karl Jaspers' Philosophy and Psychopathology* (New York: Springer, 2013), 48.

5. Erich Fromm, *The Art of Loving* (New York: Harper & Row, 1956), 43f.

6. Jerry Mander, *In the Absence of the Sacred: The Failure of Technology and the Survival of the Indian Nations* (San Francisco: Sierra Club Books, 1991).

7. Owen Barfield, *Saving the Appearances: A Study in Idolatry* (Middletown, CT: Wesleyan University Press, 1988), chap. 6.

8. Spiral Dynamics is a theory of human consciousness that claims to "explain everything." In fact, it is quite convincing and helpful in terms of understanding at what level individuals, groups, nations, and whole eras hear, process, and act on their experience. Paralleling the foundational work of Piaget, Maslow, Fowler, Kohlberg, and Graves, people like Robert Kegan, Don Beck, and Ken Wilber have made "Integral Theory" a part of much political, social, and religious discourse. "Transpartisan" thinking would often describe the higher levels of consciousness, whereas many progressive people still think "bipartisan" is as high as we can go. I have used the terms *nondualistic thinking* or *contemplation* to mean approximately the same.

9. Richard Rohr, *From Wild Man to Wise Man: Reflections on Male Spirituality* (Cincinnati: St. Anthony Messenger Press, 2005), 73f.

10. Plotkin, *Nature and the Human Soul*, 49f. In Plotkin's eight-stage wheel of development, he sees the early stages as largely ego driven, as they have to be. Until we make some kind of "soul encounter" with the deeper self, we cannot be soul drawn and live from our deeper identity. It is a brilliant analysis that parallels our own work in initiation (M.A.L.Es) and my thesis in this book.

11. Plotkin, *Soulcraft*, 91f.

12. Victor Turner, *The Ritual Process: Structure and Antistructure* (Ithaca, NY: Cornell University, 1977), 94f. This book first clarified for me the concept of liminality and why spiritual change, transformation, and initiation can happen best when we are on some "threshold" of our own lives. "Liminal space" has since become a key concept in my own work in initiation. Many people avoid all movement into any kind of liminal space, stay on cruise control, and nothing new happens.

13. Gerald May, *The Dark Night of the Soul: A Psychiatrist Explores the Connection Between Darkness and Spiritual Growth* (New York: HarperCollins, 2004).

14. As quoted in Richard Rohr, *On the Threshold of Transformation: Daily Meditations for Men* (Chicago: Loyola Press, 2010), 253.

Chapter 4: The Tragic Sense of Life

1. Miguel de Unamuno, *Tragic Sense of Life* (Mineola, NY: Dover, 1954).

2. Walter Brueggemann, *The Message of the Psalms* (Minneapolis: Augsburg, 1984), 162.

3. Julian of Norwich, *Revelations of Divine Love*, chap. 61.

4. Richard Rohr, *The Enneagram: A Christian Perspective* (New York: Crossroad, 1999). After fifty years of working with this explanation of human motivation and behavior, I am convinced that it was discovered and refined to help the "discernment of spirits" in spiritual directees. It makes very clear that our "sin" and our gift are two sides of the same coin and that we cannot fully face one without also facing the other. This tool has changed many lives.

5. Walter Brueggemann, *Theology of the Old Testament: Testimony, Dispute, Advocacy* (Minneapolis, MN: Fortress, 1999), 61f. "Israel's religion, and thus the texts, are incessantly pluralistic," according to both Brueggemann and Professor Rainer Albertz.

Chapter 5: Stumbling Over the Stumbling Stone

1. Richard Rohr, *Things Hidden: Scripture as Spirituality* (Cincinnati: St. Anthony Messenger Press, 2022), 195f. For Franciscans, Jesus did not need to change the mind of God about humanity. Instead, he came to change the mind of humanity about God. Ours was a Cosmic Christ from all eternity who revealed the eternal love of God on the cross, but God did not need any "payment" to love us.

2. Francis of Assisi, *Testament*, 3.

3. Robert L. Moore, *Facing the Dragon: Confronting Personal and Spiritual Grandiosity* (Wilmette, IL: Chiron, 2003), 69.

Chapter 6: Necessary Suffering

1. Carl G. Jung, *The Collected Works of C. G. Jung*, ed. Gerhard Adler and R. F. C. Hull (Princeton, NJ: Princeton University Press, 1980), 11:75.

2. Albert Einstein, "Fundamental Ideas and Problems of the Theory of Relativity," Lecture delivered to the Nordic Assembly of Naturalists at Gothenburg, July 11, 1923, *The Nobel Prize*, https://www.nobelprize.org/uploads/2018/06/einstein-lecture.pdf.

3. Gerard Manley Hopkins, "That Nature Is a Heraclitean Fire and the Comfort of the Resurrection," *Poems and Prose* (New York: Penguin, 1984), 65f.

4. Carl R. Rogers, *On Becoming a Person: A Therapist's View of Psychotherapy* (New York: Houghton Mifflin, 1995), 26.

5. Parker J. Palmer, "Standing and Acting in the Tragic Gap," *On Being*, December 16, 2015, https://onbeing.org/blog/standing-and-acting-in-the-tragic-gap/.

6. Thomas Merton, *New Seeds of Contemplation* (New York: New Directions, 1962). Merton's descriptions of the terms *true self* and *false self* have become a foundational

piece of modern spirituality and have clarified for many what self has to "die," according to Jesus, and what self lives forever.

Chapter 7: Home and Homesickness

1. Jung, *Collected Works* 1:483.

2. Herman Hesse, *Steppenwolf: A Novel* (New York: Picador USA, 1963), 153.

3. Paraphrased from Teresa of Ávila, *The Interior Castle*, trans. Mirabai Starr (New York: Riverhead, 2004), 129.

4. Michael J. Christiansen and Jeffery A. Wittung, *Partakers of the Divine Nature: The History and Development of Deification in the Christian Traditions* (Madison, NJ: Fairleigh Dickinson University, 2007). The process of the divinization of human persons, or *theosis,* is for me at the very heart of the meaning of the Christian message, but it has been feared and undeveloped in the Western churches.

5. C. P. Cavafy, "Ithaca," Richard Rohr rendition.

Chapter 8: Amnesia and the Big Picture

1. Olivier Clement, *The Roots of Christian Mysticism: Texts from the Patristic Era with Commentary* (London: New City, 2002). This excellent and profound book is worth reading several times and reveals how little the Western churches studied the Eastern Church fathers or the early period at all.

2. William Wordsworth, "Intimations of Immortality from Recollections of Early Childhood," in Oscar Williams, ed., *Immortal Poems of the English Language* (New York: Washington Square, 1963), 260.

3. Brian McLaren, *Why Did Jesus, Moses, the Buddha, and Mohammed Cross the Road? Christian Identity in a Multi-Faith World* (New York: Jericho Books, 2012), 211.

4. Wilber, *One Taste*, 32.

5. General audience, Pope John Paul II, June 28, 1999.

6. Philip Gulley and James Mulholland, *If Grace Is True: Why God Will Save Every Person* (New York: HarperCollins, 2004).

Chapter 9: A Second Simplicity

1. Wordsworth, "Intimations of Immortality."

2. Joseph Chilton Pearce, *The Biology of Transcendence: A Blueprint of the Human Spirit* (Rochester, VT: Park Street Press, 2002); Andrew Newberg, Eugene D'Aquili, and Vince Rause, *Why God Won't Go Away: Brain Science and the Biology of Belief* (New York: Ballantine, 2002).

3. Pierre Teilhard de Chardin, *Building the Earth and the Psychological Conditions of Human Unification* (New York: Discus, 1969), 11.

4. Carmen Adevedo Butcher, *The Cloud of Unknowing with the Book of Privy Counsel: A New Translation* (Boston: Shambhala, 2009). This new translation of an enduring classic can serve as the missing link for both modern fundamentalism and atheism, which suffer from the same deficit.

5. T. S. Eliot, "The Dry Salvages," *Four Quartets* (New York: Harcourt, Brace & World, 1971), 39.

6. Viktor E. Frankl, *Man's Search for Meaning* (Boston: Beacon, 1959).

7. Richard Rohr, *Everything Belongs: The Gift of Contemplative Prayer* (New York: Crossroad, 1999).

Chapter 10: A Bright Sadness

1. Quoted in *Newsweek*, Volume 113, 105.

2. Augustine, *Confessions*, Book 10, 27, largely my translation.

3. Merton, *New Seeds of Contemplation*, 297.

4. Hopkins, *Poems and Prose*, 27.

Chapter 11: The Shadowlands

1. Teresa of Ávila, *The Interior Castle*, trans. Mirabai Starr (New York: Riverhead, 2004).

2. Men as Learners and Elders, or M.A.L.Es, was the male spirituality program begun by the Center for Action and Contemplation that is now carried on by Illuman. It offers men's rites of passage and programs for male enrichment worldwide. See https://illuman.org/.

Chapter 12: New Problems and New Directions

1. The Center for Action and Contemplation was founded in Albuquerque, New Mexico, in 1987 to help people working for social change to develop a rich interior life. We have always said that the most important word in our long title is "and." See https://cac.org/.

2. Brian McLaren, Phyllis Tickle, Shane Claiborne, Alexie Torres Fleming, and Richard Rohr, *Emerging Church: Christians Creating a New World Together* (Albuquerque, NM: Center for Action and Contemplation, 2010), MP3, 7 hours, and Richard Rohr, *What Is the Emerging Church?* (Albuquerque, NM: Center for Action and Contemplation, 2009), MP3, 80 minutes.

3. Robert Sardello, *Silence: The Mystery of Wholeness* (Berkeley, CA: Goldenstone, 2008) and Max Picard, *The World of Silence* (Washington, DC: Regnery Gateway, 1988).

4. Richard Rohr, *The Naked Now*.

Chapter 13: Falling Upward

1. Clare of Assisi, "The Third Letter of St. Clare to St. Agnes of Prague," http://www.slr-ofs.org/uploads/9/5/5/8/95584600/3_-_the_third_letter_of_st._clare.pdf.

2. Regis J. Armstrong and Ignatius C. Brady, trans., *Francis and Clare: The Complete Works* (New York: Paulist, 1982), 204.

3. To learn more about this concept, see Martin Buber's classic book *I and Thou*, available in many editions.

Coda

1. *The Collected Poems of Thomas Merton* (New York: New Directions, 1977), 279–280.

Armstrong, Karen. *The Bible: The Biography.* London: Atlantic, 2007.

Becker, Ernest. *The Denial of Death.* New York: Free Press, 1973.

Bly, Robert. *The Sibling Society: An Impassioned Call for the Rediscovery of Adulthood.* Reading, MA: Addison-Wesley, 1996.

Bourgeault, Cynthia. *Centering Prayer and Inner Awakening.* Cambridge, MA: Cowely, 2004.

Bühlmann, Walbert. *The Coming of the Third Church: An Analysis of the Present and Future of the Church.* Maryknoll, NY: Orbis, 1980.

Butcher, Carmen Acevedo. *The Cloud of Unknowing with the Book of Privy Counsel: A New Translation.* Boston: Shambhala, 2009.

Campbell, Joseph, ed. *The Portable Jung.* New York: Penguin, 1971.

Chödrön, Pema. *Comfortable with Uncertainty: 108 Teachings.* Boston: Shambhala, 2006.

———. *Start Where You Are: A Guide to Compassionate Living.* Boston: Shambhala, 2001.

Eberle, Scott. *The Final Crossing: Learning to Die in Order to Live.* Big Pine, CA: Lost Borders, 2006.

Fowler, James. *Stages of Faith: The Psychology of Human Development and the Quest for Meaning.* San Francisco: Harper San Francisco, 1995.

Frankl, Viktor. *Man's Search for Meaning.* New York: Washington Square Press, 1984.

Freeman, Laurence. *Jesus: The Teacher Within.* New York: Continuum International, 2000.

Girard, René. *The Girard Reader.* Edited by James G. Williams. New York: Crossroad, 1996.

Goleman, Daniel. *Emotional Intelligence: Why It Can Matter More Than IQ.* New York: Bantam, 1997.

Grant, Robert. *The Way of the Wound: A Spirituality of Trauma and Transformation.* Burlingame, CA: private publisher, 1998.

Gulley, Philip, and James Mulholland. *If Grace Is True: Why God Will Save Every Person.* San Francisco: Harper San Francisco, 2003.

Gunn, Robert Jingen. *Journeys into Emptiness: Dogen, Merton, Jung and the Quest for Transformation.* New York: Paulist, 2000.

Hagberg, Janet O. *Real Power: The Stages of Personal Power in Organizations.* Minneapolis, MN: Winston, 1984.

Hanna, Charles Bartruff. *The Face of the Deep: The Religious Ideas of C. G. Jung.* Philadelphia: Westminister, 1967.

Hart, Tobin. *From Information to Transformation: Education for the Evolution of Consciousness.* New York: Lang, 2001.

Hillman, James. *The Soul's Code: In Search of Character and Calling.* New York: Warner, 1996.

Hollis, James. *Finding Meaning in the Second Half of Life: How to Finally, Really Grow Up.* New York: Gotham, 2006.

——. *The Middle Passage: From Misery to Meaning in Midlife.* Toronto: Inner City, 1993.

Inchausti, Robert. *Subversive Orthodoxy: Outlaws, Revolutionaries, and Christians in Disguise.* Grand Rapids, MI: Brazos, 2005.

James, William. *The Varieties of Religious Experience: A Study in Human Nature.* New York: Random House, 1999. (Originally published 1902.)

Johnson, Robert A. *Inner Gold: Understanding Psychological Projection.* Kihei, HI: Koa Books, 2008.

——. *Transformation: Understanding the Three Levels of Masculine Consciousness.* San Francisco: Harper San Francisco, 1991.

Johnston, William. *"Arise, My Love . . .": Mysticism for a New Era.* Maryknoll, NY: Orbis, 2008.

Julian of Norwich. *Julian of Norwich: Showings.* Translated by Edmund Colledge and James Walsh. New York: Paulist, 1977.

Jung, Carl G. *The Collected Works of C. G. Jung.* Princeton, NJ: Princeton University, 1980.

Katie, Byron. *Loving What Is: Four Questions That Can Change Your Life.* New York: Three Rivers, 2002.

——. *A Thousand Names for Joy: Living in Harmony with the Way Things Are.* New York: Harmony, 2007.

Kegan, Robert. *In Over Our Heads: The Mental Demands of Modern Life.* Cambridge, MA: Harvard University Press, 1994.

Kelsey, Morton T. *Discernment: A Study in Ecstasy and Evil.* New York: Paulist, 1978.

Lane, Belden. *The Solace of Fierce Landscapes: Exploring Desert and Mountain Spirituality.* New York: Oxford University Press, 1998.

Levinson, Daniel J. *The Seasons of a Man's Life: The Groundbreaking 10-Year Study that Was the Basis for Passages!* New York: Knopf, 1978.

Loy, David. *Nonduality: A Study in Comparative Philosophy.* New Haven, CT: Yale University Press, 1988.

Marion, Jim. *Putting on the Mind of Christ: The Inner Work of Christian Spirituality.* Charlottesville, VA: Hampton Roads, 2000.

Matthew, Iain. *The Impact of God: Soundings from St. John of the Cross.* London: Hodder and Stoughton, 1995.

McColman, Carl. *The Big Book of Christian Mysticism: The Essential Guide to Contemplative Spirituality.* Charlottesville, VA: Hampton Roads, 2010.

McLaren, Brian D. *A Generous Orthodoxy.* Grand Rapids, MI: Zondervan, 2004.

———. *A New Kind of Christianity: Ten Questions That Are Transforming the Faith.* New York: HarperCollins, 2010.

Miller, William A. *Make Friends with Your Shadow: How to Accept and Use Positively the Negative Side of Your Personality.* Minneapolis, MN: Augsburg, 1981.

———. *Your Golden Shadow: Discovering and Fulfilling Your Undeveloped Self.* San Francisco: Harper San Francisco, 1989.

Moore, Robert L. *Facing the Dragon: Confronting Personal and Spiritual Grandiosity.* Wilmette, IL: Chiron, 2003.

Murphy, Desmond. *A Return to Spirit: After the Mythic Church.* New York: Crossroad, 1997.

Naranjo, Claudio. *The Divine Child and the Hero: Inner Meaning in Children's Literature.* Nevada City, CA: Gateways, 1999.

Needleman, Jacob. *Time and the Soul: Where Has All the Meaningful Time Gone—and Can We Get It Back?* San Francisco: Berrett-Koehler, 2003.

Newberg, Andrew. *Why We Believe What We Believe: Uncovering Our Biological Need for Meaning, Spirituality, and Truth.* New York: Free Press, 2006.

O'Murchu, Diarmuid. *Quantum Theology: Spiritual Implications of the New Physics.* New York: Crossroad, 1997.

Palmer, Parker J. *A Hidden Wholeness: The Journey Toward an Undivided Life.* San Francisco: Jossey-Bass, 2004.

Panikkar, Raimon. *A Dwelling Place for Wisdom.* Louisville, KY: Westminster/John Knox, 1993.

———. *Christophany: The Fullness of Man.* Maryknoll, NY: Orbis, 2004.

Pearce, Joseph Chilton. *Spiritual Initiation and the Breakthrough of Consciousness: The Bond of Power.* Rochester, VT: Park Street, 1981.

Pearson, Carol S. *The Hero Within: Six Archetypes We Live By.* New York: Harper & Row, 1986.

Peck, M. Scott. *The Road Less Traveled: A New Psychology of Love, Traditional Values and Spiritual Growth.* New York: Touchstone, 1998.

Plotkin, Bill. *Nature and the Human Soul: Cultivating Wholeness and Community in a Fragmented World.* Novato, CA: New World Library, 2008.

———. *Soulcraft: Crossing into the Mysteries of Nature and Psyche.* Novato, CA: New World Library, 2003.

Smith, Cyprian. *The Way of Paradox: Spiritual Life as Taught by Meister Eckhart.* London: Darton, Longman and Todd, 2004.

Smith, Huston. *Forgotten Truth: The Common Vision of the World's Religions.* San Francisco: Harper San Francisco, 1976.

St. John of the Cross. *Living Flame of Love.* Translated and edited by E. Allison Peers. New York: Triumph, 1991.

Stein, Murray. *In Midlife: A Jungian Perspective.* Dallas, TX: Spring Publications, 1994.

Tarnas, Richard. *The Passion of the Western Mind: Understanding the Ideas That Have Shaped Our World View.* New York: Ballantine, 1991.

Taylor, Charles. *A Secular Age.* Cambridge, MA: Belknap Harvard, 2007.

Toolan, David. *At Home in the Cosmos.* Maryknoll, NY: Orbis, 2003.

Tracy, David. *Blessed Rage for Order: The New Pluralism in Theology.* New York: Seabury, 1979.

Tugwell, Simon. *Ways of Imperfection: An Exploration of Christian Spirituality.* Springfield, IL: Templegate, 1985.

Underhill, Evelyn. *The Ways of the Spirit.* New York: Crossroad, 1993.

Watts, Alan. *Behold the Spirit: A Study in the Necessity of Mystical Religion.* New York: Vintage, 1972.

Whyte, David. *The Three Marriages: Reimagining Work, Self and Relationship.* New York: Riverhead, 2009.

Wilber, Ken. *The Essential Ken Wilber: An Introductory Reader.* Boston: Shambhala, 1998.

———. *Integral Spirituality: A Startling New Role for Religion in the Modern and Postmodern World.* Boston: Shambhala, 2006.

———. *The Simple Feeling of Being: Embracing Your True Nature.* Boston: Shambhala, 2004.

Wilber, Ken, Jack Engler, and Daniel P. Brown. *Transformations of Consciousness: Conventional and Contemplative Perspectives on Development.* Boston: New Science Library, 1986.

Xavier, N. S. *The Two Faces of Religion: A Psychiatrist's View.* Tuscaloosa, AL: Portals, 1987.

Fr. Richard Rohr is a Franciscan priest and founder of the Center for Action and Contemplation in Albuquerque, New Mexico. An internationally recognized author and spiritual leader, Fr. Richard teaches primarily on incarnational mysticism, nondual consciousness, and contemplation, with a particular emphasis on how these affect the social justice issues of our time. Along with many recorded conferences, he is the author of numerous books, including *The Universal Christ: How a Forgotten Reality Can Change Everything We See, Hope For, and Believe* and *The Wisdom Pattern: Order, Disorder, Reorder.*

Richard Rohr bears witness to the deep wisdom of Christian mysticism and teaches how God's grace guides us to our birthright as beings made of Divine Love. To learn more about Fr. Richard's work and the Center for Action and Contemplation, please visit https://cac.org.